William Hazlitt, M. (François) Guizot

The History of Civilization

From the Fall of the Roman Empire to the French Revolution

William Hazlitt, M. (François) Guizot

The History of Civilization
From the Fall of the Roman Empire to the French Revolution

ISBN/EAN: 9783744773935

Printed in Europe, USA, Canada, Australia, Japan

Cover: Foto ©ninafisch / pixelio.de

More available books at **www.hansebooks.com**

THE

HISTORY OF CIVILIZATION

FROM THE

FALL OF THE ROMAN EMPIRE

TO

THE FRENCH REVOLUTION.

BY F. GUIZOT,

THE PRIME MINISTER OF FRANCE;
AUTHOR OF "HISTORY OF THE ENGLISH REVOLUTION OF 1640."

TRANSLATED BY WILLIAM HAZLITT.

VOLUME III.

NEW YORK:
D. APPLETON AND COMPANY,
90, 92 & 94 GRAND STREET.
1870.

CONTENTS

TWENTY-FIRST LECTURE.

Object of the lecture—Of capitularies in general—Review of the capitularies of the Carlovingian Frank kings—Of the two forms under which the capitularies have descended to us—Scattered capitularies—Collection of Angesise and of the deacon Benedict—Of the edition of the capitularies by Baluze—Erroneous idea generally entertained as to capitularies—They are not invariably laws—Great variety in these acts—Attempt at classification—Table of contents of the capitularies of Charlemagne 1. Moral legislation—2. Political legislation—3. Penal legislation—4. Civil legislation—5. Religious legislation—6. Canonical legislation—7. Domestic legislation—8. Incidental legislation—True character of the capitularies . . . . p. 9

TWENTY-SECOND LECTURE.

Of intellectual decay in Frankish Gaul, from the fifth to the eighth century—Of its causes—It ceases under the reign of Charlemagne—Difficulty of describing the state of the human mind at this epoch—Alcuin is its most complete and faithful representative—Life of Alcuin—His labors for the restoration of manuscripts—For the restoration of schools—His teaching in the school of the palace—His relations with Charlemagne—His conduct as abbot of Saint Martin of Tours—His works: 1. Theological; 2. Philosophical and literary; 3. Historical; 4. Poetical—His general character . . . . p. 18

TWENTY-THIRD LECTURE.

Classification of celebrated men of the age of Charlemagne: 1. Leidrade, archbishop of Lyons—His letter to Charlemagne upon what he has done in his diocese—2. Theodulph, archbishop of Orleans—His measures for the instruction of the people—His poem entitled *Exhortation to Judges* —3 Smaragde, abbot of Saint Michael—His treatise of morality for kings, entitled *Via Regia*—4. Eginhard—His alleged marriage with a daughter of Charlemagne—Their relations—Of what happened after the death of this prince—His letters—His *Life of Charlemagne*—Recapitulation . . . . p. 55

TWENTY-FOURTH LECTURE.

The progress and causes of the dismemberment of the empire of Charlemagne—1. State of this empire in 843, after the treaty of Verdun—Inferior state of the kingdom of France at this epoch—2. In 888, after the death of Charles le Gros—Seven kingdoms—Definitive establishment of the inheritance of fiefs in France—Twenty-nine small states, or important fiefs, founded at the end of the ninth century—3. In 987, at the fall of the Carlovingians—Four kingdoms—In France, fifty-five important fiefs—Explanation of this dismemberment—Their insufficiency—One only, the diversity of races, developed by M. Thierry, is probable, but incomplete—The true cause is the impossibility of a great state at that epoch, and the progressive rise of the local societies which formed the feudal confederation . . . . p. 75

TWENTY-FIFTH LECTURE.

History of legislation from the death of Charlemagne to the accession of Hugh Capet—Necessity of precisely determining the general characteristics of the legislation at the two terms of this epoch, in order to understand properly its progress during its course—1. State of the legislation under Charlemagne—It is personal, and varies according to races—The church and the imperial power give it some unity—2. State of the legislation after Hugh Capet—It is territorial; local customs have replaced national laws—All central legislative power has disappeared—3. History of legislation in Frankish Gaul between these two terms—Analytical tables of the capitularies of Louis le Débonnaire, Charles le Chauve, Louis le Begue, Carloman, Eudes, and Charles le Simple—Comparison of these tables according to the figures only—Comparison of the provisions of the capitularies—General results of this inquiry . . . p. 93

TWENTY-SIXTH LECTURE.

Object of the lecture—Internal history of the Gallo-Frankish church, from the middle of the 8th century to the end of the 10th—Anarchy which pervaded it in the first half of the 8th century—Twofold principle of reform—The reformation is actually undertaken by the first Carlovingians: 1. By the civil power; 2. By the ecclesiastical power—Special reforms—Order of Canons—Its origin and progress—Reformation of the monastic orders by Saint Benedict d'Aniane—They change character—Preponderance of the temporal power in the Gallo-Frankish church at this epoch—Proofs—Still the church progresses towards its future preponderance—But it is not to the profit of its own government, of the bishops of France, that this progress is to turn . . . . p. 109

TWENTY-SEVENTH LECTURE.

History of papacy—Peculiar situation of the city of Rome—Relations of the popes about the middle of the eighth century, with the Italian, Spanish, Anglo-Saxon, Gallo-Frankish, and Germanic churches—Their alliance with the early Carlovingians—Advantages which they drew from it—Donation of Pepin and of Charlemagne—Sovereignty of the Carlovingian emperors over the popes—Uncertainty of the ideas, and incoherency of the facts concerning the rights of papacy—It increases more and more in minds—It apparently acquires a legal title—False decretals—Nicholas I.—His character—Affair of the marriage of Lothaire and of Teutberge—Affair of Rhotarde, bishop of Soissons—Triumph of papacy: 1. Over temporal sovereigns; 2. Over national churches —Its decided preponderance in the west . . . . . p. 127

TWENTY-EIGHTH LECTURE.

Of the intellectual condition of Frankish Gaul, from the death of Charlemagne to the accession of Hugh Capet—Sketch of the celebrated men of this period—The theological mind—The philosophical mind—Hincmar and John Erigena are respectively their representatives—Life of Hincmar—His activity and influence as archbishop of Rheims—1. Concerning his relations with kings and popes—2. Concerning his administration in the interior of the Gallo-Frankish church and of his diocese —3. Concerning his disputes and theological works—Origin of the theology of the middle ages—Quarrel between Hincmar and the monk Gottschalk upon predestination—Numerous writings upon this subject —Councils of Kiersy, Valence, and Langres—Recapitulation . p. 144

TWENTY-NINTH LECTURE.

Object of the lecture—Of the philosophical spirit in the 9th century— Scotus or Erigena—His country—Date of his birth—Tradition respecting his travels in Greece—He settles in France at the court of Charles le Chauve—Of the School of the Palace under Charles—Ancient philosophy studied there—Encouragement of Scotus Erigena—His learning—Relations of Christianity with the Neoplatonism of Alexandria— Their struggle—Attempt at Amalgamation—History and pretended works of Dionysius the Areopagite—Fundamental differences of the two doctrines: 1 in the point of departure and the method; 2, in the bases of the questions—These differences occur between Scotus Erigena and the Christian theologians of the 9th century—Examination of his works: 1, De Prædestinatione: 2, De Divisione Naturæ—His celebrity and his death—Recapitulation . . . . p. 166

THIRTIETH LECTURE.

General summary of the course—Extent and variety of subjects—The history of civilization, its price—It is the result of all partial histories—Uni ty and variety of the existence of a people—Three essential elements in French civilization, Greco-Roman antiquity, Christianity, Germany—1. Of the Roman element, from the 5th to the 10th century—Under a social point of view—Under an intellectual point of view—2. Of the Christian element, from the 5th to the 10th century—Under a social point of view—Under an intellectual point of view—3. Of the Germanic element, from the 5th to the 10th century—Under a social point of view—Under an intellectual point of view—Two principal facts characterize this epoch: 1. The prolongation, more or less apparent, but everywhere real, of Roman society and its influence—2. The disorderly and indeterminate fermentation of the different elements of modern civilization—Conclusion . . . . p. 189

ILLUSTRATIONS AND HISTORICAL TABLES

I. Table of the organization of the court, and of the central government of the Roman empire at the commencement of the fifth century . . . . p. 203
II. Table of the hierarchy of ranks and titles in Roman society at the same epoch 209
III. Narrative of the embassy sent in 449 by Theodosius the Younger, emperor of the east, to Attila, established on the banks of the Danube 211
IV. Chronological table of the principal events of the political history of Gaul, from the fifth to the tenth century 230
V. Chronological table of the principal events in the ecclesiastical history of Gaul, from the fifth to the tenth century 233
VI. Chronological table of the principal events of the literary history of Gaul, from the fifth to the tenth century 237
VII. Table of the councils and canonical legislation of Gaul, from the fifth to the tenth century 246

SECOND COURSE.

LECTURE THE FIRST.

Object of the course—Elements of national unity—They exist and begin to be developed in France towards the end of the 10th century—Thence dates French civilization—The feudal period will be the subject of this course—It includes the 11th, 12th, and 13th centuries, from Hugh Capet to Philippe de Valois—Proof that these are the limits of the feudal period—Plan of the course: History; 1st, of society; 2d, of the human mind, during the feudal period—The history of society resolves itself into, 1st, history of civil society; 2d, history of religious society—The history of the human mind resolves itself into, 1st, history of learned literature; 2d, history of national literature in the vulgar tongue—Importance of the middle ages in the history of French civilization—The present state of opinions concerning the middle ages—Is it true that there is danger in historical impartiality and poetical sympathy for this period?—Utility of this study . . . . p. 324

SECOND LECTURE.

Necessity for studying the progressive formation of the feudal system—It is often forgotten that social facts form themselves but slowly, and in forming themselves, undergo many vicissitudes—Analysis of the feudal system in its essential elements. They are three in number: 1. The nature of territorial property; 2. Amalgamation of sovereignty and property; 3. Hierarchical organization of the feudal association—State of territorial property from the 5th to the 10th century—Origin and meaning of the word *feodum*—It is synonymous with *beneficium*—History of benefices, from the 8th to the 10th century—Examination of the system of Montesquieu concerning the legal gradation of the duration of benefices—Causes of the increase of the number of benefices—Almost all landed property became feudal . . . . p. 339

THIRD LECTURE.

Of the amalgamation of sovereignty and property, the second characteristic of the feudal system—True meaning of this fact—Its origin—It comes neither from the Roman society nor from the German band—Is it the result of conquest only?—Of the system of feudal publicists on this subject—Two forms of society in Germany, the tribe and the band—Social organization of the tribe—Domestic sovereignty is there distinct from political sovereignty—Twofold origin of domestic sovereignty among the ancient Germans—It arose from family and from conquest—What became of the organization of the German tribe, and especially of domestic sovereignty after the establishment of the Germans in Gau—What it retained of the family spirit gradually diminished; what it retained of conquest became dominant—Recapitulation and true character of feudal sovereignty . . . . p. 359

FOURTH LECTURE.

General association of the possessors of fiefs among themselves; third characteristic of the feudal system—From the very nature of its elements this association must have been weak and irregular—It, in fact, always was so—Fallacy of the view which the apologists of this system trace of the feudal hierarchy—Its incoherency and weakness were especially great at the close of the 10th century—The formation of this hierarchy from the 5th to the 10th century—Three systems of institution are seen together after the German invasion: free institutions, monarchical institutions, aristocratical institutions—Comparative history of these three systems—Decline of the two first—Triumph of the third, which yet remains incomplete and disordered . . . . p. 376

FIFTH LECTURE.

Method to be followed in the study of the feudal period—The simple fief is the fundamental element, the integrant molecule of feudalism—The simple fief contains: 1, the castle and its proprietors; 2, the village and its inhabitants—Origin of feudal castles—Their multiplication in the 9th and 10th centuries—Causes of this—Efforts of the kings and powerful suzerains to oppose it—Futility of these efforts—Character of the castles of the 11th century—Interior life of the proprietors of fiefs—Their isolation—Their idleness—Their incessant wars, expeditions, and adventures—Influence of the material circumstances of feudal habitations upon the course of civilization—Development of domestic life, condition of women, and of the spirit of family in the interior of castles . p. 395

TWENTY-FIRST LECTURE.

Object of the lecture—Of capitularies in general—Review of the capitularies of the Carlovingian Frank kings—Of the two forms under which the capitularies have descended to us—Scattered capitularies—Collection of Angesise and of the deacon Benedict—Of the edition of the capitularies by Baluze—Erroneous idea generally entertained as to capitularies—They are not invariably laws—Great variety in these acts—Attempt at classification—Table of contents of the capitularies of Charlemagne: 1. Moral legislation—2. Political legislation—3. Penal legislation—4. Civil legislation—5. Religious legislation—6. Canonical legislation—7. Domestic legislation—8. Incidental legislation—True character of the capitularies.

I ANNOUNCED to you my intention of laying before you a summary of the reign of Charlemagne, and its results, reviewing his government and his influence upon intellectual development. In the first of these respects, the picture I have placed before you appears to me sufficiently complete; it presents, I think, a clear and precise idea of the part filled by the wars of Charlemagne in the history of civilization in the west; and, moreover, I could not enter more fully into the subject, without going through an absolute and continuous narration of events. As to the government of Charlemagne and its action upon mind, what I have said in the last lecture is altogether incomplete, and I may, without losing myself in details, enter more closely into this part of the subject. I will proceed to do so. The legislation of Charlemagne will now occupy our attention: that which he did in protecting intellectual development, with an account of the distinguished men who lived and labored under his influence, will be the subject of following lectures.

It is commonly supposed that the term *capitularies* applies only to the laws of Charlemagne; this is a mistake. The word *capitula,* " little chapters," equally applies to all the laws of the Frank kings. I have no remark to make at present respecting the capitularies, in themselves of very slight importance,[1] of the first race; of those of the second race, there have come down to us 152, namely:

---

[1] The table in the twentieth lecture mentions only sixty; but there were besides five private acts, which, upon reflection, I think ought to be inserted among the capitularies.

5 capitularies of Pepin le Bref, commencing with the year 752, the period of his elevation to the title of king of the Franks.

  65 of Charlemagne.
  20 of Louis le Debonnaire.
  52 of Charles le Chauve.
    3 of Louis le Begue.
    3 of Carloman.
    1 of Eudes.
    3 of Charles le Simple.

I reckon here only the acts of such Carlovingians as reigned in France; several descendants of Charlemagne, established in Germany and Italy, also left capitularies, but with these we have nothing to do.

The capitularies enumerated have come down to us in two different forms. We have them, first, in the shape of as many separate acts, scattered through various manuscripts, sometimes with, sometimes without date; and there exists, secondly, a collection of them made in the course of the ninth century, and divided into seven books. The first four of these were compiled by Angesise, abbot of Fontenelle, one of the councillors of Charlemagne, who died in 833. He collected and classified the *capitula* of that prince, and a portion of those of Louis le Debonnaire. The first book contains 162 *capitula* of Charlemagne, relative to ecclesiastical affairs.

The second, forty-eight *capitula* of Louis le Debonnaire, in the same class of subjects.

The third, ninety-one *capitula* of Charlemagne, on temporal affairs.

The fourth, seventy-seven *capitula* of Louis le Debonnaire, on temporal affairs.

To these four books, which, immediately upon their publication, acquired such credit that Charles le Chauve, in his own capitularies, cites them as an official code, a deacon of Mayence, named Benedict, at the request of his archbishop, Otger, added, about the year 842, three new books, constituting the fifth, sixth, and seventh books of the collection, and which contain:

The fifth, 405 *capitula*; the sixth, 436 *capitula*; the seventh, 478 *capitula*. In all, 1697.

But, besides the capitularies which Angesise had omitted, and those which had been declared since the compilation of his collection, the three books of the deacon Benedict contain a number of acts with which the Carlovingian kings had nothing to do; for instance, fragments of the Roman law, extracted from the Theodosian code, from *Breviarium* of the Visigoths, from Justinian, Julien, &c. We even find there considerable fragments of the famous collection known by the name of *The false Decretals*, pretended canons, and other acts of the first popes—a collection at this time scarcely known, and which Benedict himself was one of the first to bring into vogue; so that many learned persons have assigned their fabrication to him.

Four supplements, added by anonymous compilers at later periods to the seven books already mentioned, extend the number of articles in this collection to 2100.

The capitularies have been published several times under both these forms. The best edition is unquestionably that of Baluze, in two vols. folio, Paris, 1677. It is not only the best as a matter of comparison, but it is excellent in itself. "Of all the sources of the law of the middle ages," says Savigny,[1] "I have found none more fully presented to us than the capitularies in Baluze's excellent edition." And, in fact, it is far more complete, and better edited than those of Lindenbrog, Pithon, Herold, Du Tillot, &c. Baluze had collected a great number of manuscripts, and he published fragments and whole capitularies previously inedited. His work may fairly be described as a vast and good collection of texts; but there, in truth, its merit ends. The texts themselves have been subjected to no examination, to no critical revision. Baluze has given them to us exactly as he found them, without troubling himself to inquire whether or no the copyists had confused them, or filled them with blunders. It would doubtless have been an entire misconception to have sought to introduce into the capitularies an order foreign to the ideas of the primitive legislator, to have classified them systematically, to have curtailed repetitions emanating from the legislator himself, and which are characteristic of his work. But there are, in the various manuscripts, a confusion and a want of accuracy which are manifestly attributable to the copyists alone; a multitude of words are changed, a multitude of articles wrongly placed; various readings of the same manuscript are set down as different *capitula*. I do not by any means propose to

---

[1] ii., 91.

go through a list of the blunders of this description, or to discuss the question of their rectification. All I desire to point out to you is the general fact that they exist in abundance, and that Baluze's work, consequently, valuable in many respects, is still only to be regarded as the materials for a really correct and satisfactory edition of the capitularies—an edition, however, which it would require long and arduous and scientific labor to produce.

Let us first consider the capitularies themselves.

At the first glance, it is impossible not to be struck with the confusion which pervades this word: it is indiscriminately applied to all the acts inserted in Baluze's collection; and yet, in point of fact, the greater portion of those acts differ essentially from capitularies, properly so called. What would be the effect, if some centuries hence, a compiler were to take all the acts of a government of our times, of the French administration for instance, in the last reign, and, throwing them promiscuously together in one heap, under one undistinguishing title, were to give the collection forth as the legislation, the code of the period? The result would manifestly be an utterly absurd and fallacious chaos; laws, ordinances, decrees, briefs of the crown, personal judgments, departmental circulars, would be mixed up together, hap-hazard, in utter confusion. This has been exactly the case with the capitularies. I will proceed to analyse the collection of Baluze, classifying according to their nature and objects the acts of all kinds which we meet with there. You will at once see how great is their diversity.

We find there under the general title of capitularies:

1. Ancient national laws revised; the Salic law, for example.[1]

2. Extracts from the ancient laws, Salic, Lombard, Bavarian, &c.; extracts evidently made for a particular purpose, a particular place, a particular moment of time, for a special necessity, the nature of which there is no longer anything to indicate to us.[2]

3. Additions to the ancient laws, to the Salic law, for in-

---

[1] See Baluze, i., col. 281, *sub anno* 798.
[2] Extract from the law of the Lombards, cap. a., 801; Baluze, i., col 349; from the law of the Ripuarians, cap. a., 803: *id.*, col. 395.

stance,[1] to the law of the Lombards,[2] to that of the Bavarians,[3] &c. These additions seem to have been made in a peculiar form, and with peculiar solemnities; that to the Salic law is preceded, in an ancient manuscript, by these words:

"These are articles which the lord Charles the Great, emperor, caused to be written in his councils, and ordered to be inserted among the other laws."

The legislature, indeed, appears to have required the adhesion of the people to these additions more expressly than to the other parts of the law; thus, in 803, the year in which the additions to the Salic law were made, we find Charlemagne issuing the following direction to his *missi:*

"Let the people be interrogated touching the articles which have recently been added to the law; and after they have all consented to them, let them affix to the said articles their signature in confirmation."[4]

4. Extracts from the acts of the councils, and from the entire body of canonical legislation; the great capitulary enacted at Aix-la-Chapelle, in 789,[5] and a host of articles in the other capitularies, are nothing more than such extracts.

5. New laws, of which some were passed by the general assemblies of the people, with the concurrence of the great laymen and great ecclesiastics together, or of the ecclesiastics alone, or of the laymen alone; while the rest appear to have been the work of the emperor himself, or to have been what we now call ordinances. The distinctions between these two classes of laws are not, on a close examination, very precisely marked, but they are perceptible.

6. Instructions given by Charlemagne to his *missi*, on their departure for the provinces, and designed sometimes to regulate the personal conduct of the *missi*, sometimes to guide them in their inquiries, very often as simple communications to the people in particular districts, which the *missi* were to convey. Acts of this description, very foreign, in part, at all events, to our notions of legislation, are of frequent occurrence in the capitularies;[6] articles of a totally different nature are sometimes mixed up with them.

---

[1] Cap. a., 803; *id.*, i., 387. [2] Cap. a., 801; *id.*, i., 345.
[3] Cap. l., 788; *id.*, i., 207. [4] Cap a., 803, § 19; i., 394.
[5] *Id.*, i., 200.
[6] Cap. a., 789; Baluze, i., 243; a, 802, i., 351; a., 802, i., 375; a., 803, i., 391; a, 806, i., 419.

7. Answers given by Charlemagne to questions addressed to him by the counts or bishops, or *missi dominici*, on the occasion of difficulties occurring to them in the course of their administration,[1] and wherein he solves these difficulties, which have reference sometimes to matters which we should call legislative, sometimes to points in executive administration, sometimes to private interests.

8. Questions which Charlemagne proposed to put to the bishops or counts at the next general assembly, and which he had noted down on paper that they might not, meantime, pass out of his recollection. These questions, which are among the most curious documents in the whole collection, bear in general a character of censure and reprimand of those to whom they are to be addressed. I will read a few of them to give you a practical idea of the liberality and good sense which characterized the mind of Charlemagne. My translation is literal:

"How does it happen that, both on the frontiers and with the army, wherever there is any great measure to be taken for the defence of the country, one man will not give aid to another?"[2]

"What is the meaning of these continual suits by which every one appears seeking to wrest from his neighbor that which he possesses?"[3]

"To ascertain on what occasions and in what places the ecclesiastics and the laity seek, in the manner stated, to impede each other in the exercise of their respective functions. To inquire and discuss up to what point a bishop or an abbot is justified in interfering in secular affairs, and a count or other layman with ecclesiastical affairs. To interrogate them closely on the meaning of those words of the Apostle: 'No man that warreth for the law, entangleth himself with the affairs of this life.' Inquire to whom these words apply."[4]

"Desire the bishops and abbots to tell us truly what is the meaning of the phrase always in their mouths: 'Renounce the world;' and by what signs we may distinguish those who have renounced the world, from those who still adhere to the world: is it merely that the former do not bear arms, or marry publicly?"[5]

[1] 6° Cap. a, 803: *id.*, i., 401.
[2] 1 Cap. a., 811, § 1. Baluze, i, 477
[3] *Ib.*, § 2.
[4] Cap. II., a., 811, § 4.
[5] *Ib.*

"To ask them further, whether he is to be considered as having renounced the world, whom we see laboring, day by day, by all sorts of means, to augment his possessions; now making use, for this purpose, of menaces of eternal flames, now of promises of eternal beatitude; in the name of God or of some saint despoiling simple-minded men of their property, to the infinite prejudice of the lawful heirs, who are, in very many cases, from the misery in which they are thus involved, driven by their necessities to robbing and to all sorts of disorders and crimes."[1]

Clearly such questions as these do not at all resemble articles of law.

9. Some of the *capitula* are not even questions, but mere notes, memoranda of particular things which Charlemagne, from time to time, conceived the idea of doing, and which he had put down on paper, lest he should forget them. We read, for instance, at the end of the *capitula*, or instructions to the *missi dominici*, in 803, these two articles:—

"Recollect to order that they who send us horses as presents, inscribe their names on each horse. And so with dresses that may be sent us from abbeys.

"Recollect to order that whenever vicarious persons are found doing evil, or suffering it to be done, they be expelled from their post, and replaced by others of a better character."[2]

I could cite many *capitula* of this description.

10. Other articles contain judgments and briefs of the crown and the courts, collected evidently for the purpose of jurisprudence; thus we read in a capitulary of the year 803:

"A man had suborned a slave, induced him to kill his two young masters, the one aged nine, the other eleven, and then killed the slave himself, and threw him into a ditch. Adjudged, that the said man pay a *wehrgeld* for the boy of nine years old, a double *wehrgeld* for the boy of eleven, and a treble *wehrgeld* for the slave; and undergo, moreover, our ban."[3]

This is obviously a judicial decree in a particular case, in

---

[1] Cap. II., a , 811, § 5.
[3] Cap., a., 803, § 12 Baluze, i , 398
[2] Baluze, i., 395.

serted among the capitularies as a precedent in future cases of a similar description.

11. We meet, in like manner, with acts of pure domestic financial administration, relative to the administration of Charlemagne's own domains, and which enter into the most minute details on this subject. The famous capitulary *De Villis* is an example of this, and there are several other articles of the same character scattered through the collection.[1]

12. Besides the so various acts I have enumerated, the capitularies contain purely political acts, occasional documents, nominations, recommendations, decisions upon personal and passing differences. I look, for instance, at the capitulary rendered in 794 by the assembly of Frankfort,[2] and among the 54 articles of which it is composed, I find:

(Art. 1.) Letters of pardon granted to Tassilon, duke of the Bavarians, who had revolted against Charlemagne.

(Art. 6.) Arrangements for the settlement of a dispute between the bishop of Vienne, and the archbishop of Arles and others, respecting the limits of the sees of the Tarentaise, Embrun, and Aix. It sets forth that letters from the pope on these matters were read, and that it was determined to consult anew with his holiness.

(Art. 7.) As to the justification offered, and the pardon received, by bishop Pierre.

(Art. 8.) As to the deposition of the pretended bishop Gerbod.

(Art. 53.) Charlemagne procures the assent of the assembly of bishops to the pope's license, authorizing him to retain about his person bishop Hildebold as his minister of ecclesiastical affairs.

(Art. 54.) He recommends Alcuin to the good wishes and prayers of the assembly.

There is obviously nothing legislative here.

Thus, at first glance, on the most simple examination of the nature of these various acts, and without entering into any close inspection of their contents, you see how wholly erroneous is the general, the common idea entertained of these capitularies; they constitute anything but a code; they comprise anything but laws. Let us now take a closer view, let us penetrate

---

[1] Baluze, i., 331 [2] *Id., ib.,* 26

into the interior of the collection, and examine the articles of which each capitulary is composed; we shall here find the same diversity, the same confusion; we shall here, in like manner, find how inadequate has been the attention hitherto paid to this study, and how fallacious are most of the results which have been deduced from it.

I have analyzed the sixty-five capitularies of Charlemagne, classifying under eight heads, according to the nature of the provisions, the articles which they comprise. These eight heads are:

1. Moral legislation.
2. Political legislation.
3. Penal legislation.
4. Civil legislation.
5. Religious legislation.
6. Canonical legislation.
7. Domestic legislation.
8. Occasional legislation.

I will first lay this classification before you, and then make some observations upon each head.

Analytical Table of the Capitularies of Charlemagne.

Date	Articles	Moral Legislation	Political Legislation	Penal Legislation	Civil Legislation	Religious Legislation	Canonical Legislation	Domestic Legislation	Occasional Legislation
769	18	1	3			3	11		
779	23		9	5	2	2	5		
783	1	1							
Id.	1	1							
Id.	8			4	3		1		
789	80	16	5		3	11	45		
Id.	16					2	14		
Id.	23	6	9		2	1	5		
Id.	34	3	5	18	3	3	5		
793	17	1	6		7		4		
794	54		6		4	6	27		8
797	10		5	5					
799	5						5		
800	1		1						
Id.	70							70	
Id.	5		5						
801	8			5	3				

Analytical Table of the Capitularies of Charlemagne—continued.

Date.	Articles.	Moral Legislation.	Political Legislation.	Penal Legislation.	Civil Legislation.	Religious Legislation.	Canonical Legislation.	Domestic Legislation.	Occasional Legislation.
Id.	1		1						
Id.	22		2				20		
802	41	9	10	5		1	16		
Id.	23	2	13	3			5		
803	7						7		
Id.	1						1		
Id.	1						1		
Id.	11		2	4	5				
Id.	34		20	2	8		2		2
Id.	12		3	3	6				
Id.	14	1	6	2	3	1	1		
Id.	8		4		4				
Id.	13	1	5	1	3	1	2		
Id.	3					1	2		
804	20	2	3				15		
Id.	1	1							
805	16	4					12		
Id.	25	4	13	3	4		1		
Id.	24								
Id.	16								
Id.	1								
806	20	1							
Id.	8			4	3		1		
Id.	6		3	1	2				
Id.	8		4	1	2				
Id.	19	1					2		
806	23					7	16		
807	7		7						2
808	30		11	10	6		1		
809	37	3	15	6	12		1		
Id.	16								
810	19	6	8	4					
Id.	16	5	4	3	2	2			
Id.	5		5						
811	12		4				8		
Id.	13		9			9	4		
Id.	9								
812	9		9						
Id.	11	1	9		1				
Id.	13		10		3				
813	28	3	2			3	20		
Id.	20		6	2		7	2	3	
Id.	46			39		7			

CIVILIZATION IN FRANCE.

Analytical Table of the Capitularies of Charlemagne—continued.

Date.	Articles.	Moral Legislation.	Political Legislation.	Penal Legislation.	Civil Legislation.	Religious Legislation.	Canonical Legislation.	Domestic Legislation.	Occasional Legislation.
year uncertain.	59	5	13		3	9	29		
Id.	14					14			
Id.	13					9	4		
Id.	13	2	8		2		1		
Id.	9					9	9		
	1150	80	273	130	110	85	309	73	12

Let us now examine a little more closely the contents of this table; the examination will be a very rapid one, but sufficient, I hope, to give you an idea of the true character of the government of Charlemagne, and of the monuments which exist of it in this collection.

I. *Moral Legislation.*—I have classed under this title those articles which are neither commanding nor prohibitory; which, in truth, are not laws at all, but mere advice, suggestions, or moral precepts. For instance:

"Avarice consists in desiring the possessions of others, and in not giving to others a share of that which we ourselves possess; according to the apostle, it is the root of all evil, and it should, therefore, be carefully avoided.[1]

"Those who apply themselves to amass property by all sorts of ways make dishonorable gains.[2]

"All men should practise hospitality.[3]

"Keep clear of theft, of unlawful marriages, of bearing false witness, as we have often exhorted you, and as is exhorted by the Word of God."[4]

The legislator goes even further than this; he seems to think himself responsible for the conduct of each individual, and apologises for not being able to fulfil this responsibility to the extent he desires:

---

[1] Cap. a., 806, § 15; Baluze, i, 454. [2] Ib., § 16.
[3] Cap. a., 794, § 33; ib., 268. [4] Ib., 789, § 56 ib., 238.

' It is necessary," he says, "that every man should seek, tc the best of his strength and ability, to serve God and walk in the way of his precepts; for the lord emperor cannot watch over each person individually, with the necessary care, or keep each man in proper discipline.'"

Is not this pure morality? Such provisions are foreign to the laws of rising societies and to those of perfected societies: open the Salic law and our codes, you will find nothing of the kind there; they in no way address themselves to human liberty in order to give it counsel; they contain merely formally prohibitive or imperative texts. But in the passage from primitive barbarism to civilization, legislation takes another character; morality is introduced into it, and becomes, for a certain period, matter of law. Skilful legislators, founders or reformers of societies, comprehend the empire which the idea of duty exercised over men; the instinct of genius warns them, that without its support, without the free concurrence of the human will, society can neither be maintained nor developed in peace; and they apply themselves to introduce this idea into the souls of men in every kind of way, and they make legislation a kind of preaching, a medium of instruction. Consult the history of every nation, the Hebrews, the Greeks, &c., you will everywhere recognize this fact; you will everywhere find between the epoch of the primitive laws, which are purely penal, prohibitive, destined to repress the abuses of force; and the epoch of scientific laws, which have confidence in morality, in the reason of individuals, and leave all which is purely moral in the domain of liberty; between these two epochs, I say, you will always find one in which morality is the object of legislation, in which legislation formally writes and teaches it. Gaulo-Frankish society was at this point when Charlemagne governed it; and this was one of the causes of his close alliance with the church, the only power then capable of teaching and preaching morality.

I accordingly comprehend, under the name of *moral legislation*, all relating to the intellectual development of men; for example, all the provisions of Charlemagne concerning schools, what books to distribute, the reformation of ecclesiastical offices, &c.

---

[1] Cap. a., 802, § 3; *ib.*, 364.

II. *Political Legislation.*—This is one of the most considerable portions of the capitularies; it comprehends two hundred and ninety-three articles. Under this head I place—

1. The laws and measures of Charlemagne of all kinds, to ensure the execution of his orders throughout the extent of his states; for example, all provisions relative to the nomination or conduct of his various agents, counts, dukes, vicars, centeniers, &c.; they are numerous, and are constantly repeated.

2. The articles whose object is the administration of justice, the sitting of local courts, the forms to be followed there, the military service, &c.

3. The police legislations, which are very various, and sometimes go into the most minute details; the provinces, the army, the church, merchants, beggars, public places, the interior of the imperial palace, alternately form the object of them. We there meet, for example, with an attempt to fix the price of goods, a veritable attempt at a *maximum* price.

"The most pious lord our king has decreed, with the consent of the holy synod, that no man, ecclesiastic or layman, shall, whether in times of plenty or in times of scarcity, sell provisions dearer than at the price recently fixed by the bushel, namely: a bushel of oats, one denier; of barley, two deniers; of rye, three deniers; of wheat, four deniers. If he desires to sell it in loaves, he shall give twelve loaves of wheat, each of two pounds, for one denier, fifteen loaves of rye, twenty of barley, or twenty-five of oats, of the same weight, also for one denier, &c."[1]

The suppression of mendicity and a poor rate, likewise appear there.

"With regard to vagrant mendicants, we order, that each of our subjects support his own poor, whether on his fees or within his house, and not allow them to go elsewhere to beg. If such beggars are found, and they do no work with their hands, let no one think of giving them anything."[2]

The provisions relative to the internal regulation of the palace give a singular idea of the disorders and violences which were committed there:

---

[1] Cap. a., 794, § 2; vol. i., col. 263.
[2] Cap. a., 806, § 10; vol. i., col. 454.

"We will and order that none of those who serve in our palace, take upon himself to receive any man who seeks a refuge there, and comes there to conceal himself, on account of robbery, homicide, adultery, or any other crime; that if any free man violate our prohibition, and conceal a malefactor in our palace, he shall be forced to carry him on his shoulders to the public place, and there he shall be attached to the same post as the malefactor. . . . . Whoever shall find men fighting in our palace, and cannot or will not put an end to the conflict, he shall pay a share of the damage which they have caused, &c."[1]

The capitularies contain numberless analogous provisions, internal police was evidently of great importance in the government of Charlemagne.

4. I class, also, under the head of political legislation all which concerns the distinction between the lay and the ecclesiastical powers and their relations. Charlemagne made great use of the ecclesiastics—they were, in truth, his principal means of government; but he wished to make use of them, and not for them to make use of him: the capitularies attest his vigilance in governing the clergy himself, and keeping it under his power. You have seen, by some of the questions which he proposed addressing to the bishops in the general assemblies, to what a degree he was impressed with this idea.

5. It seems to me necessary, lastly, to refer to political legislation, the provisions relative to the administration of the sees conceded by Charlemagne, and his relations with the beneficiaries. This was certainly one of the leading features of his government, and one of those to which he most assiduously called the attention of the *missi*.

I need not point out to you that the general character of all this political legislation, in its various parts, is a continual, indefatigable effort towards order and unity.

III. *Penal legislation.* This in general is scarcely more than the renewal, to a certain extent, of the ancient Salic, Ripuarian, Lombard, barbarian, &c., laws. Punishment, repression of crimes, of abuse of force, is, as you have seen, almost the only object, the essential character of those laws. There was, therefore, less to do in this respect than in any

---

Cap. a., 800, § 3 and 4; vol. i., col. 343.

other. The new provisions which Charlemagne here and there added, were in general for the object of mitigating the ancient legislation, especially the rigor of the punishments inflicted upon slaves. In some cases, however, he aggravated the punishment, instead of mitigating it—when, for example, punishments were a political instrument in his hands. Thus the punishment of death, so rare in the barbaric laws, recurs in almost every article of a capitulary of the year 789, intended to restrain and convert the Saxons; almost every violation of order, every relapse into idolatrous practices, is punished with death.[1] With these exceptions, the penal legislation of Charlemagne has but little originality or interest.

VI. *The civil legislation* offers but little more. Here, also, the ancient laws, the ancient customs, remained in vigor; Charlemagne had very little to alter in them. He, however, carefully occupied himself, doubtless at the instigation of the ecclesiastics, with the condition of persons, especially with the relations between men and women. It is evident that at this epoch these relations were prodigiously irregular—that a man took and quitted a woman without scruple, and almost without formality. The result was a great disorder in individual morality, and in the state of families. The civil law was thence strongly interested in the reformation of manners, and Charlemagne understood this. Hence the great number of provisions inserted in his capitularies concerning the conditions of marriages, the degrees of parentage, the duties of husbands towards wives, the duties of widows, &c. The greater portion of these provisions are borrowed from canonical legislation; but it must not be supposed that their motive and origin was purely religious—the interest of civil life, the necessity of fixing and of regulating the family, had evidently a large share therein.

V. *Religious legislation.* By religious legislation, I mean provisions relative, not to the clergy, to ecclesiastics alone, but to the faithful, to the Christian people, and to its relations with the priests. It is thus distinguished from canonical legislation, which concerns only the ecclesiastical society, the

---

[1] Bal., vol. i., col. 251.

relations of the clergy among themselves. The following are some provisions of religious legislation:

"Let care be taken not to venerate the names of false martyrs, nor the memory of doubtful saints."[1]

"Let no one suppose that God is only to be prayed to in three languages,[2] for God is adored in all languages, and man is heard if he ask just things."[3]

"Let preaching always be performed in such a manner that the common people may be able to understand it thoroughly."[4]

These provisions have generally a character of good sense, even of liberty of mind, which one would scarcely expect to find in them.

VI. *The canonical legislation* is that which occupies the greatest place in the capitularies, and naturally so; the bishops (as I have already observed) were the principal counsellors of Charlemagne; they sat in the greatest numbers in the general assemblies; their affairs were always attended to first. Accordingly, these assemblies were generally looked upon as councils, and their laws were transmitted to the collection of canons. They are almost all drawn up in the interest of the power of the bishops. You will remember that at the accession of the Carlovingian race, the episcopal aristocracy, strong as it had been, was in complete dissolution. Charlemagne reconstituted it; under his hand, it regained the regularity, the entirety it lost, and became, for many centuries, the dominant ruler of the church. At a later period, I shall speak of this more minutely.

VII. The *domestic legislation* contains only what relates to the administration of the private property, the farms of Charlemagne; an entire capitulary, entitled *de Villis*, is a collection of various instructions, addressed at different periods of his reign to the persons employed on his domains, and which have been erroneously assembled under the form of a single capitulary. M. Anton has given, in his *History of German Agriculture in the Middle Ages*,[5] a very curious com-

---

[1] Cap. a., 789, § 41; a., 794, § 40; vol. i., col. 228, 269.
[2] Probably in Latin, Greek, and the German language.
[3] Cap. a., 794, § 50; vol. i., col. 270.
[4] Cap. a., 813, § 14; vol i., col. 505.
[5] In German, vol. i., p. 177—243.

mentary upon this capitulary, and upon all the domestic details which we find there.

VIII. The *occasional legislation* is inconsiderable in amount; only twelve articles belong to this head, and I have just cited some of them.

Here closes my examination, far too brief in itself doubtless, but still more detailed, more definite, I think, than any previously made of the legislation of Charlemagne and its object. I say *legislation*, because I wish to avail myself of words in common use; otherwise, it is quite clear that in all we have gone through there is nothing of what we understand by a code, and that Charlemagne, in his capitularies, did anything but legislate. Capitularies are, properly speaking, the whole acts of his government, public acts of all kinds by which he manifested his authority. It is evident that the collection which has come down to us is far from containing all those acts, and that a large number of them are wanting. There are whole years for which we have no capitularies; in those which we do possess we find provisions which relate to acts which are missing. The collection of Baluze is a mere collection of fragments; they are mutilated wrecks, not of the legislation only, but of the whole government of Charlemagne. This is the point of view under which any one wishing to make an accurate study of the capitularies should view them in order to comprehend and explain them.

In our next lecture, we shall begin to occupy ourselves with the state of mind at the same epoch, and with the influence of Charlemagne over intellectual development.

TWENTY-SECOND LECTURE.

Of intellectual decay in Frankish Gaul, from the fifth to the eighth century—Of its causes—It ceases under the reign of Charlemagne—Difficulty of describing the state of the human mind at this epoch—Alcuin is its most complete and faithful representative—Life of Alcuin—His labors for the restoration of manuscripts—For the restoration of schools—His teaching in the school of the palace—His relations with Charlemagne—His conduct as abbot of Saint Martin of Tours—His works; 1. Theological; 2. Philosophical and literary; 3. Historical; 4. Poetical—His general character.

I HAVE said, and I consider it established, that, from the fifth to the eighth century, decay in Frankish Gaul was constant and general; that it was the essential character of the time, and only stopped under the reign of Charlemagne.

If this character was anywhere more visible, more signal than elsewhere, it was in the intellectual order, in the history of the human mind at this epoch. Recal to mind through what vicissitudes we have seen it pass. At the end of the fourth century, two literatures, two philosophies, marched, as it were, side by side, profane literature and sacred literature, pagan philosophy and Christian theology. It is true, profane literature and pagan philosophy were dying; but they still breathed. We saw them soon disappear; sacred literature and Christian theology alone remained. We have continued on our way; Christian theology and sacred literature themselves have disappeared; we no longer meet with anything but sermons, legends, monuments of an entirely practical activity, devoted to the wants of actual life, foreign to the research and contemplation of the true and beautiful. This is the state into which the human mind had fallen in the seventh, and during the first half of the eighth century.

This decay has been generally attributed to the tyranny of the church, to the triumph of the principle of authority and faith over the principle of liberty and reason. Quite modern writers, men of impartiality and learning—Tennemann, for example, in his *History of Philosophy*[1]—have adopted this ex-

---

[1] In German, vol. viii., p 1—8.

planation. The absolute authority of the church, and the doctrine of pure and simple faith, opposed to that of rational inquiry, have, doubtless, powerfully contributed to weaken the human mind; but it was at a later period that their influence was exercised. At the epoch which occupies us, this cause, I think, had as yet acted but feebly. Recal to mind the picture I place before you of the state of the Christian church at the fifth century;[1] liberty then was great. Now, from the fifth to the eighth century, the church was not constituted with sufficient regularity or strength to exercise tyranny; none of the means of government by which, at a later period, she dominated over mind were then within her hands; the rising papacy as yet possessed only a power of influence and counsel; episcopacy, although it was the dominant system of the ecclesiastical society, was weak and disordered; councils became rare; no authority was firm and general; if there had been any true energy of mind, doubtless it would easily have forced itself into light. At a later period, from the 11th to the 14th century, the church was strong; her power was regularly organized; the principle of implicit submission to her decision reigned in the minds of men; and yet intellectual activity was far greater. There was then a real danger in struggling against the church, and yet men struggled: they resisted her pretensions, they even assailed her title. The seventh century made no attempt at attack or resistance; the ecclesiastical power and freedom of thought had not even occasion to commence a struggle.

Is it not, then, to this cause that the intellectual apathy and sterility of this epoch are to be attributed? The fall of the empire, its disorders and miseries, the dissolution of social relations and ties, the occupation and sufferings of personal interests, the impossibility of permanent labor, of tranquil leisure, such were the true causes of the moral, as well as of the political decay, and of the darkness which enveloped the human mind.

Whatever may be the cause of it, the fact is undeniable. If we considered in its entirety the history of the human mind in modern Europe, from the fifth century up to our own days, we should find, I think, that the seventh century is the lowest point to which it has descended, the nadir of its course, so to

---

[1] See vol. i., the third and fourth lectures

speak. With the end of the eighth century began its movement of progress.

It is rather difficult to characterize this movement with exactness, and to sum up in a few characteristic words the intellectual state of Frankish-Gaul under Charlemagne. No one simple idea dominates in it. The works which then occupied mind formed no whole, attached themselves to no principle. They are partial, isolated works; the activity is sufficiently great, but manifests itself by no great results; all attempt to systematize this time under a moral point of view—to reduce it to any general and striking fact, would infallibly misrepresent it.

Another method appears to me more suited to make it known and understood. We find in this period a man with mind doubtless more active and extensive than any around him, except that of Charlemagne; superior in instruction and intellectual activity to any of his contemporaries, without elevating himself much above them by the originality of his knowledge of ideas; in a word, a faithful representative of the intellectual progress of his epoch, which he outstripped in all things, but without ever separating himself from it. This man is Alcuin. It is necessary, as a general rule, to give way only with extreme reserve to the temptation to take a particular man as the image, the representative of an epoch. Such comparisons are more ingenious than solid. On the one hand, a society, however declining and sterile it may be, is almost always, intellectually speaking, greater and richer than an individual. It comprehends a body of ideas, of knowledge of facts, and of moral wants, which are not reproduced within the narrow space of an individual existence. On the other hand, a distinguished man, even when originality is not his pre-eminent characteristic, always differs greatly from the mass of his contemporaries: he is himself, and not a nation; so that, under a twofold relation, the representation is incorrect, and the image fallacious. Care should be taken, in this particular case which occupies us, not to depend too much upon it, though it is, perhaps, here more faithful than in any other instance. Alcuin is, perhaps, one of the men who best represent their epoch; still we must make many reservations. And, at the same time that I place him before you as the expression of the state of the human mind at the end of the eighth century, I should wish to be sure that you will reduce this comparison to its true value.

Alcuin was not a Frenchman. It will be sufficient to cast a glance at the last table in the previous lecture, to see that Charlemagne took great care to attract distinguished foreigners into his states, and that among those who helped to second intellectual development in Frankish Gaul, many came from abroad. Charlemagne even did more. We see, at the seventeenth century, that Louis XIV., not content with protecting letters in his kingdom, extended his encouragement and favor to them throughout Europe. Colbert wrote to learned Germans, Dutch, Alsatians, to announce to them, on the part of the king, presents and pensions, which went sometimes as high as three thousand livres. Analogous facts are met with under Charlemagne; he not only strove to attract distinguished men into his states, but he protected and encouraged them wherever he discovered them. More than one Anglo-Saxon abbey shared his liberality; and learned men who, after following him into Gaul, wished to return to their country, in no way became strangers to him. Peter of Pisa and Paul Warnefried, who remained but a short time in Gaul, experienced this. Alcuin fixed himself there permanently. He was born in England, at York, about 735. The intellectual state of Ireland and England was then superior to that of the continent; letters and schools prospered there more than anywhere else. It is rather difficult to assign any precise causes for this fact; the principal of them, I think, is the following:—Christianity was carried into Ireland by Greek missionaries, and into England by Latin missionaries. In Ireland, during the first ages which followed its introduction, no invasion of barbarians came to stop its progress, to disperse the monasteries and schools, to stifle the intellectual movement which it had set on foot. In England, when the missionaries of Gregory the Great arrived, the barbaric invasion was consummated, the Saxons well established; there also, therefore, Christianity had not to undergo, at least not at this epoch, or until the great incursion of the Danes, any social disorder; its studies and its various works were not violently interrupted. I placed before you, in the beginning of this course,[1] the view of the intellectual state of Gaul in the fourth, and at the commencement of the fifth century; neither schools nor literary men were wanting to it; and if the Visi-

---

[1] Vol. i., lectures third and fourth.

goths, the Burgundians, the Franks, had not brought chaos and ruin into it, the human mind, although weakened, had not fallen into the state in which we find it at the seventh century. This is the advantage which England possessed at that epoch; society here had not been ravaged or broken up by recent, continual invasions. The establishments for study and science which Christianity had formed there, were still erect, and quietly pursued their labors.

Whether this cause is or is not sufficient to explain it, the fact is incontestable. The schools of England, and particularly that of York, were superior to those of the continent. That of York possessed a rich library, where many of the works of pagan antiquity were found; among others, those of Aristotle, which it is a mistake to say were first introduced to the knowledge of modern Europe by the Arabians, and the Arabians only; for from the fifth to the tenth century, there is no epoch in which we do not find them mentioned in some library, in which they were not known and studied by some men of letters. Alcuin himself informs us of the instruction which they gave in the school of the monastery of York. We read in his poem, entitled, *Pontiffs and Saints of the Church of York:*

"The learned Ælbert gave drink to thirsty minds at the sources of various studies and sciences. To some he was eager to communicate the art and rules of grammar; for others he made flow the waves of rhetoric. He exercised these in the combats of jurisprudence, and those in the songs of Adonia. Some learned from him to sound the pipes of Castalia, and to strike with a lyric foot the summits of Parnassus. To others he taught the harmony of heaven, the works of the sun and the moon, the five zones of the pole, the seven wandering stars, the laws of the course of the stars, their appearance and decline, the motions of the sea, the tremblings of the earth, the nature of men, of beasts, and birds, and the inhabitants of woods; he unveiled the various qualities and the combinations of numbers; he taught how to calculate with certainty the solemn return of Easter; and above all, he explained the mysteries of the holy scriptures."[1]

Reduce this pompous description to simple terms: grammar,

---

[1] *Pontiffs and Saints of the Church of York*, v. 1431—1447; *Alcuini Opera*, vol. ii., p. 256, ed. Frohben, 1777.

rhetoric, jurisprudence, poetry, astronomy, natural history, mathematics, chronology, and the explanation of the holy scriptures, these surely form an extensive course of instruction, more extensive than was found at this epoch in any school in Gaul or Spain. He who taught these, this Ælbert whom Alcuin celebrates, became archbishop of York, and Alcuin succeeded him in his functions.

About this time, before 766, he had already made one, or even two journeys to the continent. The occasion and date of the journeys are very difficult to determine. I will not occupy you with these details of minute and complicated criticism. Some learned men have thought that at that time —at Pavia, perhaps—Alcuin saw Charlemagne. If the fact be true, it is to no purpose, for we know absolutely nothing of their first connexion. But, in 780, on the death of archbishop Ælbert, and the accession of his successor, Eanbald, Alcuin received from him the mission to proceed to Rome for the purpose of obtaining from the pope and bringing to him the *pallium*. In returning from Rome, he came to Parma, where he found Charlemagne. It is not known whether this was the first time of their seeing each other; but, at all events, the emperor at once pressed him to take up his abode in France. After some hesitation, Alcuin accepted the invitation, subject to the permission of his bishop, and of his own sovereign. The permission was obtained, and in 782 we find him established in the court of Charlemagne, who at once gave him three abbeys, those of Ferrieres in Gatanois, of St. Loup at Troyes, and of St. Josse in the county of Ponthieu.

From this time forth, Alcuin was the confidant, the councillor, the intellectual prime minister, so to speak, of Charlemagne. Let us endeavor to form somewhat of a clear and complete idea of his labors.

In doing so, we must observe a distinction between his practical activity and his scientific activity, between the immediate results of his personal influence, and those of his writings.

In the practical point of view, as intellectual prime minister of Charlemagne, Alcuin did, more especially, three things —1. He corrected and restored the manuscripts of ancient literature; 2. He revived public schools and public studies; 3. He himself taught.

1. The historians mention only in passing, and without

attaching any importance to it, a fact which really played an important part in the revival of intellectual activity at this period; I mean the revision and correction of ancient manuscripts, both sacred and profane. From the sixth to the eighth century, these had gone through the hands of copyists so ignorant that the texts had become altogether unrecognizable; infinite passages had been mutilated and misplaced; the leaves were in the utmost disorder; all orthographical and grammatical correctness had disappeared; to read and understand the works thus injured, required absolute science, and of science there was less and less every day. To remedy this evil, to restore ancient manuscripts to their proper reading and order, to correct their orthography and their grammar, was one of the first tasks to which Alcuin applied himself; a task which continued to occupy him throughout the remainder of his life, which he constantly recommended to his pupils, and in the fulfilment of which he was supported by Charlemagne's authority. We find among the capitularies an ordinance in these terms:—

"Charles, by the aid of God, king of the Francs and Lombards, and prince of the Romans, to the high ministers of religion throughout our dominions: Having it near at heart that the state of the churches should more and more advance towards perfection, and being desirous of restoring by assiduous care the cultivation of letters, which have almost entirely disappeared from amongst us, in consequence of the neglect and indifference of our ancestors, we would excite by our own example all well-disposed persons to the study of the liberal arts. To this purpose, we have already, by God's constant help, accurately corrected the books of the Old and New Testaments, corrupted by the ignorance of the copyists. We could not endure that in the divine services, amidst the sacred lessons, there should occur discordant solecisms, and we, therefore, conceived the design of reforming these lessons. We entrusted this work to our proved servant, the deacon Paul. We enjoined him diligently to go through the writings of the catholic fathers; to cull amidst those fertile meads the finest and most useful flowers, and to form of these one sweet and beneficial garland. Eager to obey our highness, he re-perused the treatises and discoveries of the various catholic fathers, and selecting the best of these, has presented to us, in two volumes, a series of divine readings, freed from inaccuracies, adapted to each sacred day throughout the year. We have examined the texts of these volumes with our sagacity, and having found them worthy of our sanction and authority, we transmit them to you to be read in the churches of Christ under your care."[1]

Whilst he was thus, by the agency of others, collecting and correcting the texts destined for divine services, Alcuin himself labored at a complete revisal of the sacred writings. He concluded it about the year 801, in the abbey of St. Martin de Tours, and sent it to Charlemagne. "I long meditated," he says, "what present I could offer you, not merely not unworthy of the glory of your imperial power, but which might form some addition to your wealth; for I could not consent that while others were laying at your feet rich gifts of every kind, my humble talents should remain so idle as not to prepare some offering to your beatitude. At length by an inspiration of the Holy Ghost, I thought of a present at once suitable in me to offer, and calculated to be agreeable to your wisdom. What, indeed, could be more worthy of you than the divine books, which I herewith send to your Most Illustrious Authority, collected into one body, and carefully freed from all errors, to the utmost of our ability and pains? If the devotion of my heart could have devised anything better, I would have offered it to you with equal zeal for the increase of your glorious fortune."[2]

This present, it would seem, excited the emulation of Charlemagne himself, for we read in Thegau, a contemporary chronicler, that, "in the year which preceded Charlemagne's death, he carefully corrected, by the assistance of certain learned Greeks and Syrians, the four gospels of Jesus Christ."[3]

Such examples, and such orders, could not fail of effect, and the ardor for the reproduction of ancient manuscripts became general; as soon as an exact revision of any work had been completed by Alcuin or one of his disciples, copies of it were transmitted to the principal churches and abbeys, where fresh copies were made for diffusion amongst the lesser churches and abbeys. The art of copying became a source of fortune,

---

[1] Constitution of Charlemagne, addressed to the bishops, in 788; Baluze, i., 203.
[2] Letters of Alcuin, i., 153, letter 103.
[3] *De la Vie e des Actes de Louis le Debonnaire*, in my *Collection des Mémoires relatifs à l'Histoire de France*, 111, 281.

of glory even; the monasteries in which the most correct and beautiful copies were executed, attained celebrity on this sole account; and, in each monastery, the monks who most excelled in the art were, in like manner, honored among their brethren. The abbey of Fontenelle, and two of its members, Ovon and Hardouin, were especially renowned in this respect. The fraternities at Reims and at Corbie sought to vie with the famed monks of Fontenelle; instead of the corrupt characters which had been in use for the past two centuries, the small Roman characters were resumed. The monastic libraries soon became very considerable in their extent; a great number of existing manuscripts date from this period; and though its zeal was more peculiarly directed to sacred literature, profane literature was not altogether neglected. Alcuin himself, it is stated, on more than one authority, revised and copied the plays of Terence.

II. At the same time that he was restoring manuscripts, and thus supplying study with sound materials, he labored with ardor at the re-establishment of schools, which had then fallen everywhere into decay: here again an ordinance by Charlemagne shows us the measures, doubtless suggested by Alcuin himself, which were taken on this subject:

"Charles, by the aid of God, &c., to Baugulf, abbot, and his brotherhood, health:

"We beg to inform your Devotion to God that, in concert with our councillors, we have deemed it beneficial that in the bishoprics and monasteries confided by the favor of Christ to our government, care should be taken, not only to live orderly and according to our holy religion, but moreover to instruct in the knowledge of letters, and according to the capacity of individuals, all such as are willing and able to learn, by God's help. For though of the two it is better to be good than to be learned, yet to have knowledge leads to the being good. In the various letters addressed to us from monasteries, announcing that the brethren continued to pray for us in their holy ceremonies, and in their private orisons, we have remarked that for the most part, while the sentiments were excellent, the language in which they were conveyed was generally rude and illiterate; that the fine thoughts and feelings which a pious devotion dictated within, an unskilful and an uneducated tongue mutilated in the delivery. This inspired us with an apprehension that the same want of ability which prevented men from writing properly, must also operate in keeping them from a due understanding of the holy scriptures. It is certain, at all events, that the allegories, emblems, and imagery of the holy writings, will be more readily comprehended in their true spiritual meanings, by those who are versed in general learning. We, therefore, would have you select from among your brethren such as may be deemed best fitted, for first acquiring themselves, and then communicating to others, a knowledge of letters; and let such proceed to their task with the least possible delay. As you value our favor, fail not to communicate copies of this communication to all the suffragan bishops, and all the monasteries around you."[1]

Many contemporary monuments give evidence that this *imperial circular*, as we should now call it, did not remain without effect; that it resulted in the re-establishment of systematic studies in the episcopal cities and in the great monasteries. From this epoch date the majority of the schools, which soon afterwards acquired such celebrity, and from which proceeded the most distinguished men of the following century; for example, of Ferrieres in Gatinois, of Fulda in the diocese of Mayence, of Richenau in that of Constance, of Aniane in Languedoc, of Fontenelle or St. Vandrille, in Normandy; while most of the men who did honor to these establishments at the period in question, had been disciples of Alcuin himself, who, amid all his avocations, was a public preacher and a public teacher of great distinction.

III. It was not, however, in a monastery, nor in any public institution, that he taught in the first instance: from 782 to 796, the period of his residence in the court of Charlemagne, Alcuin presided over a private school, called *The School of the Palace*, which accompanied Charlemagne wherever he went, and at which were regularly present all those who were with the emperor. Here, besides many others, Alcuin had for auditors:

1. Charles, son of Charlemagne.
2. Pepin   do.
3. Louis   do.
4. Adalhard.
5. Angilbert.
6. Flavius Damœtas.   } Privy councillors of Charlemagne
7. Eginhard.

---

[1] Baluze. i, 201.

8. Riculf, archbishop of Mayence.
9. Rigbod, archbishop of Trèves.
10. Gisla, sister of Charlemagne.
11. Gisla, daughter of Charlemagne.
12. Richtrude, a nun of Chelles.
13. Gundrade, sister of Adalhard; and Charlemagne himself, who took the most lively interest in the lessons given.

It is difficult to say what could have been the course of instruction pursued in this school; I am disposed to believe that to such auditors Alcuin addressed himself generally upon all sorts of topics as they occurred; that in the *Ecole du Palais*, in fact, it was conversation rather than teaching, especially so called, that went on; that movement given to mind, curiosity constantly excited and satisfied, was its chief merit. At such periods, in the days of its new birth, amid the joy of its first progress, the mind is neither regular nor fastidious; it troubles itself very slightly as to the beauty and real utility of its labors; that which it takes most especial delight in is the play of thought, it may be said to disport with itself rather than to study; it is more intent upon its own immediate activity than upon results; so that it is occupied with something which interests it, that is all it asks; let it but discover or produce something new, unexpected, and it is all delight. There has come down to us a singular specimen of the instruction given at this *Ecole du Palais*: it is a conversation entitled *Disputatio*, between Alcuin and Pepin, second son of Charlemagne, at that period a youth of fifteen or sixteen: I will lay before you a literal translation of the greater portion of this; you will judge for yourselves as to its claims to a learned character, and whether it is what we now understand by lessons.

Interlocutors: PEPIN, ALCUIN.

" PEPIN. What is writing?
ALCUIN. The keeping of history.
P. What is speaking?
A. The interpreter of the soul.
P. What is it gives birth to speaking?
A. The tongue.
P. What is the tongue?
A. The whip of the air.
P. What is the air?
A. The preserver of life.
P. What is life?

A. Happiness for the happy, misery for the miserable; the expectation of death.

P. What is death?

A. An inevitable event, a doubtful journey, a subjec. of tears for the living, the confirmation of wills, the robber of men.

P. What is man?

A. The slave of death, a passing traveller, a guest in his own abode.

P. How is man placed?

A. As a traveller exposed to the world.

P. Where is he placed?

A. Between six walls.

P. What are they?

A. That above, that below, that on the right, that on the left, that in front, that behind.

P. What is sleep?

A. The image of death.

P. What is the liberty of man?

A. Innocence.

P. What is the head?

A. The pinnacle of the body.

P. What is the body?

A. The abode of the soul.

(Next follow twenty-six questions relative to the various parts of the human body, which I suppress as wholly destitute of interest. Then Pepin goes on:)

P. What is heaven?

A. A moving sphere, an immense vault.

P. What is light?

A. The torch of all things.

P. What is the day?

A. A call to labor.

P. What is the sun?

A. The splendor of the universe, the beauty of the firmament, the grace of nature, the glory of the day, the distributor of the hours.

(I here again suppress five questions on the stars and elements.)

P. What is the earth?

A. The mother of all that grows, the nurse of all that exists, the granary of life, the gulf which swallows up all things.

P. What is the sea?
A. The highway of the daring, the limits of the earth, the hostelry of rivers, the source of rain.

(Now follow six wholly uninteresting questions as to material objects in nature. Then Pepin goes on:)

P. What is winter?
A. The exile of spring.
P. What is spring?
A. The painter of the earth.
P. What is summer?
A. The power which clothes the earth, and ripens fruits.
P. What is autumn?
A. The granary of the year.
P. What is the year?
A. The chariot of the world.

(I here omit five astronomical questions.)

P. Master, I am afraid to go upon the sea.
A. What leads you to the sea?
P. Curiosity.
A. If you are afraid, I will accompany you.
P. If I knew what a ship was, I would prepare one wherein thou mightest accompany me.
A. A ship is a wandering house, an inn ready in all places, a traveller who leaves no trace behind him.
P. What is grass?
A. The robe of the earth.
P. What are vegetables?
A. The friends of the physician, the glory of the cooks.
P. What is it renders bitter things sweet?
A. Hunger.
P. What is that of which men never get weary?
A. Gain.
P. What is the dream of the waking?
A. Hope.
P. What is hope?
A. The refreshment of labor, a doubtful event.
P. What is friendship?
A. The similarity of souls.
P. What is faith?
A. The assurance of unknown and marvellous things.
P. What is marvellous?
A. I saw the other day a man standing, a dead man walking, a man walking who had never breathed.

P. How may that have been? Explain yourself.

A. It was an image reflected in the water.

P. How could I have failed to understand you; I who have so often seen the same thing?

A. As you are a youth of good disposition, and endowed with natural capacity, I will put to you several other unusual questions: endeavor to solve them.

P. I will do my best; if I make mistakes, you must correct them.

A. Doubtless. Some one, who is unknown to me, has conversed with me, having no tongue and no voice; he was not before, he will not be hereafter, and I neither heard nor knew him. What means this?

P. Perhaps you mean a dream, master?

A. Exactly so, my son. Listen, once more: I have seen the dead engender the living, and the dead consumed by the breath of the living.

P. Fire was produced by rubbing together dead branches, and it then consumed the branches.

A. You are quite accurate.

(Then come fourteen more enigmas of the same character, and the conversation terminates as follows):

A. What is that which at one and the same time is and is not?

P. Nothing.

A. How can it be and not be?

P. It exists in name, but not in fact.

A. What is a mute messenger?

P. That which I hold in my hand.

A. What do you hold in your hand?

P. My letter.

A. Read it, my son."[1]

Clearly, as a means of education, these conversations are altogether and strangely puerile: as a symptom and commencement of intellectual movement, they merit all our attention: they evidence that eager curiosity with which mind, in its crude infancy, directs its view upon all things; that so vivid pleasure which it takes in every unexpected combination, in every at all ingenious idea; a tendency which is manifested alike in the life of individuals and in that of

---

[1] Alcuini Opera, ii., 352—354.

nations, and which gives birth to the most fantastic dreams, the vainest subtleties. It was, beyond doubt, dominant in the palace of Charlemagne, and, doubtless, led to the formation of that sort of academy there, whose members all assumed surnames derived from sacred or profane literature—Charlemagne—David, Alcuin—Flaccus, Angilbert—Homer, Friedgies—Nathaniel, Amalaire—Symphosius, Gisla—Lucia, Gundrade,—Eulalia, and so on; and the singular conversation of which I have just laid extracts before you is, in all probability, only a fair specimen of that which habitually took place, and to their no small delight, among these *beaux-esprits*, half barbarian, half cultivated.

If the influence of Alcuin had been confined within the walls of this academy, it would have effected but little worthy of our notice; but the great business of his life was in connexion with Charlemagne, and the intellectual authority of this extraordinary man was more grave and more productive of results.

To give you an idea of the relations existing between these two men, and of the prodigious movement of mind which Alcuin was entrusted with the direction of, I cannot do better than lay before you the most authentic monument of them which exists—their correspondence. There remain to us, in the whole, two hundred and thirty-two of Alcuin's letters; of these, thirty are addressed to Charlemagne; I will pass these in review before you, sometimes translating passages as I proceed, sometimes merely indicating the nature of their contents.

Review of the Letters of Alcuin to Charlemagne.

No. of the Letter.	Date.	Purport.
14	793	On the Transfiguration of Jesus Christ.
28	796	He congratulates him on his victories over the Huns (Avares), and gives him advice as to the manner in which he should proceed for their conversion: 1. By sending among them gentle-mannered missionaries; 2. By not requiring tithe from them. "It is better to lose the tithe than to prejudice the faith; we ourselves, born, bred, and educated in the Catholic religion, scarce consent to surrender a tithe of our goods; how much less readily will such consent be given by the newly-born faith, the doubtful heart and greedy spirit of these tribes?"

Review of the Letters of Alcuin to Charlemagne

No. of the Letter.	Date.	Purport.
		3 By observing a certain method of religious instruction:
		"This method, I think, should be that which the blessed Augustin has laid down in his book *On the Instruction of the Simple-minded*. The pupil should first be taught the general facts of the immortality of the soul, of a future life, and the eternity of our destiny. Then he should be told for what crimes and sins eternal punishment with the devil and his angels will be inflicted on him, and for what good actions he will be rewarded, in the presence of Christ, with eternal glory. Finally, he should have carefully inculcated upon him faith in the Holy Trinity, and have explained to him the coming of Jesus Christ into this world, for the salvation of mankind."
32	796	He recommends him to be lenient towards his Hun prisoners, and towards his enemies generally.
38	796	He gives him an account of what he is doing for the prosperity of the school at the Abbey of Tours:
		"I, your Flaccus, in obedience to your exhortation and wise desire, apply myself in serving out to some of my pupils in this house of Saint Martin, the honey of the holy writings; I essay to intoxicate others with the old wine of antique studies; one class I nourish with the fruits of grammatical science; in the eyes of another, I display the order of the stars. But I am constantly in want of most of those excellent books of scholastic erudition, which I had collected around me in my own country, both by the devoted zeal of my master, and by my own labor. I therefore entreat your majesty to permit me to send some of my people into Britain that they may bring these flowers thence into France.... In the morning of my life I sowed the seeds of learning in Britain; now, in its eventide, though my blood is less warm within me, I do not cease sowing these seeds in France, and I hope that by the grace of God they will prosper in both countries."
61	797	He gives him a detailed explanation of the lunar cycle.
64	798	He recommends several persons to his favor.
65	798	He explains to him the origin of the names of Septuagesima and Sexagesima. (The sixty-sixth letter is a reply from Charlemagne, who puts forward several objections to his views.)
67	798	He recurs to the subject, and defends himself from the imputation of obstinacy.

Review of the Letters of Alcuin to Charlemagne.

No. of the Letter.	Date.	Purport.
		"As to what you say in the conclusion of your letter, in a most friendly spirit, and solely for my good, that, if there be anything to correct in my opinions on the matter, I should correct them promptly and humbly, I would reply that, thanks to God, I have never been obstinately pertinacious in error, nor over confident in my own opinion; I yield without a struggle to superior judgment, attentive to the maxim that it is better to make use of the ears than of the tongue. I entreat your wisdom, then, to believe that I address myself to you, not as to a disciple but as to a judge, and that I offer you my humble ideas, not as to one ignorant of the matter, but as to one fully competent to correct the views of others."
68	797	On the course of the sun and the phases of the year; and on the heresy of Felix, bishop of Urgel.
69	798	On astronomy and chronology: he replies to several questions which had been addressed to him by a woman, probably Gisla, Charlemagne's sister.
70	798	On astronomy; he replies to several questions of Charlemagne on the course of the sun, the constellations, &c.
71	798	On the same subject.
80	799	On the state of public affairs; he urges him to be lenient towards the Saxons.
81	799	He excuses himself from accompanying Charlemagne to Rome, on the ground of ill health.
84	800	A complimentary letter, with some astronomical calculations.
85	800	He thanks him for having heard read the pamphlet he (Alcuin) had written against bishop Felix, and sends him some observations on orthography and arithmetic.
90	800	He condoles with him on the death of his wife Lintgarde, and forwards an epitaph.
91	800	On the same subject.
93	800	He congratulates him on his victories; exhorts him to clemency; speaks to him about the health of pope Leo; excuses himself for not having written, and refuses to go to Rome.
102	801	He felicitates himself upon the return of Charlemagne from Italy.
103	801	Forwarding his corrected copy of the holy scriptures.
104	801	He excuses himself from going to court, on the ground of his advanced age.
105	801	He expresses his sorrow for the death of Manfred, solicits materials for the building of a church, and en-

Review of the Letters from Alcuin to Charlemagne.

No. of the Letter.	Date.	Purport.
		treats Charlemagne to be careful in avoiding the dangers of the expedition to Benevento: "Though my affection may appear insensate, at least it cannot be charged with want of consistency; and the confidence I have in your proved humility, emboldens me to say to you what I do. Perhaps some one may object: why does he concern himself with that which is not his business? But I humbly interest myself in all that concerns your prosperity, which, I declare to you, is more dear to me than my own life. You are the blessing of the kingdom, the safety of the people, the honor of the church, the protector of all the faithful in Christ; it is under the shadow of your power, the shelter of your pious care, that, by Divine grace, we are enabled to pursue a religious life, and to serve God in tranquillity: it is, therefore, just and necessary, that, with an attentive spirit and a devoted heart, we occupy ourselves with your fortune and your health, and pray God to preserve to us in health and prosperity our most excellent and most honor-worthy king David."
106	801	He thanks him for his favors, and entreats him, on account of his infirmities, to allow him to remain at St. Martin's.
115	802 or 803	He excuses himself and the fraternity of St. Martin for having given an asylum to a priest of the church of Orleans, which affair had been the occasion of a great tumult in the church of St. Martin, and of great anger to Charlemagne and Theodulf.
123	Year uncertain.	He replies to questions forwarded by Charlemagne, as to the difference between the terms *eternal* and *sempiternal, perpetual* and *immortal, age* and *time.*
124	Id.	He replies to questions from Charlemagne, on certain passages of Scripture.
125	Id.	He replies to a question by Charlemagne, why we find in none of the gospels the hymns sung by Jesus Christ after the Last Supper.
126	Id.	He replies to Charlemagne, who has asked him, on the part of a learned Greek, to whom the price of man's redemption was remitted.
127	Id.	He gives advice to Charles on the subjects of capitularies, wills, successions, &c.

It was no easy task for Alcuin to fulfil such varied relations, to satisfy all the intellectual requirements of that indefatigable master, who thought of everything and busied himself with everything—history, morals, theology, astronomy, chronology, grammar—and doubtless regarded it as a matter of course, that in these things, as in all others, his will should in every case, and immediately, be carried into effect.

There is doubtless a powerful charm in the society of a great man; but when the great man is a sovereign, it soon becomes a heavy burden to have to please him at every moment and in everything. No formal text shows it us; but Charlemagne, in his relations with Alcuin, no doubt exhibited that pitiless egoism of a superior and despotic genius, which only considers men, even those whom it best loves, and to whom it attaches the greatest importance, as tools, and progresses towards its end without troubling itself as to how dear it costs those whom it employs in the attainment. A profound weariness seized upon Alcuin—he earnestly solicited permission to retire from the court, and to live in retirement. In 796, he wrote to an archbishop, whose name is unknown:

"Your paternity must know that I your son ardently desire to lay aside the weight of worldly affairs, and to serve God alone. Every man needs with vigilance to prepare to meet God, and how especially so old men, borne down with years and infirmities!"[1]

And to his friend Angilbert:

"On thy departure, I attempted many times to take refuge in the haven of repose; but the King of all things, the Master of souls, has not yet accorded to me what he has so long made me wish."[2]

Charlemagne at length allowed him to depart, and about 796, it seems, he gave him for a retreat the abbey of Saint Martin of Tours, one of the most wealthy in the kingdom.

Alcuin hastened to take possession of it. The retreat was magnificent; there were more than twenty thousand laborers or serfs on the domains of the abbeys which he possessed, and the correspondence which he continued to keep up with Charlemagne animated without burdening his life. He did not remain idle in his new situation; he re-established rule and order in the monastery, enriched the library with manuscripts copied at York by young priests whom he sent for this purpose, and by his own teaching he gave the school a

---

[1] **Lett.** of Alcuin, 168th, vol. i., p. 228. [2] Ibid., 21st, vol. i., p. 31.

brilliancy which it had never before known. It was at this epoch that many of the most distinguished men of the following century—among others, Raban Maur, who became archbishop of Mayence, and Amalaire, a learned priest of Metz—were formed by his lessons.

Charlemagne attempted several times to recal Alcuin to his side; he wished him, among others, to accompany him to Rome, when he went there, in 800, to assume the empire of the west. "It is a reproach," he writes to him, "to prefer the smoked roofs of the people of Tours to the gilded palaces of the Romans."[1]

But Alcuin remained firm.

"I do not think," answers he, "that my weak body, broken by daily pains, can support this journey. I should have much desired it if it were practicable.[2] How can I constrain myself to new combats, and to toil under the weight of arms—I, who am left by my infirmities scarcely in a state to raise them from the earth?[3] . . . I implore you to leave me to finish my career at Saint Martin; all the energy, all the dignity of my body has flown; I admit it; less and less is daily left me, and I shall never again recover it in this world. I had of late desired and hoped once more to see the face of your beatitude, but the deplorable increase of my infirmities has proved to me that I must renounce that hope. I conjure, then, your inexhaustible goodness that the so holy spirit, that the so benevolent will, which are in you, be not irritated against my weakness; grant, with a pious compassion, that a wearied man may repose himself, that he may pray for you in his orisons, and that he may prepare, by confession and tears, to appear before the eternal judge."[4]

Charlemagne, it seems, insisted no longer; and Alcuin, perhaps in order to protect himself from new solicitations, resolved entirely to renounce all activity, even that to which he had given himself up in his retreat. In 801, he resigned his abbeys, and obtained that they should be divided among his principal disciples; and, free from all business, he, till the day of his death (19th May, 804), occupied himself only with his health and his salvation.

I have given somewhat of expansion to this account of his

---

[1] Lett. of Alcuin, 93d, vol. i., p. 139. [2] Ibid., 81st letter, p. 120.
[3] Ibid., 101th letter, p. 154. [4] Ibid., 106th, p. 157.

relations with Charlemagne, and the various situations of his life; it is there, more especially, that is reflected the image of this time, and that the social movement amidst which he lived is shown. I will now say something to you of his works; a few words and a few extracts will, I hope, suffice to give you at least an idea of them.

They may be divided into four classes: 1, theological works; 2, philosophical and literary works; 3, historical works; 4, poetical works.

1. The theological works are of three kinds: 1. Commentaries on various parts of the holy scriptures; commentaries whose especial object is to discover the allegorical meaning, and to determine the moral sense of the sacred writings. 2. Dogmatical treatises, the greater part directed against the heresies of the Adoptians respecting the nature of Jesus Christ; a heresy which played a rather important part at this time, which was condemned by two councils held by the order of Charlemagne, and of which Alcuin was the principal adversary. 3. Liturgical works on the celebration of ecclesiastical offices.

2. The philosophical and literary works are six in number: 1, a kind of treatise of practical morality, entitled *De Virtutibus et Vitiis*, and addressed to count Wido or Guy in a dedicatory epistle, and a peroration in the following terms:

"I recollect thy request and my promise; thou didst urgently pray me to write thee some exhortations in a concise style, in order that, amidst the occupations given thee by military affairs, thou mightest constantly have before thine eyes a manual of maxims and paternal counsels, where thou mightest examine thyself, and excite thyself to seek eternal beatitude. I very willingly comply with so worthy a request; and be assured that, although these counsels may appear to thee written without eloquence, they are dictated by holy charity. I have divided this discourse into separate chapters, so that my advice may be more easily fixed on the memory of thy piety; for I know thou art much occupied with worldly affairs. Let the holy desire to thy salvation, I beseech thee, make thee often have recourse to this reading, as to a useful refreshment: so that thy soul, fatigued with external cares, may enter into itself, there find enjoyment, and understand properly to what it ought especially to apply itself.

"And do not allow thyself to be deterred by the lay habit which thou wearest, or by the secular life which thou leadest, as though in that habit thou couldst not pass through the gates of celestial life. For as the beatitude of the kingdom of God is preached to all without distinction, so the entry to that kingdom is open equally, with only a distinction as to merits, to each sex, to all ages, to all ranks; there no heed is taken as to whether a man on earth has been layman or priest, rich or poor, young or old, master or slave, but eternal glory crowns each according to his works."[1]

Thirty-five chapters then follow upon the various virtues and vices, wisdom, faith, charity, indulgence, envy, pride, &c. We find nothing here particularly original or profound; but practical utility is aimed at with much good sense, and human nature is sometimes observed and described with a highly intellectual delicacy. The following two chapters prove it.

" Of Sorrow.

" There are two kinds of sorrow, the one beneficial, the other pernicious. Sorrow is beneficial when the soul of the sinner is afflicted with his sins, and is so afflicted with them that it aspires to confession and penitence, and desires to be converted to God. Very different is worldly sorrow, which works the death of the soul, become incapable of accomplishing any good; this latter troubles man, and often depresses him to that point that he loses the hope of eternal good. Of this sorrow are born malice, rancor, cowardice, bitterness, and despair, often even disgust at this life. It is conquered by spiritual joy, hope of future blessings, the consolation given by the scriptures, and by fraternal conversation, animated with spiritual enjoyment."[2]

" Of Vain Glory.

" That pest, vain glory, is a passion with a thousand forms, which glides on all sides into the heart of the man who is occupied in striving against vices, and even of the man who has conquered them. In the deportment and the beauty of the body, in step, word, action, fasts, prayer, solitude, reading, science, silence, obedience, humility, long-suffering, patience, it seeks a means of overcoming the soldier of Christ;

---

[1] Alcuin Oper., vol. ii., pp. 129, 145. [2] Chap. 38, vol. ii., p. 152.

it resembles a dangerous rock concealed under swollen billows, and which prepares a terrible storm for those who sail the most successfully, and when they are all unsuspecting. This man, who does not take pride in fine and splendid clothing, the demon of false glory endeavors to inspire with a pride in the foulness and coarseness of common clothing; another has resisted the temptations of ambition, he will be lost by those of humility; a third has not allowed himself to be puffed up by the advantages of science and eloquence, he will be subdued by the gravity of silence. One publicly fasts, and vain glory possesses him; to escape it he fasts in secret; it insinuates its poison into the swelling heart of the internal man; for fear of succumbing he avoids long prayer before his brothers, but what he does in secret does not protect him from the excitements of vanity; it puffs one, because he is very patient in his works and labors; another because he is very prompt to obey; this man because he surpasses all others in humility; that, because of his zeal in science; a third, by reason of his application to reading; a fourth, because of the length of his watches. A terrible evil, which strives to sully man, not only in works of the world, but even in his virtues."[1]

There is here a rather skilful observation of human nature, and a tolerable art in expressing the results.

The title of the second work of this class is *De Ratione Animæ* (*of the nature of the soul*), and it is addressed to Gundrade, sister of Adalhard, and surnamed Eulalia, one of the women who were present at the lectures of Alcuin in the school of the palace. It is a more purely philosophical attempt than the preceding, and in which, under all its forms, the idea of the unity of the soul is expressed with subtlety and energy.

" The soul," says he, " bears divers names according to the nature of its operations: inasmuch as it lives and makes live, it is the soul (*anima*); inasmuch as it contemplates, it is the spirit (*spiritus*); inasmuch as it feels, it is sentiment (*sensus*); since it reflects, it is thought (*animus*); as it comprehends, intelligence (*mens*); inasmuch as it discerns, reason (*ratio*); as it consents, will (*voluntas*); as it recollects, memory

---

[1] Chap. 31, vol. ii., p. 144.

(*memoria*). But these things are not divided in substance as in name, for all this is the soul, and one soul only."

And elsewhere:

"The soul, in its very nature, has an image, as it were, of the Holy Trinity, for it has intellect, will, and memory. The soul, which is also called the mind, the life, the substance which includes these three faculties within itself, is one; these three faculties do not constitute three lives, but one life; not three minds, but one mind; not three substances, but one substance. When we give to the soul the names of mind, life, or substance, we regard it in itself; but when we call it the memory, the intellect, or the will, we consider it in its relation to something. These three faculties make but one, inasmuch as the life, the mind, the substance, form one. They make three, inasmuch as they are considered in their external relations; for the memory is the recollection of something; the intellect is the understanding of something; the will is the will of something, and in this they are distinguished. And still there is in these three faculties a certain unity. I think that I think, that I will, and that I remember; I will to think, and to recollect, and to will; I remember that I have thought and willed, and that I have remembered, and thus these three faculties are combined in one."[2]

In other respects, there are in this treatise nothing but scattered ideas, and no systematic character.

After these two moral essays, come four treatises; 1. On grammar; 2. On orthography; 3. On rhetoric; 4. On logic, which I shall only mention; for to make known the contents and merits of them would render it necessary to enter too far into detail. The last two are in the form of a dialogue between Alcuin and Charlemagne, the object of which is evidently to instruct Charlemagne in the methods of the ancient sophists and rhetoricians, especially in what concerns logic and judicial eloquence.

3. The historical works of Alcuin are of little importance; they are confined to four lives of the saints, Saint Waast, Saint Martin, Saint Riquier, and Saint Willibrod. The latter, however, contains some rather curious details for a history of manners. It is said that Alcuin wrote a history of Charle-

---

[1] Vol. ii., p. 119.

magne, in particular of his wars with the Saxons, but this, if it ever existed, is now lost.

4. His poetical works, although numerous, are also but of little value; there are two hundred and eighty pieces of verse, upon all kinds of subjects, most of them upon the incidents of the day. The principal is a poem upon the bishops and saints of the church of York; it is worth reading, as an indication of the intellectual state of the age.

I regret that I am unable to enter more fully into these monuments of a mind so active and distinguished. Some will, perhaps, think I have dwelt too long upon them as it is · for myself, I fear that I have scarcely thrown a glance at them; and if we were to make a profound study of them, we should unquestionably find both profit and pleasure in it: but we must restrict ourselves. To sum up, the following seems to me to be the general character, the intellectual physiognomy of Alcuin and of his works. He is a theologian by profession, the atmosphere in which he lived, in which the public to whom he addresses himself lived, is essentially theological; and yet the theological spirit does not reign alone in him, his works and his thoughts also tend towards philosophy and ancient literature; it is that which he also delights in studying, teaching, and which he wished to revive. Saint Jerome and Saint Augustin are very familiar to him; but Pythagoras, Aristotle, Aristippus, Diogenes, Plato, Homer, Virgil, Seneca, Pliny, also occur to his memory. The greater part of his writings are theological; but mathematics, astronomy, logic, rhetoric, habitually occupy him. He is a monk, a deacon, the light of the contemporaneous church; but he is at the same time a scholar, a classical man of letters. In him, at length, commenced the alliance of these two elements of which the modern mind had so long borne the incoherent impress, antiquity and the church—the admiration, the taste, the regret, shall I call it, for pagan literature, and the sincerity of Christian faith, the zeal to sound its mysteries, and to defend its power.

TWENTY-THIRD LECTURE.

Classification of celebrated men of the age of Charlemagne: 1. Leidrade, archbishop of Lyons—His letter to Charlemagne upon what he has done to his diocese—2. Theodulph, archbishop of Orleans—His measures for the instruction of the people—His poem entitled *Exhortation to Judges*—3. Smaragde, abbot of Saint Michael—His treatise of morality for kings, entitled *Via Regia*—4. Eginhard—His alleged marriage with a daughter of Charlemagne—Their relations—Of what happened after the death of this prince—His letters—His *Life of Charlemagne*—Recapitulation.

When I placed before you the view of the celebrated men of the age of Charlemagne, I comprehended therein those who died and those who were born in his reign, his contemporaries, properly so called, and those who long survived him; the former discovered, as it were, and employed by him, the second, formed under his influence: an important distinction, if we would justly estimate an epoch and the influence of a man. A sovereign arrives at power in the midst of circumstances, and under the influence of causes, anterior to, and independent of his own will; and which have planted around distinguished men; he gathers them, but he has not made them: his merit consists in knowing how to recognize them, to accept them, to make use of them; but they are not the result of his action; we must not judge of this by them. We have in modern times a striking example of this distinction. Most of the men who constituted the glory of the reign of Louis XIV. were formed entirely independently of him, while the religious struggles still resounded in France, amidst the troubles of the Fronde, and in a liberty which soon vanished. The true fruit of the influence of Louis XIV. belongs to the last period of his reign; it is the manners and the men of that time which are necessary to be considered in order to judge properly of the effects of his government, and the direction which it impressed upon mind. The distinction is great, and should be well observed.

We shall find no such difference among the men whom Charlemagne found, and those who were formed under him. The latter were in no way inferior to their predecessors, but they were different, and the truth of the distinction which I have pointed out is equally evident.

I spoke in our last lecture of the chief, and, without contradiction, the most distinguished cotemporary of Charlemagne. The men of whom I am about to speak, at least almost all of them, belong to the same epoch, to the same class; like Alcuin, they were not formed by Charlemagne; he discovered and made use of them. Two among them, Leidrade and Theodulph, were, like Alcuin, foreigners; and without Charlemagne, would probably never have appeared in Frankish Gaul.

I. Leidrade was born in the province which the Romans called Norica, situated on the confines of Italy and Germany. He was first attached to Arnon, bishop of Salzburg, and made himself distinguished at an early age by his mind and knowledge. Charlemagne first engaged him as a librarian, and employed him in various missions. The *missi dominici*, the principal instruments, as you have seen, of his government, were almost all men of this kind, whom he had attracted from all parts, and whom he habitually retained near him, in order to send them, according to need, to inspect some portion of his states, until, sooner or later, he separated from them, conferring upon them some great ecclesiastical or civil charge. It thus happened to Leidrade. After numerous missions, the last of which, in Southern Gaul, prevented him for some time from being consecrated, he was nominated, in 798, archbishop of Lyons. The church of Lyons had always been one of the most considerable of the south of Gaul, and, at the same time, one of those in which disorder had been the greatest, and calculated to give the greatest trouble to repair. It was on this ground, and to satisfy this want, that Charlemagne confided it to Leidrade. A curious monument has come down to us of what the new archbishop did in his diocese. This is a letter in which he himself gives a detailed account to Charlemagne of his labors and their results. I will read it entire, despite its emphatic prolixities. It is necessary to bear with them in order to form a true idea of the turn of mind of the age, and the relations of an archbishop with the sovereign. The date of this letter is not exactly known, but it probably belongs to the early years of the ninth century.

" *To Charles the Great, Emperor.*

" To the powerful Charles, emperor, Leidrade, bishop of Lyons, health. Our lord, perpetual and sacred emperor, I supplicate the clemency of your highness, to hear read this short epistle with a favorable countenance, so that your pious prudence may know what it contains, and that your noble clemency may know the purport of my request. You deigned awhile ago to entrust the government of the church of Lyons to me, the most infirm of your servants, incapable and unworthy of that charge. But since you treat men far less according to their merit, than according to your accustomed bounty, you have acted with me as it has pleased your ineffable piety; and without any title thereto on my part, you have been pleased to charge me with the care of this church, and to act in such a manner that the abuses which have been committed in it may be for the future reformed and avoided. Many things were wanting to this church, both externally and internally, as much in what concerns the holy offices, as for the edifices and other ecclesiastical wants. Listen, therefore, to what I, your very humble servant, have effected in it, since my arrival, with God's aid and yours. The all powerful Lord, who sees into consciences, is my witness, that I do not expose these things in order to draw profit therefrom, and that I have in no way arranged, and communicate this to you in order to procure any advantage to myself, but because I expect each day to leave this life, that because of my infirmities I think myself very near death. I tell you these things to the end that, having attained your benign ear, and being weighed with indulgence, if you think that they have been effected suitably, and according to your will, they may not, after my death, be allowed to languish and perish.

" When, according to your order, I had taken possession of this church, I acted with all my power, with all the strength of my weakness, to bring the ecclesiastical offices to the point at which, with the grace of God, they have nearly arrived. It pleased your piety to grant at my request the restitution of the revenues which formerly belonged to the church of Lyons; by means of which, with God's grace and yours, there has been established in the said church, a psalmody, where is followed, as far as we are able, the ceremonies of the sacred palace, in all that the divine office requires. I have schools of singers, many of whom are already sufficiently instructed to be able to teach others. Moreover, I have schools of readers, who no only acquit themselves of their functions in the church, but who, by meditation on the holy scriptures, assure themselves the fruits of understanding of spiritual things. Some can explain the spiritual sense of the Evangelists; others have understanding of the prophecies; others, of the books of Solomon, the Psalms, and even Job. I have also done in this church what lay in my power, as to copying books. I have likewise procured clothing for the priests, and what was necessary for the offices. I have omitted nothing which lay in my power for the restoration of the churches, so that I have roofed the great church of this town, dedicated to Saint John the Baptist, and I have reconstructed a portion of the walls; I have also repaired the roof of the church of Saint Etienne; I have rebuilt the church of Saint Nizier, and that of Saint Mary, without counting the monasteries and episcopal houses, of which one in particular was almost destroyed, and which I have repaired and re-roofed. I have also constructed another with a high platform. This I have prepared for you, in order that if you come into these parts you may be received there. For the priests, I have constructed a cloister in which they now live all united in one edifice. I have also repaired other churches in this diocese, one of them dedicated to Saint Eulalia, where there is a nunnery dedicated to Saint George; I have had it re-roofed, and part of the walls built up from the foundations; another house in honor of Saint Paul has also been re-roofed. I have entirely repaired the church and house of a nunnery dedicated to Saint Peter, where rests the body of Saint Annemond, martyr, and which was founded by that holy bishop himself. Thirty-two virgins of the Lord now live there under the monastic rule. I have also repaired, by renewing the roof and part of the walls, the royal monastery of l'Isle Barbe; ninety monks now live there under a regular monastic rule. We have given to its abbot the power to bind and unbind; the same as his predecessors had—Ambrose, Maximian, Licinius, illustrious men who have governed this place, and which Euchere, Loup, Genest, and the other bishops of Lyons, when they were absent and could not fulfil in person, delegated, in order to take care that the catholic faith was believed with sincerity, and that heretical feuds did not abound.

"These abbots were even charged, if the church of Lyons was without its chief, to serve it in all things as guides and counsellors, until, with the grace of God, it was provided with a worthy pastor. We have likewise given this power to their successors. Above all things, we have ordered that the decrees of the ancient kings of France should be executed, to the end that, as it was by them ordained in their statutes respecting sales and augmentations, these monks may for ever possess without dispute, that which they have at present, that which by the grace of God they may one day acquire."[1]

I shall spare all commentary: the letter is sufficiently detailed to show what an archbishop did at that time, who wished to re-establish religion, society, and learning, in his diocese. Leidrade passed his life in works of this kind; we find him quitting his church but twice to go into Spain, by the order of Charlemagne, to discuss and preach against the heresy of the Adoptians. His eloquence, it is said, gained for him there brilliant triumphs, and thousands of heretics were converted by him. However this may have been, in 814, almost immediately after the death of Charlemagne, whether from sorrow or prudence, he resigned his bishopric, and shut himself up in the monastery of Saint Medard at Soissons. He was taken thence for awhile, by Louis le Debonnaire, who charged him with re-establishing order in the church of Macon. No chronicler pronounces his name after this epoch, and with the exception of the letter which I have just read, there only remain of his writings two or three short and very insignificant theological pieces.

II. We are better acquainted with a friend of Leidrade, his companion in the great mission entrusted to him by Charlemagne, in Narbonnese Gaul; I mean Theodulph, bishop of Orleans. Like Alcuin and Leidrade, he was a foreigner, a Goth by nation, and an Italian by birth. Charlemagne sent for him, it is unknown at what epoch; we find him established in Gaul in 781, and between 786 and 796, he was bishop of Orleans. He took especial care to re-establish schools in his diocese. We have by him, concerning the duties of priests, a capitulary in forty-one articles, which displays rather elevated views of order and morality, and contains, among others, the two following articles:

"If any priest wishes to send his nephew or any other of

---

[1] *Sanct. Agobardi Opera*, vol. ii., pp. 125—129, ed. of Baluze, Paris, 1665.

his relations to school, we allow him to be sent to the church of St. Croix, or to the monastery of Saint Aignan, or of Sain Benedict, or of Saint Lifard, or to any other monastery confided to our government.

"Let the priests hold schools in villages and districts, and if any of the faithful wish to confide their young children to them, in order to have them study letters, let them not refuse to receive and to instruct them; but, on the contrary, teach them in perfect charity, remembering that it is written: 'And they that be wise, shall shine as the brightness of the firmament, and they that turn many to righteousness, as the stars for ever and ever.'[1] And while instructing children, let them exact no price therefor, and receive nothing, except when the parent shall offer it them, willingly, and out of affection."[2]

This last article is almost the only monument of this epoch which positively institutes a teaching destined for others than priests. All the measures, whether of Alcuin or Charlemagne, which I have hitherto spoken of, have the literary education of priests for their object; here are included the faithful in general, the people; and not only the people of towns, but of the country districts, which were far more neglected as regards instruction. There is nothing to show us the results of the recommendations of Theodulf in his diocese, and they were probably almost null; but the attempt deserves remark.

About the year 798, Theodulph was sent by Charlemagne, with Leidrade, into the two Narbonnese, to observe and reform the administration of those provinces. On his return he composed a poem of 956 verses, entitled, *Parænesis ad Judices* (Exhortation to Judges), and destined to instruct magistrates in their duties in such missions. The course of the work is simple. After a religious preamble, which terminates with an eulogy on Charlemagne, Theodulph describes the route followed by Leidrade and himself, and the principal towns through which they passed, Vienne, Orange, Avignon, Nimes, Agde, Beziers, Narbonne, Carcassonne, Arles, Marseilles, and Aix. To this enumeration succeeds a view of the dangers which assail the probity of magistrates, and of all the attempts which were made to corrupt Leidrade and

---

[1] Daniel, xii., 3. [2] Theod., cap. § 19, 20.

himself. Then come his exhortations to the judges, exhortations over which he takes pleasure in dwelling at length, as a man who has seen the evil, and as a bishop accustomed to give everything the form of a sermon. The poem abruptly finishes with this general exhortation to the great men of the world:

" Mortal, always be prepared to treat mortals with mildness; the law of nature is the same for them and for thee. However different may be thy course here below, thou and they start from the same point; it is to the same point that you tend. One sacred spring runs for them as for thee, and throws upon them, as upon thee, the same paternal blot. . . . The Author of life died for them as well as for thee, and he will extend his gifts to each according to his merits. Let us here fold the sails of my book, and let the anchor retain my ship on this shore."[1]

There is, in all this, you see, very little invention or art: but, as an historical and moral monument, the poem is devoid neither of merit nor interest. The most curious passage, in my opinion, is that where Theodulph describes all the attempts at corruption which he had to resist:

" A large crowd," says he,[2] " pressed around us, of both sexes and of every age: the child, the old man, the young man, the young woman, the girl, the boy, he who had attained his majority, he who had reached puberty, the old woman, the full grown man, the married woman, she who was still a minor. But why did I stay? The entire nation earnestly promise us gifts, and think that at that price whatever they desire is as good as done. This is the machine by which all endeavor to throw down the wall of the soul, the battering-ram with which they wish to strike in order to seize it. Here one offered me crystals and precious stones of the east, if I would make him master of the domains of another; a second brings me a quantity of gold money, impressed with the tongue and character of the Arabians, or upon whose brilliantly white silver surface a Latin style has engraved words, with which he wished to acquire lands, fields, and houses; another secretly called one of our servants, and said to him

---

[1] *Parænesis a l Judices*, v. 917—956, in the *Opera Varia* of P. Germand, vol. ii., p. 1046.
[2] Ibid., v. 163—290; vol. ii., p. 1032—1034.

with a low voice the following words, which were to be repeated to me: 'I possess a vase remarkable for its chasing and its antiquity; it is of a pure metal and of considerable weight; on it is engraved the history of the crimes of Cacus, the faces of the shepherds bruised by the blows from clubs of iron, and soiled with blood, the signs of his numerous robberies, a field inundated with the blood of men and herds; we see Hercules who in fury breaks the bones of the son of Vulcan, and the latter with his ferocious mouth vomiting the terrible fires of his father; but Alcides presses his knee upon the stomach of Cacus, his sides with his feet, and with his club shatters his face and throat, whence issue torrents of smoke. You next see Alcides bringing out of the cavern the stolen oxen, which seem to fear being dragged a second time backward. All this is on the hollow part of the vase, with a circle around it; the other side, covered with smaller designs, shows the child of Tyrinthus strangling the two serpents, and his ten famous labors are there placed in their order. But frequent use has so polished the exterior, that, effaced by time, the figures which represent Hercules, the river Chalydon, and Nessus fighting for thy beauty, Dejanira, have almost completely disappeared. We see also the fatal mantle, poisoned with the blood of Nessus, and the horrible fate of the unhappy Lychas, and Antæus, who could not be conquered or fought upon earth, like other mortals, strangled in the formidable arms of Hercules. This, then, will I offer to the lord (for he even called me lord), if he will favor my wishes. There is a great number of men, women, young people, children of both sexes, to whom my father and mother have granted the honor of liberty, and this numerous group find themselves enfranchised; but, by altering their charters, we shall enjoy, thy master the possession of this antique vase; I, of all this people; and thou, of my gifts.'

"Another says: 'I have mantles dyed in various colors, which came, as I believe, from the ferocious Arabians. We see there the calf following its mother, and the heifer the bull, the color of the calf and that of the heifer exact to nature, as are those of the bull and the cow. See how brilliant they are, how pure are the colors, and with what art the larger parts are joined to the smaller. I have a quarrel with some one about some beautiful herds, and I offer on this occasion a fitting present, since I offer bull for bull, cow for cow, ox for ox.'

"Here one promises me beautiful cups, if by that means he can obtain what I ought not to give him; the inside of one of them gilt, the outside black, the color of the silver having the dye of sulphur. Another says: 'I have cloths fit to cover splendid beds and beautiful vases; I will give them if my desires are granted.' 'A well watered estate, ornamented with vines, olives, meadows, and gardens, was left by my father,' says one; 'my brothers and sisters claim from me a share, but I wish to possess it without partition; I shall obtain the accomplishment of this wish, if it find favor before thee; and if thou acceptest what I give thee, I shall reckon upon thy giving me that which I request.' One wishes to seize the house of his parent, another his estates; of these two, one had already taken, the other wished to take what did not belong to him; both burned with the desire, that to keep, this to acquire: one offered me a sword and casque, the other bucklers; one brother is in possession of the inheritance of his father, his brother likewise lays claim to it; one offers me mules, the other horses.

"Thus do the rich act; the poor are not less pressing, and the will to give is not more wanting. With various means, the conduct is alike: as the great offer great presents, the lower offer small. Here behold some who display prepared skins which take their name from thee, Cordova; one brings white, the other, red; this offers fine linen, that woollen stuffs, to cover my head, my feet, or my hands. Such a one offers as a gift one of those cloths which are used to wash, with a little water, our face and hands; others bring boxes. There was even one, who, with an air of triumph, presented round wax candles. How can we enumerate all these things? all were confident in their gifts, and no one supposed that he could obtain anything without presents. Oh wicked pest spread over all places! oh, crime, oh, fury! oh, vice, worthy of horror, which may boast of its having subdued the universe! nowhere is there wanting people who give and people who receive wrongfully. They hastened to gain me; and they would not have thought to find me susceptible of corruption, if they had not found my predecessors susceptible. No one seeks wild boars in the water, fish in the forest, a wood house in the sea, water in fire. . . . They expect to find each thing where they have been accustomed to find it, and mortals think that what has happened will always happen. When they see that the darts of their words are broken, and that the arms of their promises in no degree avail them when they see that I remain firm as a fortress after an ineffectual siege, and that I do not allow myself to be deceived by any of their artifices, every one forthwith occupies himself only with his own business; every one receives what he is entitled to, and no more; thus, a man who sees closed up a passage, through which he has been accustomed to go for the purposes of robbery, turns aside, and proceeds hopelessly elsewhere. But, in order not to show myself deficient in moderation and discreet judgment, to manifest that I acted openly and frankly, to guard against my conduct exciting too much astonishment by its entire novelty, and that the so recent evil might not bring good into hatred, I did not refuse that which was offered to me by real benevolence, by that noble feeling which, joining souls together, causes them readily to take and receive from each other. I accepted with thanks the little presents made me, not by the hand of anger, but by that of friendship—fruit, vegetables, eggs, wine, bread, hay. I took the young fowls, and birds, smaller in size than they, but good to eat. Happy the virtue which is tempered, adorned, and maintained by discretion, the nurse of all virtues."

The invasions and their disasters, so often renewed, had not destroyed, as you see, in the cities of southern Gaul, all the wealth, and there still remained abundance wherewith to tempt the avidity of magistrates.

Independently of these details concerning the state of society, the poem of Theodulph is remarkable for the gentleness of the sentiments which pervade it; one is astonished to find, amidst barbarous disorders and tyrannies, that delicate goodness which seems to belong only to times of great civilization and peace. He exhorts the judges to treat considerately all who present themselves before them:

"If one," says he, "has lost his father, another his mother, another her husband, take particular care with their cause; be their protector, their advocate; be to the one her husband, the other his mother. If any ever come to thee weak, infirm, or ill, infantine, or aged, bear towards him a charitable help; cause him who cannot stand erect, to sit; take by the hand him who cannot raise himself; sustain and encourage him whose heart, voice, hand, or legs, are about to fail him; with thy words raise him who is cast down; appease him who is irritated; give strength to him who trembles, recal to order him who is excited."¹

I will cite the original text of this passage; the style, although very faulty, is of a remarkable conciseness and energy:

> "Qui patre senue matre orbatur, vel si qua marito
> Istorum causas sit tua cura sequi
> Horum causiloquus, horum tutela maneto,
> Pars hæc te matrem noverit, illa virum,
> Debilis, invalidus, puer, aeger, anusve, senexve,
> Si veniant, fer opem his miserando piam;
> Fac sedeat qui stare nequit, qui surgere prende;
> Cui cor, voxque tremit, pesque, manusque juva;
> Dejectum verbis releva, sedato minacem;
> Qui timet, huic vires, qui furit, adde metum."

Independently of this poem, there are seventy-one various pieces of Theodulph remaining, divided into five books, but they are of little value. Two small theological treatises, and some fragments of sermons by him, have also been collected. After the death of Charlemagne, Louis le Debonnaire still employed Theodulph in various missions; but in 817, compromised in the conspiracy of Bernard, king of Italy, against the emperor his uncle, he was exiled from his diocese, and banished to the town of Angers, where he died in 821.

III. Smaragde, abbot of Saint Mihiel, in the diocese of Verdun, was a man of the same character and the same position as the two bishops of whom I have just spoken. It is neither known in what country he was born, nor at what epoch Charlemagne took him into his service; but we find him abbot of Saint Mihiel before 805, and employed, in 809, in various negotiations with Rome. In the diocese of Verdun he took particular care of schools, and in the schools with the teaching of grammar. To expound and discuss the precepts of Donatus, a grammarian of the fourteenth century, who was preceptor of Saint Jerome, Smaragde wrote a large Latin grammar, which was celebrated in his time, and of which many manuscripts still exist. It has never been printed. We have two other works by him: the first, entitled *Via Regia*, is a treatise of morality for the use of princes, divided into thirty-two

---

¹ Verse 621.

chapters, and addressed either to Charlemagne, or to Louis le Debonnaire; it is not exactly known which. The ideas are wise and benevolent, but common; one fact alone merits remark: this is, the far more moral than religious character of the work. The church occupies but little place therein, and, with the exception of some general recommendations, the author only speaks of it in a cursory manner, and to exhort the prince to watch over it. If the book was addressed to Louis le Debonnaire, the emperor was far more of a monk than the abbot of Saint Mihiel.

The second work of Smaragde, entitled the *Diadem of the Monks*, is purely religious, and has no other object but that of giving to the monks advice on the means of sustaining or reanimating their fervor. The abbot of Saint Mihiel took an active part, among others, in the council of Aix-la-Chapelle in 817, in all measures for the reform of monastic orders. He died, it would appear, shortly after 819.

These were the most remarkable men among priests whom Charlemagne employed. Their origin is clear; their knowledge made their fortune; it was in their character of literary men that Charlemagne distinguished them, and called them near him. By the side of these, we meet men of another nature, of another origin; politicians, military men, who acquired a taste for learning, and ended by devoting themselves to it, after having been engaged at first in an entirely different career. Charlemagne employed literary men in affairs of state, and inspired statesmen with an esteem for letters. Among these last, three especially merit our attention, all three unconnected in the early part of their life, both with the church and with learning, soldiers or counsellors of Charlemagne, occupied in the business of civil government, taking part in warlike expeditions, and who, however, all three ended by study and by a religious life, and have left us monuments of their intellectual activity. These are Angilbert, Saint Benedict d'Aniane, and Eginhard.

I shall merely mention the names of the first two: they wrote but very little; of Angilbert we have only some poems, and some documents concerning the abbey of Saint Riquier, to which he retired; and when we shall especially occupy ourselves with the history of the church at this epoch, we shall again find Saint Benedict d'Aniane, who, after having led a life of war in his youth, became the second reformer of monastic orders. Eginhard alone fills an important place in the literature of this time, and we shall at present occupy ourselves with him.

He was of the Frankish race, born, perhaps, beyond the Rhine, and calls himself " a barbarian, but little versed in the language of the Romans."[1] Charlemagne took him into his service while very young; caused him to be brought up with his children in that school of the palace of which Alcuin was the head; and when Eginhard arrived at the age of manhood, he not only made him superintendent of all those works which we in the present day call public works, roads, canals, buildings of all kinds, but his councillor and private secretary.

Traditions go farther; they attribute to Eginhard the honor of having married Emma, the daughter of Charlemagne; and the adventure which they say led to this marriage is one of the most popular traditions of our old history. Here it is as we have it in the chronicle of the monastery of Lauresheim,[2] the only ancient monument which makes any mention of it:

"Eginhard, arch-chaplain and secretary of the emperor, Charles, acquitted himself very honorably of his office in the court of the king, was welcomed by all, and especially loved with very lively ardor by the daughter of the emperor, herself named Emma, and who was promised to the king of the Greeks; each day love increased between them; fear restrained them, and, out of apprehension of the royal displeasure, they dared not incur the grave danger of seeing each other. But love, ever on the alert, conquered everything: at last this excellent young man, burning with irremediable fire, and not daring to address himself through a messenger to the ear of the princess, suddenly took confidence in himself, and secretly, in the middle of the night, repaired to where she lodged. Having knocked softly, and as if to speak with the young girl by order of the king, he obtained permission to enter, and then alone with her they yielded to the tender impulses of love. But when at the approach of the light of day, he wished to return through the last shadows of night, to the place whence he came, he perceived that a great deal of snow had suddenly fallen, and dared not go out, for fear

---

[1] *Preface* to his *Life of Charlemagne*, in my *Collection*, vol. iii., p. 121.

[2] Lauresheim, or Lorch, in the diocese of Worms, and four leagues from Heidelberg. This chronicle extends from the year 763 or 764 the period of the foundation of the monastery, to the year 1179.

that the traces of a man's feet should betray his secret. They were both full of anguish at what they had done, and seized with fear, remained within; at length, as in that trouble, they deliberated upon what to do, the charming young girl, whom love rendered daring, gave her advice, and said that, stooping, she would take him on her shoulders, that she would carry him before day close to his dwelling, and that having deposited him there, she would return, carefully following the same steps.

"Now, the emperor, by the Divine will, as it is believed, had passed the night without sleep, and rising before day, was looking from the tower of his palace. He saw his daughter walking slowly, and with steps tottering under the weight which she bore, and when she had deposited it in a convenient place, quickly retracing her steps. After having long looked at them, the emperor, seized at once with admiration and grief, but thinking that it could not have happened thus without a providential interposition, restrained himself, and preserved silence upon what he had seen.

"In the meantime, Eginhard, tormented with what he had done, and quite sure, in some way or other, the thing could not long remain unknown to the king, his lord, at last resolved in his anguish to seek the emperor, and on his knees demand a mission of him, saying that his services, already great and numerous, had received no suitable recompense. At these words, the king discovering nothing of what he knew, held silence for some time, and then assuring Eginhard that he would shortly give him an answer, he named a day for doing so. He immediately convoked his councillors, the chief of the kingdom, and his other familiar adherents, ordering them to repair to him. This magnificent assembly of various lords thus met, he commenced, saying that the Imperial majesty had been insolently outraged by the guilty love of his daughter for his secretary, and that he was greatly troubled at it. Those present remaining struck with stupor, and some of them still appearing to doubt, the thing was so unheard of and daring, the king satisfied them by evidence, recounting matters exactly as he had seen them with his own eyes, and asked them their advice upon the subject. They pronounced various sentences against the presumptuous author of the deed: some wished him to be punished with chastisement hitherto without example, others that he should be exiled, others again that he should be subjected to such or such a penalty, each speaking according to the sentiment which animated him. Some, however, as much more benevolent as they were more wise, after having deliberated among themselves, earnestly implored the king to examine this affair himself, and to decide according to the wisdom which he had received from God. When the king had well observed the affection which each bore him, and amongst the various opinions offered had selected that which he had determined to follow, he spoke thus to them: 'You know that men are subject to various accidents, and that it often happens that things which commence with a misfortune have a more favorable issue; we must not grieve for this affair, which, by its novelty and gravity, has surpassed our foresight, but rather piously seek for and respect the intentions of Providence, who is never deceived, and who knows how to turn evil to good. I shall not therefore subject my secretary, for this deplorable affair, to a chastisement which will increase instead of effacing the dishonor of my daughter. I think that it is more wise, and that it better becomes the dignity of our empire, to pardon their youth, and unite them in legitimate marriage, and thus give to their disgraceful fault a color of honor.' Having listened to this advice of the king, all loudly rejoiced, and loaded with praises the grandeur and benevolence of his soul. Eginhard was ordered to enter; the king saluting him as had been resolved, said to him with a tranquil countenance: 'You have laid before us your complaints that our royal munificence has not worthily rewarded your services. To speak truly it is your own negligence which should be accused, for despite so many and so great affairs of which I alone have borne the burden, if I had known anything of your desire, I would have accorded to your services the honors which are due to them. Not to detain you with a long discourse, I shall, however, put an end to your complaints by a magnificent gift: as I wish always to see you faithful to me as heretofore, and attached to my person, I will give you my daughter in marriage, your *bearer*, she who, girding up her robe, has shown herself so docile in carrying you.' Immediately, according to the orders of the king, and amidst a numerous suite, his daughter entered, her face covered with a charming blush, and the father put her hands within the hands of Eginhard, with a rich dowry, many domains, much gold and silver, and other valuable property. After the death of his father, the most pious emperor Louis likewise gave Eginhard the domain of Michlenstadt and that of Mühlenheim, which is now **called** Seligestadt."¹

This is the graceful narrative upon which all the tales, all the poems, all the dramas of which this adventure has been the subject, are founded. The chronicler wrote at an epoch near to the event in an abbey which Eginhard endowed, and the monks of which might have been well acquainted with the incidents of his life. Still this is the only monument of the time in which the event is stated. Moreover, it seems denied by the silence of Eginhard himself, and by some passages in his life of Charlemagne. Among the children of this prince, whose name he enumerates, we do not find Emma or Imma: he names seven boys and eight girls, whom Charlemagne had by his wives or his mistresses; none of his daughters is called Imma;² and in none of the other lists which have come down to us of the history of Charlemagne do we meet with this name. Moreover, we read in the *Life of Charlemagne:*

"His daughters were very beautiful, and he passionately loved them. Accordingly, to the astonishment of all, he would never consent to any of them ever marrying either to his own people or to a foreigner; he kept them all about him, and with him, until his death, saying that he could not deprive himself of their society. Although happy in all else, he experienced the malignity of fortune with regard to his daughters; but he concealed his vexation, and conducted himself as if they had never given rise to injurious suspicions, as if no reports went about concerning them."³

If the adventure which I have just read were true, how could such a passage be found in the work of Eginhard? How would he himself have spoken of the report which went

---

¹ *Recueil des Historiens des Gaules et de la France,* vol. v., p. 383.
² According to Eginhard, Charlemagne had:—
  1. By Hildegarde, three sons, Charles, Pepin, Louis; three daughters, Rotrude, Bertha, Gisla.
  2. By Fastrade, two daughters, Thebrade, Hildrade.
  3. By a concubine (Himiltrude), one daughter, Rothaide.
  4. By Mathalgarde (a concubine), one daughter, Rothilde.
  5. By Gersuinthe,   (id.)   one daughter, Adelrude.
  6. By Regina,   (id)   two sons, Drogon, Hugo.
  7. By Adalinde,   (id.)   one son, Theodoric.
  8. By a concubine, one son, Pepin.—In all, seven sons and eight daughters.—*Life of Charlemagne,* pp. 142—145.
³ Life of Charlemagne, p. 145.

abroad concerning the conduct of the daughters of Charlemagne, when his own wife would have been the principal object of them? It is impossible to resolve this little historical problem; but if I must give an opinion, I should strongly doubt the recital of the chronicle of Lauresheim.

However this may be, the affection of Charlemagne for his secretary was great, and they lived together in close intimacy. It was especially out of gratitude that Eginhard wrote the life of the emperor.

"Another motive," says he, "which seems to me not unreasonable, would moreover suffice in deciding me to compose this work; brought up by this monarch, from the time when I began to be admitted to his court, I lived with him and his children in constant friendship, which imposed upon me after his death, as during his life, all the ties of gratitude towards him. People would therefore be justly authorized to believe and declare me to be an ingrate if I retained no recollection of the benefits heaped upon me, and should say not a word of the high and magnificent actions of a prince who has acquired so many titles to my gratitude, and if I were to consent that his life should remain the same as if he had never existed, without a written memorial, and without the tribute of eulogy which is his due."[1]

Charlemagne never separated himself from his secretary; he did not employ him in any extraordinary missions: once only, in 806, he sent him to Rome to get his will confirmed by the pope; with this exception, he constantly kept him near him.

After the death of Charlemagne, Eginhard enjoyed the same favor with Louis le Debonnaire; but he soon became full of a distaste for that prince, and only desired to retire from the court. Among the sixty-three of his letters which have come down to us, many are curious monuments of the situation and despondency of the companions of Charlemagne, when they found themselves separated from that prince, and forced to live under the deplorable government of his son.

"I do not ask thee," writes Eginhard to one of his friends, "to write me anything concerning the affairs of the palace, for nothing done there can please me to know: I only desire

---

[1] Preface to the *Life of Charlemagne*, by Eginhard, vol. iii, p. 120, in my *Collection*.

to learn where my friends are, and what they do, if there remain there any of them but thou."[1]

Elsewhere he conjures one of the officers of the palace to excuse him to the emperor for not coming to court:

"The queen, in quitting Aix, ordered me to rejoin her at Compiégne, for I could not set out with her. To obey her orders, I proceeded with great difficulty, and in ten days, to Valenciennes. Thence, not in a state to mount my horse, I came by water to Saint Bavon. But I am alternately attacked with pains in the kidneys, and with relaxed bowels, in such a manner that since my departure from Aix I have not passed a single day without suffering from one or other of these evils. I am likewise struck with that which cast me down last year, with a continual numbness in the right thigh, and an almost intolerable pain in the liver. Amidst these sufferings, I had a very sad life, and almost devoid of every enjoyment; but what most afflicts me is, that I fear I shall not die where I wish, and that I shall have to occupy myself with something other than the service of the holy martyrs of Christ."[2]

Domestic troubles were soon combined with political annoyances. Whether or not she was a daughter of Charlemagne, Eginhard had married an Imma, of whom he speaks several times in his letters, and whom he tenderly loved. In their old age, as it very often happened at this epoch, she separated from him to devote herself to a religious life. She died in 836, in the nunnery, whither she had retired; and Eginhard wrote to his friend Loup, abbot of Ferrieres:

"All my labors, all my cares for the affairs of my friends or for my own, are nothing to me; all is effaced, all sinks before the cruel sorrow with which the death of her who was formerly my faithful wife has struck me, who was also my sister and my cherished companion. It is a misery which cannot end, for her merits are so deeply engraven in my memory, that nothing can tear them thence. What redoubles my grief, and each day aggravates my wound, is, to thus see that all my wishes have been without effect, and that the hopes which I have placed in the intervention of the holy martyrs are deceived. Accordingly, the words of those who attempt to console me, and which have often succeeded with

---

[1] Letter 47, in the *Recueil des Historiens de France*, vol. ii., p. 382.
[2] Letter 41, Ibid., vol. vi., p. 350.

other men, do nothing but re-open and cruelly envenom the wound of my heart; for they call upon me to support with courage sorrows which they do not feel, and ask me to congratulate myself upon a trial wherein they are incapable of pointing out to me the slightest subject for contentment."[1]

The language of sorrow, infected, in most of the monuments of this age, with a cold and dry religious jargon, which reduces it to monotonous common-place, is here frank and simple, and proves that Eginhard had not imprisoned his soul as well as his life in the monastic habit.

He did not long survive his wife: he died in 839, in the monastery of Sligestadt, which he founded.

Independently of these letters, we have remaining of his: —1, the *Life of Charlemagne;* 2. *Annals of his times.* Of these two works, the first is, without comparison, the most distinguished piece of history from the sixth to the eighth century—indeed, the only one which can be called a history, for it is the only one in which we recognize any traces of composition, any political and literary pretension. I have as yet only had occasion, for the most part, to speak to you of miserable chroniclers. The *Life of Charlemagne* is not a chronicle: it is a genuine political biography, written by a man who was present at the events he narrates, and who understood them. Eginhard commences by describing the state of Frankish Gaul under the last Merovingians. We see that their dethronement by Pepin was still a subject of discussion with a certain number of men, and caused some disquietude to the race of Charlemagne. Eginhard took care to explain how it could not be otherwise; he minutely describes the humiliation and powerlessness into which the Merovingians had fallen; proceeds from this exposition to recount the natural accessions of the Carlovingians; says a few words upon the reign of Pepin, upon the beginning of that of Charlemagne, and his relations with his brother Carloman; and enters at last into the account of the reign of Charlemagne alone. The first part of the account is devoted to the wars of that prince, and especially his wars against the Saxons. From wars and conquests, the author passes to the internal government, to the

---

[1] Letter from Eginhard to Loup, abbot of Ferrieres, *Recueil des Historiens de France*, vol. vi., p. 402.

administration of Charlemagne; lastly, he comes to his domestic life, his personal character.

It is evident that this is not written at hazard, without plan or aim; we here recognize intention, a systematic composition—there is art, in a word; and since the great productions of Latin literature, no historical work had borne such characteristics. The work of Gregory of Tours itself, without comparison the most curious which we have encountered on our road, is a chronicle, like the others. The *Life of Charlemagne* is, on the contrary, a true literary composition, conceived and executed by a reflecting and cultivated mind.

With regard to the *Annals* of Eginhard, they have no value beyond that of a chronicle. His title to them has been disputed, and they have been attributed to other writers, but everything leads us to believe that they are by him.

It is said that he composed a detailed history of the wars against the Saxons. Nothing of it has come down to us.

Alcuin and Eginhard are, without doubt, the two most distinguished men of the reign of Charlemagne. Alcuin, a man of letters, employed in government affairs; Eginhard, a statesman, who became a man of letters. We are about to see this momentary splendor of the reign of Charlemagne disappear; we are about to be present at the dismemberment of his empire. The intellectual movement, of which we have observed the first steps, will not perish; we shall see it perpetuated as it began; on the one hand, in men who direct the affairs of the world; and, on the other, in those who devote themselves to solitary study and learning. Society will often change its state and forms; intellect, reanimated, will now, without stopping, traverse all its revolution.

TWENTY-FOURTH LECTURE.

The progress and causes of the dismemberment of the empire of Charlemagne—1. State of this empire in 843, after the treaty of Verdun—Inferior state of the kingdom of France at this epoch—2. In 888, after the death of Charles le Gros—Seven kingdoms—Definitive establishment of the inheritance of fiefs in France—Twenty-nine small states, or important fiefs, founded at the end of the ninth century—3. In 987, at the fall of the Carlovingians—Four kingdoms—In France, fifty-five important fiefs—Explanation of this dismemberment—Their insufficiency—One only, the diversity of races, developed by M. Thierry, is probable, but incomplete—The true cause is the impossibility of a great state at that epoch, and the progressive rise of the local societies which formed the feudal confederation.

WE read in a chronicle of the century in which Charlemagne died:

"Charles, who was always travelling, arrived by chance unexpectedly at a certain maritime town of Narbonnese Gaul. Whilst he was dining, and was as yet unknown by any one, Norman corsairs came to execute their piracies even in the port. When the people saw the vessels, they supposed that they were merchants; according to these, Jews; according to those, Africans; according to others, Britons; but the able monarch, perceiving by the construction and speed of the vessels that they carried not merchants, but enemies, said to his people: 'These vessels are not filled with merchandize, but with cruel enemies.' At these words, all his Franks, in emulation of one another, ran to their vessels, but in vain. The Normans, learning that he whom they used to call Charles le Marteau, was there, feared lest their whole fleet should be taken in his port, or perish by wreck; and they avoided, by an inconceivably rapid flight, not only the sword, but even the eyes of those who followed them. Still the religious Charles, seized with a just awe, rising from the table, went to the window which looked towards the east, and long remained, with a countenance covered with tears. No one daring to interrogate him, this valiant prince, explaining to the great men who surrounded him the cause of his action and his tears, said to them: 'Know you, my friends, why I weep so bitterly? Truly, I fear not that these men should succeed in harming me by their miserable piracies; but I am deeply affected that, I living, they have dared to touch this shore; and I am troubled with a violent sorrow when I foresee with what evils they will overwhelm my successors and their people.'"[1]

By a singular chance, we know the precise date of this anecdote: it was written about the month of June, 884—that is to say, seventy years after the death of Charlemagne, from the account of a man who had taken part in many of his expeditions against the Saxons, the Slaves, the Avares, &c. Omitting the emphasis and tears, which the chronicler doubtless added, we see therein that at the end of his life Charlemagne was occupied with the perils which menaced his kingdom on all sides. Many other texts, less precise, indicate the same uneasiness in him. He was still, surely, very far from foreseeing how brief a space this empire would survive him, and to what a degree the dissolution would be carried.

I do not propose recounting to you the events of this dissolution, but I wish to place before you the principal crises, and to point out their causes.

It took place between the death of Charlemagne, in 814, and the accession of Hugh Capet, in 987. All this epoch was employed in the accomplishment of this great work. It was by the fall of the race of the Carlovingians, and the accession of the Capetians, that it was definitively consummated.

At the death of Charlemagne, his empire extended from the north-east to the south-west, from the Elbe, in Germany, to the Ebro, in Spain; from north to south, it extended from the North Sea to Calabria, almost at the extremity of Italy. His power was, doubtless, exercised very unequally in this vast territory; upon many points he was not obeyed,—people did not even hear him spoken of, and he cared not for this: that was still his empire.

At the end of twenty-nine years, in 843, after the treaty of Verdun, by which the sons of Louis le Debonnaire, Lothaire, Charles le Chauve, and Louis le Germanique, shared this em-

---

[1] *Faits et Gestes de Charles le Grand*, by a monk of Saint Loup, in my *Collection des Mémoires relatifs à l'Histoire de France*, vol. iii., p. 251

pire, this was its arrangement: it formed three kingdoms, divided according to this table:—

Table of the Dismemberment of the Empire of Charlemagne, in 843.

1. Kingdom of France. Charles le Chauve. 840—877.	2. Kingdom of Germany. Louis le Germanique, 840—876.	3. Kingdom of Italy. Lothaire I., emperor, 840—855.
It comprehended the countries situated between the Scheldt, the Meuse, the Saone, the Rhone, the Mediterranean, the Ebro, and the Ocean.	It comprehended the countries situated between the Rhine, the north sea, the Elbe, and the Alps.	It comprehended, 1. Italy, with the exception of Calabria; 2. The countries situated between the Rhone, the Saone, and the Meuse, to the West, the Rhine, and the Alps to the East, that is, Provence, Dauphiné, Savoy, Switzerland, la Franche-Comté, a part of Burgundy, Lorraine, Alsace, and a part of the Netherlands.

Let it not be supposed that each of these kingdoms was compact unity; in that of France, the only one concerning which we have especially to occupy ourselves, two princes, Pepin II., in Aquitaine (from the year 835), and Nomenoé, in Brittany (from the year 840), likewise assumed the title of king, and took from Charles le Chauve the sovereignty of a considerable portion of his territory.

The dismemberment followed its course: forty-five years after this epoch, in 888, on the death of Charles le Gros, the last of the Carlovingians, who seemed to unite for a moment all the states of Charlemagne, this was the point to which it had come. Instead of three kingdoms, we find seven:

Table of the Dismemberment of the Empire of Charlemagne, about the end of the Ninth Century.

Kingdoms.	Reigning kings.	Accession and death.	Extent.
1. Kingdom of France.	Charles le Simple.	893—929	The countries included between the Scheldt, the Meuse, the Saone, the Rhone, the Pyrenees, and the Ocean, and a portion of the north of Spain beyond the Pyrenees, formerly the county of Barcelona.
2. Kingdom of Navarre.	Fortun le Moine.	880—905	Almost all the north of Spain, between the Pyrenees and the Ebro.
3. Kingdom of Provence, or cis-Juran Burgundy.	Louis l'Aveugle.	890—928	The countries included between the Saone, the Rhone, the Alps, the Jura, and the Mediterranean.
4. Kingdom of trans-Juran Burgundy.	Raoul I.	888—912	The countries between the Jura, the Pennine Alps, and the Reuss, that is, Switzerland, Valais, the country of Geneva, Chablais, and Bugey.
5. Kingdom of Lorraine.	Zwentebold.	895—900	The countries between the Rhine, the Meuse, and the Scheldt.
6. Kingdom of Germany.	Arnoul.	888—899	The countries between the Rhine, the North Sea, the Elbe, the Oder, and the Alps.
7. Kingdom of Italy.	Bérenger I.	888—924	All Italy to the frontier of the kingdom of Naples, then the principality of Bénévento, and Calabria.

I return to the internal state of the kingdom of France. In 843, two princes only, a king of Aquitaine, and a duke of Brittany, shared his territories with Charles le Chauve. In 888, the dismemberment was carried still farther, and by a cause which was not destined to stop. Every one knows that the possessors of domains and royal offices, that is to say, the beneficiaries and the dukes, counts, viscounts, centeniers, and other governors of provinces or districts, were constantly bent upon rendering themselves independent and hereditary, and assuring themselves the perpetual possession of their lands and governments. In 877, we find a capitulary of Charles le Chauve conceived in the following terms:

"If, after our death, any of our faithful subjects, seized with the love of God and our person, desire to renounce the world, and if he have a son or any other relation capable of serving the public, let him be at liberty to transmit his fees and honors as he pleases."[1]

And, in another article:

"If a count of this kingdom be about to die, and if his son be near us, we desire that our son, with those of our subjects who are most nearly related to the defunct count, as well as the other officers of the said county, and the bishop of the diocese in which it shall be situated, shall provide for his administration, until the death of the said count be announced to us, and we have been able to confer upon his son, present at our court, the honors with which he was invested. If the son of the defunct count be a child, let the same son, the bishop, and the other officers of the place, in like manner see to the administration of the county, until, informed of the death of the father, we have accorded the same honors to the son."[2]

Here we find the inheritance of benefices and of royal offices legally consecrated: and it is written in the manners, as in the laws; for numerous monuments attest that at this epoch, when, on the death of the governor of a province, the king attempted to give his county to any other than to his descendants, not only was he resisted therein by personal interest, but that such a measure was considered as a violation of right, a veritable injustice. Wilhelm and Engelschalk occupied two countships on the confines of Bavaria, under Louis le Begue: on their death, their offices were given to count Arbo, to the exclusion of their sons: "Their children and their relations, looking upon this as a great injustice, said that things should be otherwise, and that they would die by the sword, or that Arbo should quit the county of their family."[3]

This principle bore its fruits: About the end of the ninth century, twenty-nine provinces, or fragments of provinces, were already erected into small states, the ancient governors of which, under the names of duke, count, viscount, had become their true sovereigns. Twenty-nine fiefs, in fact, which have played an eminent part in our history, are traceable to this period.

---

[1] *Cap. Car. Calv.*, a., 877, tit. 53, § 10; Bal., vol. ii., p. 264.
[2] Id., § 9 and 3; Bal., vol. ii., p. 263—269.
[3] *Aune, Fuld,* a., 887, *Recueil des Historiens de France,* vol. viii., p. 48.

Table of the Feudal Dismemberment of the Kingdom of France, about the end of the Ninth Century.

Nos.	Title of the fief.	Date of becoming hereditary.	Name of the possessor at the end of the ninth century.	Date of his accession and of his death.
1	Duchy of Gascony.	872	Sanche Mittara II.	
2	Viscounty of Bearn.	819	A son of Centulf II.	
3	County of Toulouse.	850	Eudes.	875—918
4	Marquisate of Septimanie.	878	William le Pieux.	886—918
5	County of Barcelona.	864	Wifred le Velu.	864—906
6	County of Carcassonne.	819	Acfred I.	904
7	Viscounty of Narbonne.	...	Mayeul.	911
8	County of Roussillon.	...	Raoul.	Abt. 905
9	County of Urgel.	884	Suinifred.	884—950
10	County of Poictiers.	880	Eble le Batard.	892—932
11	County of Auvergne.	864	William le Pieux.	886—918
12	Duchy of Aquitaine.	id.	The same.	id.
13	County of Angoulême.	866	Alduin I.	886—916
14	County of Perigord.	id.	William.	886—920
15	Viscounty of Limoges.	887	Adelbert.	914
16	Lordship of Bourbon.	...	Adhemar.	Abt. 921
17	County of the Lyonnese.	890	William II.	890—920
18	Lordship of Beaujolais.	id	Berauld I.	
19	Duchy of Burgundy.	887	Richard le Justicier.	877—921
20	County of Châlons.	886	Manasses de Vergy.	
21	Duchy of France.	830	Robert II.	898—923
22	County of Vexin.	878	Aledran.	
23	County of Verman.	Abt. 830	Herbert I.	902
24	County of Valois.	id.	Pepin.	
25	County of Ponthieu.	859	Helgaud II.	878—926
26	County of Boulogne.	Abt. 860	Regniel.	882
27	County of Anjou.	870	Foulque le Roux.	888—938
28	County of Maine.	853	Gottfried.	
29	County of Britany.		Alain III.	877—907

The importance of these states is not equal, nor their independence absolutely alike; some still keep up frequent relations with the king of France; others are under the protection of a powerful neighbor; certain ties unite them, and hence certain reciprocal obligations result which will become the constitution of the feudal society. But the dominant feature is not any the less isolation, independence; they are evidently as many small states, born of the dismemberment of a great territory—local governments, formed at the expense of the central power.

From the end of the ninth century I pass at once to the end of the tenth, to the termination of the epoch which occupies us, to the complete fall of the Carlovingians, who give place to the Capetiens.

Instead of seven kingdoms, the ancient kingdom of Charlemagne then could number only four.

1. The kingdoms of Provence and Transjuran Burgundy were united, in 933, by Raoul II., king of Transjuran Burgundy, and formed the kingdom of Arles, governed, from 937 to 993, by Conrad le Pacifique.

2. The kingdom of Lorraine, from which many great fiefs were detached, was nothing more than a duchy, possessed, from 984 to 1026, by Thierry I.

3. Otho the Great, in 964, united the kingdom of Italy to the empire of Germany.

In the interior of the kingdom of France, the dismemberment was continued: instead of 29 small states or fiefs which we encountered at the end of the ninth century, we find therein, at the end of the tenth, fifty-five fully established.

Table of the Feudal Dismemberment of the Kingdom of France, about the end of the Tenth Century.

Nos.	Title of the Fief.	Date of the hereditary foundation.	Name of the possessor in 987.	Date of his accession and of his death.
1	Duchy of Gascony.	872	Bernard William	984–1010
2	Viscounty of Bearn.	819	Centuf Gaston II.	984–1004
3	Viscounty of Bigorre.	End of 9th century.	Garcia Arnould I.	
4	County of Fezenzac.	920	Aimery I.	983–1032
5	County of Armagnac.	960	Gerard Trancalion	
6	County of Lectoure and Lomagne.	End of 10th century.	Raymond Arnaud.	
7	County of Astarac.	About 930	Arnaud II.	
8	County of Toulouse.	850	William Taillefer.	950–1037
9	County of Barcelona.	864	Borrel, count of Urgel.	967– 993
10	County of Rouergue.	820	Raymond III	961–1010
11	County of Carcassonne	819	Roger I.	957–1012
12	Viscounty of Narbonne	End of 9th century.	Raymond I	966–1023

Table of the Feudal Dismemberment of the Kingdom of France, &c.—continued.

Nos.	Title of the Fief.	Date of the hereditary foundation.	Name of the possessor in 987.	Date of his accession and of his death.
13	County of Melgueil.	Commencement of 10th cent.	Bernard II.	
14	Lordship of Montpelier.	975	William I.	975–1019
15	County of Rousillon.	Middle of 9th cent.	Gauffred I.	
16	County of Urgel.	884	Borrel.	950– 993
17	County of Poictiers.	880	William Fier-a-Bras.	963– 997
18	Duchy of Aquitaine.	864	The same.	
19	County of Auvergne.	Id.	Guij I.	979– 989
20	County of Angoulême.	866	Arnaud le Bâtard.	975–1001
21	County of Perigord and of La Haute-Marche.	Id.	Adalbert I.	968– 995
22	County of La Basse Marche.	Id.	Bosson II.	968–1032
23	Viscounty of Limoges.	887	Gerard.	963–1000
24	Viscounty of Turenne.	Middle of 9th cent.	Archambaud Jambe-Pourri.	
25	Viscounty of Bourges.	927	Geoffrey II.	1021
26	Lordship of Bourbon.	End of 9th century.	Archambaud II.	
27	County of Macon.	920	Alberic II.	979– 995
28	Duchy of Burgundy.	877	Henry le Grand.	965–1002
29	County of Chalons.	886	Hugues I.	987–1039
30	Lordship of Salius.	920	Humbert II.	
31	County of Nevers.	987	Othon William.	987–1027
32	County of Tonnerc.	End of 10th century.	Gui.	987– 992
33	County of Sens.	941	Renaud le Vieux.	951– 996
34	County of Champagne.	End of 9th century.	Herbert II.	968– 993
35	County of Blois.	834	Eudes I.	978– 995
36	County of Rethel.	Middle of 10th cent.	Manasses I.	
37	County of Corbeil.	Id.	Bouchard I.	1012
38	Barony of Montmorency.	Id.	Bouchard II	1020
39	County of Vexin.	878	Gauthier I.	
40	County of Meulent.	959	Robert I.	
41	County of Vermandois.	880	Herbert III	987–1000
42	County of Valois.	Id.	Gauthier I.	
43	County of Soissons.	End of 10th century.	Gui, Count of Vexin.	

Table of the Feudal Dismemberment of the Kingdom of France, &c.—continued.

Nos.	Title of the Fief.	Date of the hereditary foundation.	Name of the possessor in 987.	Date of his accession and of his death.
44	County of Reucy and Rheims.	940	Gilbert.	739
45	County of Ponthieu.	859	Hugues.	
46	County of Boulogne.	860	Guy Barbe Blanche.	
47	County of Guines.	965	Adolphe.	966
48	County of Vendôme.	End of 10th century.	Bouchard I.	1007
49	Duchy of Normandy.	912	Richard-sans-Peur.	943– 996
50	County of Anjou.	870	Foulques Nerra.	987–1040
51	County of Maine.	853	Hugues I.	955–1015
52	Lordship of Bellême.	940	Ives I.	997
53	County of Brittany.		Conan I.	987– 992
54	Barony of Fougeres.	End of 10th century.	Meen I.	1020
55	County of Flanders.	862	Arnauld II. (younger)	965– 989

And these were not, as was the case under the Merovingians, accidental momentary dismemberments, the fruit of the general uncertainty of property and power; they were permanent, consummated results. These fifty-five duchies, counties, viscounties, lordships, had a long political existence; sovereigns hereditarily succeeded sovereigns; laws, customs, were regularly established therein. Men might write, indeed have written, their separate histories; for a long period they formed the history of France.

Such is the actual picture of the progressive dismemberment of the empire of Charlemagne, which commenced before the middle of the ninth century, and was accomplished at the end of the tenth. This dissolution was a subject of great sorrow and fear to some contemporaries, as in the fall of the Roman empire, elevated minds thought they saw in it a new invasion of barbarism and of chaos. A talented man, Florus, deacon of the church of Lyons, under the reign of Louis le Debonnaire and of Charles le Chauve, has deplored it in a kind of lament, of which the following is the literal translation:—

"A beautiful empire flourished under a brilliant diadem; there was but one prince and one people; every town had judges and laws. The zeal of the priests was sustained by frequent councils; young people repeatedly read the holy scriptures, and the minds of children were formed to the study of letters. Love, on the one hand, on the other fear, everywhere kept up good order. Thus the Frankish nation shone in the eyes of the whole world. Foreign kingdoms, the Greeks, the barbarians, and the senate of Latium, sent embassies to it. The race of Romulus, Rome herself, the mother of kingdoms, was subject to this nation; it was there that its chief, sustained by the help of Christ, received the diadem by apostolic gift. Happy if it had known its good fortune, the empire which had Rome as a citadel, and the door-keeper of heaven as a founder! Now fallen, this great power has lost at once its splendor and the name of empire; the kingdom lately so well united is divided into three parts; there is no one who can be looked upon as emperor; instead of a king, we see a kinglet; instead of a kingdom, a piece of a kingdom. The general good is annulled; each occupies himself with his own interests; they think of nothing else; God is forgotten. The pastors of the Lord, accustomed to meet, can no longer hold their synods amidst such division. There is no longer any assembly of the people, no longer any laws; an embassy arrives in vain there where there is no court. What will the neighboring nations of the Danube, the Rhine, the Rhone, the Loire, and the Po, become? Anciently united by the ties of concord, now that the alliance is broken, they will be troubled by unhappy dissensions. To what end will the wrath of God bring all these evils? Scarcely is there one who thinks thereon with fear. Who meditates on what is passing and is afflicted? men rather rejoice at the breaking up of the empire, and they call an order of things peace, which offers none of the benefits of peace."[1]

Two facts clearly appear in this poem: on the one hand, the sorrow which the dismemberment of the empire caused to enlightened men; on the other, the popular satisfaction; the people felt as if restored to themselves, and disencumbered of a burden. The dissolution was evidently brought about by general, necessary causes. The bonds which the will and conquests of Charlemagne had established between so many

---

[1] *Recueil des Historiens des Gaules et de la France,* vol. vii., p. 303 and following pages.

different nations, so many distant and separate territories, the unity of country and power, were factitious, and could not subsist.

What, upon regarding more nearly, were the causes of the phenomenon, whose principal crises we have just followed? How was the dismemberment effected? What internal transformation did society in the end then undergo?

A crowd of solutions, all equally unsatisfactory, have been given of this problem. Some people have assigned the decay of the empire of Charlemagne to the incapacity of his successors; of Louis le Debonnaire, of Charles le Chauve, Charles le Gros, and Charles the Simple; if they had had the genius and the character of the founder of the empire, the empire, say they, would gloriously have subsisted. Others have imputed its fall to the avidity of the dukes, counts, viscounts, beneficiaries, and other royal officers of all kinds; they sought to render themselves independent; they usurped the power, dismembered the state. According to others, it is the Normans who should answer for its ruin; the continuity of their invasions, and the misery into which the people had fallen, brought about all the evil. The explanations are evidently narrow and puerile. One only has more value, and merits a serious inquiry: this is that which M. Augustin Thierry has recently developed, in his *Lettres sur l'Histoire de France*, and especially in the second edition.[1] I do not entirely agree with it; I do not think that it is sufficient to account for the facts; but it is ingenious, lofty, and, without doubt, contains much truth.

According to M. Thierry, the dismemberment of the empire of Charlemagne was brought about by the diversity of races. On the death of Charles, when the terrible hand which forcibly held together so many different nations had lost its hold, they first separated, and then grouped themselves according to their true nature, that is to say, according to origin, language, manners; and under this influence was accomplished the formation of the new states. Such is the general physiognomy and explanation which M. Thierry assigns to this great event. Let us see how he applies the particular facts, and in what successive crises he supposes he can recognize the development of this cause. I shall perhaps give a more

---

[1] Letters xi. and xii., pp. 191–247.

precise, more systematic form to his ideas, than they have in the letters themselves; but, at bottom, I shall neither add nor retrench anything.

Between the death of Charlemagne, and the accession of Hugues Capet, M. Thierry distinguishes two great epochs. The first extends from the death of Charlemagne to that of Charles le Gros, after which seven kingdoms (M. Thierry reckons nine) shared the territory of the empire. The second extends from the end of the ninth century to the end of the tenth, to the accession of Hugues Capet. To these two epochs correspond two phases of the dismemberment, two revolutions different in object and character, although arising from the same causes, and tending to the same end.

To the first epoch belongs the national struggle of races, by which the great events which fill it are naturally explained. The two principal are incontestably the quarrel between Louis le Debonnaire and his sons, and that of the sons of Louis le Debonnaire among themselves. What is the true meaning of these two crises? Let us hear M. Thierry himself:

"From the commencement of the civil wars between the emperor Louis 1. and his children. . . . a great divergency of political opinion became visible between the Franks living in the midst of the Gaulish population, and those who remained upon the ancient German territory. The first, connected, despite their descent, with the interest of the people conquered by their ancestors, in general took part against the emperor, that is, against the empire, which, for the Gaulish aborigines, was a government of conquest. The others united in the contrary party, with all the Teutonic colonies, the ancient enemies of the Franks. Thus all the Teutonic nations, leagued apparently for the rights of a single man, defended their national cause by maintaining against the Gallo-Franks and the Welskes, a power which was the result of the German victories. . . . According to the testimony of a cotemporary, the emperor Lodewig mistrusted the Gallo-Franks, and put confidence only in the Germans. When, in 830, the partisans of a reconciliation between father and son proposed, as a means of attaining it, a general assembly, the evil-disposed labored to procure that this assembly might be held in a town in Roman France. "But the emperor," says the same historian, "was not of this opinion, and he obtained, according to his desires, that the people should be convoked at

Nimeguen: all Germany repaired thither in great numbers, in order to aid him."¹

"Shortly afterwards, Germany herself, hitherto so faithful to the empire, separated her national cause from that of the new Cæsars. When Lodewig I. at his death, left the Frankish dominion shared between his three sons, Lother, Lodewig, and Karle; although the first had the title of emperor, the Teutonic nations attached themselves to the second, who was only king. The question of the pre-eminence of the empire over the kingdoms was soon discussed between the brothers at the point of the sword; and from the commencement of the war, the eastern Franks, the Almanni, the Saxons, and the Thuringians took part against the *keisar* (emperor).

"Reduced to the government of Italy, Helvetia, Provence, and a small portion of Belgian Gaul, the emperor Lother also had as few partisans on the borders of the Rhine and the Elbe, as upon those of the Seine and the Loire: "Know," he wrote to his brothers, who prayed him to leave them in peace each in his kingdom, "know, that the title of emperor was given to me by superior authority, and consider what extent of power and what magnificence should accompany such a title." This haughty answer was, properly speaking, a manifesto against the national independence of which the people felt the want; they answered to it, in a terrible manner, by that famous battle of Fontanet, near Auxerre, where the sons of the *Welkses* and the *Teutskes* fought under the same banner for the overthrow of the political system founded by Charles the Great."²

Despite the diversity of combination, both quarrels have, then, the same character: and, in this continued effort against unity and empire, it was always according to races that the dismemberment tended to operate.

In all the events comprehended between 814 and 888, as in these two, M. Thierry thinks the action of the same cause may be recognized, and he comes thus to the formation of the nine kingdoms that it raised upon the ruins of the empire. He reckons nine, for he looks upon Aquitaine and Brittany as kingdoms, although at the end of the ninth century the count

---

¹ *Recueil des Historiens des Gaules et de la France*, vol vi., p. 3.
² Letter xi., pp. 195—199.

of Brittany and the dukes of Aquitaine did not bear the title of king. Then commenced the second epoch, and the second revolution.

In this epoch it is no longer the breaking up of states according to the difference of race that is in question; this work was already consummated. But Frankish Gaul remains under the empire of foreign sovereigns: the population which inhabits it is mixed; even Gauls dominate in it; and the descendants of Charlemagne are pure Germans. To expel them, to put in their place princes of a more national origin, such, according to M. Thierry, was the constant effort of France, properly so called, from 888 to 987; such is the secret of all the vicissitudes, of all the struggles of the 10th century, and especially, 1st, of the struggle of the elective king Eudes against the legitimate king, Charles le Simple; 2, of that of Hugues the Great, duke of France, against Louis d'Outre Mer; 3, of the definitive fall of Louis V. and of the succession of Hugues Capet.

"The race of Charles the Great," says M. Thierry, "entirely German, and attaching themselves by the ties of tradition and the affections of parentage, to the countries of the Teutonic language, could only be looked upon by the Franks as an obstacle to that separation upon which their independent existence had just been founded. The idiom of the conquest, fallen into disuse in the castles of the lords, was preserved in the royal house. The descendants of the Frank emperors deemed it an honor to understand this language of their ancestors, and collected pieces of verse composed by the poets beyond the Rhine. . . . Doubtless, in the events which followed 987, the premature death of Lodewig, the son of Lother, we must attribute a large share to the ambition and character of the founder of the third dynasty. . . . Nevertheless it may be affirmed that this ambition, hereditary in the family of Robert le Fort, for a whole century was maintained and aided by the movement of national opinion. Even the expressions of the Chronicles, dry as they are at this epoch of our history, lead us to suppose that the question of the change of dynasty was not then looked upon as a personal affair. According to them, the matter in hand was an inveterate hostility, an enterprise undertaken long since with the view of rooting up the posterity of the Frank kings from he kingdom of France. . . . The accession of the third race was the accomplishment of this enterprise; it was, properly speaking, the end of the kingdom of the Franks, and the substitution of a national royalty instead of the government founded by the conquest."[1]

From Charlemagne to Hugh Capet, the history of France reduces itself into two great facts: 1, the separation of nations according to the diversity of races; 2, the expulsion of the sovereigns of a purely German race, in order to give place to sovereigns of Gallo-Frankish, that is to say, national origin.

Such is the system of M. Thierry; a rare knowledge of events, a lively feeling of the situation and of manners are displayed therein, at each step. But a few observations will suffice, if I do not deceive myself, to show that it is incomplete, and too exclusive.

1. In the various alliances and combinations which took place under Louis le Debonnaire, and his children, the nations were far from being always connected or separated according to races; many other causes determined their movements, and the consideration of race often appears very subordinate therein. I desire for proof only, the facts of which M. Thierry himself has spoken. In the wars of Louis against his children, the nations of purely German race seem to defend the emperor and the empire; in the wars of the sons of Louis, it is they who combat him; and among those who defend it in the train of Lothaire, there are Romans, Gauls, Goths, Burgundians, Franks; nor are all the kingdoms ranged against the imperial pretensions of Lothaire, for the king of Aquitaine, Pepin II. allied himself with him against Louis le Germanique and Charles le Chauve. The geographical position, personal interests, numerous changing and special causes evidently, exercised an influence over their alliance which was often more decisive than the origin and relationship of nations.

5. This relationship is not more decisive as to the formation of kingdoms: those of Cis-Juran and Trans-Juran Burgundy clearly show this; all the races are there mixed, and there the demarcation is determined by entirely other motives.

3. The consideration of race is still more foreign to the

---

[1] Letter xii., pp. 228, 235, 287,

formation of three small states, duchies, counties, lordships, &c., into which each kingdom was subdivided. There was here no struggle of origin or nationality, and yet there was separation, dismemberment, the same as among the great masses of populations of which kingdoms are formed.

Other causes than the diversity of races presided, then, at the dissolution of the empire of Charlemagne, and at the formation of the new states. That, doubtless, contributed to it: but it should not be looked upon as a general, dominant cause: for the same facts are brought about when it did not act, as when it did act. Now it is the general and dominant cause which we seek. Since the diversity of races does not furnish us with it, let us endeavor to find it elsewhere.

You will recollect that, in exhibiting the state of Roman Gaul and its inhabitants, ancient and modern, after the great invasion,[1] I established that the two primitive associations of the German nations—the tribes, administered according to the principles of liberty; and the warrior-band, in which military and aristocratic patronage prevailed—were equally broken up in passing to the Roman soil, for their institutions no longer suited the new situation of the conquerors, at once proprietors, and dispersed over a vast territory.

You have also seen the Roman society, its general organization, at least, as to the force which presided over it, the imperial administration, dissolve after the invasion: so that at the commencement of the eighth century, Roman society and German society had alike perished in Frankish Gaul, now abandoned to the most heterogeneous anarchy.

The attempt of Charlemagne was to entirely resuscitate it; to restore the empire and its unity, by re-establishing on the one hand the Roman administration, on the other, national German assemblies, and military patronage. He in some sort renewed all the modes of association, all the means of government which the empire and Germany had known, and which lay disorganized and powerless, in order to replace them in vigor for his own good. He was at once chief of the warriors, president of the national assemblies, and emperor. He succeeded for a moment, and on his own account. But this was, as it were, a galvanic resurrection; applied to a

---

[1] Lecture viii., vol. i.

great society, the principles of the imperial administration, those of the wandering band, and those of the free tribes of Germany, were equally impracticable. No great society could be maintained. It is necessary to find its elements, on one hand in the minds of men, on the other in social relations. Now the moral and the social state of the people at this epoch equally resisted all association, all government of a single and extended character. Mankind had few ideas, and did not look far around. Social relations were rare and restricted. The horizon of thought and of life was exceedingly limited. Under such conditions, a great society is impossible. What are the natural and necessary bonds of political union? on the one hand, the number and extent of the social relations; on the other, of the ideas whereby men communicate, and are held together. Where neither of these are numerous or extensive, the bonds of a great society or state are nonexistent. Such was the case in the times of which we now speak. Small societies, local governments, cut, as it were, to the measure of existing ideas and relations, were alone possible; and these alone succeeded in establishing themselves.

The elements of these petty societies, and petty local governments, were ready at hand. The possessors of benefices by grant from the king, or of domains occupied by conquest, the counts, dukes, governors of provinces, were disseminated throughout the country. These became the natural centres of corresponding associations. Round them was agglomerated, voluntarily, or by force, the neighboring population, whether free or in bondage. Thus were formed the petty states called fiefs; and this was the real cause of the dissolution of the empire of Charlemagne. Power and the nation were dismembered, because unity of power and of the nation was impossible; all became local, because all generality was banished from interests, existences, and minds. Laws, judgments, the regulations for order, wars, tyrannies, liberties, all were compressed in small territories, because nothing could be regulated or maintained in a larger circle. When this great fermentation of the various social conditions, and of the various powers which covered France was accomplished, when the small societies which had arisen from it had invested with a more or less regular and determinate form, the hierarchical relations which united them, that result of the conquest and of the reviving civilization took the name of the feudal system. It is at about the end of the tenth century, and when the Carlovingian race disappeared, that this revolution may be looked upon as consummated. We have just followed it in the historical monuments; in the next lecture we shall study the legislative monuments of the same epoch, and if I do not deceive myself, we shall equally recognize it there.

TWENTY-FIFTH LECTURE.

History of legislation from the death of Charlemagne to the accession of Hugh Capet—Necessity of precisely determining the general characteristics of the legislation at the two terms of this epoch, in order to understand properly its progress during its course—1. State of the legislation under Charlemagne—It is personal, and varies according to races—The church and the imperial power give it some unity—2. State of the legislation after Hugh Capet—It is territorial; local customs have replaced national laws—All central legislative power has disappeared—3. History of legislation in Frankish Gaul between these two terms—Analytical tables of the capitularies of Louis le Debonnaire, Charles le Chauve, Louis le Begue, Carloman, Eudes, and Charles le Simple—Comparison of these tables according to the figures only—Comparison of the provisions of the capitularies—General results of this inquiry.

I HAVE sought the progress and the causes of the dismemberment of the empire of Charlemagne, in events, in history, properly so called. I have endeavored to distinguish what transformation Gallo-Frankish society underwent, and why. I have shown that, of the various explanations which people have attempted to give of it, none is satisfactory; that that even which contains the most truth, the diversity of races, is exclusive, incomplete, does not account for all the facts. It seemed to me that the impossibility of a sole and extensive society, in the state in which social relations and minds then were, alone fully explains this great and so rapid metamorphosis; that the formation of a multitude of small societies, that is to say, the establishment of the feudal system, was the necessary consequence, the natural course of events; that since their meeting, Roman and German society had tended towards this end, and that they had, in fact, attained it at the end of the tenth century, when the dismemberment of the empire of Charlemagne was definitively accomplished.

If this explanation is established, if such was the progress of facts from Charlemagne to Hugh Capet, we ought to find it in the history of laws as in the history of events. Between the development of legislation and that of society, there is an intimate correspondence; the same revolutions are accomplished therein, and in an analogous order. Let us now study the history of the laws during the same epoch, and let us see if they will lead us to the same result, if we shall see the same explanation arise from it.

The history of laws is more difficult to understand thoroughly than that of events, properly so called. Laws, from their very nature, are monuments more incomplete, less explicit, and consequently more obscure. Besides, nothing is more difficult, and yet more indispensable, than to take fast hold of and never lose the chronological thread. When we give an account of external facts, wars, negotiations, invasions, &c., their chronological concatenation is simple, palpable; each event bears, as it were, its date written on its face. The actual date of laws is often correctly known; it is often known at what epoch they were decreed; but the facts which they were designed to regulate, the causes which made them to be written in one year rather than another, the necessities and social revolutions to which the legislation corresponds, this is what is almost always unknown, at least, not understood, and which it is still necessary to follow step by step. It is from this study having been neglected, from the not having rigorously observed the chronological progress of laws in their relation with that of society, that confusion and falsehood have so often been thrown into their history. For example, you constantly hear speak of the feudal laws as already in vigor at the sixth century, immediately after the conquest, and of barbarous laws as being still in vigor at the eleventh century, under the feudal system. The resemblance of certain facts, of certain words, which are equally met with in the two epochs, causes this mistake: a little more attention to the chronological development of laws and of the social state, would have prevented it. Numerous errors in this matter, some of them the result of mere ignorance, many systematic and learned, have no other origin.

In order to prevent falling into it in the study with which we have now to occupy ourselves, one means only seems to me efficacious, that is, to determine precisely the two terms between which this study is comprised, that is, the general state of Gallo-Frankish society, first at the death of Charlemagne, and then at the accession of Hugh Capet. When we correctly know these two facts, when we know what the legislation was throughout its progress, we shall not be so liable to deceive ourselves concerning the route which it had followed in the interval; and if the study which we make of its history, between the two terms, gives a clear account of its transition from one to the other, we shall be justified in confiding in it.

It will be understood that I only intend here to point out the general characteristics of legislation under Charlemagne and under Hugh Capet; but that will suffice for our purpose.

At the first epoch, at the commencement of the ninth century, the essential characteristic feature of the legislation is that it is personal and not territorial; that is to say, that each people, each race, has its law, and that wherever men, of such or such a race, live, they follow its law, and not that of the territory which they inhabit. The Romans are governed by the Roman law; the Franks by the Salic or the Ripuarian law; the Burgundians by the Burgundian law; the Lombards by the Lombard law; the Saxons by the Saxon law, &c. Nationality is inherent in the legislation; in the diversity of races, and not in that of places, resides the principle of the variety of laws.

Above this variety hover certain principles of unity. And first, the canonical legislation is one, the same for all people, whatever their origin or name. The religious society is essentially one; unity is the standard of the church; hence the unity of the ecclesiastical legislation, in the midst of the most various national laws.

Civil legislation itself, taking this word in its most extensive sense, and as opposed to religious legislation, is not devoid of all unity. The king, the emperor, with or without the concurrence of the national assemblies, decrees certain laws applicable to all the inhabitants of his empire, Romans, Franks, Lombards, Burgundians, &c. There is evidently universality in many of the capitularies of Charlemagne; they are addressed to the whole territory, and are obligatory upon all.

To speak in a general way, and leaving aside exceptions, it is more especially in respect to civil and penal law that diversity according to races pervades the legislation of this period. Unity is complete in the religious legislation, and tends to prevail in the political legislation, which comes under the influence of the central power.

Such are the general characteristics of legislation at the commencement of the ninth century. I pass at once to the commencement of the eleventh, the term at which the epoch which we are studying stops, and when the feudal system had taken her definitive consistency in France, and truly possessed society. What metamorphosis is brought about in the laws!

Their diversity, according to races, has disappeared. There still remains some traces of it; we still find the Saxon, Salic, Lombard law spoken of; but these are only rare instances, the faint echo of an order of things becoming extinct. The laws vary, not according to races, but, on the one hand, according to conditions; on the other, according to places. The social legislation, from being personal, has become territorial. There are different laws for different kinds of property, different degrees of liberty. Accordingly, in each small state formed by the feudal subdivisions of the territory, arise peculiar laws. The diversity of races has been replaced by that of classes and of places. To the national laws have succeeded privileges and customs. This is the first characteristic, the essential feature of the new physiognomy that legislation has taken.

Another great change also took place. You have just seen that in the beginning of the ninth century, the unity of the imperial power was, notwithstanding the variety of the national laws, a principle of unity in the laws. In the commencement of the eleventh century, nothing of the kind existed; there was no longer any central, general legislative power; the variety of laws established according to places, to circumstances—that is to say, the variety of privileges and customs was no longer combated or modified by any principle of unity derived from a higher sphere. There was no unity existing but in the legislation of the church, which alone remained superior to all diversities.

The great revolutions, then, which occurred in the legislation from the ninth to the tenth century, may be thus stated: 1. Legislation, according to races, had given way to legislation according to social conditions, to local circumstances. 2. Central legislative power, and the unity thence resulting to certain branches of legislation, more especially in political legislation, had disappeared.

This is the transformation which the history of legislation from the ninth to the eleventh century has to describe. Let us exhibit its course.

I have already spoken to you of the legislative monuments which remain of this period, the capitularies of the Carlovingian kings. You remember the analysis to which I subjected those of Charlemagne, and the results I derived from that analysis. I classed them, as you recollect, under eight principal heads: 1. Moral legislation; 2. Political legislation; 3. Penal legislation; 4. Civil legislation; 5. Religious legislation; 6. Canonical legislation; 7. Domestic legislation; 8. Occasional legislation. I have applied the same method to the capitularies of Charlemagne's successors, with these results:

Analytical Table of the Capitularies of Louis le Debonnaire.

Date.	Articles.	Moral Legislation.	Political Legislation.	Penal Legislation.	Civil Legislation.	Religious Legislation.	Canonical Legislation.	Domestic Legislation.	Occasional Legislation.
815	7	..	..	..	..	..	..	..	7
816	1	..	..	..	..	..	1	..	
Id.	29	..	..	4	..	1	24	..	1
Id.	1								
817	18	..	18						
Id.	80	..	..	..	..	..	80		
Id.	3	..	3						
Id.	1	..	1						
819	21	1	4	12	4				
Id.	9	..	9						
Id.	12	..	..	6	6				
Id.	8	..	6	..	2				
Id.	29	2	24	..	..	..	3		
Id.	11	2	3	..	..	..	6		
821	5	..	5						
822	6	..	6						
Id.	8	..	..	..	..	..	..	..	8
823	28	11	16	..	..	..	1		
826	7	..	..	5	..	..	2		
827	1	..	..	..	..	..	..	..	1
828	10	..	4	..	..	..	6		
829	46	..	20	9	10	..	6	..	1
832	1	..	..	..	..	..	..	..	1
834	1	..	..	..	..	..	..	..	1
837	14	..	14						
Id.	5	..	3	..	2				
26	362	16	136	36	24	1	129		20

Analytical Table of the Capitularies of Charles le Chauve.

Date.	Articles.	Moral Legislation.	Political Legislation.	Penal Legislation.	Civil Legislation.	Religious Legislation.	Canonical Legislation.	Domestic Legislation.	Occasional Legislation.
844	6	..	6						
Id.	9	..	..	..	..	..			
845	6	..	6						
Id.	12	..	4	..	..	..	5	..	3
Id.	8	..	8						
844	10	..	..	..	..	..	..	..	10
846	19	..	10	..	..	..	9		
847	11	..	7	..	..	..	..	..	4
Id.	12	..	8	..	..	..	..	..	4
851	8	..	8						
853	19	..	6	..	..	..	6	..	7
Id.	3	..	..	..	..	..	..	..	3
Id.	15	..	12	..	..	..	3		
Id.	13	..	7	5	..	..	..	..	1
854	13	..	10	1	..	..	1	..	1
Id.	7	..	1	..	..	..	..	..	6
Id.	1	..	..	..	..	..	..	..	1
856	1	..	1						
Id.	15	..	6	..	..	..	..	..	9
Id.	5	1	..	..	..	..	..	..	4
Id.	6	1	..	..	..	..	..	..	5
Id.	1	..	..	..	..	..	..	..	1
857	10	..	9	..	..	1			
Id.	8	..	4	4					
Id.	5	..	..	..	..	..	..	..	5
858	15	..	15						
859	12	..	8	..	..	..	..	..	4
Id.	13	..	..	..	..	..	..	..	13
Id.	13	..	..	..	..	..	..	..	13
860	19	..	19						
Id.	18	..	18						
861	1	..	1						
862	4	..	..	..	..	..	..	..	4
Id.	20	..	..	..	..	..	..	..	20
864	43	..	32	3	4	..	..	1	3
865	23	..	5	..	..	..	4	..	14
868	12	..	8	..	..	..	4		
Id.	1	..	..	..	..	..	..	..	1
869	17	..	12	..	..	..	5		
Id.	7	..	..	..	..	..	..	..	7
870	1	..	..	..	..	..	..	..	1
Id.	2	..	..	..	..	..	..	..	2
872	3	..	..	..	..	..	..	..	3
873	12	..	8	4					
874	3	..	..	..	..	..	..	..	3
876	15	..	9	..	..	1	5		

Analytical Table of the Capitularies of Charles le Chauve—contin'd.

Date.	Articles.	Moral Legislation.	Political Legislation.	Penal Legislation.	Civil Legislation.	Religious Legislation.	Canonical Legislation.	Domestic Legislation.	Occasional Legislation.
876	9	..	..	..	..	..	..	..	9
Id.	4	..	..	..	..	..	..	..	4
877	1	..	..	..	..	..	..	..	1
Id.	1	..	..	..	..	..	..	..	1
Id.	37	..	11	..	..	..	..	..	26
51	529	2	259	17	4	2	51	1	193

Analytical Table of the Capitularies of Louis le Begue—877-9.

Date.	Articles.	Moral Legislation.	Political Legislation.	Penal Legislation.	Civil Legislation.	Religious Legislation.	Canonical Legislation.	Domestic Legislation.	Occasional Legislation.
877	5	..	..	..	..	..	..	..	5
878	8	..	3	1	..	..	4	..	..
879	9	..	3	..	..	..	..	..	6
3	22	..	6	1	..	..	4	..	11

Analytical Table of the Capitularies of Carloman, son of Louis le Begue—(879-884).

Date.	Articles.	Moral Legislation.	Political Legislation.	Penal Legislation.	Civil Legislation.	Religious Legislation.	Canonical Legislation.	Domestic Legislation.	Occasional Legislation.
882	1	..	..	..	..	..	..	..	1
Ib.	14	..	12	2	..	..	..	..	..
883	3	..	..	3	..	..	..	..	..
3	18	..	12	5	..	..	..	..	1

Capitulary Table of Eudes, King of France (887--898)

Date.	Articles.	Moral Legislation.	Political Legislation.	Penal Legislation.	Civil Legislation.	Religious Legislation.	Canonical Legislation.	Domestic Legislation.	Occasional Legislation.
888	..	..	..	..	..	..	..	..	1

Analytical Table of the Capitularies of Charles le Simple
(893—929).

Date.	Articles.	Moral Legislation.	Political Legislation.	Penal Legislation.	Civil Legislation.	Religious Legislation.	Canonical Legislation.	Domestic Legislation.	Occasional Legislation.
907	1	..	..	..	..	..	..	..	1
921	8	..	..	..	..	..	..	..	8
926	1	..	..	..	..	..	..	..	1
3	10	..	..	..	..	..	..	..	10

CIVILIZATION IN FRANCE.

Comparative Analytical Table of the Capitularies of Charlemagne, Louis le Debonnaire, Charles le Chauve, Louis le Begue, Carloman, Eudes, and Charles le Simple.

	Date.	Articles.	Moral Legislation.	Political Legislation.	Penal Legislation.	Civil Legislation.	Religious Legislation.	Canonical Legislation.	Domestic Legislation.	Occasional Legislation.
Charlemagne. (768—814.)	65	1151	87	293	130	110	85	305	73	12
Louis le Debonnaire. (814—840.)	26	362	16	136	36	24	1	129	..	20
Charles le Chauve. (840—877.)	51	529	2	259	17	4	2	51	1	193
Louis le Begue. (877—879.)	3	12	..	6	1	..	..	4	..	11
Carloman. (879—884.)	3	19	..	12	5	..	..	..	..	2
Eudes. (887—898.)	1	1	..	..	..	..	..	..	..	1
Charles le Simple. (893—929.)	3	10	..	..	..	..	..	..	..	10
	152	**2094**	**105**	**706**	**289**	**139**	**88**	**489**	**74**	**249**

Before we enter into an examination of the provisions themselves, thus classified under these different heads, let us consider their numerical aspect: the mere comparison of figures will develope important facts.

Between the reign of Charlemagne and that of Louis le Debonnaire, if we merely look to the number of articles in moral, political, penal, religious, &c., legislations, we shall notice very little difference; the various classes of capitularies are, as to mere figures, in very nearly the same respective proportions. The occasional legislation is somewhat fuller in the latter reign, but not sufficiently so to arrest our attention. We must penetrate quite into the interior of the legislation to discover that it has become changed in its character, that it is no longer the work of the same government in the latter as in the former case.

We perceive a further distinction under Charles le Chauve; here the numerical proportion of the various classes of legislation is changed. Under the heads of moral, penal, civil, religious, canonical, and domestic legislation, we find very few articles, while, on the other hand, the list of political and occasional measures is much fuller; a certain indication of a great change in the state of society and of power. To what interests does moral, penal, civil, religious legislation address itself? To interests which affect society far more nearly than they do power; important, doubtless, for power itself, but of an importance which has nothing direct or selfish about it, which has relation to the public functions of government, and not to distinct and personal existence. Political and occasional legislation, on the contrary, affects power in its personality; it is power which such measures serve or impede; it is power, more especially, and often power alone which they contemplate in their effects. Accordingly, whenever, in whatever epoch, or under whatever form, you see political and occasional laws multiply, be assured that the government is in danger, that it has enemies against whom it is defending itself, that it is not simply and solely occupied in fulfilling its public character, that it is not principally intent upon social interests, but that it is its personal interests which guide and rule its action. In the course of the Revolution of England, and of our own, in all similar crises, what classes of legislation fill the statute books? Political and occasional laws. The name and character of law is given formally to all the measures of government; but, in point of fact, they are merely acts of government, acts framed in the view above all to the interest of power, and for its service, rather than for the public service. This fact manifests itself clearly in a simple numerical comparison of the different classes of capitularies under Charlemagne and under Charles le Chauve. Under Charlemagne, occasional legislation is very limited; it is evidently a tranquil government, having full confidence in itself, occupied solely with the idea of accomplishing its task and conducting the affairs of the society. Under Charles le Chauve, it is to political and occasional measures that legislation applies itself; this, assuredly, is a tottering government, desperately endeavoring to regain the force and order which are abandoning it. Weakness and disorganization in the central power are manifested in the very fact.

How stands the matter under the successors of Charles le Chauve? What do the figures tell us here?

Political and occasional legislation still predominate in the capitularies, but even that is more and more limited; even the legislative measures in which power is personally interested, become fewer and fewer. It is clear that, not only as under Charles le Chauve, the central government is in peril, but that it is disappearing altogether; before, it defended itself; now, it makes no attempt to do so; it abandons itself, it takes no heed to itself; it has, indeed, no self to take heed to, for it is non-existent.

Thus, without any examination of the contents of the capitularies, by a simple comparison of the figures which indicate the various classes of laws, we identify the same progress, we are present at the same spectacle that has been exhibited to us by the history of events. Legislation is stamped with the impress of the revolutions which the country underwent. The government of Charlemagne, like his Empire, is dismembered and dissolved.

Let us examine the interior of this legislation, the contents of the capitularies: we shall arrive at precisely the same results.

This examination is susceptible of great extension, and might be made the topic of a vast number of curious observations; but I am compelled to limit myself to general facts. Of these, the most important are as follow:

1. In describing to you the capitularies of Charlemagne, I pointed out their extreme diversity; they are not, as you will remember, merely laws, but comprise acts of every kind;

ancient laws re-enacted, fragments of ancient laws, applied specially to particular portions of the empire; additions to the ancient laws; new laws of the emperor, decreed sometimes with the concurrence of the laity and ecclesiastics together; sometimes with that of the ecclesiastics alone, sometimes, again, of the emperor in person, independently of any assembly at all; instructions given to the *missi dominici;* questions addressed to the *missi;* answers by the emperor to questions from the *missi;* notes made by the emperor for his own use; memoranda of questions that he proposed to put, in the next general asembly, to such and such persons, bishops, counts, &c. In a word, the prodigious variety of the acts comprehended under the general title of capitularies was one of the facts upon which I particularly dwelt.

But, however great their variety, it was always from Charlemagne himself that these acts emanated; he was on all occasions the author and centre of the legislation. Whether old or new laws were in question, whether instructions or private memoranda, whether questions or answers, his presence and his power were everywhere felt; he was everywhere active and sovereign.

Under Charles le Chauve, the case was altogether different. The diversity of the acts comprised under the title of capitularies still subsisted, but a far different diversity had introduced itself: that of legislators. It is no longer the emperor alone who speaks and ordains; it is no longer from him alone that all things emanate. Among the capitularies which go under the name of Charles le Chauve, there are several acts with which he had nothing to do.[1] 1. Petitions from certain bishops to the king, requiring him, and that sometimes in a very imperious tone, to establish order, and to protect the church. 2. Counsels addressed by bishops to the king respecting the government of his states, and even as to that of the interior of his palace.[2] 3. Acts of bishops regulating the administration of their affairs in the different kingdoms among themselves, entirely without any reference to the king himself.[3] 4. Acts of the pope, with respect to the affairs of the king and of the kingdom.[4] Finally, treaties, conventions

---

[1] Cap. Car. Calv., a. 845, 856; Baluze, ii., 7, 14.
[2] Ib., a. 808; ii, 101. [3] Cap. Car. Carlo., a. 859; ii., 121.
[4] Ib., a. 877; ii., 251.

entered into between the king and his brothers, or his nephews, or his *fideles.* So that the sources of the acts constituting this collection are as various as the nature of the acts themselves. A most significant fact, which a glance at the title and first two or three lines of each capitulary fully enables us to recognize.

2. There is another no less deserving of attention. Not only does political legislation, under Charles le Chauve, occupy a larger space than under Charlemagne; it is wholly different in itself, has no longer the same object in view. The political laws of Charlemagne have almost always reference to truly public interests, to the business of general government, sometimes relating to the conduct of the imperial delegates, the dukes, counts, centeniers, *missi dominici, scabini,* &c.; sometimes to the holding of the assemblies, local or general, in which justice was administered. The relations of Charlemagne with his beneficiaries and with the church, make their appearances indeed, but more occasionally and more briefly. Under Charles le Chauve the case is reversed: provisions bearing upon administration, properly so called, upon the conduct of the royal officers, on the holding of assemblies, on really public business, are rare; the predominant feature, that, in fact, which constitutes the political legislation of this reign, is provisions having for their object the arrangements of the king with his beneficiaries, and with the church, that is to say, with the portion of the government, further removed from the public, nearer to the king himself, whether the other parties in these cases are ecclesiastics or laymen, it is always class or personal interests that we find in question; it is always some personal or class grievance for which redress is sought at the hands of the king, or some extension of privileges solicited. The representations made are more or less powerful, more or less legitimate, but it is no longer the body of the people that is in question, nor the government of the people; political legislation is no longer a public legislation; it has changed its character; its object is wholly private interests.

I. It has, at the same time, changed its tone. The legislation of Charlemagne is, in general, concise and imperious; it commands or prohibits summarily, without taking up the time in roundabout phrases and dissertations, and such is the proper method. Laws are not theses of philosophy nor specimens of eloquence; it is not their business to maintain doctrines nor to move the passions; to command, to forbid, is their purpose, and they always suffer when they deviate in any way from it. The legislation of Charlemagne, for the most part, went straightforward to this object. Such was by no means the case with the legislation of Charles le Chauve. However closely we examine that legislation, you can scarce detect either command or prohibition, amid the heaps of ratiocination, exhortation, advice, entreaty. The capitularies of Charles le Chauve are not regular laws, but either sermons addressed to minds sought to be brought over to particular views, or negotiations with men whose obedience was only to be hoped for by a certain degree of obedience in return.

This leads us to the greatest legislative change which is seen between these two epochs, to the really new character of the legislation of Charles le Chauve, and of his successors, the character in which the approach of the feudal system is clearly shown.

I have just said that in the capitularies of the last Carlovingians, we find many acts which do not emanate from the king only, from the central legislative power, and especially many treaties; between Charles le Chauve, for example, and his brothers, his nephews, or other princes, in possession of some portion of the territory of the empire of Charlemagne. Out of the fifty-one capitularies of Charles le Chauve, there are nine treaties of this kind. But this is not all : almost the entire legislation at this epoch is a series of negotiations between separate and independent powers. Under Charlemagne, however various they may have been, whether they were addressed to the agents of power or to its subjects, all the acts bore the character of a superior who commands inferiors. Social and political unity was strongly marked on it. Under Charles le Chauve, the unity disappeared; it is evidently no longer a general power which commands; it is a special power which treats with other powers, a government which defends its territory and rights against other governments. Out of the 529 articles which the capitularies of Charles le Chauve contain, more than a hundred have this appearance; legislation has become diplomacy. Now what is the dominant characteristic of the feudal society? Precisely the facts which we here observe; petty states, petty governments, considering themselves each independent in its territory, or nearly so, quarrel, dispute, reciprocally send ambassadors, hold conferences, form conventions. During a long period the relations of royalty with the feudal lords dispersed throughout the French territory are nothing else; its laws, its charters, are treaties; its progress is concession or acquisition. This is what distinguishes, what characterizes feudal society when considered in its whole. Now, under the last Carlovingians, this characteristic already appears in the laws: there is no longer any legislation, properly so called: there is diplomacy between independent states.

You see the history of legislation leads us to the same results to which history, properly so called, conducted us. We have just put to laws the corresponding question to that which we have addressed to events; the answer is the same: we have discovered not only the same tendency, but the same progression in the development of facts so different. This, if I do not deceive myself, is the best confirmation of our view of the dismemberment of the empire of the Carlovingians. We have had reason to lay aside as incomplete that which is drawn from the diversity of races, for you see it is contradictory to the history of legislation; from the ninth to the eleventh century, the diversity of races, instead of exercising any more empire over laws, ceased to be a dominant principle, and the source of variety: the laws vary not according to races, but according to classes and to places.

The diversity of races, then, will never explain the history of the legislation at this epoch, whilst the progressive development of the feudal society, the necessary formation of a multitude of petty states and petty powers,—one sole state and one sole power having become impossible—alike accounts for the vicissitudes of legislation and the vicissitudes of society.

I will go no further into the history of the laws under the Carlovingians. I should find there the texts for many curious observations; but they would require too much detail, and would carry us further than we have time to go. In our next lecture we will examine the history of the church, of religious society at the same epoch; and then see if it will give us results analogous to those which have been furnished us by the history of civil society. Before, however, I close this lecture, I will place before you a particular fact which did not come naturally within the scope of the considerations I have been suggesting to you, but which yet it is desirable that you should be acquainted with. This is the distribution of the *missi dominici*, sent throughout the kingdom by Charles le Chauve in 853, the only year in reference to which the details of this distribution have come down to us. France was then divided into eighty-six districts or territorial circumscriptions. The coincidence of this number with that of our present department, though very singular, is pure matter of chance; some of these eighty-six districts are described as comprehending several counties. They were divided among twelve companies of *missi*, whose total number was forty-three. We have their names and their quality. Of the forty three, thirteen were bishops, five abbots, and twenty-five lay men, without any particular title; at the head of each mission was a bishop; at least a bishop occurs first in each list.

The consequences to be deduced from this table are unimportant, but the document is a curious one in itself.

TWENTY-SIXTH LECTURE.

Object of the lecture—Internal history of the Gallo-Frankish church, from the middle of the 8th century to the end of the 10th—Anarchy which pervaded it in the first half of the 8th century—Twofold principle of reform—The reformation is actually undertaken by the first Carlovingians: 1. By the civil power; 2. By the ecclesiastical power—Special reforms—Order of canons—Its origin and progress—Reformation of the monastic orders by Saint Benedict d'Aniane—They change character—Preponderance of the temporal power in the Gallo-Frankish church at this epoch—Proofs—Still the church progresses towards its future preponderance—But it is not to the profit of its own government, of the bishops of France, that this progress is to turn.

I have already given the history of the Gallo-Frankish church up to the accession of the Carlovingians, towards the middle of the eighth century. I then considered it under the two points of view to which all questions which may arise with regard to a religious society attach themselves; on the one hand, without, in its relations with the civil society, with the state; on the other, within, in its organization and internal government. And not only the church in general, but those two distinct elements, the priests and the monks, the secular clergy and the regular clergy, have been the subject of a twofold inquiry.[1]

It conducted us, you will remember, to this result—that at the commencement of the eighth century, the Gallo-Frankish church was a prey to an ever-increasing anarchy. Externally, far from simplifying and fixing itself, its relations with the state became more and more confused, disordered, uncertain; the spiritual power and the temporal power "lived from day to day without principles, without fixed conditions; they encountered everywhere, running against each other, confounding, disputing the means of action, struggling and meeting in darkness and at chance."[2] Internally, in its own government, the situation of the church was no better—

---

[1] See the 19th Lecture. [2] See the 12th Lecture.

episcopacy had entirely usurped it; the inferior clergy in vain struggled to maintain some rights, to assure themselves some guarantees. And, after having usurped everything, the episcopal aristocracy itself fell into a powerless anarchy: scarcely were there any more councils, scarcely any more metropolitan power; egotism penetrated there as in civil society; each bishop governed his diocese at his will—despotic towards his inferiors, independent of his superiors and his equals. The monasteries presented almost the same phenomena. So that, taking all things together, a little before the middle of the eighth century, that which dominated in the heart of the church, as in the state, in Frankish-Gaul, was disorganization.

Still, at the same time that we recognized this fact, we caught a glimpse on the two banks of the Rhine, both for church and for state, of the first glimmering of another destiny. There were growing up together, on the one hand, that race of the Pepins which was to give Frankish-Gaul new masters; on the other, that Germanic church which, regularly and strongly organized under the influence of papacy, might serve for the reform of the other churches in the west, as a fulcrum and model.

It so, in fact, happened. You have seen, under the first Carlovingians, order and life re-enter into civil government: we are about to be present at the same fact in the church, at the same epoch, and from the same causes.

There is no need of demonstration; it breaks forth on all sides. From Pepin le Bref to Louis le Debonnaire, it is impossible not to be struck with the movement of reform which speaks out and propagates itself in the Gallo-Frankish church. Activity and rule appear in it at the same time. The temporal government labors with all its strength to introduce them. Pepin and Charlemagne commenced by drawing the episcopacy out of the anarchy and indolence into which it had fallen; they restored the power of the metropolitans, frequently assembled the bishops, occupied themselves with giving back to ecclesiastical government its entirety and regularity. Towards 747, at the request of Pepin, pope Zachary sends a collection of canons to him. In 774, Adrian I. sends a second, much more complete, to Charlemagne: and Charlemagne does not confine himself to circulating these codes of ecclesiastical discipline; he carefully watches over their observation; he causes new canons to be decreed; religious administration is evidently one of the principal affairs of his government. He succeeded in re-awaking in the church that general, regular activity which so long since had almost died away. Twenty councils only were held in the seventh century, and only seven in the first half of the eighth. Dating from Pepin, they once more became frequent. The following is a table of those which met under the Carlovingian race:

Kings.	Date of accession and death.	Number of Councils.	
Pepin le Bref,	752—768	14	in 16 years.
Charlemagne,	768—814	33	in 46 years.
Louis le Debonnaire,	814—840	29	in 26 years.
Charles le Chauve,	840—877	69	in 37 years.
From the death of Charles le Chauve, to the accession of Hugh Capet.	877—987	56	in 110 years.
		201	in 235 years.

This fact alone attests the return of activity and life into ecclesiastical society; and this activity did not content itself with holding councils, with regulating the immediate and special affairs of the clergy; it extended itself to the wants of religious society in general; of all the Christian people, in the future as in the present. This was the time of the definitive improvement of the liturgy; writings upon the ecclesiastical offices, their celebration, their history, abound; and rules establish themselves in the train of these treatises. It is also the time when the greater part of the *penitentials*, or codes of ecclesiastical punishment, were drawn up, which regulated the relation between sins and penances; they often vary from diocese to diocese, and appear in great number before any had acquired the least extended authority. Then, also, homiliaries or collections of sermons for the use of priests and the faithful, were multiplied. In a word, everything at this epoch gives testimony of a great ardor for labor and reform, a reform which, whether pursued by the civil power, which concurred very actively in the government of the church, or by the church itself, was applied to re-establish rule and progress in its own bosom.

Two special reformations, undertaken and accomplished by isolated individuals, the formation of the order of canons, and the re-establishment of rule among the monks, attest the same movement, and powerfully contributed to accelerate it.

About the year 760, Chrodegand, bishop of Metz, struck with the disorder which pervaded the secular clergy, and with the difficulty of governing the scattered priests, living isolately and each in his own fashion, undertook to subject those living in his episcopal diocese to an uniform rule, to make them live in common—in fact, to constitute of them a society analogous to that of monasteries. Thus arose the constitution of canons; the institutions of the times were its occasion, the monastic order its model. Chrodegand applied himself to render the assimilation as complete as he could. The rule, in thirty-four articles, which he gave to the first canons is almost literally borrowed from the rule of Saint Benedict. Labors, relaxations, duties, the whole employment of the time of the canons, are regulated in it; meals are to be taken in common, clothing to be uniform. It is true, a fundamental difference exists between the two orders; the canons may possess private property, while, with the monks, the monastery alone is possessed. But in the details of life the resemblance is minute, and it has evidently been sought.

The institution must have answered to the wants of the age, for it was rapidly propagated. Many bishops imitated Chrodegand; the organization of the clergy of episcopal churches into chapters became general; in 785, 789, 802, 813, we find the civil and ecclesiastical power eagerly sanctioning it. At length, in 826, Louis le Debonnaire, in a council held at Aix-la-Chapelle, had a rule of canons drawn up in 145 articles, which reproduced and extended that of Chrodegand, and he sent it to all the metropolitans of his kingdom, in order that it should everywhere be applied, and become the uniform discipline of churches.

It seems that this discipline encountered much resistance in the secular clergy; it deprived them of the disorderly liberty which they had so long enjoyed; it imposed an uniform and rather rough yoke upon them. But a circumstance to which most historians have paid but too little attention, almost everywhere removed these obstacles, and powerfully favored the extension of the new order.

I have already observed,[1] that the possessions of the church in each diocese were at the disposition of the bishop, who administered and distributed her revenues almost alone and arbitrarily; so that the simple priests, and not only the priests dispersed through the country districts, but those of the episcopal city, of the cathedral church itself, depended entirely on the bishop for their support, for the first and most imperious wants of life. And as a great number of bishops gave themselves up to infinite disorders, and spent on their own account the revenues of the church, the existence of the priests was very miserable and precarious; poverty, even distress, was often their condition.

The evil was so real, that when many bishops wished to imitate what had been done by the bishop of Metz, to unite the priests of their cathedral in the same edifice, and make them live in common, the temporal and spiritual powers thought it their duty to interfere, in order to prevent this being done, unless there were means of subsistence, a secured livelihood for the new establishment. The council of Mayence ordered, in 813, that the reform should be carried out, "where there were the means;" and that of Aix-la-Chapelle, in 816, enjoined bishops in the admission of canons to regulate themselves according to the revenues of the church.

But this difficulty did not last long. When the people saw priests thus confined, disciplined, and leading a life as regular and severe as the monks, it felt a redoubled respect and fervor for them. Gifts flowed to chapters as well as to monasteries. Never, perhaps, had so many and so well-endowed churches been founded; most of the cathedrals were rapidly enriched, and many donations were especially addressed to the canons, now become an object of edification and admiration. Simple priests thus escaped, in many places, from the state of distress and dependence into which they had been cast; the secular clergy became favorable to the new order, although it bore its yoke; and the order of canons soon played a very important part in the movement of reformation of the church at this epoch.

At the same time, a new reformation of monks was accom-

---

[1] 13th Lecture

plished, by the influence of a man who took the name of their first reformer in the west, Saint Benedict d'Aniane.

Benedict was not his original name; it is not known what that was; he was a Goth by race, and was born in 751, in the diocese of Maguelonne, in Septimania, of which his father was count. Sent in his childhood to the court of Pepin-le-Bref, he was page, cup-bearer, warrior, and took part in many expeditions of Charlemagne. In 774, without any details remaining to us concerning the adventures of his lay life, we find he has renounced it, become a monk in the abbey of Saint Seine, the foundation of which I have already recounted.[1] There he soon became the most respected of the monks; so much was he respected, that the abbot being dead, they wished to confer the title upon him: a singular resemblance, you perceive, between his destiny and that of the great reformer, whom he had adopted as a model. As Saint Benedict of Nursia at first opposed the wishes of the monks of Vicovaro, Benedict d'Aniane repelled those of the monks of Saint Seine: they were not, he said, capable of supporting the severe rule which he wished to establish; they would not be long before they rose up against him. The monks insisted; but Benedict, more obstinate than his patron, resolved to quit the abbey. About the year 780 he returned into southern Gaul, and, still faithful to the example of Saint Benedict, he became a hermit on the borders of a small stream, the Aniane, in the diocese of Maguelonne. His celebrity accompanied him, increased even, in his hermitage; a crowd of companions, already monks, or eager to become so, assembled around him, and he soon found himself obliged to build a large monastery, where he put in force the reformation which he proposed, in all its rigor.

This reformation was, at bottom, but a return to the primitive rule of Saint Benedict, concerning which I spoke to you in detail,[2] and which the relaxation of discipline, in most monasteries, had caused to be abandoned. Benedict d'Aniane published it anew, at the same time collecting the various rules given to monasteries, from that up to his own day; he formed of them the *codex regularum*, a regular body of law for the monastic society, and circulated it in Frankish Gaul. Not content with thus placing the law before the eyes

---

[1] 17th Lecture.   [2] 14th Lecture.

of those who were to obey it, he undertook the practical reform of monasteries; and, either in his own person, or by disciples of his choice, in point of fact, accomplished it in those of Gellon in Languedoc, of l'Isle Barbe, near Lyons, of Saint Savin in Poitou, of Cormery in Touraine, of Massay in Berry, of Saint Mesmin near Orleans, of Marmunster in Alsace, and many others.

So great a work soon attracted the consideration of the people and of Charlemagne to its author. In 794, we see Benedict seated at the council of Francfort, and there taking part in the condemnation of the heresy of the Adoptians, in the person of Felix, bishop of Urgel. In 799, by order of Charlemagne, he repaired to Urgel, with archbishop Leidrade, to preach to the heretics. Lastly, in 816, Louis le Debonnaire called him near his person, made him abbot of a large monastery, which he had just founded at Inde, in the vicinity of Aix-la-Chapelle, and in 817, Benedict presided at the special assembly, held at Aix-la-chapelle, for the reformation of monastic orders, an assembly entirely composed of monks and abbots, and the convocation of which he probably brought about.

From this assembly there went forth a great capitulary, destined to accomplish, in a general manner, and by the instrumentality of the public power, that reformation which Benedict followed in detail so long ago; it contains eighty articles, and should be looked upon as the completion and commentary of the rule of Saint Benedict. But the commentary differs greatly from the text, and here is shown, in the monastic mind, a revolution which it is necessary for us to characterize.

It will be recollected how, in analyzing the rule of Saint Benedict, we found it, despite the severe enthusiasm of which it is the fruit, to be feeling, even liberal—that is to say, foreign to all minute details, to all narrow views; humane and moderate with regard to practical life, in the heart of a very rigid general thought. Utterly different is the character of the additional rule which the capitulary of 817 contains. It seems, at first, to have no other object than that of again putting the primitive rule in vigor. The first three articles impose upon every abbot the obligation of re-perusing it upon re-entering his monastery, and of penetrating thoroughly into its purpose; upon every monk, that of learning it by heart. But to this succeeds a legislation most foreign to the text and spirit of the ancient law; a legislation overcharged with puerile details, with minute forms and vain observances; the following are some examples:

"Let the monks not shave during Lent, unless it be Holy Saturday. During the rest of the year, let them shave once a fortnight, and at the octave of Easter."[1]

"Let the bath be used according to the directions of the prior."[2]

"Let them not eat poultry either within or without the monastery, except by reason of sickness; let no bishops order monks to eat poultry. At Christmas and at Easter let them eat poultry for four days, if there be any; if not, they shall not demand it as their due."[3]

"Let them eat no fruit nor salad, except with their other food."[4]

"Let the length of the hood be two cubits."[5]

"Let his portion of meat and drink be given separately to each brother, and let no one give any of his own share to another."[6]

"Let no fixed time be observed for bleeding, but let every one be bled according as he needs it; and at such times have some especial indulgence as to eating and drinking."[7]

And so on of eighty-one articles, twenty-one are of a kind entirely foreign to all religious sentiment, to all moral tendency; and contain nothing but miserable prescriptions of this kind. Assuredly nothing less resembled that enthusiasm, that gravity, with which the primitive rule is marked; nothing more clearly attests the decay of the monastic mind, and its rapid tendency towards a miserable superstition. Benedict d'Aniane, like Benedict of Nursia, wished to reform the monasteries; but the reformation of the sixth century was at once extensive and sublime; it addressed itself to what was strong in human nature: that of the ninth century was puerile, inferior, and addressed itself to what was weak and servile in man. Such, in point of fact, is the general character of the monastic order from this epoch, despite numerous attempts to lead it back towards its source; it lost its grandeur, its first ardor, and remained laden with those puerilities, those ridiculous details, which humiliate men, even when they submit to them with a good intention.

---

[1] Art. 6. [2] Art. 7. [3] 8, 9, 78. [4] Art. 10
[5] Art. 21. [6] Art. 66. [7] Art 11.

Puerile or grave, monastic or secular, all this reformation of the Gallo-Frankish church was accomplished under the inspection and with the concurrence of the temporal power. In truth, from Pepin le Bref to Louis le Debonnaire, it is the temporal power, king or emperor, which governs the church, and effects all that I have just placed before you. The proofs of this are evident.

1. All the canons, all the measures relative to the church at this epoch, are published under the name of the tempora. power; it is that which speaks, which orders, which acts. To be convinced of this, one need only open the acts of the councils.

2. These acts, and many other monuments, even formally proclaim that it is to the civil power that the ordering of such things belongs, and that the church lives and acts under its authority. The canons of the council of Arles, held under Charlemagne, in 813, terminate as follows:—

"We have briefly enumerated the things which seem to us to require reformation, and we have decided that we shall present them to the lord emperor, invoking his clemency, to the end that if anything be wanting to his work, his prudence may supply it; that if there be anything contrary to reason, his judgment may correct it; that if anything be wisely ordered, his support, with the aid of the Divine goodness, may cause it to be carried into effect."[1]

We likewise read in the preface of the acts of the council of Mayence, also held in 813:

"Above all things, we have need of your aid, and of your holy doctrine, to warn us, and instruct us with benevolence; and if what we have drawn up below in some articles, appear worthy to you, let your authority confirm them; if anything appear to you to require correction, let your imperial grandeur order its correction."[2]

What texts can be clearer?

3. The capitularies of Charlemagne likewise prove at every step, that the government of the church was one of his principal affairs; a few articles, taken promiscuously, will show with what attention he occupied himself with it.

"Our *missi* are to inquire whether there be any cause of

---

[1] Con. Labbe, vol vii, col. 1238.   [2] Ibid, 1241.

complaint against a bishop, an abbot, an abbess, a count, or any other magistrate whatsoever, and inform us thereof."¹

"Let them examine if the bishops and the other priests live according to the canonical institution, and whether they know and properly observe the canons; whether the abbots live according to rule and canonically, and whether they thoroughly know the canons; if in monasteries the monks live according to rule; if in nunneries they live according to rule, and what is the extent of the establishment."

"Let them examine the monasteries and nunneries in each city; let them see how the churches are kept up or repaired, both as regards the edifices themselves and their ornaments; let them carefully inform themselves of the manners of each, and of what has been done with regard to what is ordered concerning readings, the chanting, and all which concerns the ecclesiastical discipline."³

"If any of the abbots, priests, deacons, &c., do not obey his bishop, let them go before the metropolitan, and let him decide the business with his suffragans; and if there is anything which the metropolitan bishop cannot reform or settle, let the accusers and the accused come to us with the letters of the metropolitan, that we may know the truth of the thing."⁴

"Let the bishops, abbots, counts, and all the powerful men, if they have between them any dispute and cannot reconcile themselves, come into our presence."⁵

This is assuredly a very direct and active intervention. Charlemagne did not govern civil affairs more immediately.

4. He exercised, besides, a very efficacious influence, although indirect; he nominated bishops. We read, indeed, in his capitularies, the re-establishment of the election of bishops by the clergy and the people, according to the primitive custom and the legal right of the church:

"Not being ignorant of the sacred canons," says he, "and to the end that in the name of God the holy church may freely enjoy her privileges, we have given our assent that the bishops be elected, according to the canonical statutes, by the

---

¹ 3d Cap. a., 789, § 11; Bal., vol. i., col. 244.
² 2d Cap. a., 802, § 2—5; vol. i., col. 475.
³ 5th Cap. a., 806, § 4, vol. i., col. 453.
⁴ Cap. a., 794, § 4, vol. i., col. 264.
⁵ 3d Cap. a., 812, § 2.

choice of the clergy and the people, in the diocese itself, without any regard to persons or presents, by the merit only of their life and wisdom ; and to the end that they may be completely able to direct those who are subject to them."[1]

But the fact continued to be but little in accordance with this right ; both after and before this capitulary, Charlemagne almost always nominated the bishops ; and even after his death, under his feeblest successors, the intervention of royalty in such matters was allowed by the most jealous of its rivals. In 853, pope Leo IV. wrote to the emperor Lothaire :

" We supplicate your mansuetude to give the government of this church to Colonna, an humble deacon, to the end, that having received your permission, we may, with the aid of God, consecrate him bishop. If it do not seem well to you that he be bishop of this church, let your serenity confer upon him that of Tusculum, which is now without a shepherd."[2]

In 879, pope John VIII. made a similar request to Carloman, in reference to the church of Verceil.[3]

The chronicles of the time are, besides, full of particular facts which can leave no doubt upon the subject, and prove that the choice of bishops was the occasion, on the part of the candidates, of a multitude of intrigues ; on the part of the prince himself, of partiality, or a singular indifference. Two anecdotes, derived from the chronicle of the monk of Saint Gall (a monument more important and more instructive than the pedantry of scholars is willing to believe), are remarkable examples of it : I shall give them literally.

" It is known that Charlemagne brought up, in the school of the palace, many young men whose learning and talent he afterwards employed.

" He made one of these pupils, who was poor, the chief and writer of his chapel. . . . . One day, when they announced the death of a certain bishop to the most prudent Charles, he asked if this prelate had sent before him into the other world any of his property and of the fruits of his labors.

" ' Not more than two pounds of silver, sire,' answered the messenger. The young man in question, unable to contain

---

[1] 1st Cap. a , 803, § 2, vol i., col. 379.
[2] Gratian. *Decret.*, p. ii., dist. 63, c. 16.
[3] Gieseler, Manual of Eccles. Hist., vol. ii., p 41, note 9.

within his breast the vivacity of his spirit, cried, in spite of himself, in the presence of the king : 'What a light viaticum for a journey so great, and of so long duration.'

"After deliberating some minutes within himself, Charles, the most prudent of men, said to the young priest : 'What sayest thou ? were I to give thee this bishopric, wouldst thou be careful to make more considerable provision for this long journey ?' The other hastening to devour these wise words, as grapes ripe before their time falling into his half-open mouth, threw himself at the feet of his master, and answered : 'Lord, it is for the will of God and your power to decide.'

" 'Conceal thyself,' said the king, 'behind the curtain, and thou shalt learn what rivals thou hast for this honorable post.' When the death of the bishop was known, the officers of the palace, always ready to watch the misfortune, or, at all events, the death of another, impatient of all delay, and each with the other, set to work the favorites of the emperor in order to obtain the bishopric. But he, firm in his design, refused them all, saying that he would not break his word to the young man. At last queen Hildegarde sent first the great men of the kingdom, and then came herself, to solicit the bishopric for her own chaplain. The king received her request with the most gracious air, assured her he could not, and wished not to refuse her anything, but added, that he could not pardon himself, if he were to deceive his young priest. In the manner of all women, when they think to make their desires and ideas predominant over the will of their husbands, the queen, dissimulating her rage, softened her naturally strong voice, and endeavoring to mollify, by caressing manners, the immovable soul of Charles, said to him : 'Dear prince, sire, why throw away this bishopric by giving it to such a child ? I conjure you, my amiable master—you, my glory and my support, grant it to my chaplain, your devoted servant.' At these words the young man, whom Charles had enjoined to place himself behind the curtain, near which he himself was seated, and to hear the prayers which each made, cried in a lamentable tone, but without quitting the curtain which surrounded him : 'Lord king, hold firm ; suffer no one to tear from thy hands the power given thee by God.' Then this prince, the courageous lover and friend of truth, ordered his priest to show himself, and said to him : 'Receive this bishopric, but take the utmost care to send before me, and before thyself, into the other world, great alms, and a good viaticum, for the long journey, from which no one returns."

This is the second:

"Another prelate was dead. Charles gave the succession to a certain young man. He, all content, prepared to set out. His servants brought him, as suited the episcopal gravity, a horse of a very quiet sort, and placed a stool for him to get into his saddle. Indignant that they should treat him as he were infirm, he sprang from the ground on to the horse so energetically, that it was with difficulty he could keep his seat, and not fall over the other side. The king, who saw what passed from the balustrade of the palace, had this man called to him and said : " My brave man, thou art lively, agile, quick, and thou hast a strong foot. The tranquillity of our empire is, as thou knowest, incessantly troubled by a multitude of wars ; we have need of such a priest as thou in our suite : remain, then, to be the companion of our fatigues, since thou canst mount thy horse so freely."[1]

I might cite many facts of this kind. This was assuredly treating the episcopacy and the church without ceremony.

5. Not only did the Carlovingians thus dispose of the bishoprics, but they often appropriated a portion of their domains to themselves. Every one knows what Charles Martel did in this way. But it is less generally known that this fact was repeated many times under the princes of his race, even the most devoted and submissive to the church. In 743, Carloman, brother of Pepin le Bref, decreed the following capitulary :

" We have resolved, with the counsel of the servants of God and the Christian people, because of the wars and the invasions of other neighboring nations which menace us, to take for a while, and by way of usufruct, some portion of the ecclesiastical domains, and to keep them, with the permission of God, for the maintenance of our army, on the condition that every year there shall be paid to the proprietary church or monastery, a sol—that is to say, twelve deniers, for each farm ; and that if he to whom the capital belongs dies, the church is to retake possession of it ; and if necessity re-

---

[1] *Deeds and Exploits of Charlemagne the Great*, by a Monk of Saint Gall, vol. iii., p. 151, of my *Collection*.

quires, or the prince orders it, this possession shall be renewed."[1]

We read also in a capitulary of Louis le Debonnaire, in 823:

"We order the abbots and *laymen* to have observed *in the monasteries which they hold from our gift,* and according to the counsels of the bishops, all which relates to the religious life of monks, canons, &c."[2]

There were, then, laymen who received from the emperor certain monasteries in the way of benefices. Abbots of this kind were still more numerous under Charles le Chauve; they had the name of *Abbacomites*.

Doubtless the church was constantly protesting; and, upon the whole this fact passed, and properly passed, for an attack on her rights, a violent usurpation. Yet it was so frequent, so open, that an idea of some kind of royal right was almost attached to it; and the church more than once seemed to acknowledge, that in extreme need, a portion of her property might be thus temporarily applied to the service of the state.

6. It was not only with ecclesiastical administration and discipline that the temporal power occupied itself at this period. It interfered even in matters of dogma, and they were governed in its name. Three questions of this kind were raised in the reign of Charlemagne. I shall merely point them out. 1. The question of the worship of images, raised in the west by a canon of the second council of Nice, in 787. The Gallo-Frankish church rejected this worship, and all that seemed to tend to it. A special work, drawn up by order of Charlemagne, probably by Alcuin, entitled, *Libri Carolini,* was published against it. The favor given by the popes to this doctrine did not operate upon the Frankish bishops nor their master, and, in 794, the council of Frankfort formally condemned it. 2. The heresy of the Adoptians concerning the nature of Jesus Christ, of which I have already spoken, and which Charlemagne also formally condemned in three successive councils, at Ratisbon, in 792, at Frankfort in 794, and at Aix-la-Chapelle, in 799. 3. The question of an addition to the symbol as to the procession of the host. These, assuredly, are matters entirely foreign to the external government of the

---

[1] 2 Cap. Carlom., a., 743; Bal. vol. i., col. 149.
[2] Cap. Lud., p. a, 823, § 8; vol. i., col. 635.

church—they are purely dogmatical. They were not the less regulated, if not by the civil power itself, at least under its authority, and with its intervention.

It may, therefore, be affirmed, without discussing the question of right, without examining whether it be good or ill that it should be thus, that at this epoch, directly or indirectly, the temporal power governed the church. The situation of Charlemagne in this respect was almost exactly the same as that of the king of England in the English church. In England, also, the civil assembly, or parliament, and the ecclesiastical assembly, or convocation, were long distinct ; and neither one nor the other decided upon, or could do anything without the sanction of royalty. Whether the matter in hand was a council or a *champ de mai*, a dogma or a proclamation of war, Charlemagne equally presided at it : in neither case did they think of dispensing with him.

But at the same time that they governed the church, and for the very reason that they did not in any way fear her independence, the first Carlovingians conferred immense advantages on her, and provided the most solid foundations for her future power.

1. It was by their support that the tithe was definitively and generally established. You have seen that the church, relying upon the Hebrew customs, had at various different times, but without any great success, attempted to appropriate this rich revenue to herself. Charlemagne gave to the tithe the aid not only of his laws but of his indefatigable will. It was under his reign that it truly took root in the legislation and practice of the west.

2. He also extended the jurisdiction of the clergy. We read in one of his capitulations :—

" We will that neither abbots, priests, deacons, nor under-deacons, nor any priests, be cited or taken before public or regular judges, for deeds concerning their person : let them be judged by their bishop, and so let justice be done them. If any complaint be carried against them before the judge concerning the domains of the church or their own property, let the judge send the complaint with one of his own messengers to the bishop, in order that he may do justice by the intervention of his advocate ; and if there arise between them any dispute which they cannot or will not settle themselves, let the cause be carried before the court or the judge by the advocate whom the law gives the bishop, and let it there be decided according to the law, respect being always paid to what has just been said with reference to the person of the priest."[1]

Whenever he had any purpose in interfering in the disputes of the bishops, whether among themselves or between them and the laymen, he made no hesitation in doing so. But in general, as the ecclesiastical jurisdiction was more enlightened and regular, he was more inclined to extend than to restrict it ; and despite the submission of the bishops during his reign, they drew from it at a later period many useful precedents in favor of their independence.

3. In the civil order also, especially in reference to marriages and wills, the power of the clergy greatly increased at this period. I have already pointed out the cause from which it drew this important attribute. I have shown how, among the barbarians, the family was unfixed, unstable, and how it was the interest of a regular government to introduce more order and fixedness into it. It was more especially for this reason that all questions of parentage, marriage, or wills, came under the ecclesiastical jurisdiction ; and the church, by penetrating into the interior of families, acquired an enormous power.

4. Lastly, Charlemagne gave up to each church, under the name of *mansus ecclesiasticus*, a farm free from all kinds of charges and taxes; an important concession at an epoch when rural property furnished almost all the public expenditure.

Despite her momentary servitude, the church assuredly had here numerous fertile principles of independence and power. These were not long in developing themselves. During the early years of the reign of Louis le Debonnaire, the order of things established by Charlemagne continues, or nearly so: it is still the emperor who governs, who, at least, appears to govern the church. But everything soon changes, and the church in her turn governs the emperor. I shall not enter with any detail into this subject. Every one knows that the usurpation of power by the clergy is the dominant characteristic of the reigns of Louis le Debonnaire and Charles le Chauve, up to the time when all general society, all central government, disappeared to give place to the feudal system.

---

[1] Cap. Car., M. A. 801, § 39, vol. i, cap. 355.

The facts are present to all minds. I shall quote but one text, possibly more clear than all the facts put together. This is Art. 2 of the accusation brought the 14th of June, 859, before the council of Touil, by Charles le Chauve, against Wenilon, archbishop of Sens, who had separated from him to ally himself with his enemies. This denunciation of a bishop by a king seems an act of the resistance and independence of royalty; it is expressed in the following terms:

"By his election, and that of the other bishops, and with the will, consent, and acclamations of all the faithful of our kingdom, Wenilon, in his own diocese, in the city of Orleans, in the cathedral of Saint Croix, in presence of the other archbishops and bishops, consecrated me king, according to the ecclesiastical custom; and in calling me to reign, he anointed me with the holy oil, gave me the royal diadem and sceptre, and led me to the throne. After this consecration, I could not be cast from the throne, nor supplanted by any one—at least, not without having been heard and judged by the bishops, by whose ministry I was consecrated king, and who have been named the throne of God. God rests upon them, and it is through them that he decrees his judgments. I have always been, and am at present ready to submit myself to their paternal corrections, and to their castigatory judgments."[1]

Truly the revolution which, in Frankish Gaul, had raised the priesthood above the empire, cannot be proved by a less suspicious and more formal testimony.

It was to the profit of the Gallo-Frankish episcopacy that this revolution seemed to be brought about; it was by the bishops that the temporal power was thus acquired and thus treated. But this sovereignty of the national church was not to subsist long, and it was not to the profit of the bishops that the church had overcome the state. It will be recollected that in seeking amidst the dissolution which invaded Gaul under the last Merovingians, what principles of civil and ecclesiastical regeneration became visible—that it was beyond the Alps, at Rome, that the principle of ecclesiastical regeneration appeared to us.[2] There, in fact, was developed the power called upon to rule the church in general, and the

---

[1] Bal., vol. ii., col. 133   [2] 19th Lecture.

Gallo-Frankish church in particular. It was in the hands of the papacy, not of the episcopacy, that the empire definitively fell. In the next lecture I shall place before you the history of the relations between the Gallo-Frankish church and papacy during this epoch, and you will see that it was papacy that took possession of the sovereignty on the decay of the Carlovingians.

TWENTY-SEVENTH LECTURE.

History of papacy—Peculiar situation of the city of Rome—Relations of the popes about the middle of the eighth century, with the Italian, Spanish, Anglo-Saxon, Gallo-Frankish, and Germanic churches—Their alliance with the early Carlovingians—Advantages which they drew from it—Donation of Pepin and of Charlemagne—Sovereignty of the Carlovingian emperors over the popes—Uncertainty of the ideas, and incoherency of the facts concerning the rights of papacy—It increases more and more in minds—It apparently acquires a legal title—False decretals—Nicholas I.—His character—Affair of the marriage of Lothaire and of Teutberge—Affair of Rhotarde, bishop of Soissons—Triumph of papacy: 1. Over temporal sovereigns; 2. Over national churches—Its decided preponderance in the west.

I HAVE shown that the Gallo-Frankish church was raised by the first Carlovingians, from the state of impotence and anarchy into which it had fallen. We have seen it re-enter into order and activity; we have seen this revolution brought about by the concurrence and under the authority of the temporal power. Pepin, Charlemagne, and even Louis le Debonnaire, on his accession, actually governed the Gallo-Frankish church. This state of things was of short duration. I have pointed out with what rapidity the spiritual power passed from docility to independence, from independence to sovereignty; I have shown its pretensions already acknowledged by the temporal power itself, particularly by Charles le Chauve. It was to the profit of the Gallo-Frankish episcopacy that this change was brought about. I announced that it would not long enjoy it, that a third power, the papacy, would soon take their scarcely acquired supremacy from the national bishops. It is with this fact—that is to say, with the history of papacy, from the eighth to the tenth century, especially in its relations with the Gallo-Frankish church, that we have to occupy ourselves at present.

There is a primitive fact with regard to the development of papacy in Europe, which, I think, has never been taken sufficiently into account. Not only was Rome always the most important city in the west; not only did the recollections of its ancient grandeur tend to the good of the bishop, who, without as yet reigning, was already the chief of its people; but Rome also had a particular advantage in the west, that of never remaining in the hands of the Barbarians, Heruli, Goths, Vandals, or others: they had many times taken and pillaged it—they never long retained possession of it. Alone, among all the great western cities, and whether as united to the empire of the west, or as independent, it never passed under the German yoke: alone it remained Roman, after the ruin of the Roman empire.

It happened, without premeditation, without labor, by the sole nature of its situation, that Rome found herself, morally at least, at the head of the ancient population disseminated throughout the new Western States. In this struggle, at first public, afterwards secret, but for a long period so active — this struggle of the conquered against the conquerors—the attention of the Gallo-Romans, of the Hispano-Romans, of all the cities desolated by their barbarous conquerors, naturally turned towards Rome, so long their sovereign, and now the only living wreck of the ancient society, alone exempt from new masters, alone capable of still preserving the respected traditions of the people that they still governed. For this reason, Rome was a name dear to the whole mass of the population in the west, the centre of recollections and ideas, the image of all which remained of the Roman world. It was under the influence of this fact that papacy took rise; it was, so to speak, its cradle; it placed it in its very origin at the head of nations; it rendered it a kind of national power for the race of the conquered.

Let us now see what was its situation with regard to the principal churches of the west, at the middle of the eighth century.

At this epoch, there were in the west five great national churches: the Italian church, or rather the Lombard—for I only speak of the north of Italy, then in the power of the Lombards—the Spanish church; the Anglo-Saxon church; the Gallo-Frankish church, and the rising Germanic church.

1. It was in Italy, in the Lombard church, that papacy was the least powerful. The bishop of Rome had never been, either as metropolitan or by any other title, the superior of the bishops of the north of Italy: the Lombard kings, who had long been Arians, and incessantly applied themselves to drive their conquests into the territory which they administered, were its natural enemies. "The perfidy of the Lom-

bards," wrote pope Pelagius I., in 584, "has caused us, despite their own oaths, so many tribulations and evils, that no one can recount them." The correspondence between the Lombard bishops and the popes, became, therefore, difficult and rare; and that church which reached almost to the gates of Rome, was stranger to them than any other.

2. For a long time, on the contrary, their influence over the Spanish church was great and progressive. Under the domination of the Arian Visigoths, the catholic and persecuted clergy of Spain maintained frequent and intimate relations with the bishop of Rome, who, in the name of the catholic church, supported it in its resistance. It happened, moreover, that in the course of the fifth and sixth centuries, two illustrious Spanish bishops, Torribius, bishop of Astorga, and Leandro, bishop of Seville, were the secretaries and friends—the one of Leo the Great (440–461), the other of Gregory the Great (590–604), and established habitual relations between their church and that of Rome. Accordingly, it is on the subject of the Spanish church that the pretensions of papacy are the most openly manifested at this epoch. In 538, pope Vigilius writes to Profuturus, bishop of Braga:

"As the holy Roman church possesses the primacy over all churches, it is to her, as the chief of the church, that all important affairs are to be sent, the judgments and complaints of bishops, as well as great questions of ecclesiastical matters. For that church, which is the first, in confiding her functions to the other churches, called upon them to share in her labors, not in her plenitude of power."[1]

There was, at that time, no other church in the west to which the bishop of Rome addressed language like this. Accordingly some doubts have been raised as to the authenticity of this letter; still it seems to me probable. The power of the papacy in Spain was so real, that in 603 two Spanish bishops, Januario of Malaga, and Stephen, having been irregularly deposed, Gregory the Great sent an envoy, named John, with orders to inquire into the affair: and without convoking any council, without seeking the adhesion of the Spanish clergy, John declared that the deposition was illegal, annulled it, and reinstated the two bishops, thus exercising the rights of the most extended ecclesiastical supremacy.

---

[1] Baluze, *Nov. Coll. Conc.*, vol. i., coll. 1465.

It was not, however, so well established as one would suppose. The Visigoth kings, dating from Ricared (586–601), had become Catholics. At first, the papacy profited by it; the fact which I have related proves it. But the struggle between the national clergy and the temporal government having ceased, the clergy grew more closely connected with the government, and less so with the foreign bishop, whom they had taken for a chief. Accordingly, we see the power of papacy a little weakened in Spain during the course of the seventh century, and the national church acting with more independence. At the commencement of the eighth century king Witiza quarrelled with the pope, interdicted all recourse to Rome, rejected the Roman discipline, and, it is said, even authorized the marriage of priests. Some years afterwards, the invasion of the Arabs took place, and the greater part of Spain was lost both for papacy as well as for Christianity. In the middle of the eighth century, it preserved power only among the Christian refugees in the north of the Peninsula, or at the foot of the Pyrenees; and there even the disorder was such, and society so agitated or weak, that there was scarcely anything for a distant and systematic influence to do.

3. With regard to the Anglo-Saxon church, you know, that, founded by the popes themselves, it was placed, from its very origin, under their most direct influence; it was still in the middle of the eighth century in the same situation.[1]

4. The situation of the Gallo-Frankish church was different. You have seen that during the course of the seventh century her relations with Rome had become very rare.[2] It was in the middle of the eighth century, precisely at the opening of the epoch with which we are about to occupy ourselves, that they again became more frequent and efficacious. I will resume this history presently.

5. The Germanic church, as you know, owed its success to the labors of the Anglo-Saxon missionaries, of Saint Boniface, more especially; and her founders, in creating her, as it were, to the papacy.[3]

Such was the situation of the popes with regard to the great national churches in the West, when, about the middle of the eighth century, the first Carlovingians closely allied themselves with them. It is easy to recognize the happy effects upon the papacy of this alliance.

---

[1] 19th Lecture.   [2] Ibid.   [3] Ibid

And, first, it acquired an ascendency in the Italian church which it had never before possessed. After the defeat of the Lombards by the Franks, the bishop of Rome did not become the metropolitan of the Lombard bishops; he did not receive the title of patriarch; but he was invested with a superiority without example, indefinite, and so much the greater.

The Lombard clergy saw him respected by the Frank conquerors, who in general looked upon him as their representative and minister beyond the Alps, and it was through him accordingly that tne clergy treated with the conquerors. No one in the Lombard church could think of equalling it; and the church itself rapidly fell under his authority.

He also acquired fresh authority in the Gallo-Frankish church. It was with his aid, and by supporting themselves with his name and opinions, that the first Carlovingians labored to reform her. Even before their elevation, Saint Boniface wrote to pope Zachary, that Carloman, brother of Pepin le Bref, asked him to repair to Gaul: "Protesting that he wished to amend and reform the state of religion and the church, which, for at least seventy or eighty years, had been abandoned to disorder, and crushed under foot."[1]

It was under the presidence and influence of Saint Boniface, in his character of legate of the pope, that councils were held, formerly so rare, but now again become frequent. The acts of the council of 742, called *Germanicum*, commence in the following terms:

"I, Carloman, duke and prince of the Franks, with the counsel of the servants of God and our great men, have convoked the bishops of my kingdom, and Boniface, who is sent from Saint Peter, that they may give me counsel," &c.

The same fact reappears in the council held the following year at Lestines or Leptines, in the diocese of Cambray, and at the assembly of Soissons (752), where Pepin was consecrated king. Not content with thus serving as mediator between the temporal sovereigns and the popes, Saint Boniface undertook to unite closely to the see of Rome the metropolitans, or archbishops, whose power he was establishing; he induced those of Rouen, of Sens, and of Reims, at the time of their nomination, to demand the *pallium*—the sign of their new dignity—from the pope, and thus to claim of him a sort of inves-

---

[1] S. Bon., ep. 51, p. 107.

titure. Only one among them followed his counsel, and the pope testified to Boniface his disappointment that the other two had not done the same. Lastly, it was not the sovereigns or the clergy only who were reconciled to papacy, and contracted a more intimate alliance with it. The same movement was manifested among the faithful, the people: the number of pilgrims who repaired to Rome with pious intentions rapidly increased. We read in a capitulary of Pepin le Bref:

"As regards pilgrims who make a pilgrimage in the service of God, let no one demand toll of them."[1]

And it is evidently to the pilgrimage of Rome that this provision relates.

Though we had no other proof of the ascendant movement of papacy in the Gallo-Frankish church, but the tone in which it is there spoken of, this were sufficient; not only the language of the clergy, but of writers in general, the temporal sovereigns themselves, becomes extremely pompous—magnificent and respectful epithets increase. The pope was no longer simply the bishop of Rome, the brother of other bishops; titles were given to him, and expressions employed towards him which were not employed towards or given to any other. Certain phrases of Alcuin, who in his capacity of favorite to Charlemagne, cannot be suspected of wishing to sacrifice the power of his master to a foreign power, will say more concerning those titles and expressions than any generalities. In 796, he addressed pope Leo III. (695–816) in these words:

"Most holy father, elected pontiff of God, vicar of the apostles, heir of the fathers, prince of the church, guardian of the only dove without stain."[2]

And in another place, in 794, to Adrian I. (761–795):

"Very excellent father, even as I recognize thee for the vicar of the blessed Peter, the prince of the apostles, so do I regard thee as the heir of his miraculous power."[3]

Again, in writing to Charlemagne, in 799:

"Hitherto there have been in the world three persons of supreme rank: the sublimity of the apostolical vicar who occupies the seat of the blessed Peter, the prince of the apostles; the dignity of the emperor who exercises the secular

---

[1] Cap. Pipp., a. 755, p. 22; Bal., vol. i., col. 175.
[2] Letter 20, vol. i., p. 30.   [3] Letter 15, vol. i, p. 25.

power in the second Rome; the third is the royal dignity with which the will of our Lord Jesus Christ has invested you, that you may govern the Christian people."[1]

It is true that it would be improper to accept these expressions literally; we must not believe that the pope possessed, in its whole extent, the power which they attribute to him; but they show what moral and religious supremacy he already possessed in the mind of the people. His intellectual dominion, the source of all other species of his dominion, really dates from this period.

His temporal power received at the same time a notable accretion. When Pepin had conquered the Lombards, he compelled them to restore to the bishop of Rome the lands which they had taken from him, and he, moreover, added a part of those which he had himself conquered, especially in the exarchy of Ravenna. After the complete ruin of the Lombard kings, Charlemagne, in appropriating these states, made new and considerable donations of the same kind to Adrian the First. The authenticity of these two gifts has been called into question, and it is true that the original act is, in neither case, extant. Nevertheless, they are, directly or indirectly, mentioned by contemporary writers; and numerous chronicles and monuments of various kinds attest, or suppose their existence. The extent of the lands thus conceded may be disputed: in the succeeding centuries the pope greatly exaggerated it, no doubt; but I conceive that it is impossible reasonably to question the reality of these donations. They present nothing which is not perfectly natural, and in harmony with the entire history of the eighth century. We ought rather to have been surprised had they not occurred.

It is more difficult to determine the true meaning and political bearing of such concessions. Two hypotheses have been maintained upon this point. According to some, Pepin and Charlemagne gave to the pope no more than the civil proprietorship, the *dominium utile*, the revenue of the lands, and of the slaves and laborers who inhabited them—not the sovereignty, the government of the territory. According to others, political sovereignty was attached to the concession; the popes exercised all the rights of political sovereignty, as had been done before them by the exarch of Ravenna, and the other

---

[1] Letter 80, vol. i., p. 117.

delegates of the emperor of the East, who, even after the donations had been made, preserved, for a while, some shadow of supremacy over these lands, but soon completely lost it, leaving the pope as their only successor.

In my opinion, neither one nor the other of these hypotheses can be maintained; each of them depends upon an oblivion of the condition of minds in the time which it relates to. In those days, people did not acquire such clear and precise ideas of sovereignty, power, and rights, as are formed of them by us, in the present day. They did not distinguish with such strictness between the *dominium utile* and political government, between property and sovereignty. All this science of modern civilians was foreign to men's minds and to facts, in the middle of the eighth century. The proprietor, as proprietor, exercised in his domains a portion of those rights which are at present ascribed to the sovereign alone. He maintained order, did justice or caused it to be done, led or sent to war the men upon his lands, not in virtue of a special power, called political, but in virtue of his proprietorship itself, in the idea of which the most various powers were confounded. Thus, on the one hand, when, in the ninth century, we see the popes exercising the greater part of those rights which we name political, in the domains which they had received from Pepin and Charlemagne, we must not therefore conclude that real, complete, and independent sovereignty had been conferred upon them; and, on the other hand, neither must we any more believe that Charlemagne, in retaining a certain sovereignty over the territory which he had given to the popes, thought that he ought to, and, in fact, did, reserve to himself all the rights which, in the present day, appear to us to be attached to the word. At the same time that the pope, in the name of proprietor, had ministers, judges, and even military chiefs, chosen by and dependent upon himself, on his domains, Charlemagne received taxes from them, and sent them, as to the rest of his states, *missi dominici*, charged with the inspection of all matters, the suppression of abuses, &c. In a word, complete sovereignty was attributed neither to the pope nor to the emperor; it fluctuated between the two, in a divided and uncertain state; and from this fact arise all the difficulties of a question which does not exist in the eyes of any one who is acquainted with and understands the period of which we are speaking.

Whether or no he possessed such sovereignty, there can

be no doubt but that the acquisition of such vast domains, and of all the rights of proprietorship, was a great increase of temporal power for the bishop of Rome. He found himself, from that time, beyond any comparison, the richest bishop in Christendom, and without a peer materially as well as morally.

Thus, the early Carlovingians, and especially Charlemagne, were the most useful allies to the papacy: 1st, in ensuring to the pope a power over the Italian church, which they had not hitherto possessed; 2dly, in giving them a very active influence in the affairs of the Gallo-Frankish church; 3dly, in recognizing in these, by language and all demonstrations which strike the imagination of nations, a majesty and supremacy which had not yet been admitted by princes; 4thly, and finally, in increasing, whether by wealth, or by its indirect consequences, their temporal power.

Nevertheless, you must not believe that, in their relations with the papacy, they had abdicated their empire. As you have seen that Charlemagne favored the influence of the clergy within the Gallo-Frankish church, and yet subjected them to his own power, so he ruled the popes even while he prepared for them the means of ruling his successors. In the first place, their election was not complete until it had received the approbation of the emperor. Facts and texts abound in proof of this. In 796, Charlemagne wrote to pope Leo III. who had just been elected:

"After having read your excellency's letter, and noticed the decree, we were greatly rejoiced both with the unanimity of the election and with the humility of your obedience, and with the promise of fidelity which you have made to us."[1]

In 816, the election of Stephen IV. took place in the presence of the commissaries of Louis le Debonnaire, to whom the decree was sent in order that it should receive his confirmation. In 817, Pascal I. excuses himself for the precipitation of his ordination. In 825, at the time of the election of Eugenius II., Louis le Debonnaire sent his son Lothaire to Rome, and it was determined that commissaries of the emperor should always be present at the ordination of the pope.

This consent of the emperor has sometimes been represented as a nomination; it has been pretended that he named the

---

[1] Cap., vol. i., col 271.

pope like the other bishops. Nothing is less founded than this assertion. The pope was elected at Rome by the clergy, and sometimes, too, with the concurrence of the people of Rome; but in order to his consecration, the approbation of the emperor was necessary. The concurrence of the temporal power went no further than this.

The language of many popes at this period expressly witnesses their dependence, and the positive superiority of the imperial power. Leo III. wrote to the emperor:

"If we have done anything incompetently, and if, in the affairs which have been submitted to us, we have not rightly followed the path of the true law, we are ready to reform what we have done, according to your judgment and that of your commissaries."[1]

Leo IV. wrote to Lothaire the First:

"We promise that we will always do all that shall be in our power to keep and observe inviolably the statutes and decrees as well of yourself, as of your predecessors."[2]

Moreover, in France, within the Gallo-Frankish church, the emperors governed alone, without, in any respect, sharing the power with the papacy. That influence upon the Gallo-Frankish church which I have just exhibited to you as being in the hands of the popes, was only indirect. They did not convoke the councils; the emperor alone called them. The decision of these assemblies did not require their approbation. All ecclesiastical supervision or administration belonged either to the national bishops or to the delegates of the emperor, and the pope only interfered indirectly, by way of advice.

There existed, moreover, with the public, both laity and clergy, a certain idea of an ancient and general legislation of the church, to which the popes were bound to submit, as well as the other bishops. People made no precise estimate of its source and its authority; they were not fully aware from what power it ought always to emanate; the question was not, as it afterwards was, very clearly laid down between the councils and the popes; but it was the firm impression of the public that, above the popes, were the canons, discipline, and general law of the church, and that of themselves they had no right to change them.

---

[1] Gratian. Decret., p. 11, caus. 2, quot. 7, col. 41.
Gratian. Decret., Distinct. 10, c. 9.

Such was the situation of the papacy, more especially in its relations with the Gallo-Frankish church, at the commencement of the ninth century, and at the end of the reign of Charlemagne. You see that much incoherence and confusion reigned in it. We thus meet with a multitude of contradictory facts; some bear witness to the independence of the national churches; others exhibit the papal power above the national churches. Here appears the superiority of the temporal power; there, that of the spiritual power enthroned at Rome. In 833, Gregory IV. interfered to reconcile Louis le Debonnaire and his sons, reproaching the bishops of Frankish Gaul with their conduct: they protested against his interference, and contested with him the rights which he assumed, declaring that "they would by no means submit to his will, and that if he came to excommunicate, he should depart excommunicated; for the authority of the ancient canons permitted nothing of this kind." Nevertheless, in his answer, Gregory reproaches them with having employed, in writing to him, the titles *frater* and *pater*, by turns, "whereas it would have been much more becoming to have exhibited towards him nothing but a filial respect;" and, upon this, not only did they not expostulate again, but the word *frater* gradually disappeared from their language. In 844, the bishops of Frankish Gaul refused to acknowledge Drogon, archbishop of Metz, the natural son of Charlemagne, a vicar of pope Sergius II., who had given him his diploma; and, in 849, they menaced Nomenoe, king of Brittany, with excommunication, because he received with disdain a letter of pope Leo IV., "to whom God had given the primacy of the entire world." I might multiply examples; I might exhibit temporal sovereigns, popes, and national churches, turn by turn, conquerors or conquered, arrogant or humble. Nevertheless, through all these contradictions, we plainly perceive that the papacy was making progress; it reigned, if not in fact, at least in the minds of men. The conviction that the pope was the interpreter of the faith, the chief of the universal church, that he was above all other bishops, above national councils, and above temporal governments, in matters of religion, and even in temporal affairs, when they related to religion; this conviction, I say, became more and more established in the minds of men. In the middle of the ninth century, we may regard it as definitively formed; the conquest of the intellectual order was then completed for the profit of the papacy.

It had also to make the conquest of the legal order; the mind of nations attributed it to the sovereignty of law, but there were wanting titles in which its laws should be written, and in the name of which it might assert their historical antiquity, as well as their national legitimacy. These it soon found.

Collections had been making, for a long time, of the canons of the church. The first collection of this kind, in the west, had been compiled in the sixth century, by a Roman monk, named Denis le Petit. It soon became a kind of ecclesiastical code, and the object of general emulation. Many similar collections were written in the different states of the west. Spain, in particular, had one of them, to which the name of *Isidore* was given, although St. Isidore, bishop of Seville, had evidently no hand in it. It was more extensive than that of Denis le Petit, and contained a greater number of letters of the popes, as well as of canons of councils, and particularly of the Spanish councils. It spread itself beyond Spain, and very soon obtained great credit, particularly in Gaul.

In the first half of the ninth century, between the years 820 and 849, there suddenly appeared, still under the name of St. Isidore, a new collection of canons, much more important than that which I have already mentioned. It is in the north and east of Frankish Gaul, in the dioceses of Mayence, Trèves, Metz, Reims, &c. &c., that we first meet with it; there it had no obstacle opposed to its circulation; very few were the doubts which arose here and there concerning its authenticity, and in a short time it acquired a sovereign authority. This is the collection which is called The False Decretals. It has received this name, because it contains numerous pieces which are manifestly false, and because it bears all the characters of a lying fabrication. It begins with sixty letters of the most ancient bishops of Rome, from Saint Clement (91—100) to Melchiades (311—214); letters of which no monument had yet made mention, and of which the falsehood appears at the first glance. The popes of the three first centuries are therein continually made to employ St. Jerome's translation of the bible, which was not produced until the end of the fourth century; they also allude to facts and to works of the sixth and seventh centuries. In short, the fabrication cannot in the present day be called into question by a man of any sense or information.

The author of this fabrication is not known. Since we meet with it first of all in the dioceses of Trèves and Mayence, and on account of other minor indications with which will not occupy your time, it has been attributed to Benedict, deacon of Mayence, whom I have already named to you, and who made the second collection of the statutes of Charlemagne. Whoever he may have been, his work spread rapidly: many took it for the ancient collection already known by the name of Saint Isidore: others, believing it to be new, neglected even to examine its contents. It had for patrons, not alone the popes and their partisans, but also nearly all the bishops; for, in fact, it was not written exclusively in the interest of the papacy. It even seems, all things considered, in its primitive intention to have been more especially destined to serve the bishops against the metropolitans and the temporal sovereigns. The greater portion of the fabricated pieces, even whilst displaying with pomp the power of the popes, have for their principal object the establishing of the independence of the bishops, and it is above all against the metropolitans and the temporal princes that the power of the pope is invoked.

The false decretals had, therefore, from the first, the support of the bishops; and, far from calling them into question, they eagerly adopted them, pre-occupied, as has so often happened, with the interest of the moment, and not troubling themselves to perceive that one day the fraud would turn to the profit of the pretensions of the papacy, rather than to their own advantage.

About the middle of the ninth century the pope had thus triumphed both in the intellectual and in the legal orders; they were in possession of a rational right and a written title; this sovereignty reposed not only upon public belief, but also upon traditions.

Thus founded, and invested with such forces, their power was naturally not slow to display itself practically. About the same period, in fact, all the consequences of the principles set down, either in the general opinions of the time, or in the false decretals, made their appearance in certain particular events.

In 856 a nephew of Charles le Chauve, and great-grandson of Charlemagne, Lothaire, king of Lorraine, had married

Teutberge, daughter of Boson, a Burgundian count. In 857 she displeased him, and he put her away; he accused her of all kinds of crimes, among others, of incest with Hubert, her brother. He lived openly with another woman, Waldrade, sister of Gunther, archbishop of Cologne, and niece to Teutgaud, archbishop of Trèves, whom he had loved, it is said, for a long time, and to whom he had even promised marriage.

In 858, Teutberge, with the assistance of a champion, justified herself by the proof of boiling water, and Lothaire found himself forced to take her back again, but he never ceased in his efforts to get rid of her. Whether truly, or through fear, she permitted herself to avow the crime of which she was accused; and between 860 and 862, three councils held at Aix-la-Chapelle solemnly condemned her, annulled the marriage, and allowed Lothaire to wed Waldrade.

But, pretty nearly about the same time, in 858, the holy see was assumed by a monk of severe manners, ardent character, and inflexible spirit, who had not, without great difficulty, determined upon leaving his cloister to become pope, and who, once pope, desired to reign over Christianity indeed. Hear how a contemporary chronicler speaks of Nicholas the First:

"Since the blessed Gregory, no bishop exalted, in the city of Rome, to the pontifical see, may be compared with him; he reigned over kings and tyrants, and subjected them to his authority, as if he had been the master of the world. He showed himself humble, benign, pious, and benevolent towards religious bishops and priests, and those who observed the precepts of the Lord—terrible and extremely severe towards the impious, and those who wandered from the right way; so that he might be taken for another Elias, resuscitated in our days by the voice of God, if not in body, at least in spirit and in virtue."[1]

In the year 859, it appears that Teutberge addressed herself to Nicholas I., and claimed his interference. He made her wait for some time. It was not till 862, and after the holding of the three councils of Aix-la-Chapelle, that he sent two legates to Lorraine, with orders to investigate the matter anew. For this purpose a council was convoked at Metz,

---

[1] Chron. de Reginon, ad a. 868.

in 863. Whether the facts with which Teutberge was charged appeared sufficiently proved, or whether Lothaire (which seems the most probable) succeeded in winning over the two legates, the councils at which they assisted sanctioned the conclusions of former councils, and the matter appeared to be terminated, with the accord of all judges and all powers.

But when the news of this decision came to Rome, whether with or without reason (and, for my part, I believe that it was with reason), Nicholas perceived in it nothing more than the effect of obsequiousness, or, to speak plainly, of servility and corruption, whether upon the part of the bishops of Lorraine, or upon that of his own legates. The general voice accused them; the two archbishops who had directed the council were relations of Waldrade. Nicholas resolved to take no half measures; and, without convoking any council at Rome, he, with his single authority, not only annulled the acts of the council of Metz, but deposed the archbishops of Trèves and Cologne, and commanded Lothaire to receive his wife again. He had, to excuse him in adopting this bold and despotic conduct, upon one hand, public opinion, which was strongly pronounced against Lothaire and Waldrade; on the other hand, as far as we can judge at this distance of time, truth and justice: against him were the rights of the bishops and councils, and all the ancient discipline of the church; but the text of the false decretals furnished him with a point of support against these last objections. Strong in the austerity of his conscience and the approbation of the people, he persisted in his resolution, and not content with avenging morality, called also to his aid the spirit of liberty. In 863, he wrote to Adventius, bishop of Metz:

"Examine well whether these kings and princes, to whom you profess yourselves subjected, are really kings and princes. Examine whether they govern well, first, themselves—next, their people: for he who is worth nothing for himself, how can he be good for another? Examine whether they reign according to justice; for, otherwise, they should be regarded as tyrants rather than as kings; and, in such case, we ought to resist and oppose, instead of submitting to them. Were we to submit to them, were we, not to rise up against them, we should be obliged to encourage their vices."[1]

---

[1] Mansi.

Against such arms the temporal princes, aided even by their own clergy, as Lothaire was upon this occasion, were too weak. Nicholas I. triumphed at the same time over Lothaire and over the clergy of Lorraine; both one and the other submitted to, whilst they expostulated against, his decision.

Nearly at the same moment, a second matter presented itself, which furnished him with the occasion of a second victory. Hincmar, archbishop of Reims, with whom I shall occupy you more in detail by and bye, desired to reign almost as despotically in the Gallo-Frankish church, as Nicholas reigned in the church universal. One of his suffragans, Rohade, bishop of Soissons, had deprived a priest of his diocese of his rank, on account of misconduct; three years after this condemnation, under the pretext that it was unjust, and rather, as it appears, from ill-humor against Rothade, than from any other motive, Hincmar re-established the priest in his parish, against the will of his bishop, and excommunicated the latter for his disobedience. A dispute was thus established between the bishop of Soissons and the archbishop of Reims. The bishop deposed in 862, by the council of Soissons, appealed from it to the pope; Hincmar, by means of stratagems and violence, eluded, for some time, the effects of their appeal, and even prevented its arrival at Rome; but Nicholas I. received it at last, and in 865, having called a council upon this subject, he said, in his opening discourse:

"The bishops of Gaul, having convoked a general council (which it is permitted to none to do), without the order of the apostolic see, have there cited Rothade . . . . Even though the council had not been called, he ought not to have been deposed without our knowledge, for the sacred statutes and the canonical decrees have remitted to our decision the trials of bishops, together with all other important matters."[1]

This was to misunderstand and to brave all canonical rules, all the examples of the past, all the customs of the church But upon this particular occasion, as upon the former, Nicholas had right and the public voice on his side; and he upheld justice and the popular opinion. He triumphed again; Rothade was re-established, and the national churches were conquered in the person of Hincmar, as the temporal sovereigns had been in the person of Lothaire.

---

[1] Mansi, t. xv., p 686.

This double victory was not undisputed: more than once, in the course of the tenth century, resistance reappeared; and the successors of Nicholas I., among others Adrian II., were not all of them so skilful or so fortunate in their enterprises as he had been. Nevertheless, on the whole, their power and the maxims which supported it, were making progress in external things, as well as in the minds of men; and it is from the reign of Nicholas I. that the sovereignty of the papacy really dates.

I approach my limits. I have occupied you with the internal history of the Gallo-Frankish church from the eighth to the tenth century, as regards its relation with the temporal sovereign. I have placed before you its external history, its relations with its foreign sovereign. And to this I confine my picture of the Carlovingian ecclesiastical society. It remains for us to study intellectual development in the same period. You have already seen what this was under Charlemagne, and up to the time of Louis le Debonnaire. The study of it, from the reign of Louis le Debonnaire to the accession of Hugh Capet, will be the object of our next meetings.

TWENTY-EIGHTH LECTURE.

Of the intellectual condition of Frankish Gaul, from the death of Charlemagne to the accession of Hugh Capet—Sketch of the celebrated men of this period—The theological mind—The philosophical mind—Hincmar and John Erigena are respectively their representatives—Life of Hincmar—His activity and influence as archbishop of Reims—1. Concerning his relations with kings and popes—2. Concerning his administration in the interior of the Gallo-Frankish church and of his diocese—3. Concerning his disputes and theological works—Origin of the theology of the middle ages—Quarrel between Hincmar and the monk Gottschalk upon predestination—Numerous writings upon this subject—Councils of Kiersy, Valence, and Langres—Recapitulation.

In exhibiting the intellectual revival of Frankish Gaul under Charlemagne,[1] I affirmed that the movement which was then given to mind, did not cease under his successors. It is to the progress of this movement, in the ninth and tenth centuries, that I purpose to direct your attention to-day.

When I arranged the table of the celebrated men of the times of Charlemagne,[2] I included in it, you remember, those alike, whom he found, and those whom he formed, his contemporaries, properly so called, and their immediate disciples. I have treated in detail only of the first, confining myself, as regards the last, to the indications of their names and their works. The majority of these—for instance, the historians Thegan, Nithard the astronomer, the theologians Raban, Florus, Walfrid Strabo, Paschase Radbirt, Ratramne, and many other erudite and literary men, and poets, who were comprised in the last part of the table which I have placed before you, belong to the epoch whereupon we are now to be engaged; and in adding to this table that of the celebrated men who appeared towards the end of the ninth, and in the course of the tenth century, I complete a summary of the intellectual activity of Frankish Gaul under the Carlovingian line. Here is this supplement:

---

[1] Lecture 23d. [2] Lecture 20th.

Name.	Country.	Born.	Died.	Condition.	Works.
1 St. Remi.	Gaul.	Beginning of the ninth century.	878	Archbish'p of Lyons.	Theological writings; amongst others, writings upon predestination and free-will.
2. St. Ado.	Diocese of Sens.	800	875	Archbish'p of Vienna.	1. Theological writings; 2. An universal chronicle.
3 Hincmar	Gaul.	806	882	Archbish'p of Rheims.	1. Theological writings; among others, writings on predestination; 2. Political writings and decrees; 3. Letters.
4. Remi.	Bungundy.	About the middle of the ninth century.	About 908	Monk of St. Germain d'Auxerre.	1. Commentaries upon the scriptures; 2. Theological writings; 3. Commentaries upon the ancient grammarians and rhetoricians.
5. Abbo.	Gaul.	Idem.	About 924	Monk of St. Germain des Prés.	1. A poem upon the siege of Paris by the Normans, in 885; 2. Manuscript sermons
6. Hucbald.	Flanders	About 840	930	Monk of St. Amand.	1 Poems; 2. Lives of the Saints.
7. St. Odo.	Maine.	879	942	Abbot of Cluny	1. Theological writings; 2. Lives of the Saints; particularly Gregory of Tours; 3. Sermons.
8. Frodoard	Epernay.	894	966	Canon of Reims.	1. Poems; 2. History of the church of Reims; 3. A chronicle, from 919 to 966.
9. Gerbert. (Silv. II.)	Aurillac.	In the first half of the tenth century.	1003	Pope.	1. Works on mathematics; 2. On philosophy; 3. On theology; 4. Poems; 5. Letters

Now, in endeavoring to go further than this series of names, dates, and titles, of works, I experience the same embarrassment which I experienced when I desired to depict the intellectual condition of France under Charlemagne. The works of all those men whom I have just named form no united whole, do not connect themselves with any great idea, or with any general and fruitful system, around which we may group them, or which may be employed as a thread of connection in this study. Their works are detached, partial, little varied, and more remarkable for the activity they manifest than for the results they have produced. In the absence of a systematic summary, shall I take these men one by one, relating the life, and describing the writings of each? Such biographies would be uninteresting and uninstructive unless they were very minute; but we have little time to devote to them. I will solve the question as I solved it in the case of the reign of Charlemagne. I referred the intellectual picture of his epoch to the life of one man, of a man who seemed to me its most faithful representative: I traced in the destiny and works of Alcuin, the delineation of the condition and general movement of mind. I shall adopt the same method for the following epoch: I shall seek for some man who is the image of it, in whom the intellectual life of his contemporaries is reflected: and I shall endeavor to make him thoroughly understood, well assured that, considering the shortness of the time to which I am limited, this will be the best way of making you acquainted with the entire period. Two men will enable us to arrive at this result.

In studying the life and writings of Alcuin, we were led to recognize therein a double tendency, a double character: "Alcuin," I said, "was a theologian by profession; the atmosphere in which he lived was essentially theological; but nevertheless the theological spirit did not reign in him alone; his labors and his thoughts also tended towards philosophy and ancient literature. He was familiar with St. Jerome and St. Augustine; but Pythagoras, Aristotle, Aristippus, Diogenes, Plato, Homer, Virgil, Seneca, and Pliny, lived also in his memory. He was a monk, a deacon, the light of the contemporary church, but he was also a man of learning and classical literature. In him, in fact, commences the alliance of the two elements of which the modern mind has so long carried the discordant impress: antiquity and the church; admiration, love—shall I say regret?—for pagan literatuie; with sincerity of Christian faith, and eagerness to fathom its mysteries and defend its power."[1]

The same fact is the predominant character of the epoch with which we now occupy ourselves; but it is no longer in any one man that we find its image; the Christian and the Roman mind, the new theology and the ancient philosophy manifest themselves equally, but in a separate and even hostile state. We meet with two men who may be considered as the distinct representations of these two elements. One, Hincmar, archbishop of Reims, is the centre of the theological movement; the other, Scotus or Erigena, is the philosopher of the time. With the life of Hincmar the events and labors of contemporaneous theology connect themselves; in that of Erigena, the modes of ancient philosophy are revealed. In the history of these two men appear the two forces of which the struggle for a long time constituted all the intellectual history of modern Europe; I mean the doctrinal church, and free thought. I shall endeavor to make you acquainted both with one and with the other. It is with Hincmar that I shall begin.

He was born about the year 806, in Frankish-Gaul, properly so called, that is to say, in the north-east of present France. His family was one of the most considerable of the time: the famous Bernard II., count of Toulouse, and another Bernard, count of Vermandois, were his relations. He was brought up from his childhood in the monastery of St. Denis, under the abbot Hilduin. Louis le Debonnaire, when he ascended the throne, whether it was that he already knew Hincmar, or whether he took an interest in his family, caused him to come to his court, and retained him near him. You know the efforts that were made by this prince, from 816 to 830, to reform the church, and particularly the monasteries. The monastery of St. Denis, like many others, greatly required reform; discipline and knowledge were there equally declining. Hincmar, young as he was, labored and powerfully assisted, in 829, to enforce their regeneration. He did more: he himself entered the monastery, and led the most rigid life there; but he was not permitted to remain in peace long; the abbot Hilduin took part, about 830, in the quarrels of Louis le Debonnaire with his sons; he declared himself

---

[1] Lecture 22.

against the emperor; and when Louis recovered power, Hilduin was dispossessed of his monastery and banished to Saxony. Whether from affection to his abbot, or from other considerations with which we cannot now become acquainted, Hincmar followed him there, and nevertheless retained sufficient credit, not only to allow of his son returning to the court himself, but to enable him to cause Hilduin to be recalled and reinstated.

To begin from this epoch, we see him sometimes with the emperor, sometimes in his monastery, leading, by turns, the life of a favorite priest, and that of an austere monk. It is difficult, at this distance of time, to decide upon what were the parts taken in his actions by worldly ambition and by religious fervor. What appears certain is, that neither one nor the other was ever wholly absent from him, and that, in the entire course of his life, as at this epoch, he was almost equally taken up with his fortune and his salvation.

At the death of Louis le Debonnaire, in 840, Charles le Chauve took Hincmar into the same favor. From 840 to 844, he lived at the court of this prince as his most intimate confidant, and his principal agent in all ecclesiastical affairs. Charles gave him many abbeys. In 844, he assisted at the council of Verneuil. The archbishopric of Reims had been vacant for nine years, in consequence of the deposition of the archbishop Ebbo—a complicated and obscure business, into the details of which I will not enter. The clergy demanded, at last, that this important see should be filled, and the following year, in 845, at the council at Beauvais, Hincmar, then thirty-nine years old, was elected archbishop of Reims.

His activity and influence in the Gallo-Frankish church dated from this epoch. He was archbishop of Reims for thirty-nine years, from the year 845 to the 23d of December, 882. In this long space of time we find his signature below the acts of thirty-nine councils, not to speak of many minor ecclesiastical assemblies, of which there remain no records. In the greater part of these councils he presided and directed affairs.[1]

---

[1] Hincmar assisted,

In 844, at the council of Verneuil.	In 847, at the council of Paris.
845,	of Beauvais.	849,	of Kiersy.
id.	of Meaux	id.	of Paris.

The historian of the church of Reims, Frodoard, who had the archives of the church at his disposal, especially mentions four hundred and twenty-three of his letters, and, at almost every page, indicates the existence of a great many others. These letters are directed to kings, queens, popes, archbishops, bishops, abbots, priests, dukes, counts, &c. He was evidently in habitual and familiar correspondence with all the considerable men of the time. Finally, there remain to us sixty-six of his works, great or small, religious or political, collected by father Sirmond, in two folio volumes, to which another Jesuit, father Cellot, afterwards added a third volume; and we know with certainty that there are many other writings of Hincmar which have not reached us.

Assuredly we have here an active and powerful life. In order to appreciate it well, and to draw from it much light concerning the general history of the time, we must classify, to some degree, the facts which filled it, considering Hincmar under three principal points of view:

I. Without the Gallo-Frankish church and his own diocese, in his relations whether with the national civil power, the kings of France, or with the foreign ecclesiastical power, the pope. II. Within the Gallo-Frankish church and his own diocese, in his ecclesiastical influence and his episcopal administration. III. In his scientific and literary activity as theologian and writer. All the important and instructive facts of Hincmar's life come under one or other of these three aspects.

In 850, at the council of Moret.		In 863 at the council of Senlis.	
851,	of Soissons.	id.	of Verberie.
853,	id.	866,	of Soissons
id.	of Kiersy.	867,	of Troyes.
id.	of Verberie.	869	of Verberie.
857,	of Kiersy.	id.	of Metz.
858,	id.	id.	of Pistes.
859,	of Metz.	870,	of Attigy.
id.	of Toul.	871,	of Douzy.
860,	Place uncrt'n.	873,	of Senlis.
id.	of Toul.	874,	of Douzy.
861,	of Soissons.	875,	of Châlons.
862,	of Sens.	876,	of Pontion.
id.	of Sablonniere.	878,	of Neustria
id.	of Pistes.	id.	of Troyes.
862,	of Soissons.	881,	of Fismes.
id.	of Pistes		
	(transferred to Soissons.)		

I. Considered in his relations with the national civil power, Hincmar appeared, throughout his entire life, as the bishop of the court of France, the director of two kings. It is advisedly that I say the bishop of the court of France. We find him, indeed, at the head of all the events of the court, of all official ceremonies. Four coronations, four consecrations of kings and queens took place in this epoch, and Hincmar presided at them all. In 856, at Verberie, he crowned Judith, daughter of Charles le Chauve, who married Ethelwolf, king of the Anglo-Saxons. In 866, at the council of Soissons, he crowned Hermentrude, wife of Charles le Chauve. In 869, at the council of Metz, he crowned Charles le Chauve himself king of Lorraine. In 877, he crowned Louis le Begue, king of France. In a word, it was always Hincmar who, upon all great occasions, within or without his diocese, in ecclesiastical or civil assemblies, represented the church amidst the court, and presided at the alliance of religion with royalty.

In matters of a graver nature than ceremonies, in politics properly so called, the remarkable characteristic of the life of Hincmar was his constant fidelity to the direct line—to the legitimate descendants of Charlemagne; a difficult task in his time, amidst all the vicissitudes of the throne, and the dissensions of the reigning family. Whether by attachment, principle, foresight, or skill, the faith of Hincmar never lost itself in this labyrinth; he always kept himself at a distance from the party which history has qualified as the rebellious; and those princes who are recognized as having formed the series of true kings of France ever counted him among their defenders. We find him, nevertheless, keeping himself, at the same time, on good terms with their enemies and rivals. It would be unjust to say that, in history, Hincmar bears the appearance of an intriguer; there is nothing to indicate that he sought out intrigue, that he pursued, at all cost, opportunities of acting, influencing, and prevailing; but everything shows that, when need was, he knew how to employ intrigue with activity and dexterity, and that he excelled in acquiring or preserving influence wherever the interest of his position, in the state or in the church, made it necessary to him. He, in consequence, possessed great credit with all kings and contemporary powers during the long period of his life. We see his intervention not only in the relations of princes with the church, but in civil government itself; he was employed upon difficult missions, consulted in delicate questions. And not only does this political activity appear in his history, but there are written monuments remaining of it. We have five works by him, either upon government in general, or upon the events and affairs wherein he took part, which abound in valuable information upon the ideas and political condition of France at that epoch. These works are:

I. A treatise, in thirty-three chapters, addressed to Charles le Chauve, and entitled: *De regis persona et de regio ministerio;*[1] a work upon morality rather than upon politics, judging according to our present ideas, but which, in the ninth century, was truly political, for it was in the name of morality, and in developing its precepts, that the ecclesiastics influenced governments. In the treatise of Hincmar, morality is moreover mingled with a great number of maxims of prudence and practical wisdom, very like those which, in the fifteenth century, constituted all political science, and of which the book of the *Prince* is the type.

II. A letter addressed to Louis le Begue, after his coronation, at the end of the year 877, containing advice upon the government of his states, and terminating with this remarkably sensible paragraph:

" I address to your majesty, by letter, what I would say in words if I were near you. As to the affairs properly so called of the church and of the kingdom, I ought not to give counsel upon this subject without the general concurrence and advice of the great, and I cannot, and dare not, decide concerning it of myself. If, in the interim, there should befal any cause of trouble (from which may God preserve us), and if it should please your majesty to inform me of it, I will endeavor to assist you with my advice and services, according to my knowledge and my power."[2]

III. A letter to the emperor Charles le Gros, engaging him to superintend the education of the two young kings of France, Louis III. and Carloman, and to provide them with good councillors.

IV. A long letter, addressed to the grandees of western France, who had consulted Hincmar concerning the government of king Carloman, in which he transmits to them long extracts from, perhaps an entire copy of, the work of Adal-

---

[1] Hinc. Op., vol. ii., p. 184. [2] Ibid.

hard, *de ordine palatii*, in which is exhibited Charlemagne's method of government, and of which I have already treated.[1]

V. Finally, advice upon the government of Carloman, addressed to the bishops of his kingdom in 882, the year of Hincmar's death, and written at Epernay, where he had just fled from his episcopal town, besieged by the Normans; so much did the affairs of the states, in the government of which he had assisted, continue to engage him.

We must not believe that this desire of political importance, this court popularity which Hincmar constantly enjoyed, cost nothing to the independence, say, rather, to the pride of the bishop. He was not, as you have seen, of the number of those insolent and shuffling prelates, who, under Louis le Debonnaire and Charles le Chauve, delighted in humiliating royalty before them; but he professed, as a general position, the principles upon which their pretensions were founded, and, more than once, he opposed to the desires of the temporal power, language very similar to theirs. We read, in his treatise upon the divorce of Lothaire and Teutberge, a quarrel of which I have already spoken :

"Some wise men say that their prince, being king, is not subject to the laws or to the judgments of any one, unless it be God himself. . . . . who made him king . . . . and that, as he must not, whatever he may have done, be excommunicated by his bishops, so he cannot be judged by other bishops; for God alone has a right to command him. . . . . Such is not the language of a Catholic Christian; it is full of blasphemy and of the spirit of evil . . . . The authority of the apostles says that kings ought to be subject to those whom it establishes in the name of the Lord, and who watch over their souls, in order that this task may not be a source of trouble to them. The blessed pope Gelasius wrote to the emperor Anastasius: 'There are two principal powers by which this world is governed: the pontifical authority and the royal dignity; and the authority of pontiffs is so much the greater, inasmuch as they must account to the Lord for the souls of kings themselves.' . . . When it is said that the king is not subject to the laws or judgments of any one, save God alone, no more than the truth is said, if he be indeed king as his name indicates him to be. He is called king because he rules and governs;

---

[1] Lecture 20.

if he governs himself according to the will of God, if he directs the good in the right way, and corrects the wicked, in order to lead them from the bad way into the good, then he is king, and is subject to no judgment save that of God alone... for laws are made, not for the just, but for the unjust... but if he be an adulterer, a murderer, partial, or avaricious, then ought he to be judged, in secret or in public, by the bishops, who are the throne of God."[1]

Assuredly, the maxims of ecclesiastical sovereignty were never more formally set forth.

In fact, the life of Hincmar was full of acts of resistance to the very sovereigns whom he served with most zeal, and his language towards them was that of the most inflexible haughtiness. I will cite but one example:

In 881, under the reign of Louis III., a dispute had occurred between this prince and the council of Fismes, touching the election of a bishop of Beauvais; the king had protected and obstinately supported a clergyman, named Odacre, whom the council thought unworthy. Hincmar wrote to Louis:

"As regards what you have written to us, saying that you will do nothing other than what you have already done, know that, if you do it not, God will himself do that which is pleasing to him. The emperor Louis (le Debonnaire) did not live so many years as his father Charles. King Charles (le Chauve), your grandfather, did not live so many years as his father; your own father (Louis le Begue) did not live so many years as his father; and, even while living amidst that pomp in which your father and grandfather lived at Compiegne, cast your eyes where your father rests; and, if you do not know, ask where your grandfather died and reposes; and do not let your heart swell before the face of Him who died for you and for us all, and who afterwards rose from the dead, to die no more. And be sure that you must die: you know not at what day, nor at what hour; and you have therefore need, as we all have, of being ever ready for the call of the Lord.... You will pass away soon; but the holy church, with its heads, under Christ, its sovereign head, according to his promise, shall never pass away."[2]

I might multiply these quotations: the writings, like the entire life of Hincmar, prove that, without carrying them as

---

[1] Hincm. Op., de Divort. Loth. et Teuth., vol. i., pp. 693–695.
[2] Hincm. Op., vol. ii., p. 199.

far as rebellion and usurpation of the civil power, he professed, concerning the relations of the two powers, all the maxims which, since the death of Charlemagne, had developed themselves in the Gallo-Frankish church, and that he knew, when need was, to take advantage of them as means of resistance.

As regards his relations with another power, with the foreign sovereign of the church, the pope, they are more difficult to determine, as also are the ideas which he entertained upon this subject; there is much contradiction and uncertainty touching this matter. Hincmar appears often to have been in high favor at Rome: Leo IV., upon sending him the *pallium*, gave him the right, which (said he) had scarcely ever been given to other archbishops, of wearing it every day. Adrian II., John VIII., shaped their conduct by his advice, and accorded to him all that he asked of them. In the great struggle of Nicholas I. against king Lothaire, concerning Waldrade and Teutberge, Hincmar took the part of the court of Rome, supported its cause, and received from it many marks of esteem and good will. Upon other occasions, on the contrary, we find him not only opposing but combating the court of Rome, by which, on such occasions, he is very ill-treated. I have already spoken to you of the check he met with in the affair of Rothade, bishop of Soissons.[1] I will instance another matter in which Nicholas the First was not more favorable to him. Ebbo, the predecessor of Hincmar in the see of Reims, had appointed a certain number of priests or deacons, among others, one called Wulfad: it was maintained that this appointment was not canonical; that Ebbo, not having been legitimate archbishop of Reims, had not possessed the right of conferring orders, and that they ought to be withdrawn from these pretended clergymen. In 853, the question was carried before the council of Soissons, and after a long and curious process, whether it was by the influence of Hincmar, or by the real opinion of the council, the priests and deacons ordained by Ebbo were dismissed. They appealed to Rome; and, in 866, Nicholas the First commanded the revision of the matter: a new council took place at Soissons; and the pope addressed to the assembled bishops a long letter, in which the conduct of Hincmar, in that of 853, was harshly censured:

---

[1] Lecture 27.

"There," said he, "we saw the archbishop sometimes laying aside, sometimes reassuming his rights; sometimes submitting himself to the council, sometimes presiding over it; by turns, the accused, accuser, and judge; ruling all things after his own fancy, changing his part unceasingly, and thus taking the semblance of a certain animal, which is not always of one and the same color."[1]

Opposed by such reproaches and by the influence of Charles le Chauve himself, who, this time, showed favor to his adversaries, the predominance of Hincmar in the Gallo-Frankish church failed; the dismissed clergymen were re-established in their canonical rank; and, notwithstanding the discretion which the pope recommended them to observe towards Hincmar in their conquest, the defeat was a marked one for him.

The same struggle with the same result was renewed upon other occasions, with the detail of which I will not occupy your time. Upon such occasions, we find Nicholas the First sometimes keeping fair with, sometimes severely reprimanding Hincmar; and the latter, upon his part, in his correspondence with the pope, appears singularly embarrassed and fluctuating in his maxims and language. Sometimes he himself recognizes, and, in magnificent terms, proclaims the sovereignty of the pope; sometimes he defends the rights of archbishops and of bishops, and seems even to lay the foundations of a national independent church; and then he presently abandons all that he has said upon the subject, as if he feared to be accused of maxims and intentions, which, nevertheless, he could not suppress, which, haply, he wished to become apparent. His letters to the pope, inserted by Frodoard is his *Histoire de l'Eglise de Reims*, betray, at every word, this uncertainty of ideas and desires.

All things considered, and remembering the vast difference of mind and times, there was, in the situation and conduct of Hincmar, whether towards the civil power or the papacy, some analogy with the situation and conduct of Bossuet, in nearly similar questions, in the seventeenth century. Not that these two great bishops bear the least resemblance to one another as writers: a talent for writing, a genius for expression, brilliancy of imagination and style were wholly want-

---

[1] Labbe, Concil., vol. 8, col. 834.

ing to Hincmar; and, looking merely to his works, the idea would never arise of tracing any relation between him and Bossuet. But when we look deeper, the analogy becomes substantial, and the two men are explained and elucidated one by the other. Through all the fluctuations, all the changes of his language, we recognize in Hincmar a firm and bold mind, a powerful logician, who, when he had once conceived a principle or a system, unfolded its consequences skilfully, and, in the freedom of his thought, followed them without hesitation to their last results. But he was, at the same time, a man of strong common sense, and of great practical understanding, who saw what obstacles were opposed to his ideas by external circumstances, and did not allow himself to be deceived by the seduction of logic, concerning the possibility or expediency of their application. In writing, he laid down or deduced maxims with that loftiness of thought which seems to delight in its own bold and free development. In acting, no fact, no detail of the true situation escaped him; he comprehended all that ought to influence the conduct of the matter, all that was required in order to succeed; he wisely measured the possible, and attempted that and no more. Hence the embarrassment which sometimes appears in his ideas and words; sometimes it is the logician, sometimes the man of business that predominates; he fluctuates, so to speak, unceasingly between the strict steadfastness of his thought and the practical impartiality of his reason.

Thus it was with Bossuet, placed in very different society and circumstances. That lofty genius, that simple and irresistible reasoner, who arrived, by a glance, at the last consequences of a principle, and grasped them, like a club, to let them fall at a single blow, upon the head of his adversaries, more than once exhibited himself, in practice, uncertain, dilatory, anything but logically strict, inclined to cautious and to middle courses. Was this mere weakness of soul, compliance, and a tendency to yield? Sometimes perhaps, but assuredly, not always. Another cause led to this contrast. When the mind of Bossuet was free and in the presence only of its ideas, whatever might be the system upon which he was engaged, whether it concerned the pontifical power or a national church, authority or free inquiry, and whether he wished to attack or to defend it, he boldly embarked, as M. Turgot expresses himself, upon the faith of an idea, and voyaged at full sail as far as it would carry him; but when it became necessary to act, when he was called upon actually to regulate the relations of different powers, of different rights, then all the considerations, all the difficulties of action presented themselves to him; he saw what was required by his times, by the state of society and of mind; the clear perception and impartiality of his good sense suppressed the boldness of his thought; and a prudence and caution, which seemed like servile compliance, took the place of that intractable dialectic and of that haughty eloquence which lately characterized him. It is a difficult problem to ally the height and rational consequence of philosophy with the flexibility of mind and the common sense of the practical man. Hincmar and Bossuet did not solve it; but they knew how to place themselves, by turns, under the two different points of view; they deemed themselves capable, if not of reconciling, at least of playing the two parts, and it is precisely this superiority that casts their deficiencies into relief.

You will pardon me for having paused awhile upon this analogy, which seems like a digression; but to be just towards great men, we must understand them well; and in order to understand them, we must turn for a long time around them, for they have a thousand different faces to show us.

II. Within his diocese, in ecclesiastical administration properly so called, Hincmar had no such difficulties to surmount; he was alone, and master; he could, at least almost always, regulate facts according to his ideas; he governed despotically, sometimes even tyrannically, but generally with wisdom, and to the true interest of the clergy, and of the faithful who were under him. We have written monuments of his government; that is to say, capitularies, addressed to his priests, as those of kings are addressed to their courts, *missi dominici*, or other agents. The capitularies of Hincmar which remain to us, are of four different epochs. The first, addressed in 852, to the clergy of his diocese, after an assembly of the same clergy, held at Reims, under his presidency, contain forty-three articles, of which seventeen are in the form of precepts upon the conduct of priests, and twenty-six in that of interrogations and inquiries upon the same subject. The second, in three articles, are of the year 857; the third, in five articles, of 874; the fourth, in thirteen articles, of 877.[1] These capitularies are generally very judicious; their object is either

---

[1] Hincm. Op., vol. i., pp. 710—741

to recommend to the clergy regularity of behavior, knowledge, and a gentle and legal administration, or to prevent the vexations of the archdeacons, who were placed between the simple priest and the bishop, and who often oppressed those who were under them, or, finally, to protect the diocese against the invasions of the civil magistrate, the disorders and the depredations of the laity, &c. They bear witness to an active, provident, and skilful government, one that was taken up with the advancement of the moral and material welfare of its objects.

III. Hitherto, I have endeavored to show you in Hincmar, the spiritual or temporal governor, the bishop or councillor of kings. It remains for us to consider him in his intellectual activity as theologian; and this is the point of view which in the present day, at least, and in the questions upon which we are now occupied, is the most important to us.

Christian theology suffered, at this epoch, that is to say, in the course of the ninth century, a revolution which has not generally been recognized. From the sixth to the eighth century it had been dormant, as, indeed, had been every department of human thought. We do not find that any great religious questions were discussed in this period: there were bishops, priests, and monks, but no theologians. It was under Charlemagne that theological discussion recommenced; you remember that we then met with discussions upon the worship of images, the nature of Jesus Christ, the procession of the Holy Ghost; and intellectual activity, once set in motion in this direction, ceased not to advance in it. But it soon changed its character. Created in the first five centuries by the Greek and Roman fathers, Christian theology, even in combating, received the impress of that ancient civilization, in the bosom of which it had been born. The system of dogmas, put forth and arranged by St. Basil, St. Athanasius, St. Jerome, St. Hilary, St. Augustin, &c., differed essentially from all the systems of the stoics, platonists, peripatetics, neoplatonists, &c., and yet it connected itself with them; it was a philosophy, a doctrine, of which the decisions of the church were not the only source, nor its authority the only support. When, after a sleep of a hundred and fifty years, the theological movement recommenced in the west, the fathers of the first centuries, especially St. Augustin, were regarded as irrefragable authorities, as masters of the faith. They were to the theologians who then began to arise, what the apostles and the holy books had been to themselves. But the condition of society, both civil and religious, was completely changed; and the new theologians, in adopting the fathers as masters, found it impossible to reproduce or even to imitate them. There was an abyss between the theology of the first five centuries, which was born in the bosom of Roman society, and the theology of the middle ages, which was born in the bosom of the Christian church, and truly commenced in the ninth century. I cannot pretend to treat in this place of the new and important question of their difference and its causes; I can do no more than indicate its existence, by the way, and in one particular subject.

Two kinds of religious questions re-appeared at this period; 1st, questions purely Christian, that is to say, which belonged especially to Christianity, and which do not necessarily arise in all religious philosophies, because they are not connected, or are, at least, very remotely connected, with the general nature of man; such, for instance, are the questions relating to the nature of Jesus Christ, the Trinity, transubstantiation, &c. 2d, general questions which are met with in all religions and in all philosophies, because they arise from the very essence of human nature, as for instance, the question of the origin of good and evil, that of atonement, that of free-will and predestination, &c.

I have nothing to say to the first; they belong to pure Christian theology; the second come within the general domain of thought. I will select from the latter the questions of free-will and predestination, to which I have already called your attention, that arose in the ninth century, and upon which Hincmar and all the great minds of that epoch were long and intensely occupied.

I pray you call to mind, as accurately as you can, the state in which we left this question at the beginning of the ninth century, after the struggle of St. Augustin and his disciples against Pelagius and his successors. Two great heresies present themselves to our view: 1st, that of the Pelagians and of the anti-Pelagians, who attributed to the free choice and free-will of man the principal part in his moral life, and greatly abridged the action of God upon the human soul, over which they yet endeavored to preserve it; 2d, that of the predestinarians, who well nigh annul human freedom, and attribute the moral life and destiny of man to the direct action of the Divinity. We have seen the predestinarians pretending to be alone the faithful disciples of St. Augustin, and deducing their principles from his works. We have seen St. Augustin disowning them, refusing to abolish human freedom; and we have seen the church, after his example, placing herself, with more good sense than philosophical consequence, between the two parties, condemning, on the one hand, the predestinarians, on the other, the Pelagians or semi-Pelagians, and at once maintaining, without reconciling, the freedom of man and the all-powerful action of divine grace upon his soul. It was at this point we left the discussion.[1]

When it was recommenced in the ninth century, minds were much changed; the fathers of the first centuries, St. Augustin among others, had regarded all questions, and especially this, under a triple aspect: 1st, as philosophers examining things in themselves; 2d, as heads of the church charged with governing it; 3d, as teachers of the faith, and called upon to maintain orthodoxy—that is to say, to harmonize the solution of all questions with the essential principles of Christianity. I have endeavored to show how the combination of these various characters was calculated to exert, and, in fact, did exert, the greatest influence upon the quarrel originated by Pelagius. In the ninth century, nothing of the kind existed; minds had no longer so much freedom and greatness; no one was any longer like St. Augustin, at once a philosopher, head of the church, and teacher of the faith; the theologians, above all, had become total strangers to the philosophical point of view. Their doctrine reposed exclusively upon the texts of the fathers who had preceded them, and applied itself only to the deduction of consequences from rules of belief already laid down. From the epoch at which we are now, the essential character of the theological spirit is, never to examine things in themselves, but to judge of all ideas by their relations to certain determined principles. The theologians in this respect have played the same part in modern Europe as was played by the jurisconsults in the Roman world. The Roman jurisconsults did not examine what we call the general principles of law, or natural law; they had for their point of departure, certain axioms, certain legal precedents; and their skill consisted in sul tilly unravel ing the consequences, in order to apply them to particular

---

[1] Lecture 5

cases, as they presented themselves. Thus the Roman juris-consults were logicians of admirable ingenuity and accuracy, but they were never philosophers. The theologians of the middle ages were similarly constituted; they applied themselves to the same kind of work, and attained the same excellences—namely, accuracy and logical subtlety—and fell into the same faults—namely, want of attention to facts themselves, and of any feeling for reality.

Now, in the question of free-will and grace, in particular, St. Augustin had laid down all the principles. His doctrines were made the obligatory point of departure, from which no one dared to confess that he deviated. Whatever opinion a man desired to maintain, whether human freedom or predestination, it was only by reasoning upon texts of St. Augustin, and taking them for his rule, that he was allowed to defend his system. The discussion, in short, became a matter of logic; it was no longer a question of philosophy. It was under this banner and these conditions that the dispute recommenced. I will tell you how, and upon what occasion.

A monk, Saxon by birth, named Gottschalk, lived in the abbey of Fulda, under the discipline of the abbot Raban, whom I have already mentioned, and who was afterwards archbishop of Mayence, and one of the most celebrated theologians of the time. Gottschalk, we know not for what reasons, did not wish any longer to remain as monk in this abbey, and he succeeded in annulling his monastic engagement. Raban conceived a strong antipathy to him on this account. Gottschalk quitted the abbey of Fulda, and retired into that of Orbais, situated in the diocese of Soissons, and, consequently, under the jurisdiction of Hincmar, as archbishop. About the year 847, Gottschalk (it is not known upon what occasion) went upon a pilgrimage to Rome. In returning, he stopped in a valley of Piedmont, at the house of a count of the place, named Eberhard. There he had, either with count Eberhard, or with Noting, bishop of Verona, who was also staying there, long theological conversations, and he maintained that the good and the bad, the elect and the reprobate, were equally and from all time predestinated by the divine omnipotence and omniscience to their present and future fate. The bishop of Verona, shocked at this opinion, whether because it was new to him, or because it had long been repugnant to him, denounced it to Raban, now become archbishop of Mayence, and prevailed upon him to combat it. Raban, already prepossessed against Gottschalk, wrote to count Eberhard, informing him that he harbored a heretic in his house. Gottschalk, accused, departed immediately, in order to defend himself. We find him at Mayence, in 848, addressing to Raban a justification of his conduct. But it was condemned by the council which assembled the same year at Mayence; and, by order of the council, Raban wrote to Hincmar:

"Know, your Dilection, that a certain wandering monk, named Gottschalk, who affirms that he was ordained priest in your diocese, is come from Italy to Mayence, disseminating new superstitions, and a pernicious opinion concerning the predestination of God, seducing people into error; for he says that there is a predestination of God, as regards the good as well as the wicked, and that, in this world, there are certain men whom the predestination of God forces to pursue the path of death, not being able to correct their error and their sin, as if God in the beginning had created them incorrigible. . . . . Having lately heard this opinion from his own mouth, at a council held at Mayence, and having found him incorrigible, by the consent and order of our very pious king Louis, we have decided, after having condemned him, as well as his pernicious doctrine, to send him to you, in order that you may retain him in your diocese, from whence he irregularly went forth, and that you may not permit him any longer to teach error, and seduce the Christian people. According to report, he has already seduced many persons, and has rendered them less devoted to the work of their salvation; for they say: 'To what purpose shall I labor in the service of God? If I am predestinated to death, I shall never escape from it; and if I am predestinated to life, even though I do wickedly, I shall, no doubt, arrive at eternal rest.'"

Hincmar was at bottom little of a theologian; the spirit of government and practical dexterity predominated in him, and he had not made a very attentive study of the fathers. When the letter of Raban reached him, he judged of Gottschalk and his opinions according to the instinct of common sense, rather than according to any profound and extensive acquaintance with theology. He was, moreover, haughty and despotic. Gottschalk agitated the faithful, and resisted his superiors. Hincmar forthwith (in 849) condemned him by a council held at Kiersy-sur-Oise, and, thinking to subdue him by force, ordered him to be publicly scourged, and summoned to retract his opinions and to cast his writings into the fire. But the arrogance of despotism can never force the obstinacy of conscience. Gottschalk resisted all, and was shut up in the prison of the monastery of Hautvilliers, where he was treated with extreme severity.

The matter soon became noised about. Hincmar was not well acquainted with the spirit of his contemporary theologians, nor with the power which an argument, drawn from St. Augustin, could exercise over them. Whether from pity for Gottschalk, who had been so barbarously treated, or rather through the prevalence of the theological spirit, a loud clamor was raised against the conduct of the archbishop of Reims. Some very influential men in the Gallo-Frankish church, Prudence, bishop of Troyes, Loup, abbot of Ferrieres, Ratramne, monk of Corbie, and many others, attacked him, nearly all at the same time. They did not positively take the part of Gottschalk, but they declared against the treatment which he had suffered, protested against the meaning that was attributed to his words, and maintained the doctrine of predestination, rejecting only so much of it as seemed contrary to divine justice.

Hincmar was not prepared for such a storm. He wrote to Raban, who had drawn it upon him, to persuade him to defend what they had thought and done in common; Raban, intimidated, did not write, and left Hincmar exposed to the danger alone. Seeking upon all sides for champions, the archbishop of Reims addressed himself first of all to a priest of Metz, named Amalaise, who, at his request, wrote a work against Gottschalk, which is now lost. A man of much talent and learning, Scotus Erigena, concerning whom I shall soon speak more in detail, was at that time in great favor at the court of Charles le Chauve. Hincmar persuaded him to write against predestination, and he readily consented; but Erigena was a philosopher and a free thinker; he made the fact of human liberty much greater than any other had represented it, mingled in his defence a number of opinions repugnant to the theological world, and compromised Hincmar instead of serving him. The explosion was far more violent against him than it had been against the archbishop of Reims; controversial writings became multiplied; triumphant theologians discovered a thousand heresies in the work of Scotus Erigena. The church of Lyons, in particular, under its archbishop Remi, took a very active part in this war. An ill-suppressed struggle had always existed between the south and north of

Gaul. The south of Gaul had preserved more considerable remains of Roman civilization; the character of the north was much more German. The archbishop of Lyons was the most important prelate of southern Gaul, as the archbishop of Reims was the most important of northern Gaul. The rivalry of sees became coupled with the opposition of doctrines. Compromised by his writers, Hincmar, in order to defend himself, had recourse to the arms of authority. A council, held at Kiersy, in 853, laid down, in four articles, the opinions which it pronounced orthodox upon this matter, and Gottschalk found himself condemned thereby for the second time. But the archbishop of Lyons was also able to invoke councils and to cause articles to be written; and he summoned one at Valence, in 855, and the articles of Kiersy were condemned by it in their turn. Hincmar again invoked the aid of learning and argument; but this time he determined to entrust the work to no one, and he himself, in 857 and 859, wrote two works upon predestination, of which one is lost; the other, which remains to us, is addressed to Charles le Chauve, and is divided into forty-four chapters, including six chapters of epilogue. The whole course of the controversy is herein reproduced, with a great display of theological erudition; but, in reality, the theological spirit is wanting; there is more of good sense exhibited in the general ideas than of subtlety in the argumentation; and, as theologians, properly so called, the adversaries of Hincmar had the advantage over him.

His works failed, therefore, in putting a stop to the quarrel; and the matter ended by its being carried to Rome, like all other great questions of the time. It is difficult to affirm that Nicholas the First took any positive part, or that he declared either one or other of the opinions to have been the doctrine of the church. Nevertheless, we see plainly that he inclined to the ideas of Gottschalk, and to the canons of the councils of Valence, confirmed in 889 by the council of Langres. His correspondence and his conduct in this matter are unfavorable to Hincmar.

The dispute was thus prolonged, becoming, however, cooler, until the death of Gottschalk, which happened suddenly on the 30th of October, 868 or 869. A little while before, when they saw him very ill, the monks of Hautvilliers, where he was in prison, consulted Hincmar as to what they were to do in his case: the inflexible bishop replied that it was absolutely necessary that he should retract his opinions, and that otherwise they must refuse him confession and the sacrament. Not less inflexible than his persecutor, Gottschalk again refused to retract, and died beneath the severities which he was suffering. Hincmar survived him only three years. He died, in his turn, on the 21st of December, 882, driven from his episcopal city by an incursion of the Normans, and still engaged in writing, at Epernay, where he had taken refuge.

It is time for me to pause; one remark will conclude my account of this great controversy. You may see three elements appearing in it; the three spirits, so to speak, of which the coexistence and the struggle for a long while constituted the intellectual history of modern Europe: 1. the logical spirit which predominated among theologians by profession, engaged exclusively in arguing, in deducing consequences from principles, which were never called into question; 2. the political spirit, peculiar, in general, to the heads of the church, who were, above all, charged with the duties of government, and were much more engaged with the practical than the logical point of view, with business than discussion; 3. finally, the philosophical spirit, existing in certain free-thinkers, who yet endeavor to regard things in themselves, and to seek for truth, independently both of practical aim and predetermined principle. The theological spirit, the political spirit, and the philosophical spirit, were all openly at work in this affair; Hincmar represented the politicians, Gottschalk the theologians, Scotus Erigena the philosophers. The last I have scarcely more than named to you; I shall treat of him at full in my next lecture.

TWENTY-NINTH LECTURE.

Object of the lecture—Of the philosophical spirit in the 9th century—Scotus or Erigena—His country—Date of his birth—Tradition respecting his travels in Greece—He settles in France, at the court of Charles le Chauve—Of the School of the Palace under Charles—Ancient philosophy studied there—Encouragement of Scotus Erigena—His learning—Relations of Christianity with the Neoplatonism of Alexandria—Their struggle—Attempt at amalgamation—History and pretended works of Dionysius the Areopagite—Fundamental differences of the two doctrines: 1, in the point of departure and the method; 2, in the bases of the questions—These differences occur between Scotus Erigena and the Christian theologians of the 9th century—Examination of his works: 1, De Prædestinatione; 2, De Divisione Naturæ—His celebrity and his death—Recapitulation.

I REMINDED you, in the last lecture, of the two fundamental elements to which we may ascribe the intellectual development of modern Europe: Christianity, on the one part, and ancient literature on the other; Christian theology and pagan philosophy, religious polemics and classical learning; already, at the end of the eighth century, at the moment of the intellectual revival of Frankish Gaul, under Charlemagne, we have recognized the presence of these two elements in Alcuin, whom we considered as the most faithful image of the state of the mind at this epoch. In proportion as this influence developed itself, they became distinct and separate: about the middle of the ninth century, two men appeared to us as the representatives, one of the theological, the other of the philosophical element. I named to you Hincmar and John Erigena; I led you to a consideration, in the history of Hincmar, of the theological life of his time: let us now try to ascertain if any philosophical life corresponded to it; it is from the history of John Erigena that we shall learn it.

There exists amongst scholars much uncertainty respecting the date of his birth and his country. The uncertainty respecting his country appears to me not well founded: his double name indicates it clearly. John Erigena, or John Scotus, means John of Ireland. Ireland was anciently called *Erin*, and its people were of the same race as the population of the highlands of Scotland, the Scots. The name Erigena points out therefore his country, that of Scotus his race and nation. All the little difficulties, all the elaborate conjectures of the learned, fall to the ground before this simple fact.

With respect to the date of the birth of John, it is more difficult to determine anything, and I will not enter upon a minute and purposeless discussion of this subject. All that can be affirmed is, that he was born in the early part of the ninth century, from the year 800 to 815. We do not know where he passed his childhood, or where he followed his first studies. The peculiarities of his knowledge, however, agreeing with natural probabilities, give rise to the belief that it was in Ireland. Of all the western countries, Ireland was, as you know, that wherein letters maintained themselves and prospered, amidst the general confusion of Europe.

A tradition which we find prevailing at an early period, attributes to John Scotus travels in the east, in Greece particularly; we read, in a manuscript deposited in the library of Oxford, a passage of his which seems to point at them:

"I quitted," said he, "no place or temple where the philosophers were accustomed to compose or deposit their secret works, without inspecting it; and there was not one amongst such scholars, as might be supposed to possess any knowledge of philosophical writings, whom I did not question."[1]

He does not indicate, you see, any place or period; yet his words seem to relate to a country where the ancient philosophers lived and labored. No other document sheds further light upon these travels; and the knowledge possessed by John Erigena of Greek literature does not appear to me a conclusive proof. However the case may have been, about the middle of the ninth century, we find him settled for life at the court of Charles le Chauve. There has also been much dispute about the date of his arrival; it has been placed as far forward as the year 870; but the error of this appears evident to me. Many documents indicate that John was connected with Saint Prudence before the latter became bishop of Troyes in 847. It was probably, therefore, between the years 840 and 847 that John Erigena went into France, perhaps attracted thither by a formal invitation from Charles le Chauve.

---

[1] Wood's *Hist.* and *Antiquit Univers. Oxon.*, in fol. 1674, vol. i., p 15.

History gives a very false idea of this prince and his court—not certainly under the political point of view; all that it says of the weakness of the government and the falling condition of France is well founded; but under the intellectual point of view there was much more activity and liberty of spirit, much more taste for letters than is commonly supposed. The school of the Palace, so flourishing under Charlemagne, and under the teaching of Alcuin, had greatly fallen away under Louis le Debonnaire. Louis had been engaged much more with the church than with science, and much more with the religious reform of the monasteries than with the progress of study. The School of the Palace was thus a subject little considered, a sure proof of its decay; for the social state was not then such that it could subsist by itself, and without powerful protection. Charles le Chauve revived it; he summoned thither foreign scholars, especially Irish and Anglo-Saxons; he treated them with marked favor; he appreciated their works and their conversation, and lived on familiar terms with them. The School of the Palace resumed such a splendor that contemporaries were struck with it as with a novelty. To judge by the words of Herric, a monk of Saint Germain l'Auxerrois, and of Wandalbert, a monk of Prum, in the diocese of Trèves, the prosperity of the studies at those places became such that Greece might have envied the fortune of France, and that France had nothing for which to envy antiquity. There is, no doubt, great monastic emphasis in the phrase; but, at all events, the public at the time were so struck with the revival of letters in the court of Charles le Chauve, that instead of saying *the School of the Palace* (*Schola Palatii*) they said, *the Palace of the School* (*Palatium Scholæ*). What, then, was the direction of mind in this flourishing school? what studies were preferred? We may, I think, affirm that ancient philosophy and literature held a high place there. Of this we have abundant and apparently undeniable proofs.

The first are deducible from the works of John Erigena himself, chief of the School of the Palace, and teacher there. Of these works, ancient philosophy, as you will presently see, is generally the object. Not only did the original works which he has left emanate from this source; not only did he translate many treatises of the Neoplatonic school of Alexandria; but it appears certain that there exist in manuscript in many libraries, especially in that of Oxford, commentaries by him on several works of Aristotle; and in the twelfth century, at the very moment when the peripatetic philosophy resumed in the west a despotic empire, Roger Bacon lauded Scotus Erigena as a very faithful and clear-sighted interpreter of Aristotle, and awarded him the merit of having preserved, pure and authentical, certain of his writings.

It is said, also, that Scotus Erigena applied himself to the study of the works of Plato; and in some sentences of his on these two masters of antiquity, he has passed so strong and precise a judgment upon them, as to negative the supposition that he knew them merely from the writings of certain of their disciples, or from vague traditions. He calls Plato "the greatest philosopher in the world," and Aristotle "the most subtle investigator, among the Greeks, of the differences of natural things."[1]

It is not to be doubted that he understood Greek well, since he translated the treatises attributed to Dionysius the Areopagite, and gave a Greek title to his principal work. There is also reason to think that he understood Hebrew, by far the most unusual accomplishment of his time; for, in citing a verse of Genesis, he corrects the Vulgate; and instead of saying as St. Jerome, "*Terra autem erat invisibilis et incomposita,*" he says, "*Terra erat inanis et vacua;*" a translation far more exact, and nearer the original.[2]

Lastly, a celebrated scholar of his time, named Mannon, succeeded Scotus Erigena as director of the School of the Palace, and held that office, until the death of Louis le Begue, and Mannon, like Erigena, made ancient philosophy his principal study. Many contemporaries praised the learned lectures which he gave on this subject; there exist, we are assured, in some libraries of Holland, commentaries by him on Plato's discourses on *Laws*, and on *the Republic*, and also on Aristotle's *Ethics*.

Were all these indications wanting, or were they to prove unworthy of credit—were we to possess no direct and positive assertion concerning the study which Scotus Erigena made of the Greek philosophers, the language of his contemporaries would reveal clearly the tendency and character of his works.

---

[1] Scot. Erig., *De Divisione Naturæ*, vol. i., c. 33, c. 16.
[2] Ibid vol ii , chap 20.

I have told you what an uproar was created amongst theologians by his treatise on predestination, written at the request of Hincmar, against Gottschalk. The following are the terms in which Florus, a priest of the church of Lyons, immediately attacked him:

"In the name of our Lord Jesus Christ," commences the book of Florus, "against the follies and errors of a certain presumptuous man named John, on predestination and divine prescience, and the true liberty of human thought.

"There have reached us, that is, the church of Lyons, the writings of a certain vain and ostentatious man, who, disputing upon divine prescience and predestination by means of arguments of a purely human, and, as he himself boasts, philosophical kind, has dared, without assigning any reason, and without alleging any authority from the scriptures and holy fathers, to affirm certain things, as though they ought to be received and adopted on his sole and presumptuous assertion. By the assistance of God, readers, who are faithful and well exercised in the sacred doctrine, easily judge and reject these writings, which are so full of vanity, falsehood, and error, and which offend the faith and divine truth, and are to them an object of contempt and derision. Nevertheless, from what we have heard say, this same man is much admired by many persons, for being learned and versed in the knowledge of the schools: whether by speaking or writing, he casts some in doubt, and others he draws away with him in his error, as though he uttered something remarkable; and, by the vain and pernicious flow of his words, he so takes possession of his hearers and admirers, that they no longer yield themselves to the divine scriptures, nor the authority of the fathers, but prefer following his fantastic reveries. We have, therefore, judged it necessary, through charitable zeal, and for the sake of our city and our order, to reply to his insolence," &c.[1]

You observe that the character of the writings and ideas of Scotus Erigena is clearly portrayed in the accusation here put forth against him; he is denounced for *purely human*, and, according to his own words, *philosophical arguments*, and as being *learned and versed in the knowledge of the schools*. It

---

[1] *Veterum Auctorum qui ix. sæculo de Prædestinatione et Gratiâ scripserunt Opera et Fragmenta,* published by the president Mauguin; 2 vols. in 4to, v. i., p. 555. Paris, 1650.

was, in short, as a philosopher that he was condemned. In 855, the council of Valence decreed as follows:

"We banish absolutely from the pious ears of the faithful, as useless, nay, even as hurtful and contrary to the truth, the four articles (*capitula*) adopted with so little foresight by the council of our brethren,[1] and the nineteen other *capitula*, very foolishly set down in syllogisms, wherein no ability,[2] though they are lauded in this respect, shines in the secular point of view, and wherein we find an invention of the devil, rather than any argument for the faith. By the authority of the Holy Spirit, we interdict them everywhere, and we think that those who introduce novelties ought to be punished, in order to prevent the necessity of having afterwards to strike harder."[3]

Some years after, in 859, the council of Langres renewed the same sentence of condemnation against Scotus Erigena. Both accusers and judges, the simple clergy and the assemblies of the church, were then unanimous in their judgment of Scotus Erigena, and the character of his works. Let us see what he says himself; he describes and paints himself as his enemies have painted him.

His treatise on predestination begins thus:—

"Since, in earnestly investigating and attempting to discover surely the reasons of all things, every means of attaining to a pious and perfect doctrine, lies in that science and discipline which the Greeks call *philosophy*, we think it necessary to speak in a few words of its divisions and classifications. 'It is believed and taught,' says St. Augustine, 'that philosophy, that is, the love of wisdom, is no other than religion; and what proves it is, that we do not receive the sacraments in common with those whereof we do not approve the doctrine.' What, then, is the object of philosophy but to set forth the rules of true religion, whereby we rationally seek and humbly adore God, the first cause and sovereign of all things? From thence it follows that true philosophy is true religion, and conversely, that true religion is true philosophy."[4]

---

[1] The council of Kiersy.
[2] The nineteen chapters of Scotus Erigena's treatise on *Predestination*.
[3] Council of Valence in 855, can. 4.
[4] *Divina. Prædest.*, c. i., col of Maug., v. i., p. 221.

Is not this evidently the language of a man who is much more a philosopher than a theologian, and who takes his point of departure in philosophy, attempting to mix, or at least to reconcile it with religion, either because he considers them as one and the same science, or because he has need of the shield of religion to protect himself against the attacks of which he is the object?

Again, in his work *On the Division of Nature*:—

"We must follow in all things the authority of the holy scriptures, for the truth is there enclosed as in a secret sanctuary; but we must not think that, in order to endow us with the divine nature, the holy scripture always employs precise and literal words and signs; it makes use of similitudes, strained and figurative expressions, adapts itself to our weakness, and raises, by a simple mode of teaching, our dull and immature spirits."[1]

Who does not recognize here an effort, very often made, to avoid the strict interpretation of texts or dogmas, and to introduce into the study of religion some liberty of thought, under the veil of explanation and allegory?

We cannot doubt it: even before examining deeply into the ideas of Scotus Erigena, and judging only by the traditions which remain to us respecting his works, by the language of the church and of his enemies, and by his own, the philosophical character appears vividly in the life and spirit of this man; he differs from theologians essentially; it is to antiquity that he belongs, it is of ancient knowledge that he discourses to his contemporaries.

His character was by no means a cause of disfavor with Charles le Chauve. It is well attested, on the contrary, that Charles often attended his lectures, took a lively interest in them, and consulted him upon all the affairs, upon all the intellectual difficulties, so to speak, which arose in his kingdom. An anecdote in a manuscript of William of Malmesbury, a chronicler of the thirteenth century, will show you to what an extent the familiarity of the king with the philosopher was carried:

"John," says he, "was seated at table in front of the king, who sat at the other side of the table; when the viands had disappeared, and jokes began to circulate, in a light humor

---

[1] *De Nat. Divis.*, v. i., c. 66.

and after some other pleasantries, seeing John do something which shocked the Gallic politeness, the king rebuked him mildly, saying, '*Quid distat inter sottum et Scotum?*' (what separates a sot from a Scot?) 'Nothing but the table,' replied John, returning the quip to its author."[1]

Are not these the liberties of a licensed *bel-esprit*, who believes all things are permitted to him because he amuses and pleases?

It was, I am much disposed to think, this encouragement of Scotus Erigena by Charles le Chauve, that suggested to Hincmar the idea of gaining his interference in his quarrel with Gottschalk, by engaging him to write on his behalf. Hincmar (as I have already remarked) was more of a politician than theologian, more filled with the idea of governing than reasoning, and rather aiming at success than truth. He found himself in a difficult position; most of the theologians of Frankish Gaul were rising against him; the celebrated Raban, after having compromised him, refused to support him. He applied to Scotus Erigena, wishing, doubtless, to profit at once by his interest and by his knowledge, and hoping to find in him an able and influential defender.

But Hincmar knew not what an ally he was calling to his assistance, and in what a strife he was again about to engage. In order to make clearly understood the turn which the question then took, and the part which Scotus Erigena played in it, I am obliged to ascend a step higher.

Christianity, in order to establish itself, had had to vanquish all sorts of enemies, governments, nations, priests, and pagans, civil as well as religious power, and laws as well as customs. But in the intellectual order, the Alexandrine neoplatonism had been its sole adversary.

Properly speaking, it was between the Neoplatonists of Alexandria, and the Christians, that the question lay. From the second century, some attempts had been made by the rival schools at conciliating, or rather at amalgamating the two doctrines. St. Clement of Alexandria, who died in 220, and Origen, from 185 to 254, were disciples of the Alexandrine philosophy, Neoplatonists become Christians, and who endeavored to accommodate their philosophical doctrines to

---

[1] *William of Malmesbury*, in his unpublished work, *De Pontificibus*.

the Christian creeds which were developing themselves and taking the form of a system. In the course of the third or fourth centuries, these attempts were once more renewed: but it was in the middle of the sixth, that they became most vigorous. The victory was then completely on the side of Christianity; the Alexandrian Neoplatonism, abandoned by princes, and decried, and persecuted, had no alternative but to lose itself in the bosom of its enemy, preserving of itself only so much as Christianity would consent to receive. We see, indeed, at that time most of the philosophers of this school, become or near becoming Christians, blending their old opinions with their new faith, by endeavoring to make them agree. To this epoch belongs, for example, the dialogue of Æneas of Gaza, a disciple of Hierocles, entitled, "*Theophrastus; or on the immortality of the soul and the resurrection of the body,*" and that of Zacharius the Scholastic, entitled, "*Ammonius; or on the construction of the world, against the philosophers;*" writings, the design of which was evidently to introduce into the theology of St. Athanasius, St. Jerome, and St. Augustin, such ideas and forms of the expiring philosophy as would accommodate themselves with it. There were then, assuredly, many more works of this kind than are now remaining to us; the proof of which is, that they were composed with a view to being ascribed to the ancient philosophers, in the hope of thereby enforcing upon them more authority. In the middle of this fifth century there appeared, under the name of Dionysius the Areopagite, several treatises bearing the character which I have just described. Dionysius the Areopagite was one of the most illustrious names in Christian traditions, one of the most glorious conquests of nascent Christianity. He is mentioned for the first time in the 17th chapter of the *Acts of the Apostles.* This chapter is so remarkable, and carries in itself, independently of all external evidence, such indications of authenticity, that I beg your permission to read the text of the principal passages. Nowhere is the preaching of Christianity in the midst of ancient society painted with so much truth and clearness: the sacred chronicler relates the sojourn of St. Paul at Athens:

"Now when Paul waited for them at Athens, his spirit was stirred in him, when he saw the city wholly given to idolatry. Therefore disputed he in the synagogue with the Jews, and with the devout persons, and in the market daily with them hat met with him. Then certain philosophers of the epizureans and of the stoics, encountered him. And some said, 'What will this babbler say?' other some, 'He seemeth to be a setter forth of strange gods:' because he preached unto them Jesus, and the resurrection.

"And they took him, and brought him unto Areopagus, saying, 'May we know what this new doctrine whereof thou speakest is? For thou bringest certain strange things to our ears: we would know, therefore, what these things mean.'" (For all the Athenians and strangers which were there, spent their time in nothing else, but either to tell or hear some new thing.)

"Then Paul stood in the midst of Mars' Hill, and said,—'Ye men of Athens, I perceive that in all things ye are too superstitious. For as I passed by and beheld your devotions, I found an altar with this inscription—*To the unknown God*. Whom, therefore, ye ignorantly worship, him declare I unto you. God that made the world and all things therein, seeing that he is the Lord of heaven and earth, dwelleth not in temples made with hands; neither is worshipped with men's hands, as though he needed anything, seeing he giveth to all life, and breath, and all things. That they should seek the Lord, if haply they might feel after him, and find him, though he be not far from every one of us: for in him we live, and move, and have our being; as certain also of your own poets have said, For we are also his offspring. Forasmuch, then, as we are the offspring of God, we ought not to think that the godhead is like unto gold, or silver, or stone, graven by art and man's device. And the times of this ignorance God winked at; but now commandeth all men everywhere to repent; because he hath appointed a day, in the which he will judge the world in righteousness, by that man whom he hath ordained; whereof he hath given assurance unto all men, in that he hath raised him from the dead.'

"And when they heard of the resurrection of the dead, some mocked: and others said—'We will hear thee again of this matter.' So Paul departed from among them.

"Howbeit, certain men clave unto him, and believed: among the which was Dionysius the Areopagite."[1]

Such a convert would naturally have been cherished by the new society: accordingly, since that epoch, the name of

---

[1] Acts of the Apostles, chap. 17, ver. 16-34.

Dionysius the Areopagite frequently occurs in Christian narrations. In the second century, particularly, Saint Justin, one of the earliest and most able defenders of Christianity, mentions him on several occasions with honor. Tradition relates that, towards the end of the first century, in 95, Dionysius being burnt alive at Athens, obtained the honors of martyrdom. The fact is possible, but does not rest on any sure proofs.

Whatever may have been the truth of the case, towards the end of the fifth century, there appeared under the name of Dionysius the Areopagite, several works designed to effect the amalgamation of the Alexandrian Neoplatonism with Christian theology; they are entitled: 1. *On the Celestial Hierarchy*; 2. *On the Ecclesiastical Hierarchy*; 3. *On Divine Names*; 4. *Mystical Theology*; lastly, to the dogmatic writings are subjoined ten letters. The forgery is evident: the books and letters could not have been written before the middle of the fifth century: facts and customs which did not belong to the Christian church before that epoch, are therein mentioned; and at every step we meet with ideas and forms of style, of which Dionysius the Areopagite could not have had the least notion. Accordingly, in the first half of the sixth century, about the year 532, at Constantinople itself, Hypatius, a rhetorician, attacked the authenticity of these pretended works of the Athenian senator. But they agreed very well with the nature of an attempt, at that time very actively prosecuted, and very important in the then state of society; their object was to effect that reconciliation, that amalgamation of Christian dogmas with Neoplatonic ideas which formed the intellectual problem of the age. Public credulity was great, true criticism almost dormant; the writings of which I speak, easily passed into circulation. Several scholars, amongst others Maximus the Confessor (in 622), added commentaries to them; and they continued to bear the name of the illustrious Christian to whom they had been attributed.

At the commencement of the ninth century, a particular circumstance gave them immense popularity in the west, and especially in Frankish Gaul. A Saint Denis passed for having been, about the middle of the third century, the apostle of the Gauls and the first bishop of Paris. It entered the heads of some monks to maintain that this Denis and Dionysius the Areopagite were one and the same man. The Christianity of the Gauls was thus referred to an antiquity far more remote, and might thus boast of a far more illustrious founder. In 814, Hilduinus, abbot of Saint Denis, the same by whom Hincmar was educated, wrote a book, entitled *Areopagetica*, to uphold the opinion in point. It rapidly gained credit, and became in Gaul a sort of national creed. The works of Dionysius the Areopagite were from that time forward the object of eager curiosity, and in 824, Michael the Stammerer sent a copy of one of them to Louis le Debonnaire. The precious MS. was deposited and preserved in the abbey of Saint Denis; but it was in Greek, and few persons could understand it. Charles le Chauve engaged Scotus Erigena to translate it. He undertook this translation, which was probably the work that, of all others, most extended the fame of his learning in Gaul.

Historically, then, the character of the works of Scotus Erigena is incontestable. He was in the ninth century the representative and interpreter of that attempt, commenced in the second century, and so active in the fifth, at an amalgamation of the Alexandrine Neoplatonism and Christian theology. It is under this aspect that he presents himself in the succession of facts and proper names. He was the last link of that chain whose first link a pious delusion had attempted to trace to Athens herself, to the bosom of the schools of ancient philosophy.

Let us now quit history, and let us penetrate into the ideas themselves: let us judge from the works of Scotus Erigena, by comparing them, on the one hand, with those of the Neoplatonists of Alexandria—on the other, with those of the Christian theologians of his time, whether they indeed connect themselves with Neoplatonian doctrines, and vainly attempt to reproduce them and infuse them into Christianity.

I cannot, as you may easily understand, think of here offering any very extensive or strict comparison between Alexandrine Neoplatonism and Christianity. I am forced to limit myself to a few broad features, to the most general characteristics of the two doctrines; they will suffice, I hope, to distinguish them, and to show clearly to which Scotus Erigena properly belonged.

At first sight, and neglecting minor questions, two essential differences are remarkable between the Alexandrine Neoplatonism and Christianity. 1st. Neoplatonism is a philosophy, Christianity a religion. The first has human reason for its point of departure; it is to her that it addresses itself, her that it interrogates, in her that it confides. The point of departure of the second is, on the contrary, a fact exterior to human reason; it dictates to, instead of interrogating her. From thence it follows, that free inquiry predominates in Neoplatonism; it is its fundamental method and habitual practice; whereas Christianity proclaims authority for its principle, and proceeds by means of authority. From thence it again follows that, although the Alexandrine Neoplatonism, to judge of it by the language and character of its writings, presents itself under a profoundly mystical aspect, its principle at the bottom is rational; whilst primitive Christianity, the character of which is in no degree mystical, which is, on the contrary, very positive and simple, has, nevertheless, a supernatural principle. There is, then, in the starting points of these two doctrines, a radical difference.

2d. If we pass over this question of the point of departure, and of the preliminary method of every philosophy, and examine ideas to the very bottom, a second essential difference will strike us. The main doctrine of Alexandrine Neoplatonism is pantheism, the identity of substance and being, individuality reduced to the condition of a simple phenomenon, of a transitory fact. Individuality, on the contrary, is the fundamental belief of Christian theology. The God of the Christians is a distinct being, who communicates and treats with other beings, to whom the latter address themselves, who replies to them, whose existence is sovereign, but not sole. Among many other indications, the diversity of the two doctrines reveals itself clearly in the idea which they respectively involve concerning man's future state beyond his present one of actual existence. How does Neoplatonism view the condition of human beings at the moment of their death? As being absorbed in the bosom of the great all; all individuality having been abolished. How, on the other hand, does Christianity view them? It regards individuality as perpetuated even to infinity; and an eternity of punishments and rewards is substituted for the absorption of individual beings; so that, casting but a rapid glance at the two doctrines, we notice a radical difference both in the foundation and in the point of departure of the ideas—a difference which especially appears in the two essential features to which I have now drawn your attention.

Is it not true, then, that if we find these very same differences between the philosophy of John Scotus Erigena, and the Christian theology of his time; the filiation of his ideas and their affinity with Alexandrine Neoplatonism will be as certain by the very essence of the ideas, as it has appeared to us by historical traditions?

Independently of his translation of the pretended works of Dionysius the Areopagite, and of some treatises now lost, or still in manuscript,[1] there remain to us two great works of Scotus Erigena: 1st, his treatise, *De Prædestinatione*, of which I have already spoken to you; 2d, a treatise entitled Περὶ Φύσεως Μερισμοῦ, *Concerning the Division of Nature*, which contains the systematic exposition of his ideas on man and the universe.

From these two works alone I shall select the quotations to be presently offered to your view. The first is found in the collection of writings relative to the quarrel between Hincmar and Gottschalk, published by the president Mauguin. But, by an ill fortune, which I have attempted in vain to remedy, I shall be unable to present you with an analysis, whose accuracy I could guarantee, of the second, which is of most importance, for I could discover it in none of the libraries of Paris. It was published in Oxford in 1681, by Thomas Gale, in one volume, folio. Great kindness has been shown towards me, at the different public libraries, in the efforts that have been made to find it; but, unfortunately, none of them contain it. I have also made inquiries for it in England, but have not yet obtained it. I have therefore been obliged to content myself with the extracts and numerous quotations which I have found in several histories of philosophy, and particularly in two German dissertations, whereof Scotus Erigena is the special object.[2] I should say, also, by the way, that it has been demonstrated to me, by the attentive examination which I have made of them, that many foreign writers who have spoken of this work have not had it before them, any more than myself, in its entire state. Of this they ought to have made their readers aware.

---

[1] Among others, a treatise on the *Vision of God*, of which Mabillon had seen the MS. in the library of Clairmarest near St. Omer, and which commenced with these words: *Omnes sensus corporei nascuntur ex conjunctione animæ et corporis.*

[2] One is entitled, *John Scotus Erigena*, or, *On the Origin of a Christian Philosophy and its Holy Mission*, by P. Hioart, Copenhagen, 1823; the other, *The Mysticism of the Middle Ages in their Infancy*, by H Schmid, Jena, 1824.

I begin with the first question, the preliminary question of every doctrine, that of the point of departure and the method. I have just shown you what, with respect to this, was the radical difference between Alexandrine Neoplatonism and Christian theology, and how one had reason for its principle, —the other, authority. The following are some of the passages wherein Scotus Erigena expresses his thoughts on this subject:

I.

"Nature" (by nature he means the universe, all created things) "and time were created together, but authority does not date from the origin of time and nature. Reason is born at the commencement of things, with time and nature. Reason itself demonstrates it. Authority is derived from reason, and not reason from authority. An authority which is not acknowledged by reason seems valueless. Reason, on the contrary, invincibly resting on its own strength, has no need of the confirmation of any authority. Legitimate authority appears to me to be but truth unfolded by the force of reason, and transmitted by the holy fathers, for the use of future generations."[1]

II.

"We should not allege the opinions of the holy fathers, especially if they are known to most people, unless it be necessary thereby to strengthen arguments in the eyes of men, who, unskilful in reasoning, yield rather to authority than to reason."[2]

III.

"The salvation of faithful souls consists in believing what we have reason to affirm concerning the sole principle of all things, and in comprehending what we have reason to believe."[3]

IV.

"Faith is nothing more, in my opinion, than a certain principle from which the knowledge of the Creator takes its derivation in a reasonable nature."[4]

---

[1] *De Divisione Naturæ*, v. i., p. 39.
[2] *De Divisione Naturæ*, v. ii., p. 81
[3] Ibid., v iv., p 81.
[4] Ibid., v i, p. 41.

V.

"The soul in itself is unknown; but it begins to manifest itself to itself and to others in its form, which is reason."[1]

VI.

"I am not so fearful of authority, and I do not so dread the rage of minds of small intelligence, as to hesitate to proclaim aloud the things which reason clearly unfolds and with certainty demonstrates; there are, moreover, subjects of which we need only discourse with the learned, for whom nothing is more sweet to hear than the truth, and nothing more delightful to investigate, or more beautiful to contemplate, when found."[2]

Assuredly, no philosopher has ever more clearly expressed the rational character of his point of departure, which is that of all philosophy. The last passage also clearly indicates that the contest was then being waged between this principle and that of authority, and that Scotus Erigena hesitated not to engage in it. Devotion to truth and liberty is thus in a few words indicated with striking power:—

He goes further, and points out here and there in the course of his work some of the principles of philosophical method, with a precision so much the more remarkable that he often violates it himself, and like the rest of the Neoplatonic school, does often the very reverse of proceeding from the known to the unknown, and by the path of observation. The following are a few of these passages:—

VII.

"The true course of reasoning may be from the natural study of things sensible, to the pure contemplation of things spiritual."[3]

VIII.

"If we do not desire to study and to know ourselves, it is because we do not desire to raise ourselves up to what is above us, that is to our cause; for there is no other way of attaining to the most pure contemplation of the sovereign model than to well regard his image, which is nigh unto us."

---

[1] *De Divisione Naturæ*, v. ii., p. 74.
[2] *De Divisione Naturæ*, v. v., p. 227.
[3] Ibid., v. i., p. 39.
[4] Ibid., p. 268.

IX.

"Far from being of little importance, the knowledge of things sensible is greatly useful to the understanding of things intellectual. For, in the same manner as, by the senses, we arrive at intelligence, so, by the creature, we return to God."[1]

Are not the scientific spirit, and the method of observation and induction, clearly opposed, in these places, to the theological spirit, to the method of authority and deduction?

Let us pass the vestibule of the philosophy; let us go into the interior of the temple. There, the affinity of Scotus Erigena with the Alexandrine Neoplatonism will not be less apparent. He is likewise essentially a pantheist, and he hesitates not to say so, with all that confusion, it is true, which is inherent in this doctrine, and dooms it to incoherency and absurdity in the very terms by which it attempts to declare itself, yet he does so as openly and as consequently (if the word *consequence* may be here used) as his more illustrious predecessors.

X.

"The cause of all things, which is God, is at the same time simple and multiple. The divine goodness (essence) spreads itself, that is, multiplies itself in all things which exist . . . . and lastly, by the same paths, disengaging itself from the infinite variety of things which exist, again returns and concentrates itself in the simple unity which comprehends all things, which is in God and is God. Thus, all is God and God is all."[2]

XI.

"In the same manner that, originally, the river flows entire from its source; and as the water which first gushes out from the spring, spreads itself constantly and without ceasing in the bed of the river, whatever be the length of its course, in the same manner the goodness, essence, wisdom, divine life, and all which is in the source of all things, spreads itself first in the first causes, and makes them to subsist; then passes from the first causes into their effects, according to an ineffable mode, and thus circulates by uninterrupted

---

[1] *De Divisione Naturæ*, v. iii., p. 149. [2] Ibid., v. iii., c. 4

degrees from things superior to things inferior, and finally returns to its source by the most subtle and secret ways of nature."[1]

XII.

"God, who alone truly exists, is the essence of all things, as Dionysius the Areopagite says: 'The existence of all things is what remains in them of divinity.'"[2]

XIII.

"God is the beginning, the middle, and the end: the beginning, because all things come from him and participate in his essence; the middle, because all things subsist in him and by him; the end, because all things move towards him in order to attain repose, the limit of their motion, and the stability of his perfection."[3]

XIV.

"All things which are said to be, are images of God (*Theophaniæ*) . . . . all that we perceive and comprehend is but an apparition of what we see not, a manifestation of what is hidden . . . . opened a way towards the apprehension of that which we have no comprehension of, a name of that which is ineffable, a step towards that which we cannot attain . . . . a form of that which does not possess form, &c."[4]

XV.

"We can conceive nothing in the creature which is not the Creator, who alone truly *is*. Nothing out of himself can be called really essential; for all things, coming from him, are nothing more, inasmuch as they exist, than a certain participation in the existence of him who alone comes from no other and subsists of himself."[5]

XVI.

"We ought not to conceive the Lord and the creature as two beings distinct one from the other, but as one and the same being. For the creature subsists in God, and God, in a

---

[1] *De Divis. Nat.*, v. i., c. 3.   [2] Ibid., c. 12.   [3] Ibid., v. iii. c. 4
[4] *Dedic. ad S. Maximi Schol. in Gregorium Nazianz.*
[5] *De Divis. Nat.*, v. ii., c. 2.

marvellous and ineffable manner, creates himself, so to say, in the creature in whom he manifests himself, and thus renders the invisible visible, and the incomprehensible comprehensible."

XVII.

"All that the human soul, by its intelligence and its reason, knows of God and the principles of things, under the form of unity, it perceives under the multiple form, and by the senses, in the effects of causes."[2]

Although I have not the complete work before me, it would be an easy matter for me to continue these quotations; but I have given enough, doubtless, to establish the Pantheism of Scotus Erigena, and to show that he was really, with respect to the ground of his ideas, as also indeed of his method, the representative, in the ninth century, of that Alexandrian philosophy, which was for a long time the intellectual adversary of Christianity, and which from the second century had sought, if not to reconcile itself, at least to amalgamate itself with the nascent theology.

Since the attempt had not succeeded from the second to the fifth century, when Alexandrine Neoplatonism was still popular and powerful, far more reason was there for its failing in the ninth, when it had only for its organ and defender a wandering philosopher, favored by a king without power. I will not return to what I told you in the last lecture, about the clamor which was raised against Scotus Erigena; it was as general as it was violent, and greatly injured the cause of Hincmar, who had chosen him for his defender. Scotus Erigena had foreseen this, and was obliged to protect himself by all the precautions in his power. We read at the head of his treatise on predestination, dedicated to Hincmar:—

"Of this opuscule, then, which we have written at your command, and in proof of your orthodox faith, adopt and assign so much to the catholic church as you shall judge true —reject what appears to you false; and, simply human as we are, pardon us for it. As regards what seems doubtful, believe it, until authority teaches you that it must be rejected, or taken for truth, and believed always."[3]

But the precaution was in vain: we cannot deceive or

---

[1] *De Divis. Nat.*, v. ii., p. 74.   [2] Ibid
[4] *De Div. Præd. Praf.*, Col of Maug v. i., p. 110.

lull to sleep intellectual adversaries. Not only did a crowd of theologians write against the philosopher—not only was he condemned by councils, but the rumors of his opinions soon arrived at Rome, and pope Nicholas I. addressed to Charles le Chauve—probably between 865 and 867—a letter conceived in these terms:

"It has been reported to our apostleship that a certain John, of Scotch origin, has lately translated into Latin the work which the blessed Dionysius wrote in the Greek language, on divine names and celestial orders. This book ought to have been sent us, according to custom, and approved by our judgment; the more so, that this John, though he is cried up as possessed of great knowledge, has not always, it is everywhere said, been sound in his views upon certain subjects. We recommend, therefore, very strongly, that you cause the said John to appear before our apostleship, or at least that you do not permit him any longer to reside at Paris, in the school of which he is stated for a long time to have been the chief, in order that he may no longer mingle his tares with the wheat of the holy word, giving poison to those who seek for bread."[1]

There is much difference of opinion amongst scholars as to the consequences which this formidable attack produced with regard to Scotus Erigena. According to some, Charles le Chauve, after having for a long time supported him, was at last obliged to abandon him; and Erigena fled to England, where king Alfred then reigned, who gave him a favorable reception, and placed him at the head of the university of Oxford. This opinion is founded on a passage of Matthew of Westminster, an English chronicler of the thirteenth century. We there read, under the date 883—

"This year came to England, Master John, of Scottish origin, a man of a very penetrating mind, and of singular eloquence. A long while before, having quitted his native country, he went to Gaul, to the court of Charles le Chauve, and, being received by him with great honor, became his boon companion and bedfellow... At the request of this same king, he translated from the Greek into Latin, the Hierarchy of Dionysius the Areopagite, and gave to the world another book,

---

[1] Collection of P. Maugnin, v. i., p. 105; Boulaz., *Univ. Hist*, Paris, v. i., p. 181

which he entit.ed περὶ φύσεως Μερισμοῦ, that is, *Concerning the Division of Nature*,—'very useful,' says he, 'for resolving divers questions scarcely soluble;' we must excuse him on certain occasions, whereupon he has strayed from the path pursued by the Latins, for he had his eyes especially directed towards the Greeks. He has accordingly by some been judged heretical. A certain Florus has written against him: we are ignorant who this man was, who condemned the writings of John by perverting them. There are indeed many things in this book which, if we do not examine them with care, appear contrary to the catholic faith. (He then speaks of the letter of Pope Nicholas I.) ... In consequence of this reproach, this same John quitted France and came into England, where, some years after, he was stabbed to death by his own pupils with their styles, and died in great agony. For some time he had only an humble grave in the church of St. Laurence: but a ray of celestial light having fallen upon that place, the monks, encouraged by such signs, transported him to the cathedral, and honorably deposited him on the left of the altar."[1]

A mass of objections are raised against this narrative of a chronicler who lived more than three centuries after the occurrence of the facts which he relates. He appears to have confounded Scotus Erigena with another of the same name, whom king Alfred in effect summoned from the continent about the year 884, with the view of entrusting to him the direction of the university of Oxford. Such is the account of Asser, a biographer contemporary with Alfred, who adds, that in 895, John the Saxon, having become abbot of Ethelingay, was slain by strokes of the style in a commotion of monks, and that, being a very strong man, he defended himself a long while. But, in 895, Scotus Erigena must have been eighty years old; he could not, therefore, have been *very strong*, nor have *defended himself a long while* against his assassins. Thus the details given by his contemporaries are absolutely inapplicable to him, and the whole story of his return to England becomes very doubtful. Most French scholars contend that he remained in France, and even that he died there before Charles le Chauve, that is, before 877; and, independently of the circumstances which I have just noticed,

---

[1] *Collection* of Mauguin, v. i., p 106.

their opinion seems confirmed by a letter of Anastasius, librarian of Rome, to king Charles, written about 876, wherein he speaks to him of Scotus Erigena, as of a man deceased. Contemporary testimony has, in my opinion, more authority than that of Matthew of Westminster, and I am disposed to side with this latter opinion.

However that was, the philosophical movement which Erigena had prolonged or re-animated declined with him. His history is nearly the last glimmer which marks the presence and activity of the Alexandrian Neoplatonism in the bosom of Christianity. With him ended all the attempts whether at warfare or at amalgamation between these two great intellectual adversaries. Dating from this epoch, Christian theology became more and more a stranger to ancient philosophy, and the tenth century witnessed the birth of the theology of the middle age, the true ecclesiastical theology, that which was to bring forth the creeds and the Christian church, alone and free in their development.

Scotus Erigena, however, preserved to himself a great reputation, and I meet with a fact, in the thirteenth century, which loudly attests it. It appears that at this epoch, when the great heresy of the Albigenses burst forth, his works, particularly his treatise *De Divisione Naturæ,* and his translation of Dionysius the Areopagite, were known and much esteemed in southern France ; to such an extent was this the case that Pope Honorius III. ordered that a search should be made for the manuscripts of them in all libraries, and that they should be sent to Rome to be there burnt. No document, no narration attaches this fact to the history of Scotus Erigena himself, and I am not in a condition to follow, from the ninth to the thirteenth century, the traces of his writings and of their influence ; but the fact, though isolated, is the no less certain and curious.

I have detained you a long time upon the life and writings of a man much forgotten in the present day. But, in the first place, it was but justice to restore to his proper rank this strong and great intellect, which appeared as a phenomenon in the middle of his age ; on the other, I desired to show you that this phenomenon had in it nothing strange, and that, in he case of philosophy as of legislation, ancient society, the Greco-Roman society, had not so completely or so hastily perished as we have been accustomed to think. I will here conclude my description of Frankish Gaul from the eighth to the tenth century; and in our next lecture, which will be the last—I shall endeavor to sum up all the facts which I have placed before your notice, and to trace rapidly that course of French civilization, under the two first races, which we have now been considering.

THIRTIETH LECTURE.

General summary of the course—Extent and variety of subjects—The history of civilization, its price—It is the result of all partial histories—Unity and variety of the existence of a people—Three essential elements in French civilization, Greco-Roman antiquity, Christianity, Germany—1. Of the Roman element, from the 5th to the 10th century—Under a social point of view—Under an intellectual point of view—2. Of the Christian element, from the 5th to the 10th century—Under a social point of view—Under an intellectual point of view—3. Of the Germanic element, from the 5th to the 10th century—Under a social point of view—Under an intellectual point of view—Two principal facts characterize this epoch: 1. The prolongation, more or less apparent, but everywhere real, of Roman society and its influence—2. The disorderly and indeterminate fermentation of the different elements of modern civilization—Conclusion.

We are come to the termination of this course. I would now take a review of the whole, noticing the chief and predominant facts, which appear to me to result from it, and which characterize, during that long period, the history of our civilization.

I gave at the commencement a description of Gaul prior to the German invasion, at the end of the fourth and the beginning of the 5th century, under the Roman administration. We considered its social and intellectual state in civil and in religious society.[1]

After I had thus made you acquainted with Roman-Gaul, I took you across the Rhine. I directed your view towards Germany, prior to the invasion also, and in the infancy of its institutions and manners.

The Germans having invaded Gaul, we examined what were the consequences, whether immediate or probable, of this first contact of Roman with barbarous society. I drew your attention to their abrupt and violent collision.[2]

From the sixth century to the middle of the eighth, we followed the progressive amalgamation of the two societies.

---

[1] Lect. 2—6.   [2] Lect. 7.   [3] Lect. 9.

In the civil order, we saw barbarous laws arise, and the Roman law perpetuated. I labored to explain the character generally misunderstood, in my opinion, of these first rudiments of modern legislation.[1] We passed from thence to religious society; and considering it in its double element, priests and monks, the secular and regular clergy, we gave an account both of its relations with civil society, and of its own internal organization.[2]

Such has been our progress, from the sixth to the eighth century, in the history of the social state; but we had also to consider the intellectual state of Frankish-Gaul at the same period; we searched both in sacred and profane literature, and we endeavored to ascertain their distinctive character and reciprocal influence.[3]

We thus arrived at the great crisis which signalized the middle of the eighth century, the fall of the Merovingian kings and the accession of the Carlovingians; I attempted to characterize this revolution, and to assign its real causes.[4]

The Carlovingian revolution being comprehended, the reign of Charlemagne specially occupied us; I considered it in its events, properly so called, in its laws, in its action on mind. I desired particularly to distinguish that which he attempted, and that which he effectually accomplished, that which perished with him, and that which survived him.[5]

After the death of Charlemagne, the rapid dissolution of his vast empire struck our attention; we endeavored to take an account of it, and to make known to ourselves the progress as well as the causes of that phenomenon; we pursued it, on the one hand, in its events, on the other, in its laws; we inquired into the political and the legislative revolution, which, from the death of Charlemagne to the accession of Hugh Capet, led to the feudal system.[6]

To this history of civil society, from the middle of the eighth to the end of the tenth century, succeeded the history of religious society at the same period, that is to say, the history of the Gallo-Frankish church, considered firstly in itself, that is, in its national existence; secondly, externally, in its relations with the government of the universal church, that is, the popedom.

---

[1] Lect. 9—11. [2] Lect. 12—15. [3] Lect. 16, 18.
[4] Lect. 19.   [5] Lect. 20—23. [6] Lect. 24—25.

Lastly, always remaining true to the essential idea of civilization, and always mindful to consider it under its double aspect, with respect to society and the human soul, the intellectual state of Frankish-Gaul, from the eighth to the tenth century, was our concluding study. We saw ancient philosophy expire, and ecclesiastical theology arise: and we determined with some precision the profane and the sacred elements which have contributed to the modern development of the human mind.[1]

Such is the vast career, the steps of which we have followed; such is the immense variety of objects which have passed under your view. Certainly, I have not arbitrarily or from mere fancy led you into this vast expanse, causing you continually to be changing the point of view of subject. The very nature of our study rigidly exacted it: the history of civilization can only be given at this expense.

This history is a new work, scarcely more than sketched. The idea of it has been first conceived in the eighteenth century, and it is in our own times, under our own eyes, that we see its true fulfilment begin. It is not, however, only in the present day that history is made a study of; not only facts, but their connection and their causes, have been studied; philosophers and scholars have equally labored in this field. But up to the present times, we may say, the study of history, both philosophical and scholastic, has been partial and limited; political, legislative, religious, and literary histories have been written; learned researches have been made, brillian' reflections have been presented on the destination and development of laws, manners, sciences, letters, arts, of all the works of human activity; but they have never been regarded together, at one view, in their intimate and fertile union. And wherever there has been an attempt to grasp at general results, or a desire to form a complete idea of the development of human nature, it is altogether on a partial foundation that the edifice has been raised. The *Discours sur l'Histoire Universelle*, and the *Esprit des Lois*, are glorious essays on the history of civilization; but who cannot see that Bossuet has almost exclusively confined his search to religious creeds, and Montesquieu to political institutions? These two geniuses have thus narrowed the horizon of their view. What

---

[1] Lect. 28, 29

are we to say concerning minds of an inferior order? It is evident that, scholastic or philosophical, history up to the present day has never really been general; it has never at one time followed man in all the careers wherein his activity exhibits itself. And yet the history of civilization is possible only under this condition; it is a summary of all histories; it requires them all for materials, for the fact which it relates is the summary of all other facts. An immense variety, without doubt; yet do not think that unity is destroyed thereby. There is unity in the life of a people, in the life of the human race, just as there is in that of an individual; but, as in fact all the circumstances of destiny and activity in an individual contribute to form his character, which is one and the same, so the unity and history of a people must have for its basis all the variety of its entire existence.

It is, then, wholly of necessity, and driven by the very nature of our subject, that we have gone over the political, ecclesiastical, legislative, philosophical, and literary history of Frankish Gaul, from the fifth to the tenth century: if we have arrived at any precise and positive results, we owe them to this method. You may have observed, especially, how much we have been enlightened by placing civil and religious society continually in juxta-position, both of which are incomprehensible if we leave them separate. Let us now endeavor to understand clearly these results, which we have obtained. I think, with some certainty; let us endeavor to determine the point of departure of Gaulish civilization in the fifth century, and the point at which it had arrived at the end of the tenth.

You are aware that the essential, fundamental elements of modern civilization in general, and of French civilization in particular, reduce themselves to three: the Roman world, the Christian world, and the Germanic world; antiquity, Christianity, and barbarism. Let us see what transformation these three elements underwent between the fifth and tenth centuries, what they became in this last period, and what remained of them in the civilization of that period.

I. I commence with the Roman element. I wish to cast a slight glance at what the Roman world has furnished to France, under a social and an intellectual point of view; and we must discover what remained of it in the tenth century, in society and in mind.

Under the first point of view—that is to say, the influence

of Roman on Gallo-Frankish society, from the fifth to the tenth century, the result of our inquiries is, that the Roman world, when it broke up, bequeathed to the future the wrecks of three great facts—1st, central sole power, empire, and absolute royalty; 2d, imperial administration, government of provinces by the delegates of the central power; 3d, the municipal system, the primitive mode of existence of Rome and most of the countries which had successively formed the Roman empire.

What are the changes which these three facts underwent between the fifth and tenth centuries?

1. With respect to the central power, sole and sovereign, it perished, as you know, in the invasion; in vain some of the first barbarous kings tried to restore it, and to exercise it to their advantage; they were baffled in the attempt; imperial despotism was too complex an instrument for their rude hands. At the fall of the Merovingians, Charlemagne attempted to revive it, and to use it; the attempt had a momentary success; central power re-appeared: but, after Charlemagne, as after the first invasion, it broke asunder, and was lost in the chaos. Nothing, surely, less resembled imperial power than the royalty of Hugh Capet. Some remembrance of it, nevertheless, lay in the minds of men: Empire had left behind it profound traces. The names of emperor, imperial authority, sovereign majesty, had still a certain virtue, and recalled a certain type of government; these were now only words, yet words still powerful, and sufficient to produce deeds if the occasion offered. Such was the state in which, at about the end of the tenth century, this first legacy of the Roman world manifested itself.

2. The imperial administration underwent very nearly the same vicissitudes; the barbarous chiefs tried to use it, but with no better success. This mode of governing the several parts of a state was too complicated, too exact; it required the concurrence of too many agents, and intelligence of too developed a kind; the administrative machine of the empire was speedily deranged, if I may so speak, in the hands of its new masters. Charlemagne attempted to give it regularity and motion; it was a necessary consequence of the restoration of central power; and, by an analogous consequence, together with the central power of Charlemagne, perished also the provincial administration, which he had, as well as he could, reconstructed. After the complete dissolution of the new

empire, however, when the feudal system had prevailed, and when the holders of fiefs had succeeded the ancient delegates of the sovereign, there remained, in the thoughts of the people and of the possessors of fiefs themselves, some recollection of their origin. That origin, I have been careful to point out to you, was of a double kind; the fiefs originated on the one hand in benefices, or lands conceded, whether by the sovereign or by other chiefs; on the other hand, in offices or appointments of dukes, counts, viscounts, centeniers, &c., that is, of officers, invested by the sovereign with local administration. This second origin was not, therefore, absolutely effaced from memory: it was vaguely remembered that these lords—now sovereigns, or nearly so—had formerly been delegates of a greater sovereign: that they had been the representatives of a general and superior power; and that instead of being then proprietors of the sovereignty on their own account, they were only magistrates or administrators in the name of another, and that the portion of that sovereignty which they possessed might have been usurped from this sole and remote monarch, who was now lost sight of. This idea, which pervades the course of our history, and which has been the favorite theory of jurisconsults, and other writers upon public laws, is clearly a wreck of the ancient Roman administration—an echo which had survived the ruin of that vast and learned hierarchy. Such is all that we discern of it towards the end of the tenth century; but a potent germ of life lay buried under this remembrance.

3. The third fact bequeathed by the Roman to the modern world is the municipal system. You know what the state of towns was, at the end of the tenth century, into what depopulation, decay, and distress they had fallen. Nevertheless, so much as still remained of internal administration, especially in southern Gaul, was Roman in its origin; here was still some shadow of the curia, of consuls, duumvirs, and other ancient municipal magistrates. The Roman law presided over the acts of civil life, donations, contracts, &c. Municipal magistrates, deprived of their political importance, were become in a manner simple notaries who registered civil acts, and preserved records of them. A new municipal system, of a different principle and character, the system of the commons of the middle age, was about to raise itself upon the ruins of the Roman municipality; but as yet it had scarcely

begun to dawn; and, in general, all that we can discern as existing in the tenth century, of distinct administration in towns, is Roman. Let us now see what remained of Greco-Roman antiquity under an intellectual point of view, what the mind of the tenth century still retained of it. I cannot here enter into detail; I do not mean to search, in the theological tenets and popular opinions of that time, for those which were allied to Roman philosophy and opinions; I merely wish to characterize, in its most general features, the intellectual heritage which ancient society has bequeathed to us, and the condition of it at the end of the tenth century. An important fact, and far too little noticed, in my opinion, first strikes me; it is that the principle of liberty of thought, the principle of all philosophy, reason being its own point of departure and guide, is an idea essentially the daughter of antiquity, an idea which modern society holds from Greece and Rome. We have received it evidently neither from Christianity nor from Germany; for it was included in neither of those elements of our civilization. It strongly prevailed on the contrary in Greco-Roman civilization: there is its true origin; there the most valuable legacy which antiquity has left to the modern world: the legacy which has never been absolutely set aside and without value; for you have seen the idea which is the mother of philosophy, namely, the right of reason to act from itself, animating the works and life of Scotus Erigena, and the principle of liberty of thought still prevailing in the ninth century, in face of the principle of authority. A second intellectual legacy of Roman civilization to ours, is the body of beautiful works of antiquity. In spite of the general ignorance, in spite of the corruption of language, ancient literature has always been presented to the mind as a worthy object of study, of imitation, and of admiration, and as the type of the beautiful. The influence of this idea was very great, you are aware, from the fourteenth to the sixteenth century; it has never been lost completely, and in the eighth, ninth, and tenth centuries, we have encountered it at every step.

The philosophical and the classical spirit, the principle of liberty of thought and the model of the beautiful, are the gifts which the Roman has transmitted to the modern world, and which still survived to it in the intellectual order at the end of the tenth century.

II. I pass to the Christian element; I desire to ascertain

what was its condition at this epoch, and what effects it had produced.

You have followed the changes of Christian society from the fifth to the tenth century; in its birth you have seen the origin and model of all the modes of organization, of all the systems which subsequently appeared; therein you have recognized the democratical, aristocratical, and monarchical principles; you have seen the lay community one while associated with the ecclesiastical community, and at another, excluded from all participation in power: all the combinations, in short, of religious social organization offered themselves to your view. During the period which we have considered, the aristocratic system prevailed; episcopacy became soon the ruling and almost the sole power. At the end of the tenth century, the popedom raised itself above episcopacy, the monarchical overcame the aristocratic principle. Under a social point of view, therefore, the state of the church at that time reduced itself to two facts:—the preponderance of the church in the state, and the preponderance of papacy in the church. Such are the results which at this epoch we may regard as established.

Under an intellectual point of view, it is more difficult, and still more important, to render to ourselves an account of what the Christian element had at that time furnished to modern civilization. Let me here ascend a step higher, and compare for a moment what has passed in antiquity with that which passed in Christian society.

Spiritual and temporal order, human thought and human society, developed themselves amongst the ancients parallel rather than together, not without an intimate correspondence, but without exercising a prompt and direct influence one upon the other. I will explain myself: without speaking of the earlier times of philosophy, but taking it at the epoch of its highest glory, Plato, Aristotle, and most of the philosophers, whether of Grecian, or more latterly of Greco-Roman antiquity, had full liberty of thought, or nearly so. The State, public policy interfered but little with their labors to cramp them and give them a particular tendency. They, on their part, concerned themselves little about politics, nor cared much to influence immediately and decisively the society in which they lived: undoubtedly they exerted that indirect and remote influence which belongs to all great human thought cast into the midst of mankind; but the ancient philosophers made few pretensions to the action or direct influence of thought over exterior facts, of pure knowledge over society; they were not essentially reformers; they aspired to govern neither the private conduct of individuals, nor society in general. The ruling character, in one word, of intellectual development in antiquity, is liberty of thought and its practical disinterestedness; it is a development essentially rational and scientific. Upon the triumph of Christianity in the Roman world, the character of intellectual development changed: that which was philosophy became religion; philosophy was enfeebled more and more; religion usurped the understanding; the form of thought was essentially religious. It aspired from that time to much more power over human affairs; the end of thought, in religion, is essentially practical; it aspires to govern individuals, frequently even society. The spiritual order, it is true, continued to be separate from the temporal order; the government of nations was not directly and completely committed to the clergy; its lay society and ecclesiastic society developed themselves independently. Nevertheless, the spiritual penetrated much further into the temporal order than it had done in ancient times; and whereas liberty of thought, and its purely scientific activity, had been, in Greece and Rome, the ruling character of the intellectual development; its practical activity and pretension to power, was the distinguishing trait of intellectual development amongst Christian nations.

From this there resulted another change, which was not of less importance In proportion as human thought, under the religious form, aspired to more power over the conduct of mankind, and the fate of states, it lost its liberty. Instead of remaining open and free to competition, as amongst the ancients, intellectual society was organized and governed; instead of philosophical schools, there was a church. It was at the cost of its independence that thought purchased empire; it no longer developed itself in all directions, and according to its simple impulse; but it acted forcibly and immediately on mankind and on societies.

This fact is important; it has exercised a decisive influence on the history of modern Europe, so decisive, as still to subsist and to manifest itself around us in our own days. The religious form has ceased to hold exclusive dominion in human thought; scientific and rational development has recommenced; and yet what is come to pass? Have philosophers thought, have they wished to treat pure knowledge in the same manner as those of antiquity have done ? No: human reason aspires in the present day to govern and reform societies after its own conceptions, to rule the exterior world according to general principles; that is to say, the thought, again become philosophical, has preserved the pretensions it held under the religous form; with this immense difference, it is true, that it would unite the liberty of thought with its power, and that even whilst it tries to take possession of societies, to govern them, and place the power in the hands of intelligence, it does not wish intelligence to be organized nor subjected to forms and a legal yoke. It is in the alliance of intellectual liberty, as it shone in antiquity, with the intellectual power, as it showed itself in Christian societies, that we find the great and original character of modern civilization; and it is, without doubt, in the bosom of the revolution effected by Christianity in the relations of the spiritual and temporal orders of thought and of the exterior world, that this new revolution has taken its origin and its first point of support.

At the epoch to which we are now come, at the end of the tenth century, the double fact which characterizes the first revolution, I mean the abdication of the liberty of the human intellect, and the increase of its social power, was already consummated. From the tenth century, you observe spiritual society pretending to the government of temporal society, that is, announcing that thought has a right to govern the world; and, at the same time, you observe thought subjected to the rules, the yoke of the church, and organized according to certain laws. These are the two most considerable results of the vicissitudes which intellectual order has suffered from the fifth to the tenth century, the two principal facts which the Christian element has thrown into modern civilization.

III. We come to the third primitive element of this civilization, the Germanic world or barbarism. Let us see what modern society has already received from it in the tenth century.

When we considered the condition of the Germans prior to the invasion, two facts especially, two forms of social organization, struck us:

1. The tribe formed of all the proprietary chiefs of family, governing itself by an assembly, where justice was rendered, and where public business was transacted—in one word, by the common deliberation of free men; a system very incom-

plete and precarious, without doubt, in such a state of socia relations and manners, but of which, however, glimpses may be caught of the principal rudiments.

2. Side by side with the tribe, we have met with the war like band, a society where the individual lived in so free a manner, that he could adopt it or reject it, according to his taste, and where the social principle was not equality of free men, and common deliberation, but the patronage of a chief towards his companions, who served him, and lived at his expense, that is to say, aristocratic and military subordination; words which ill answer to the idea which must be formed of a band of barbarians, but which describe the system of social organization which was about to issue from it.

Such are the two principles, or rather the two germs of principles, which Germany has furnished in the earliest times, to modern society in its nascent state. The principle of common deliberation of free men no more existed in the Roman world, unless in the bosoms of the municipal system; it was the Germans who restored it to the political order. The principle of aristocratic patronage, combined with a large portion of liberty, was become equally foreign to Roman society. Both the one and the other of these elements of our social organization are of German origin.

From the fifth to the tenth century they underwent great changes. At the end of this period, the assemblies, or government, by the voice of common deliberation, had disappeared; in fact there remained scarcely any trace of the ancient *mâls*, fields of Mars and May, or Germanic courts. The remembrance, however, of national assemblies, the right of free men to join together, to deliberate and transact their business together, resided in the minds of men as a primitive tradition and a thing which might again come about. It was with the ancient German assemblies as with imperial sovereignty: neither the one nor the other any longer existed; government by the voice of free deliberation and absolute power had equally fallen, yet without absolutely perishing. They were germs buried under immense heaps of ruins, but which yet might one day reappear and be fruitful. Such was, in fact, what really happened.

With respect to the patronage of the chief towards his companions, the acquisition of large domains and the territorial life had much changed this relation of the ancient Germans. We can no more find, in any degree worth mentioning, the same liberty which used to reign in the wandering band. Some had received benefices, and were settled in them; others had continued to live around their chief in his house and at his table. The chief was become eminently powerful, there was introduced into this little society much more inequality and fixedness. Nevertheless, although the aristocratic principle and the inequality which accompanies it, and which constitutes even it, had assumed a great development, they had not destroyed all the ancient relation between the chief and his companions. The inequality did not draw servility after it; and the society which resulted therefrom, and with which we will occupy ourselves more in detail hereafter, the feudal society reposed, for those at least who composed part of it, that is, the proprietors of fiefs, upon the principles of right and liberty.

In the tenth century, and under the social point of view, the Germanic element then had furnished to modern civilization in its nascent state, on the one hand, the remembrance of national assemblies, and of the right of free men to govern themselves in common; on the other hand, certain ideas, certain sentiments of right and liberty implanted in the bosom of an entirely aristocratic organization.

Under the moral point of view, although eminent writers have strongly insisted upon what modern Europe holds from the Germans, their assertions seem to me vague and too general; they make no distinction of epoch or country; and I think that, in western Europe, especially in France, the energetic sentiment of individual independence is the most important, I would willingly say the only great moral legacy which ancient Germany has transmitted to us.

There was, in the tenth century, a national German literature, consisting of songs and popular traditions, which hold a high place in the literary history of Germany, and which have exerted a great influence on its manners. But the part played by these traditions, and by all primitive German literature, in the intellectual development of France, has been very limited and fugitive; this is the reason why I have not entered upon it with you, though this literature is positively full of originality and interest.

Such was the state of the three great elements of modern civilization in the tenth century; such are the changes, social and moral, which Roman antiquity, Christianity, and barbarism have experienced on our soil.

From thence flow, if I mistake not, two general facts, two great results, which it is necessary to exhibit.

The work of M. de Savigny on the History of Roman Law, after the fall of the Empire, has changed the face of the science; he has proved that the Roman law had not perished; that, notwithstanding great modification, without doubt, it was transmitted from the fifth to the fifteenth century, and had always continued to form a considerable part of the legislation of the west.

If I am not mistaken, the facts which I have laid before your view, in this course, have generalized this result. It follows, I think, evidently, that not only in municipal institutions and civil laws, as M. de Savigny has proved, but in political order and philosophy, in literature and all departments, in a word, of social and intellectual life, Roman civilization was transmitted far beyond the date of the Empire; that we may everywhere discern a trace of it; that no abyss separates the Roman from the modern world; that the thread is nowhere broken; that we may recognize everywhere the transition of Roman society into our own; in a word, that the part played by the ancients in modern civilization is greater and more continuous than is commonly thought. A second result equally arises out of our labors, and characterizes the period which is the object of them. During all this period, from the fifth to the tenth century, we have nowhere been able to pause; we have been unable to find, either in social or intellectual order, any system, any fact, which became fixed, which took a firm, general, and regular hold on society or mind. The general fact with which we have been struck is a continual and universal fluctuation, a constant state of uncertainty and of transformation. It was, then, from the fifth to the tenth century, that the work of fermentation and amalgamation of the three elements of modern civilization, namely, the Roman element, the Christian element, and the German element, was in operation; and it was only at the end of the tenth century that the ferment ceased, and the amalgamation being nearly accomplished, the development of the new order and truly modern society commenced.

The history which we have just concluded, then, is the history of its very conception and creation. All things rise out of the chaos, modern society among the rest. That which we have studied now is the chaos, the cradle of France: what we shall have to study hereafter is France herself. Dating only from the end of the tenth century, the social being which bears that name, if I may thus speak, has been formed and exists ; we might attend it in its proper and exterior development. This development will merit, for the first time, the name of French civilization. Until now, we have spoken of Gaulish-Roman, Frankish, Gallo-Roman, and Gallo-Frankish civilization ; we have been obliged to combine foreign names in order to characterize, with any justice, a society without unity and certainty. When we again enter upon our labors, it will be to speak of French civilization ; we shall date therefrom ; the question will no longer be concerning Gauls, Franks, and Romans, but of Frenchmen, of ourselves.

ILLUSTRATIONS AND HISTORICAL TABLES.

On authorizing the publication of these lectures, I promised to add to them a number of tables and documents intended to prove or to explain the ideas which I might have occasion to express. I have inserted some of these tables in the lectures themselves. There are some others for which I could not find a place there, and which seem to me no less necessary. I give them here. It would have been both easy and useful to multiply illustrations of this kind; but I have been obliged to limit myself. The object of those which I have selected is both to show in their developments facts which I have been merely able to point out, and to place before the reader those events, the knowledge of which I took for granted. They are seven in number:—

    I. Table of the organization of the court, and of the central government of the Roman empire at the commencement of the fifth century—that is to say, at the epoch which I took as the starting point of the course.
   II. Table of the hierarchy of ranks and titles in Roman society at the same epoch.
  III. Narrative of the embassy sent in 449 by Theodosius the Younger, emperor of the west, to Attila, established on the banks of the Danube.
  IV. Chronological table of the principal events of the political history of Gaul, from the fifth to the tenth century.
   V. Chronological table of the principal events of the ecclesiastical history of Gaul, from the fifth to the tenth century.
  VI. Chronological table of the principal events of the literary history of Gaul, from the fifth to the tenth century.
 VII. Table of the councils and canonical legislation of Gaul, from the fifth to the tenth century.

Unless I am much deceived, there is no occasion for me to insist upon the utility of these documents—it will speak for itself; and for persons who weigh and study them attentively, the history of our civilization, so obscure and so vague in its cradle, will appear, I think, under more clear and precise forms. This is my aim and hope in publishing them.

I.

Table of the Organization of the Court and of the Central Government of the Roman Empire, at the commencement of the Fifth Century.

It was under the reigns of Diocletian and of Constantine that the court and the central government of the Roman emperors gained that systematic and definitive organization, whose image the *notitia imperii Romani* has preserved to us. It was the same both in the empire of the east and in that of the west, with the exception of some unimportant differences occasioned by that of localities. For the basis of this table I have adopted the empire of the east, the most complete and the best known of the two, taking care to point out here and there facts which distinguish the empire of the west.

IMPERIAL COURT.

I.—*Præpositus sacri cubiculi* (grand chamberlain).

He had under his orders a large number of officers, divided into six classes, *scholæ*, and all named *palatini;* their duty in the palace was called *in palatio militare.* The principal were:—

1.—*Primicerius sacri cubiculi* (first chamberlain).—He was at the head of all those who served the emperor in his apartments, and accompanied him everywhere for this purpose; they were named *cubicularii* (chamberlains or valets de chambre); they were divided into parties of ten men, at the head of each of which was a *decanus*.

2.—*Comes castrensis* (count of the palace).—The chief of those who served the emperor at table, and took care of the interior of the palace; this was a kind of steward or maître-d'hotel. He had under his orders:—

(1.) *Primicerius mensorum*, the chief of those who, when the emperor travelled, went before to get everything prepared upon his road, and in the places where he was to stop.

(2.) *Primicerius cellariorum*, chief of all those employed in the kitchens and offices.

(3.) *Primicerius pædagogiorum*, the chief of the young pages, brought up for service in the interior of the palace.

(4.) *Primicerius lampadariorum*, the chief of those who overlooked the lighting of the palace. There was in this class a number of sub-divisions and subaltern officers.

3.—*Comes sacræ vestis* (count of the sacred wardrobe).—He was charged with the imperial wardrobe, and commanded many officers.

4.—*Chartularii cubiculi* (secretaries of the chamber).—They were generally three in number, and were the private secretaries of the emperor; and although occupied with public affairs, they were under the direction of the *præpositus sacri cubiculi*, because their service was personal.

5.—*Decurionus III. silentiariorum.*—The *silentiarii* were charged with preventing all noise in the palace: the thirty principal were subdivided into three parties of ten, each commanded by a decurion.

6.—*Comes domorum per Cappadociam.*—This was the steward of the property which the emperor of the east possessed in Cappadocia; these patrimonial estates were very considerable; the *comes domorum* directed their administration and collected the revenues: he held office as a magistrate.

II.—*Comites domesticorum equitum peditumque* (counts of the cavalry and infantry of the palace).

These were the two commanders of the select bands of cavalry and infantry who guarded the person of the emperor. These bands, who were called *protectores domestici*, were drawn from the seven schools of Armenian soldiers, called *palatini*, and destined for the military service of the palace. The seven schools formed a body of 3500 men, from among whom were taken the *protectores domestici*, who enjoyed great privileges. The counts of the domestic infantry and cavalry also had under their orders *deputati*, charged with executing their commands in the provinces.

The empress also had her court, organized in nearly the same manner as that of the emperor.

CENTRAL GOVERNMENT.

I.—*Magister officiorum* (master of the offices).

This was a sort of universal minister, whose functions were very extensive; he administered justice to almost all the officers of the palace (*palatini*), received the appeals of private citizens, presented senators to the princes, &c. His jurisdiction also extended over the officers belonging to other departments, such as the *mensores*, the *lampadarii*, and those who were in the department of the *præpositus sacri cubiculi*. He had under his jurisdiction:—

1.—The seven schools of the *milites palatini*. (1.) Schola scutariorum prima; (2.) Schola scutariorum secunda; (3.) Gentilium seniorum; (4.) Scutariorum sagittariorum; (5.) Armaturarum juniorum; (7.) Gentilium juniorum.

2.—The school of the *agentes in rebus:* these were the messengers and spies of the princes in the provinces: before Constantine they were called *frumentarii*.

3. The *mensores* and the *lampadarii*, of whom we have already spoken; also, the *admissionales*, or the gentlemen ushers of the palace, and the *invitatores*, who were charged with transmitting invitations.

4.—Four *scrinia* or officers, where the affairs of the prince with his subjects were immediately managed.

(1.) *Scrinium memoriæ*. Here were kept registers of employments and grades; hence, for the most part, issued the nominations.

(2.) *Scrinium epistolarum:* here were received the deputations and requests from cities, and hence were dispatched the answers of the prince.

(3.) *Scrinium libellorum;* hither were addressed the requests and appeals of subjects.

(4.) *Scrinium dispositionum:* the functions of this last office resembled those of the two preceding ones; it is omitted in the *notitia*, but the laws make mention of it.

Each of these offices had its own chief, *magister scrinii memoriæ, epistolarum*, &c.; the last was called *comes dispositionum;* there were numerous officers in it.

5.—The armorers of the empire. The master of the offices of the east had fifteen under his direction: Damascus, Antioch, 2; Edessa, Irenopolis, Cæsarea in Cappadocia, Nicodemia, 2; Sardis, Adrianople, 2; Thessalonica, Naissus, Ratiaria, Margus. The master of the offices of the west had nineteen: Sirmium, Acincum, Cornutum, Lauriacum, Salona, Concordia, Verona, Mantua, Cremona, Pavia, Lucca, Strasburg, Macon, Autun, Besançon, Reims, Trèves, 2; Amiens.

II.—*Quæstor* (the questor).

He judged in concert with the pretorian prefect, and sometimes alone, affairs referred to the prince: he composed the laws and edicts which the prince was to publish; he signed the rescripts; he had the superintendence of the register (*laterculum minus*), in which were enumerated the tribunes and the prefects of the camps and frontiers. He was a kind of high chancellor. He sent his edicts to the *scrinium dispositionum*, where they were kept, and copies distributed throughout the empire. He had no offices attached to his post, but he had twelve secretaries in the *scrinium memoriæ*, seven in the *scrinium epistolarum*, and seven in the *scrinium libellorum*

III.—*Comes sacrarum largitionum* (count of the sacred largesses)

This was the high treasurer of the empire; he collected and administered all the public revenues; all the payments issued from his office; Constantine put him in the place of the questors, the *præfecti ærarii*, &c.

His administration was divided into two offices, *scrinia*, at the head of which was a *primicerius*, or *magister scrinii* (chief of the office).

1. *Scrinium canonum.*—This, it seems, was the office in which was prepared the account of what each province, each town, &c., was to send to the public chest, *arcæ largitionum*.

2. *Scrinium tabulariorum*,
3. *Scrinium numerariorum*, } These two offices kept an account of the moneys received and expended by the treasury.

4. *Scrinium aureæ massæ.*—This office was occupied in keeping account of the bullion which was sent to the treasury, and of the use made of it in coining money, in the decoration of public monuments, in crown jewels, &c.

5. *Scrinium auri ad responsum.*—They here regulated and furnished the sums of money, whether intended to supply the expenses of the officers whom the prince sent into the provinces, of the armies, &c., or whether to be sent into the different parts of the empire, or for tribute paid to allies, barbarians, &c.

6. *Scrinium ab argento.*—This was the office where were deposited silver in ingots, the imperial plate, vases, &c.

7. *Scrinium vestiarii sacri.*—This was the office from whence issued the funds for the clothing of troops, the monarch, the imperial family, the people of his court, to whom he furnished clothing.

8. *Scrinium annularense vel miliarense.*—According to the first reading, this office would be intended to preserve the rings and jewels of the emperor; according to the second, which seems to me the most probable, its intention was to strike and distribute the small silver money, called *miliarensium*, of which the value was the tenth part of an *aureus*.

9. *Scrinium à pecuniis.*—Pancirollus thinks that it was this office which directed the coining of money throughout the empire.

10. *Scrinium exceptorum.*—The clerks of this office wrote out the account of the cases which had been judged by the count of the sacred largesses.

The attributes of these various offices were very uncertain, their names are obscure, and we can only conjecture their object. It seems that they afterwards added an eleventh office, called *scrinium mittendariorum*, and composed of officers who were sent into the provinces to get the payment of taxes hastened and completed.

Besides these offices attached to his service, the count of the largesses had a great number of subordinates in the provinces, charged with directing the affairs of his department. The principal were:—

1. Six *comites largitionum*, in the east, in Egypt, in Asia Minor, in Pontus, in Thrace, and Illyria; there were five of these in the west. They were charged with paying the salaries of the generals, soldiers, and other officers, and to overlook the collection of taxes.

2. Four *comites commerciorum*, charged with buying the stuffs and jewels necessary for the imperial household, with overlooking the operations of the merchants, and watching that the duties levied upon the commodities should be correctly paid. There was but one in the west.

3. *Præfecti thesaurorum;* they received and kept, in each province, the money proceeding from taxes, until it was sent to the count of the sacred largesses.

4. *Comes metallorum*, charged with deducting, from the produce of the mines of gold, silver, or other metals, the portion which went to the prince.

5. *Comes vel rationalis Ægypti*, charged with collecting the property which fell to the prince in that province, whether by escheat, or any other cause; he also superintended the great commerce in Indian merchandise, which passed through Egypt; there were eleven *rationales* of this kind in the west.

6. *Magistri lineæ vel tinteæ vestis;* they directed all the laborers who worked in flax for the wardrobe or furniture of the emperor. Their office was filled in the west by a *comes vestiarii*.

7. *Privatæ magistri;* they directed the workmen in silk, linen, &c., for the royal household.

8. *Procuratores gynæciorum;* charged with the superintending of spun and wove fabrics.

9. *Procuratores baphiorum;* inspectors of the dying of stuffs in purple, &c. There were nine in the west.

10. *Procuratores monetarum;* mint inspectors. There were six of them in the west.

11. *Præpositi bastagarum*, charged with the superintending the transport of goods intended for the public service, or that of the emperor, corn, commodities, merchandise, silver, &c.

12. *Procuratores linificiorum*, charged with procuring the flax necessary for the imperial fabrics. There were two in the west, at Vienna and at Ravenna.

IV. *Comes rerum privatarum* (the crown treasurer).

The public treasury was called *ærarium;* the private treasure of the emperor was called *fiscus*. Although he equally disposed of both one and the other, yet there was a distinction, and they were administered separately.

The *comes sacrarum largitionum* had the administration of the *ærarium;* and the *comes rerum privatarum* had that of the *fiscus*, whose revenues were the property which devolved upon the emperor in any manner whatsoever, the produce of certain taxes, &c. He had under his orders:

1. A department directed by the *primicerius officii*, and divided into four offices.

(1.) *Scrinium beneficiorum.*—Here were managed all affairs relative to gifts of property, real or personal, to the concession of privileges, &c., which the emperor made to such or such of his subjects.

(2.) *Scrinium canonum.*—This office received the rents of the farms on the imperial property, and kept the accounts of them. The rent was paid in money or in kind.

(3.) *Scrinium securitatum.*—In this office were deposited the receipts of those who had received the money of the fisc; and the duplicates of those which had been given to people who had paid anything to the fisc.

(4.) *Scrinium largitionum privatarum.*—Here were kept the accounts of money given by the emperor to individuals, and the salaries which he paid to the people attached to his personal service.

2. *Rationales vel procuratores rerum privatarum.*—These were officers charged with collecting the revenues of the fisc, in the provinces. They were often judges in cases where the fisc was concerned.

3. *Præpositi bastagarum rei privatæ*, inspectors of transports made for the service of the prince. There were two of these in the west.

4. *Præpositi stabulorum, gregum et armentorum*, inspectors of the studs and herds of the emperor throughout the empire. There was also a *comes stabuli*, answering to our master of the horse.

5. *Procuratores saltuum*, inspector of the woods and pasturages where the herds of the emperor were taken to graze.

There were, doubtless, many other petty officers, mention of whom has not come down to us.

V. *Primicerius notariorum* (first secretary of state).

This was a magistrate charged with keeping the register in which were inscribed all the public functionaries, their duties, salaries, warrants of nomination, &c. This register was called *laterculum majus*. The people nominated to the places, paid certain fees to this *primicerius notariorum*, who thus kept the list of all the dignities which we have just enumerated. There were three classes of *notarii*.

In each province there was a provincial chest, in all one hundred and eighteen chests. The receiver of taxes transmitted the money to these chests, under the superintendence of the *præfecti thesaurorum*. These latter gave to the *comites largitionum* the sums necessary for the expenses of the province, the salary of the officers, &c. They transmitted the balance to the governor of the province, who sent it to the chest of the sacred bounty. The carriages intended to transport it, were furnished by men kept on purpose, and formed part of the public post (*cursus publicus*), which the government alone, or those whom it authorized, had to make use of.

II.

Table of the Hierarchy of Ranks and Titles in the Roman Empire at the commencement of the Fifth Century.

Rank and titles multiplied in the Roman empire, at the same epoch in which the court and central government received their definitive form, as given in the preceding table. These ranks and titles conferred important privileges upon the possessors, with reference to the other citizens, but in no degree rendered them independent of power They were mere personal distinctions attached to certain offices, and which even the holders of these offices did not enjoy, until they had been authorized to assume them by letters patent from the prince There were six principal ranks or titles, the rights of precedence among which were minutely regulated.

I. *Nobilissimi*

This was the highest of the titles; it came close to the throne, and conferred, to a certain extent, the dignity of Cæsar. It was bestowed upon the members and allies of the imperial family.

II. *Illustres.*

The persons decorated with this title were twenty-seven in number—viz.,

1. The pretorian prefect of the East.
2. The pretorian prefect of Illyria.
3. The pretorian prefect of Italy.
4. The pretorian prefect of Gaul.
5. The prefect of Constantinople.
6. The prefect of Rome.
7—11. The five generals, commanders of the army in the East
12. The general of the horse in the West.
13. The general of the infantry in the West.
14, 15. The two grand chamberlains of the East and West.
16, 17. The two masters of the offices in the East and West.
18, 19. The two questors of the palace in the East and West.
20, 21. The two counts of the sacred largesses in the East and West
22, 23. The two counts of the privy purse in the East and West.
24, 25. The two counts commanding the body-guard, cavalry, in the East and West.
26, 27. The two counts commanding the body-guard, infantry, in the East and West.

The consuls were also *illustres.* The date of the introduction of this title is not known. Augustus used to select every month, at first fifteen, and afterwards twenty, members of the senate, to form his privy council; their decisions were held as having emanated from the entire body of the senate; they were called *patricii*, while the other senators were only entitled *clarissimi.* They, in concurrence with the sovereign, discussed and directed public affairs. Constantine formed of them his *consistorium principes* (council of state), and entitled the members *comites consistoriani.* They were, with the consuls, the first honored with the title of *illustres*, which was afterwards extended, probably also under Constantine, to the magistrates above mentioned. The *illustres* were addressed thus,—*vestra tua*, or *tua, magnificentia, celsitudo, sublimitas, magnitudo, eminentia, excellentia,* &c. Those who neglected to observe the etiquette in this respect, had to pay a fine of three pounds in gold.

The *illustres* could only be tried for any offence by the prince in person, or his immediate delegates; they were entitled to have their sentences read by the registrar; they were prohibited from making a traffic of their power and influence, and from marrying women of an inferior rank; this latter prohibition, however, was recalled at a later period; neither they nor their families could be put to the torture, nor be subjected to any of the capital punishments inflicted on plebeians; they were exempted from being summoned to any court as witnesses, &c.

II. *Spectabiles*

Of these there were sixty-two.

1, 2. The first two chamberlains in the East and West. (*Primicerii sacri cubiculi.*)

3, 4. The two counts of the palace, in the East and West. (*Comites castrenses.*)

5, 6. The two chief secretaries of the emperor, in the East and West (*Primicerii notariorum.*)

7—13. The seven heads of the principal departments of the central government in the East and West. (*Magistri scriniorum.*)

14—16. The three proconsuls (governors of dioceses or provinces) of Asia, Achaia, and Africa.

17. The count of the East.

18. The prefect of Egypt. (*Præfectus Augustalis.*)

19—29. Eleven vicars, or governors of dioceses; five in the empire of the East, and six in the empire of the West.

30—37. Eight counts, or generals of armies; two in the East, and six in the West.

38—62. Twenty-five dukes, or generals of armies; thirteen in the East, and twelve in the West.

The title of *spectabiles* was also given to the senators, probably under Constantine. It seems to have had no other origin than the mania for the classification of ranks. It was very uncertain in its application, we find it given to men who are called elsewhere *clarissimi,* or *perfectissimi,* or even *egregii;* thus the *duces,* the *silentiarii* (ushers in law courts), the *notarii* (secretaries), are designated sometimes by the one, sometimes by the other of these appellations.

IV. *Clarissimi.*

We find this title already, under Tiberius, in possession of the senators and senatorial families. After a certain number of senators had become *illustres,* the rest continued to assume the title of *clarissimi,* and by degrees it became extended to all the inferior officers employed in the provinces. At the commencement of the fifth century there were, it would appear, 115 persons addressed by this title—viz.,

Thirty-seven consular personages, governors of provinces; fifteen in the East, and twenty-two in the West.

Five *correctores,* governors of provinces; two in the East, and three in the West.

Seventy-three *præsides*, governors of provinces; forty-two in the East, and three in the West.

V. *Perfectissimi.*

This title was invented by Constantine; we find it, indeed, made use of in the law of Diocletian, but it was Constantine who introduced it into his classification of ranks, and divided the *perfectissimi* into three grades. The title was given,
    To the *præsides*, or governors, of Arabia, Isauria, and Dalmatia.
    To the *rationales*, collectors of the public revenues in the provinces.
    To the *magistri scriniorum*, heads of the offices of the court of the sacred largesses.
    To the counts of the sacred largesses, or imperial collectors and paymasters in the provinces.
    And to many other persons in the public service.

VI. *Egregii.*

This last title was very common; it appertained to all the imperial secretaries, to all the persons employed in the offices of the various governors of the provinces, to priests, to the crown lawyers, and to a whole host of other persons.

III.

Narrative of the Embassy sent in 449 to Attila, by Theodosius the Younger, Emperor of the East.

INTRODUCTION.

There is scarcely any feature of the history of this period which it were more interesting to be thoroughly acquainted with, than the relations of the Roman emperors with the barbarians, the Germans, Huns, Slavonians, &c., who pressed upon their frontiers. A knowledge of this can alone enable us to form anything like a precise and accurate idea of the comparative state of Roman and of barbarian civilization. Unfortunately, the materials of this knowledge are very deficient; we have upon the subject little more than mere sentences, paragraphs, scattered throughout the Latin chroniclers, the confused traditions of the German tribes, or some old poems which, in their present form, are evidently greatly posterior to the fourth and fifth century. The narrative of the embassy sent in 449 by Theodosius the Younger to Attila, at that time master of the whole of Germany, and himself established on the Danube, is, unquestionably, the fullest and most instructive of the monuments remaining to us of this branch of history; the only one, in fact, which shows us the interior of the states, and the life of a barbarian chief, and enables us to examine closely, and, as it were, in person, his relations with the Romans: the narrative itself is of the highest authenticity; it formed part of the history of the war against Attila, in seven books, written by the sophist Priscus, of Panium in Thrace, a member of the embassy; it has come down to us among the *Excerpta legationum*, inserted in the first vo-

lume of the Collection of Byzantine historians, and which formed the
53d book of a great historical collection made by one Theodosius, by
order of Constantine VI. Porphyrogenitus (911-959). I here present you with a literal translation of this interesting production. The
narrative, it is true, relates to the empire of the east, not to that of
the west, and to Hun barbarians, not to German barbarians: but the
relative situation of the two empires and of the two classes of barbarians at this period was very nearly the same; the social state and
manners of the Huns, notwithstanding the diversity of origin and of
language, very closely resembled, in general outline, at all events,
those of the Germans. We may, therefore, in the absence of documents specially relating to the Germans or to the west, regard the
narrative before us, as a tolerably faithful image of the relations of the
expiring empire with its future conquerors.

448—449.

Embassy of Attila to Theodosius. Plot of Chrysaphus the Eunuch to
take away the life of Attila by means of Edeco and Vigilius.
Embassy of Theodosius to Attila. Details as to the manners of
the Huns; their mode of life, &c.

The Scythian Edeco, who had performed great military exploits,
again came with Orestes, in quality of envoy; the latter, a Roman by
birth, lived in Pæonia, a country situate on the Savus, and which, in
virtue of the treaty with Ætius, general of the western Romans, was
now subject to the barbarian.

This Edeco, on being admitted into the palace, presented to the emperor letters from Attila, in which the barbarian complained that the
deserters from his camp had not been brought back to him, and threat-
ened to resume hostilities unless they were forthwith restored; and,
moreover, unless the Romans at once abstained from cultivating for
themselves the territory which the fortune of war had added to his
dominions. Now this territory extended along the Danube from Pæonia to Thrace; its breadth was fifteen days' march. Moreover, the
barbarian required that the great market should no longer be held, as
heretofore, on the banks of the Danube, but at Naissus, which town,
taken and sacked by him, and distant from the Danube five days' rapid
march, was situate he said, at the limit of the Scythian and Roman
states. Finally, he ordered that ambassadors should be sent to him,
men not of common birth and dignity, but consular personages, to receive whom, he added, he would come as far as Sardica.

These letters having been read, Edeco quitted the presence in company with Vigilius, who had acted as interpreter of the words of
Attila; and after having visited the other apartments, repaired to that
of Chrysaphus, servant of the emperor, and in great favor and authority
with him.

The barbarian had greatly admired the magnificence of the imperial
abode. Vigilius, who still accompanied him as interpreter, repeated
to Chrysaphus his expressions of praise of the imperial palace, and his
feeling that the Romans must be very happy by reason of their vast
wealth. Chrysaphus hereupon told Edeco that he might himself have
a similar abode, splendidly decorated, with gilded ceilings, and be
placed in possession of every other advantage he might desire, if he

would quit Scythia to reside at Rome. Edeco replied that it was not permissible to the servant of a foreign prince to take this step without his master's sanction. The eunuch asked him whether had easy access to Attila, and what power he was invested with in his own country. Edeco replied, that he and Attila were upon terms of familiar intercourse, and that he was one of the guards who took it in turn to keep watch over that prince in his abode. The eunuch then said, that if Edeco would do a certain service for him, he would confer upon him very important advantages; but that, as the affair required deliberation, he would communicate it to him after he had taken supper, if he would then return to his apartment without Orestes and his other fellow ambassadors. The barbarian promised to do so; and, accordingly, after he had supped, again presented himself to Chrysaphus.

After they had, by means of the interpreter Vigilius, exchanged mutual oaths, the eunuch, not to propose anything to the detriment of Edeco, but solely what should be to his great advantage, the latter not to reveal what should be proposed to him, even though he should not execute it, the eunuch told Edeco that if on his return to Scythia he would kill Attila, he should pass the rest of his life in affluence and luxury Edeco consented to the proposition, and said that he should want some money to effect the business, about fifty pounds in gold, to divide among the soldiers under his orders, and in other ways to facilitate his proceedings. The eunuch offered to give him the amount he named at once; but the barbarian said that, in the first place, it would be advisable to send him back, accompanied by Vigilius, to give Attila the answer that should be determined upon respecting the deserters; that then he and Vigilius would consult further upon the best mode of executing the design, and that this being settled, Vigilius should come for the money; this, he said, would be better than for him to take the gold with him, seeing that, immediately upon his return, in the first instance, Attila would assuredly interrogate him and his fellows as to whether they had received any presents, and as to how much money the Romans had given them, and that in such case, were he to take the money at once, it would be impossible for him to keep the fact a secret, by reason of his companions. The eunuch admitted the soundness of the barbarian's view of the matter, and acted upon it.

After that Edeco had taken his leave, Chrysaphus repaired to the emperor's privy council, who immediately sent for Martial, the minister of the offices, and communicated to him the agreement entered into with the barbarian; for it was the very nature of his post that he should be made acquainted with the matter, he being on all occasions a confidential adviser of the emperor, and having under his orders all the couriers and interpreters, and all the troops entrusted with the guard of the palace. The emperor and Martial having considered the whole affair, it was determined to send to Attila not only Vigilius, but Maximin also, as ambassador. Vigilius, whose ostensible office was that of interpreter, was to fulfil the directions of Edeco; while Maximin, who knew nothing of the real affair in hand, was to deliver the emperor's letter to Attila.

The emperor's letter was to the effect, that he had sent Vigilius as interpreter, and had selected Maximin as his ambassador, who was superior to Vigilius in rank, being of illustrious birth, and employed about his own person in many affairs; that it was not fitting that Attila, violating treaties, should invade the Roman territory; that he had already sent back to him a great many deserters, and now forwarded seventeen more, being all that remained of those who had come over to him.

Besides these things which were set forth in the letter, Maximin was ordered to ask Attila, by word of mouth, not to request men of higher rank to be sent to him as ambassadors; adding, that the predecessors of the emperor had been accustomed to send to those who heretofore ruled in Scythia, merely one of their soldiers who had become a prisoner of Rome, or any other private messenger who was capable of repeating that which he was told to say. That with reference to the other matters which still kept up dissension between them, he would suggest that Attila should send him Onegeses as an envoy; that it was impossible Attila could properly receive a consular personage in a devastated place like Sardica.

Maximin having, at the earnest request of the emperor, undertaken the proposed embassy, asked me to accompany him, and we departed with the barbarians, and proceeded to Sardica, which is thirteen days' rapid march from Constantinople. On our arrival, we invited Edeco and some other principal barbarians to dine with us. Several oxen and sheep furnished by the inhabitants of the place were slaughtered and prepared in various ways, and everything being ready, we sat down to our repast. During the banquet the barbarians exalted Attila to the skies, and we the emperor. Vigilius imprudently went the length of saying that it was not fitting to compare a man with a god; that the emperor was a god, and Attila only a man. The Huns took this in very ill part, and by degrees became inflamed with the fiercest anger. We endeavored to turn the conversation, and to appease them by soft words, which we at length succeeded in doing.

On rising from table, Maximin, desirous of conciliating by presents Edeco and Orestes, gave them silk garments and precious stones of India. Orestes, Edeco having withdrawn, said to Maximin that he was the wise and prudent man who took care not to do as so many others did, and who avoided anything that might be offensive to kings. We found out afterwards that some of our people, neglecting Orestes, had invited Edeco to supper, and loaded him with presents. At the time, ignorant of this circumstance, and not understanding what Orestes meant, we asked him how and in what he had been treated displeasingly; but he gave us no answer, and quitted us.

Next day, on continuing our journey, we related to Vigilius what Orestes had said. He observed that the latter had no right to complain of not obtaining the same honors with Edeco; that he was but a servant, a common secretary of Attila, whilst Edeco, a Hun by birth, and famous for his military exploits, far surpassed him in dignity. He then addressed Edeco in the native language of the latter, and afterwards told us, whether it was true or false I know not, that he had repeated to Edeco what we had mentioned. Edeco became so angry that we had great difficulty in tranquillizing him.

On arriving at the town of Naissus, which had been taken and destroyed by the enemy, we found no inhabitants there except a few invalids, who had taken refuge in the ruins of the temples. Proceeding thence into the desert plains at some distance from the river, the banks of which were covered with the bones of those who had been killed during the war, we arrived at the abode of Agintheus, chief of the soldiers of Illyria, who dwelt not far from Naissus. We had with as orders from the emperor for him to deliver up to us five deserters, who were to complete the number of seventeen, mentioned in the letter to Attila. We went to Aginthcus and applied for them; and after he had addressed some words of consolation to them, he made them depart with us.

It was scarcely yet day when we crossed the mountains of Naissus towards the Danube. We arrived, after many turnings and windings, in a certain town which was still dark. We thought that our road should turn towards the west; but as soon as it was day, the rising sun presented itself before our eyes. Ignorant of the position of this place, we exclaimed, as if the sun, which we saw in front of us, was following another than its accustomed course, and thus indicated commotion in the regular course of things; but it was because of the inequalities of places that this part of the route turned towards the east.

From this place, by a steep and difficult road, we descended into the swampy plains. There the barbarian boatmen received us in canoes, made of a single piece, which they construct from the trunks of trees cut and scooped out, and they passed us over the river.[1] It was not for our passage that these canoes had been prepared, but for that of a multitude of barbarians whom we met upon the road, for Attila seemed marching to the invasion of the frontiers of the empire as to a hunting party. Such were the preparations for war against the Romans, and the deserters not yet being given up, merely served as a pretext for commencing it.

After having passed the Danube, and having proceeded with the barbarians the distance of fifteen stadia, they made us stop in a plain, to wait while Edeco went to announce our arrival to Attila.[2] The barbarians who were to be our guides still remained with us. Towards night, while we were at supper, we heard the sound of approaching horses: two Scythian warriors soon appeared, who ordered us to repair to Attila. We invited them first to partake of our supper; they descended from their horses, supped with us, and the next day marched before us to show us the road. About the eighth hour of the day we arrived at the tent of Attila.[3] There was also a large number of others. As we wished to plant ours on a certain hill, the barbarians hastened to prevent us, because those of Attila were placed in a valley on the side. We left them to decide at their will where our tents were to be pitched.

There soon arrived Edeco, Scotta, Orestes, and some other principal

---

[1] They probably passed the Danube near the small town of *Aquæ*, whose environs, situated between a chain of mountains and the river, must have been marshy; perhaps it was at the confluence of the Marcus with the Danube.

[2] This plain must be in the Bannet of Temeswar; the tents of Attila were, therefore, probably pitched between the Themes and the Danube.

[3] Reckoning an hour's march at a league, their tents would be about nine leagues from the Danube. The great number of boats already prepared upon the Danube for the passage of troops, and the multitude of barbarians whom the ambassadors had met, induce me to believe that they were not, in fact, more distant from it

Scythians, who demanded with what object we had undertaken this embassy. We mutually looked at each other, astonished at so ridiculous a question. They still insisted, and assembled in a crowd and tumult to force an answer from us. We answered that the emperor had commanded us to show our commission to Attila alone, and to none others. Scotta, offended at these words, said that for what he did he had received the order of his chief. "Greeks," cried he, "we well know your craft and your perfidy in affairs." We protested that the obligation had never been imposed upon ambassadors to display the object of their mission before being admitted into the presence of those to whom they were sent.

We added, that the Scythians must needs know it, since they had often sent deputies to the emperor, and that we ought in all respects to enjoy the same rights; that, otherwise, the privileges of ambassadors would be violated. They immediately went to seek Attila, and, returning soon after, but without Edeco, they openly told us all that our orders contained, and enjoined us to depart immediately, if we had nothing further to treat of with them.

These words threw us into great anxiety; we could not conceive how the projects of the emperor, which the gods themselves could not penetrate, had been discovered and revealed; but we thought it best not to show any of our orders until they had allowed us to see Attila. We answered; "whatever may be the aim of our mission, whether we may have come to treat of what you have just said, or of any other matter, it concerns only your chief, and we are resolved to speak with none but him." They then renewed their order for us to depart immediately.

As we were making our preparations for departure, Vigilius reproached us for the answer which we had just made to the Scythians: "It would have been much better to have lied," said he, "than to return without having done anything. If I had spoken with Attila, I could easily have deterred him from making war against the Romans; I have formerly rendered him many services, and I was very useful to him at the time of the embassy of Anatolius. Edeco is of the same opinion as myself." Whether he spoke true or false, his only object was to profit by the embassy, to find an occasion to make Attila fall into the snare prepared for him, and to carry back the gold which Edeco had said he required to divide among certain warriors. But Vigilius was ignorant that he was betrayed: Edeco, in fact, whether he feared that Orestes would report to Attila what had been said at the supper at Sardica, or accuse him of having secret interviews with the emperor and Chrysaphus, had revealed to Attila the conspiracy against his life, and informed him of the quantity of gold which was to be provided for this design, as well as of all the subjects concerning which we were to treat in our embassy.

Forced, therefore, to return, despite the approach of night, we were getting ready our horses, when the barbarians came to tell me that Attila ordered we should remain, by reason of the night, which opposed our departure. Men immediately came leading an ox to us, and brought us fish of the Danube,[1] which Attila sent us. After having

---

[1] The carp of the Danube were celebrated at this epoch, and formed

supped, we went to sleep. When day appeared, we hoped that Attila would be softened, and would make us some favorable answer; but the same barbarians came on his part to repeat the order for us to go, if we had no other business to speak of except that with which he was already acquainted. We answered that we had not, and we prepared to retreat, although Vigilius did all he could to get us to say that we had to speak with Attila of things which would much interest him.

As I saw that Maximin was afflicted, I took with me Rusticus, who understood the language of the barbarians: he had accompanied us into Scythia, not because of the embassy, but for some private business which he had with Constantius, an Italian by origin, whom Aetius, the general of the western Romans, had sent to Attila as a secretary. I sought Scotta (Onegeses being absent), and told him, through the medium of Rusticus, that he should receive rich presents from Maximin, if he would procure a safe interview with Attila. I added that the ambassador had to speak of things very advantageous, not only to the Romans, but to the Huns; that this embassy would be very profitable to Onegeses himself, for the emperor requested Attila to send him to his court, to terminate the differences of the two nations, and that he would return loaded with the most magnificent presents. I observed to him, that since Onegeses was absent, he could not do less than his brother would have done in so important an affair. "I know," said I, "that Attila also places great confidence in you; but we cannot reasonably believe all one has heard on this point, and it is for you to prove to us that Attila really bestows such favor upon you." "Rest content," said the barbarian immediately, "whether in speaking or acting, I have as much credit with Attila as my brother," and, mounting his horse, he departed for the camp of Attila.

I returned to Maximin, whom I found with Vigilius, very much troubled and uncertain as to the course he ought to take; I recounted to him the conversation I had just had with Scotta, and what answer he had given me; I then got him to prepare presents to make to this Hun, and to think what he should say to Attila. They immediately arose (for I had found them lying on the turf), thanked me for the trouble I had taken, and recalled those of their people who had already commenced their journey; they then discussed between them what Maximin should say to Attila, and how they should give him the presents which he brought for him on the part of the emperor.

While we were occupied with these things, Attila sent for us by Scotta; we therefore set forward toward his tent, which we found surrounded by a multitude of barbarians, who formed a guard all round it.

When we were allowed to enter, and had been introduced, we saw Attila seated on a wooden chair: we remained at some distance from the throne; Maximin advanced, saluted the barbarian, and giving the letter of the emperor, said that the emperor wished him and all his people health and prosperity. "May that happen to the Romans which they desire for me!" answered the barbarian; and immediately

---

part of the luxury of the tables of the barbarians. Cassiodorus says: *Privati est habere quod locus continet; in principali convivio hoc decet exquiri quod visum debeat admirari. Destinet carpam Danubius, a Rheno veniat ancorago.* (Vari., l. xii., ep. 4.)

turning towards Vigilius, he called him an impudent animal, asked him how he dared to present himself before him, when he must know what had been settled with reference to peace at the time when he accompanied the embassy of Anatolius, and added, that no other am. bassador ought to have approached him until all the deserters had been sent back. Vigilius attempted to reply that they had all been given up, and that there no longer remained one among the Romans; but Attila, becoming more and more heated, loaded him with reproaches and abuse, and raising his voice in fury, told him, that but for his respect for the character of ambassador which restrained his rage, he would have crucified him, and abandoned him to the vultures, to punish him for his audacity and the insolence of his language. He added, there were still many deserters among the Romans; and having a list brought on which their names were written, he ordered his secretaries to read it aloud.

After this reading had made known all who were still wanting, Attila required that Vigilius should immediately set out with Esla to carry an order to the Romans to send him all the Scythian deserters who were still in their power, and who had gone over to them since the time when Carpilion, son of Actius, general of the western Romans, had remained in his court. "I will not allow my slaves to bear arms against me," said he; "they shall not be any help to those who pretend to entrust to them the guard of lands which I have conquered. Where, throughout the whole Roman empire, is the city or fortress which can remain whole and erect, when I have decided that it shall be destroyed? After I have proclaimed my will concerning the deserters, let the envoys immediately return to me to announce whether their masters choose to return them, or whether they prefer war."

He had begun by ordering Maximin to await the answer which he should make to the letter of the emperor, but he demanded the presents forthwith. After having given them to him, we retired into our tent, where we conversed in our native tongue upon all that had just been said. As Vigilius was astonished at the abuse with which Attila had loaded him, he who had experienced so much benevolence and kindness from him in his first embassy, I told him I was very much afraid that some of the barbarians who had supped with us at Sardica had irritated Attila by telling him that Vigilius had called the emperor a god and Attila a man. This also appeared probable to Maximin, who was ignorant of the conspiracy formed against the king of the Huns: but Vigilius was in very great anxiety, and could not divine the cause of the abuse and rage of Attila; it was impossible to believe, as he afterwards said to us, that the conversation at the supper at Sardica had been reported to him, or that the conspiracy had been discovered. The fear which had overcome all hearts was such, that, with the exception of Edeco, none who surrounded Attila dare address a word to him; and Vigilius thought that Edeco would only be the more careful to keep everything a profound secret, both on account of the oath which he had taken, and by reason of the gravity of the affair. He would fear, in fact, that the crime of having been present at clandestine councils directed against Attila, would cause him to be treated as guilty, and very severely punished.

While we were a prey to this uneasiness, Edeco came in; he took **Vigilius** aside (he indeed feigned a wish to execute seriously and sin cerely the project which they had formed); he told him to bring the gold which he was to distribute among those whom ne made use of in striking the blow, and then he left us. Curiosity caused us to ask Vigilius what Edeco had just said to him; but, deceived himself, he persisted in deceiving us, and concealing the true subject of their conversation, he pretended that Edeco had reported to him that it was because of the deserters that Attila was so enraged against him; the king of the Huns required, he added, either that they should be given up to him, or that they should send him ambassadors, drawn from among the richest and most powerful men of the empire.

Our conversation was interrupted by people who came, on the part of Attila, to forbid both us and Vigilius to buy any Roman captive, or barbarian slave, or anything whatever, except the necessaries of life, until the differences between the Huns and the Romans were terminated. This prohibition was not without intention: he wished to detect Vigilius in the fact, by leaving him no pretext upon which he could excuse himself for having brought a considerable number of money. He also ordered us to wait for Onegeses, to receive from him the answer to our embassy, and that we ourselves should give him the presents sent by the emperor, and what we wished to have. Onegeses had, in fact, been sent to the Acatzires, with Attila's eldest son. After this order had been given to us, he made Vigilius and Esla set out for Constantinople, under the pretext of again demanding the deserters, but, in fact, with the intention that Vigilius should bring the gold promised to Edeco.

After the departure of Vigilius, we did not remain more than one day in this place; we departed with Attila for more distant places, towards the north. We had proceeded but a very short distance with the barbarians, when we changed the direction, according to the order of the Scythians, our guides.[1] Attila, however, stopped at a certain village, where he took for wife his daughter Esca, although he had already several wives; the laws of the Scythians allow this.[2]

---

[1] Priscus does not say what their new direction was: everything leads to the supposition that it was towards the west, and that in general their route lay almost constantly towards the north-west.

[2] This passage has been the subject of great discussion: the following is the phrase of Priscus: Ἐν ᾗ γαμειν θυγατερα Εσκαμ εβουλετο The sense which naturally presents itself is: "where he willed to espouse his daughter Esca." Still the *his* is wanting, and it would seem as though Priscus ought to have put ἑαυτου. Some learned men have inferred from this, that it was not his daughter whom Attila married, but that it was the daughter of Esca, and that it must be read, θυγατερα του Εσκαμ; they have remarked, and with reason, that the Greeks almost always made the proper names of barbarians, with which they were imperfectly acquainted, indeclinable; that if Attila had married his own daughter, Priscus would not have failed to insist upon the irregularity of such a marriage; and the desire to clear Attila from the crime of incest has made them regard this conjecture as certain. It is possibly well-founded; still they cannot dispute that the following phrase of Priscus, "The laws of the Scythians allow this," relates to Attila having married his daughter, as well as to the

Thence we proceeded across a great plain, over a level and easy road, and we met with many navigable rivers; the largest, after the Danube, are called the Dracon, the Tigas, and the Tiphisas. We crossed the most considerable upon boats of a single piece, which those who inhabit the banks of the river make use of; the others we crossed in canoes which the barbarians always have with them; for they carry them on chariots, to make use of upon ponds and inundated places. They brought us provisions from the villages, *millet* instead of wheat; *mead* instead of wine; it is thus that the inhabitants call them. Those who accompanied us to serve us, brought *millet*, and gave us a kind of drink made from barley, which the barbarians call *cam*.

At the approach of night, after a rather long journey, we set up our tents upon the borders of a morass, whence the inhabitants of the neighboring villages drew their water, which was very good to drink: but a violent hurricane, mixed with lightning, thunder, and rain, suddenly arising, our tent was overthrown, and our utensils thrown into the morass. Alarmed with this fall and with the storm, we abandoned the place; we dispersed ourselves, and each at hazard took the road which seemed best to him, amidst darkness and rain. Arrived at last, from different directions, at the huts of the village, we assembled and demanded with loud cries what we wanted. On this noise, the Scythians came out: they lighted the reeds which serve them for torches, and asked what we wanted, and why we raised such cries? the barbarians who accompanied us, answered that we had been dispersed and had lost our way in the tempest: they then granted us a generous hospitality, and made us a fire with dry reeds.

The mistress of the village, one of the wives of Bleda, sent us nourishment and beautiful women. This, among the Scythians, is looked upon as an honor. We thanked the women for the provisions which they had brought us, and we slept in our huts, without availing ourselves of the latter present of their queen. When it was day, we set about seeking for the moveables and travelling utensils which we had lost; we found part of them in the place where we had stopped in the evening, and a part on the borders of the morass or in the morass itself: the storm had ceased, the sun had risen brilliantly, and we passed the whole day in the village, drying our things. After having taken care of our horses and other beasts of burden, we went to salute the queen, and, not wishing to be inferior in generosity to the barbarians who had received us so well, we gave her silver cups, red woollen garments, Indian pepper, dates and other dry fruit: after wishing all kind of prosperity to the inhabitants of the village, in return for the hospitality which had been accorded us, we proceeded on our way.

---

plurality of his wives; and moreover, historical testimony does not allow us to doubt but that, among a large number of barbarous nations, it was allowable for a man to marry his daughter; that of Saint Jerome is positive: *Persæ, Medi, Indi, et Æthiopes, regna non modica, et Romano regno paria, cum matribus et aviis, cum filiabus et nepotibus copulantur.* (Lib. ii., *Adv. Jovinianum.*) Why should not the Huns have done the same?

After a march of six days, the Scythians, our guides, ordered us to stop at a certain village, in order that we might continue our route in the train of Attila, who was going to pass that way; we here met the ambassadors whom the western Romans had sent to him; the principal were: Romulus, invested with the title of count, Primutus, prefect of Norica, and Romanus, chief of a body of troops. With them were Constantius, whom Ætius had sent to Attila for a secretary, and Tatullus, father of Orestes, the colleague of Edeco; the latter had accompanied them not because of the embassy, but out of friendship, and by reason of their own affairs. Constantius had become united with them during his sojourn in Italy, and family reasons had determined Tatullus; his son, Orestes, had taken for wife the daughter of Romulus of Petovio, a city of Norica.

These ambassadors had been endeavoring to soften Attila, who had demanded that they should give him up Sylvanus, prefect of the imperial plate of Rome, because he had received some gold cups which had been sent to him by a certain Constantius. This Constantius, a native of western Gaul, had been given to Attila and to Bleda for a secretary, in the same way as, at a later period, another Constantius was. This man then, at the time when the town of Sirmium, in Pannonia, was besieged by the Scythians, had received some gold vases from the bishop of the city; the bishop wished, that if he survived the taking of the town, the value of these vases should be employed for his ransom, and that if he died, this money should serve to deliver the captive citizens; but Constantius, after the ruin of the town, without troubling himself as to the results of the siege, repaired to Italy on business, gave the vases to Sylvanus, received the price of them, and it was arranged between them that if Constantius repaid the capital and interest of this money within a fixed time, the vases should be returned to him; that, in the contrary case, Sylvanus should keep and use them as his own. Attila and Bleda, suspecting this Constantius of treason, had him crucified; and Attila, informed of the affair of the cups of gold, demanded that they should give up Sylvanus to him, as having stolen property belonging to him. Ætius and the emperor of the western Romans sent deputies to him, to tell him that Sylvanus had not stolen these vases, that he was the creditor of Constantius, that he had received them in pledge for the sum lent, and had sold them to the first priest who wished to buy them, seeing that it was not permitted to laymen to make use of cups consecrated to God. They were to add, in case such good reasons and respect for God did not prevent Attila from persisting in again demanding the cups, that Sylvanus would send him the price of them, but they could not give up a man who had done no wrong.

Such was the object of the mission of these deputies, who were following the barbarian in order to obtain an answer and then return.

As we were to march by the same route as Attila, we waited for him to go before us, and we followed him at a short distance with the rest of the barbarians. After having crossed some rivers, we arrived at a large town; here was the house of Attila, much higher and more beautiful than any of the other houses of his empire; it was made of highly polished planks, and surrounded with a palisade of wood, not by way of fortification, but as an ornament.

The house nearest to the king's was that of Onegeses, also surrounded with a palisade of wood, but it was neither so high nor furnished with towers like that of Attila. At some distance from the enclosure of the house was situated the bath which Onegeses, the richest and most powerful of the Scythians next to Attila, had had constructed with stones brought from Pannonia; there was, indeed, in this part of Scythia, neither stones nor large trees, and it was necessary to get materials elsewhere. The architect who had constructed this bath, made prisoner at Sirmium, had hoped that liberty would be the reward of his labor, but this sweet hope was utterly deceived; he was cast, on the contrary, into a far still harder servitude; Onegeses made him his bather, and he waited on him and all his family when they went to the bath.

When Attila arrived at this village, young girls came to meet him; they walked in a file, under pieces of fine white linen, held up on either side by many ranks of women, and so well held out, that, under each piece, walked six virgins, or even more: they sang barbarous songs.

We were already close to the house of Onegeses, past which the road leading to that of the king went, when his wife came out, followed by a multitude of women slaves, who brought meats and wine, which is regarded among the Scythians as the greatest honor. She saluted Attila, and prayed him to taste her meats, which she presented to him with the most lively protestations of her devotion. The king, to give a mark of his good-will towards the wife of his confidant, eat upon his horse. The barbarians who escorted him held the table, which was of silver, up to him. After having dipped his lips into the cup which they offered him, he entered his palace, which was much more conspicuous than any of the other houses, and stood upon an eminence.

As for us, we remained in the house of Onegeses, according to the orders of the latter, who had returned with the son of Attila; we were received by his wife and by the other illustrious chiefs of his family, and we supped there. Onegeses could not remain with us and enjoy himself at table, because he had to give an account to Attila of what he had done in his mission, and of the accident which had happened to his son, who had dislocated his right wrist; this was the first time he had presented himself before the king of the Huns since his return.

After supper, we quitted the house of Onegeses, and pitched our tents nearer to the palace of Attila, in order that Maximin, who was to have an interview with that prince, and to converse with those who acted as his council, might thus be as little distant as possible. There we passed the night.

When day appeared, Maximin sent me to Onegeses to carry him the presents which he himself offered and those which the emperor sent him, and to ask him when and where he could have a conversation. I therefore repaired to Onegeses, with the slaves who carried the presents; the doors were closed, and I was obliged to wait till they were opened, and until some came out who could inform him of my arrival.

While I passed the time in walking round the enclosure of the house of Onegeses, some one advanced whom I at first took for a barbarian of the Scythian army, and who saluted me in Greek, saying to me, Χαίρε. I was surprised that a Scythian should speak Greek, for the barbarians, shut up in their own manners, cultivate and speak none but barbarous languages, that of the Huns or that of the Goths, those who have much commercial intercourse with the Romans also speak Latin; none of them speak Greek, with the exception of the captive refugees in Thrace or in maritime Illyria; but when we meet with these latter, they are easily recognized by their wretched clothing and pale faces, signs of the ill fortune into which they have fallen. This man, on the contrary, had the air of a happy and rich Scythian; he was elegantly clothed, and had his head shaved round: saluting him in return, I asked him who he was, from whence he came into the country of the barbarians, and why he had adopted the customs of the Scythians? "You are, then, anxious to know?" said he. "My reason for asking," I answered, "is, that you spoke Greek." He then told me, smiling, that he was a Greek by birth, that he had established himself with a view to commerce, at Viminacium, a town of Mœsia on the Danube, that he had long remained there, and had there married a rich wife; but that, at the taking of the town, all his fortune vanished, and that in the subdivision of booty his goods and himself had fallen to Onegeses. It is, indeed, the custom among the Scythians, for the principal chiefs, after Attila, to put aside the richest captives and share them afterwards. My Greek had afterwards courageously fought against the Romans; he had assisted in subjecting the nation of the Acatzires to his barbarous master, and, according to the Scythian laws, he obtained liberty as a reward, with the possession of all which he had acquired in war; he had married a barbarian wife, by whom he had children; he was the companion of Onegeses, and his new mode of life appeared to him far preferable to the old. In fact, those who remain among the Scythians, after having supported the fatigues of war, pass their life without any trouble; each enjoys the property that fate has granted him, and no one interferes with or troubles him in any way whatever.

While we thus conversed, one of the domestics of Onegeses opened the gates. I hastened towards him, and asked for Onegeses; I added, that I had to speak with him on the part of Maximin, the ambassador from the Romans: he answered, that if I waited a little, I might soon see him, for he was going out; shortly afterwards, indeed, I saw Onegeses advancing; I went towards him, saying, "The ambassador from the Romans salutes you, and I bring you presents on his part, as well as the gold sent you by the emperor." As I tried to ask him when and where he would converse with us, he ordered his people to take the gold and presents, and told me to inform Maximin that he would repair to him soon.

I therefore returned to tell Maximin that Onegeses was about to visit him; almost immediately afterwards he arrived at our tent, and, addressing himself to the ambassador, thanked him for the gifts of the emperor and his own, asking him what he wished, since he had required him to come. Maximin answered him, that the time approached when he might acquire great glory, by repairing to the emperor, terminating the contentions of the Huns and the Romans, and by his wisdom establishing a solid peace between the two nations; a peace which would not only be very advantageous to them, but which would be of so much value to him and to all his people, as his family would then experience an eternal gratitude from the emperor and all the imperial race. Onegeses then asked how he could render himself agreeable to the emperor and terminate these contests: Maximin answered him that he had bu; to take part in the present affairs, go to thank the emperor, carefully study the causes of discord, and interpose his credit to arrange the differences, according to the conditions of treaties. "But," said Onegeses, "I long since informed the emperor and his councillors of the will of Attila concerning this affair: do the Romans think that their entreaties will induce me to betray my master, and to hold no reckoning of the advantages which I have found among the Scythians for my wives and children? Is it not better to serve with Attila, than to enjoy the greatest riches with the Romans? As to the rest, I shall be much more useful to them in remaining at home, in calming and softening the rage of my master, if he is forming any violent project against the empire, than by repairing to Constantinople, and exposing myself to suspicions, if I were to do anything which appears contrary to the interests of Attila." At these words, thinking that I should be charged to converse with him, upon what we desired to learn (such an interview little suiting the dignity with which Maximin was invested), he withdrew.

The next day, I went into the interior enclosure of the house of Attila, to carry presents to his wife, who was called Creca; he had three children by her; the eldest already reigned over the Acatzires, and the other nations which inhabited Scythia, around the Pontus Euxinus. Within this enclosure there were many edifices, partly constructed of carved planks, elegantly arranged: partly of uncarved beams, well formed with the adze, and polished, with round pieces of wood mixed with them; the circles which united them, rising from the ground, were elevated and distributed, according to certain proportions. Here lived the wife of Attila. The barbarians who guarded the gates allowed me to enter, and I found her lying on a soft couch; the floor was ornamented with carpet, upon which we walked: numerous slaves surrounded her in a circle; and opposite to her, maid servants, seated on the ground, were making piece work, composed of linen of various colors, which the barbarians wear over their dress as ornaments.

After having saluted Creca, and offered her the presents, I withdrew, and, while waiting for Onegeses to return from the palace, whither he had already repaired, I went through the other buildings of the enclosure where Attila dwelt. While I was there, with many other persons (as I was known to the guards of Attila and the barbarians of his train, they allowed me to go everywhere), I saw a numerous crowd advancing in tumult, and with a great noise. Attila came out with a grave air; all eyes were directed towards him; Onegeses accompanied him, and he seated himself before his house. Many people who had causes approached him, and he delivered judgments upon them. He then re-entered his palace, where he received deputies from barbarian nations, who had come to seek him.

While I waited for Onegeses, Romulus, Promutus, and Romanus, the deputies who came from Italy about the affair of the gold vases, Rusticus, who was in the train of Constantius, and Constantiolus, a native of Pannonia, then under Attila, spoke to me, and asked me if we had received our dismissal. "It is to know this of Onegeses," said I, "that I wait in this enclosure." I asked, in my turn, whether they had obtained any favorable answer concerning the object of their mission. "Not at all," answered they; "it is impossible to change Attila's determination; he threatens war, unless they give him up Sylvanus."

As we were expressing our mutual astonishment at the intractable pride of the barbarian, Romulus, a man of great experience, and who had been charged with many very honorable missions, said to us: "This pride arises from his happy fortune, which has placed him in a rank so elevated; his fortune gives him great power, and he is so inflated with it, that reason has no access to him, and he only thinks that just which he has once taken into his head; none of those who have reigned, whether in Scythia or elsewhere, have done such great things in so short a time; he has subdued all Scythia, he has extended his dominion to the islands of the ocean, he has made the Romans his tributaries; not content with this, he meditates still greater enterprises; he still wishes to drive back the frontiers of his empire, and he is preparing to attack the Persians."

One of us asked what road led from Scythia to Persia; Romulus answered that the country of the Medes was situated not very far from that of the Scythians, and that the Huns knew the road well, having often gone it. During the ravages made in their country by a famine, and the tranquillity in which the Romans, occupied elsewhere, left them, Basich and Currich, warriors of the royal family of the Scythians, and chiefs of numerous troops, had penetrated into the country of the Medes; these chiefs lately come to Rome to treat for an alliance, related that they had journeyed across a desert country, that they had traversed a morass, which Romulus believed to be the Palus-Mæotis, and that after fifteen days, after having ascended certain mountains, they descended into Medea; that there, while they were pillaging and making incursions in the country, there suddenly came a Persian army, which darkened the air with its arrows; that at the sight of such danger, they had retired, repassed the mountains, and brought but a small part of their booty, because the Medes had regained the greater portion; that to avoid the shock of the enemy, they had taken another route, had crossed places strewn with marine stones which burnt,[1] and at last arrived at their native country after a journey, the duration of which Romulus could not recollect: it was easy to see from this that Scythia was not very far from the country of the Medes.

Romulus added, that if, in consequence, the idea of attacking the Medes seized upon Attila, the invasion would cost him neither much care nor fatigue, and that he would not have a long road to take in order to fall upon the Medes, the Parthians, and the Persians, and oblige them to pay him tribute. He had such an immense number of troops, that no nation could resist him. We then set about forming the wish that Attila might attack the Persians, and thus turn the weight of the war from us. "It is to be feared," said Constantiolus, "that the Persians once conquered, he will treat the Romans not as a friend but as a master. Now we send him gold, because of the dignity with which we ourselves have li vested him; but if he subjugates the Medes, the Parthians, and the Persians, he will no longer spare the the Romans, who form, on this side, the boundaries of his empire; he will regard them as his slaves, and will force them to obey his terrible and insupportable will."

---

[1] These stones were the bitumen which abounds upon the borders of the sea of Azof and the Black Sea.

The dignity of which Constantiolus spoke, was that of the genera of the Roman armies, an honor which Attila had received from the emperor, receiving at the same time the salary attached to this title. Constantiolus thought that Attila would without scruple violate the duties of this dignity, or of any other with which it might please the Romans to invest him, and that he would force them to give him the name of king instead of that of general. Already, when he was out of humor, he said that the generals of his armies were his slaves, and that his generals, in his eyes, were the equals of the Roman emperors.

The discovery of the sword of Mars had greatly added to his power. This sword, formerly worshipped by the kings of the Scythians, as being sacred to the god of war, had disappeared for many centuries, and had just been again found on the occasion of the wounding an ox. While we discussed the matter rather eagerly, Onegeses came out; we approached and asked him concerning the affairs with which we were charged. After conversing with some barbarians he told me to ask Maximin what consular personage the Romans proposed to send to Attila. I returned to our tent, and related to Maximin what Onegeses had just said to me; we deliberated upon what answer to make to the barbarians. I then returned to Onegeses and told that the Romans eagerly desired that he should repair to Rome, and that he should be charged with arranging their differences with Attila; but that if they were deceived in this hope, the emperor would send whatever ambassador he pleased. He ordered me immediately to fetch Maximin; and directly he came he conducted him to Attila. Maximin returning soon after, told us that the barbarian declared that he positively willed the emperor to send him as an ambassador, Nomius or Anatolius, and that he would receive no other. Maximin observed to him that it was not proper to make the deputies who should be sent to him suspected of the emperor, by designating them, but Attila answered that if the Romans refused him he would terminate the quarrel by taking arms.

We had scarcely entered our tent when the father of Orestes came to say: "Attila invites you both to a banquet which is to take place about the ninth hour of the day." At the hour mentioned, we repaired to the invitation, and in company with the ambassadors of the western Romans we presented ourselves before the entry of the hall in front of Attila; there, the cup-bearers, according to the usage of the country, presented us a cup, in order that, before sitting down, we should offer libations; after having performed this, and having tasted of the cup, we occupied the seats upon which we were to sup.

Seats were prepared on each side the hall, along the walls; in the midst was Attila, upon a couch, opposite to which was another couch, and behind that the steps of a staircase which led to where this prince slept. This couch was ornamented with cloths of various colors, and resembled those which the Romans and the Greeks prepare for married people. It was then arranged that the first rank of guests should seat themselves on the right of Attila, and the second rank on the left; we were placed in the second rank with Berich, a very considerable warrior among the Scythians, but Berich was above us. Onegeses occupied the first seat on the right of the king, and opposite him were two of the sons of Attila; the eldest lay upon the same couch as his father, not by his side but below him, and he always kept his eyes cast down out of respect for his father

Every one being seated, Attila's cup-bearer presented him a cup of wine; on receiving it, Attila saluted him who occupied the first place. At this honor the latter immediately rose: he was not allowed to re-seat himself until Attila, tasting the cup, or emptying the contents, had returned it to the cup-bearer. Attila, on the contrary, remained seated, while the guests, each receiving a cup in his turn, gave him homage, by saluting him and tasting the wine. Each guest had a cup-bearer, who took his place after Attila's had gone. All the guests were honored in the same manner; Attila, when it came to our turn, saluted us in the manner of the Thracians. After these ceremonies of politeness, the cup-bearers retired.

By the side of Attila's table were prepared four other tables, made to receive three or four, or even more guests, each of whom, without disarranging the order of seats, could take upon plates with his knife whatever he pleased. In the middle, first the servant of Attila came forward, carrying a dish full of meat, then those who were to serve the other guests covered the tables with bread and meats. There had been prepared for the barbarians, and for us, meats and ragouts of all kinds, and they served them to us upon plates of silver, but Attila had only a wooden plate, and eat nothing but plain meat.

In all things he showed the same simplicity; the guests drank from cups of gold and silver; Attila had only a wooden cup; his clothes were very simple, and were only distinguished from the other barbarians because they were of one color, and were without ornaments; his sword, the cords of his shoes, the reins of his horse, were not, like those of the other Scythians, decorated with plates of gold or precious stones.

When the meats served in the first plates were eaten, we arose, and no one again sat down until he had drank a full cup of wine to the health and prosperity of Attila, according to the forms which I have just described. After rendering him this homage, we re-seated ourselves. They then brought to every table fresh plates with other meats; and when each was satisfied, we arose, again drank as at first, and again sat down.

On the approach of night the meats were taken away; two Scythians advanced, and recited before Attila verses of their own composition, in which they sang of his victories and warlike virtues. The attention of all the guests was fixed upon them; some were charmed by the verses, others were excited by the description of battles; tears flowed down the cheeks of those whose strength had been worn away by age, and who could therefore no longer satisfy their thirst for war and glory. After these barbarian songs were ended, a buffoon came and went through all sorts of extravagances and ridiculous gesticulations and sayings, which made those present laugh heartily.

The last person who came in was the Moor, Zercho: Edeco had told him to come to Attila, and promised to employ all his influence to have his wife brought to him; the Moor had married but some years before in Scythia, where he enjoyed great favor with Bleda, but on quitting that country had left her behind him. When Attila sent the woman as a gift to Aetius, Zercho at first hoped to see her again; but this hope had been frustrated by reason that Attila had been angry at his returning into his own country. Availing himself of the occasion of this festival, the Moor again sought permission to have his wife brought to him, and his face, his demeanor, his pronunciation, and his strange mixture of Hunnish, Latin, and Gothic words, excited such mirth and transports of joyousness, that the shouts of laughter on all sides appeared undistinguishable.[1]

Attila alone preserved an unaltered visage; he was grave and motionless; he neither said nor did anything indicating the slightest disposition to participate in the merriment around him; the only change that we observed in him was, that when his youngest son, named Irnach, was brought in, he looked at him with eyes of affection and pleasure, and patted him on the cheek. I was wondering why Attila paid so little attention to his other children, and seemed only to care for this one, when a barbarian, who sat next to me, and who spoke Latin, after having made me promise that I would not repeat what he was about to say to me, told me that the diviners had predicted to Attila that all his race would perish except this boy, who would once more restore it.

As the banquet seemed likely to be extended to a late hour of the night, and as we did not wish to remain drinking any longer, we withdrew.

Next day we went to Onegeses, to tell him that we desired to be dismissed, not wishing to lose any more time; he replied, that such also was the intention of Attila, who had determined upon our departure. He then held a council of the principal chiefs upon the subject of the resolution which had been formed by Attila, and drew up the letter which we were to carry to the emperor. He had with him his corresponding secretaries, and among them Rusticus, a native of Upper Mœsia, who, having been made prisoner by the barbarians, had been raised to this post in consequence of his talent for composition.

After the council, we entreated Onegeses to restore to liberty the wife and children of Sylla, who had been reduced to slavery at the taking of Ratiaria; he was not indisposed to grant our request on our paying a considerable ransom. We earnestly supplicated him to be merciful, in consideration of their former condition, and of their present misery. At length, as he was taking his leave, Onegeses granted us the liberty of the woman for 500 *aurii*, and made the emperor a present of that of his sons.

Meantime Recca, the wife of Attila, who superintended his domestic affairs, had sent to invite us to supper.[2] We accordingly proceeded to her apartments, and found her surrounded by a great number of Scythian chiefs; she overwhelmed us with kindness, and gave us a magnificent banquet. Each of the guests rose, presented to us a cupful of wine, and kissed us on the forehead in taking it back, which among the Scythians is a mark of great good will. After supper we retired to our tents for the night.

Next day Attila invited us to another banquet: the same ceremo-

---

[1] Is it not singular to find a harlequin at the court of Attila? yet such is the origin of these buffoons. The color of the black slaves, the strangeness of their face and manners, caused them to be sought after by the barbarians as excellent ministers of mirth; to complete the singularity, Zercho asks his wife at the hands of Attila, closely paralleling harlequin demanding columbine.

[2] The learned have warmly discussed the question whether this Recca was the same with that wife of Attila of whom Priscus has already spoken, and whom he then named Creca.

nies were observed as on the first occasion, and we diverted ourselves very much; this day it was not the eldest son of Attila who was seated on the same couch with the chief, but his uncle Oebar, whom Attila regarded in the light of a father.

Throughout the banquet Attila conversed with us in the kindest manner; he ordered Maximin to induce the emperor to give to his secretary Constantius the wife he had promised him. This Constantius had gone to Constantinople with the deputies of Attila, and had offered his services in maintaining peace between the Romans and the Huns, in consideration of a rich wife being given him; the emperor had consented to this, and had promised him the daughter of Saturnillus, a man of noble family and large fortune; but Athenais, or Eudoxia (the empress went by both these names), put Saturnillus to death, and Zen, a consular personage, prevented the emperor from fulfilling his promise. This Zen, at the head of a numerous body of Isaurians, was at that time guarding the city of Constantinople, menaced by war, and had, besides, the general command of the armies of the east; he withdrew the young girl from the prison in which she had been placed, and gave her to one Rufus, a relative of his. Thus disappointed in his marriage, Constantius had earnestly entreated Attila not to suffer the affront which had been put upon him, to pass, but to insist upon a wife being given him; either the one just snatched from him, or some other woman with a rich dowry: accordingly, during supper, the barbarian desired Maximin to tell the emperor that Constantius was not to be disappointed of his hopes, and that it was contrary to the dignity of an emperor to be a liar; Attila took this interest in the matter because Constantius had promised him a large sum of money in the event of his obtaining by the barbarian's influence a rich Roman wife.

On the approach of night we withdrew from the banquet.

Three days afterwards we were dismissed, after having received a present each of us. Attila sent with us, as his ambassador, Berich, one of the leading Scythian chiefs, lord of many villages in that country, and who, at the banquet, had been placed on the same side of the table with us, and, indeed, above us. Berich had before this been received as ambassador at Constantinople.

On our way, as we were entering a certain village, the barbarians who accompanied us part of the road, took prisoner a Scythian who was acting as spy for the Romans. Attila ordered him to be crucified. Next day, again, as we were passing through another village, there were brought to us, their hands tied behind their backs, two slaves, who had killed those whom the fortune of war had rendered masters of their life and death; their heads were fastened between two pieces of wood, and they were then crucified.

Berich, so long as we journeyed in Scythia, travelled with us, and treated us with kindness; but no sooner had we passed the Danube, than he became an enemy, upon some miserable pretexts furnished by our servants. He began by taking from Maximin the horse he had given him; Attila had required all the Scythian chiefs who accompanied him to make presents to Maximin, and they had all offered him horses, Berich among the rest: but Maximin, wishing to show his moderation, had refused most of these offers, accepting only two or three horses. Berich now took the one he had given him, and moreover, would no longer converse with us, nor even follow the same route. Thus, this pledge of a hospitality contracted in the country of the barbarians themselves, was withdrawn. We proceeded to Adrianopolis through Philippolis, and stopped for awhile to repose ourselves; while there, we addressed Berich, who had also reached the city, and asked why he so pertinaciously observed silence towards men who had given him no offence. He was pacified by our words, accepted an invitation to supper, and we departed the next day from Adrianopolis in company together.

On our way, we met Vigilius, who was returning to Scythia, and after informing him of the manner in which Attila had received us, continued our journey. On arriving at Constantinople, we thought that Berich had altogether forgotten his anger, but our kindness and courtesy had not overcome his naturally fierce and vindictive disposition; he accused Maximin of having said that the generals Areobindus and Aspar enjoyed no credit with the emperor, and that since he had become acquainted with the frivolous and unstable character of the barbarians, he had no faith whatever in their alleged exploits.

IV.

Chronological Table of the Principal Events of the Political History of Gaul, from the Fifth to the Tenth Century.

A.D.
406—412 General invasion of the Germans into the empire of the west, and especially into Gaul.
411—413 Establishment of the Burgundians in eastern Gaul.
412—419 Establishment of the Visigoths in southern Gaul.
418—430 Establishment of the Franks in Belgium and northern Gaul.
451 Invasion of Attila into Gaul. His defeat in the plains of Châlons in Champagne.
476 Definitive fall of the empire of the west.
481—511 Reign of Clovis. Establishment of the kingdom of the Franks. Their conquests in eastern, western and southern Gaul.
27 Nov., 511 Death of Clovis. Division of his domains and states between his four sons.
523—534 Wars between the Franks and the Burgundians. Fall of the kingdom of the latter.
558—561 Clotaire I., fourth son of Clovis, sole king of the Franks
587 Treaty of Andélot, between Gontran, king of Burgundy, and Childebert II,, king of Metz.
613—628 Clotaire II., son of Chilperic I., and of Fredegonde, sole king of the Franks.
628—714 Progressive elevation of the family of the Pepins among the Austrasian Franks.
656—687 Struggle between the Franks of Neustria and the Franks of Austrasia.
687 Battle of Testry. Triumph of the Austrasian Franks.
715—741 Government of the Franks by Charles Martel.
714—732 Invasion and progress of the Arabs in southern and western Gaul.

CIVILIZATION IN FRANCE.

A.D	
Oct., 732	They are defeated near Tours, by Charles Martel.
1st Oct., 741	Death of Charles Martel. Division of Gaul between his sons, Pepin and Carloman.
747	Carloman enters a monastery. Pepin sole chief of the Franks.
752	Childeric III., last of the Merovingian kings, is deposed. Pepin, surnamed Le Bref, is declared king of the Franks, and crowned at Soissons by Winfried (Saint Boniface) archbishop of Mayence.
754	Pope Stephen II., who visits France, again crowns Pepin and his family.
754, 755	Pepin makes war in Italy against the Lombards. His alliance with the popes.
750—759	The wars of Pepin in southern Gaul against the Saracens. He makes himself master of Septimania.
745—768	The wars of Pepin in the south-west of Gaul against the Aquitani. He seizes upon Aquitaine.
Sept., 768	Death of Pepin. Division of his states between his two sons, Charles and Carloman.
771	Death of Carloman. Charlemagne sole king of the Franks.
769	Expedition of Charlemagne against the Aquitani.
772, 774—776, 778—780, 782—785, 794—796, 797—798, 802, 804	Expeditions of Charlemagne against the Saxons.
773—774	Expeditions of Charlemagne against the Lombards.
776	He defeats their kings, and possesses himself of their states.
787, 801	Expeditions of Charlemagne against the Lombards of Benevento.
778, 196—797, 801, 806, 807, 509, 810, 812	Expeditions of Charlemagne against the Arabs of Spain, Italy, Sardinia, &c.
788, 789, 791, 796, 805, 812	Expeditions of Charlemagne against the Slaves and the Avares in eastern Europe.
	Relations of Charlemagne with the emperors of the east.
14 Oct., 800	Charlemagne enters Rome.
15 Dec., 800	He is proclaimed emperor of the west.
801	Embassy of Haroun-al-Raschid to Charlemagne.
806	Charlemagne divides his states between his three sons, Charles, Pepin, and Louis.
808—814	The Normans begin to ravage the coasts of Frankish-Gaul.
21 Jan., 814	Death of Charlemagne.

A.D	
816	Coronation of Louis le Debonnaire, at Reims, by Pope Stephen IV.
817	Louis associates with himself his son Lothaire, and give to his two youngest sons, Pepin and Louis, the kingdoms of Aquitaine and Bavaria.
828—833	Intrigues and revolts of the sons of Louis le Debonnaire against their father.
1 Oct., 833	The assembly of Compiegne meet to degrade Louis.
2 Nov., 833	Public penance and degradation of Louis at Soissons.
835	The assembly of Thionville annuls the acts of that of Compiegne.
838	The assembly of Kiersy-sur-Ouise, when Louis deprives his eldest sons, Lothaire and Louis, in favor of the youngest, Charles le Chauve.
30 May, 839	Louis le Debonnaire is reconciled with his son Lothaire. New division of the empire between Lothaire and Charles le Chauve.
20 June, 840	Death of Louis le Debonnaire.
840—843	War between the sons of Louis le Debonnaire.
29 June, 841	Battle of Fontenay.
843	Treaty of Verdun. Definitive division of the empire.
862—877	Charles le Chauve reunites successfully a great part of the states of Charlemagne.
25 Dec., 875	He is crowned emperor at Rome.
877	He acknowledges in the assembly of Kiersy-sur Oise, the right to the hereditary possession of fees and royal offices.
6 Oct., 877	Death of Charles le Chauve.
836—877	Continued and augmenting visions of the Saracens, and of the Normans, in Frankish Gaul.
877—879	Reign of Louis le Begue, son of Charles le Chauve.
10 April, 879	Reign of Louis le Begue.
879—882	Reigns of Louis III. and Carloman, sons of Louis le Begue.
5 Aug., 882	Death of Louis III.
882—884	Reign of Carloman.
6 Dec., 884	Death of Carloman.
884—888	Reign of Charles le Gros.
885—886	The Normans besiege Paris during one year.
12 Jan., 888	Death of Charles le Gros.
887—898	Reign of Eudes, count of Paris, son of Robert le Fort, elected king during the life of Charles.
877—888	Formation of a number of independent lordships.
28 Jan., 893	Coronation of Charles le Simple, son of Louis le Begue.
1 Jan., 898	Death of king Eudes.
893—929	Reign of Charles le Simple.
911	By the treaty of Clair-sur-Esste, he gives to Rollo, a Norman chief, that part of Neustria which has since taken the name of Normandy.
922	Robert, duke of France, brother to king Eudes, is elected king.
15 June, 923	He is killed near Soissons in a battle with Charles le Simple.
923	Raoul, or Rodolph, duke of Burgundy, is elected king of France.

A.D
923—929 Captivity of Charles le Simple in the hands of Herbert, count of Vermandois. He is set at liberty for a time, but soon imprisoned again.
7 Oct., 929 Death of Charles le Simple.
15 Jan., 936 Death of king Raoul.
936—954 Reign of Louis IV., surnamed d'Outre-Mer, son of Charles le Simple. He is sometimes friendly, sometimes hostile; on one hand with the emperor Otho I., master of eastern France, on the other with the independent lords of central and western France.
10 Sept., 954 Death of Louis d'Outre Mer.
954—986 Reign of Lothaire, son of Louis. His wars with Otho II.
2 Mar., 986 Death of Lothaire.
986, 987 Reign of Louis V., son of Lothaire.
21 May, 987 Death of Louis V.
3 July, 987 Hugh Capet, count of Paris, is crowned king of France, at Reims.

V.

Chronological Table of the Principal Events of the Religious History of Gaul from the Fifth to the Tenth Century.

A.D.
11 Nov., 400 Death of St. Martin, archbishop of Tours.
400—407 Writings of Vigilantius, priest, against the relics of the martyrs, and some other practices of the church. Answered by St. Jerome.
400—420 Foundation of monasteries in southern Gaul; amongst others, those of St. Victor, at Marseilles, and of Lerens.
418 St. Germain, bishop of Auxerre.
420 The Burgundians embrace arianism.
423 Birth of semi-Pelagianism in southern Gaul. St. Augustin combats it.
428 St. Loup, bishop of Troyes.
429 A numerous council. Place uncertain.[1]
— St. Hilary, bishop of Arles.
441 Council of Orange.
450 Contest between the bishops of Arles and Vienna, upon the extent of their metropolitan jurisdiction.
452 Council of Arles.
455 Council of Arles.
462 Faust, bishop of Riez; his discussion with Claudienus Mamertius, upon the nature of the soul; he is accused of semi-Pelagianism; he writes against the predestinarians.

---

[1] I only indicate in this table the principal councils, without mentioning their object. The seventh table is especially devoted to the history of the councils and canonical legislation of Gaul at this period

A.D	
470	Institution of the Rogations by St. Mamertius, bishop of Vienne.
472	St. Sidonius Apollinaris, bishop of Clermont.
475	Council of Arles.
490	St. Avitus, bishop of Vienne.
496	Clovis embraces Christianity.
499	Conference held at Lyons, in the presence of Gondebaud, king of Burgundy, between the Catholic and Arian bishops.
501	St. Cesaire, bishop of Arles.
506	Council of Agde.
510	Sigismond, a Burgundian prince, abandons Arianism.
511	Council of Orleans.
517	Council of Epaone, in the diocess of Vienne.
529	Council of Orange.
—	Council of Vaison.
533	Council of Orleans.
538	Council of Orleans.
541	Council of Orleans.
543	Introduction of the rule of St. Benedict into Gaul. Reform and progress of monasteries. Monastic life receives the name of *religio*.
549	Council of Orleans.
554	Council of Arles.
555	St. Germain, bishop of Paris.
557	Council of Paris.
573	St. Gregory, bishop of Tours.
—	St. Senoch, and several other hermits, render themselves celebrated by their austerities.
576	Childebert II., king of Austrasia, obliges the Jews to receive baptism.
578	Council of Auxerre.
585	Council of Macon.
—	Arrival of St. Colomban in Gaul.
590	He founds the monastery of Luxeuil.
590—600	Disorder in the monasteries. Impostors overrun Gaul, and give themselves out to be Christ.
600—650	Progressive incorporation of the monks into the clergy.
615	Council of Paris.
—	Clotaire II. allows to the people and clergy the right of electing bishops, reserving to himself the confirmation of their choice.
625	Council of Reims.
626	St. Amand, a missionary bishop, labors at the conversion of the infidels in Belgium.
628	Dagobert I. obliges the Jews to receive baptism.
—	Foundation of the abbey of St. Denis.
638	Council of Paris.
639	St. Eloy, bishop of Noyon.
639	St. Ouen, bishop of Rouen.
640—660	Foundation of numerous monasteries
650	Council of Châlons.
658	Saint Leger, bishop of Autun.
—	Progress of the temporal power of the bishops.

A.D	
670—700	Preaching of Anglo-Saxon and other monks, sustained by the mayors of the palace of Austrasia, amongst the people beyond the Rhine, such as the Saxons, the Frisons, the Danes, &c.
	Tyranny of the bishops over the monasteries—Charters obtained by the monasteries—Protection afforded them by the kings and popes.
715—755	Preaching and institutions of Saint Boniface in Germany—Foundation of the bishoprics of Salzburg, Freysingen, Ratisbon, Wurtzburg, Passau, Eichstædt, &c.
720—741	Charles Martel seizes a part of the domains of the clergy.
739—752	Relations of the popes with Charles Martel and Pepin le Bref.
743	Council of Leptines.
751—800	Progress of the papacy by means of its alliance with Pepin and Charlemagne.
752	Council of Wermerie.
755	Council of Verneuil.
—	Pepin le Bref gives to the church of Rome the dominions taken from the Lombards.
761	Recommencement of the dispute upon dogmatical questions—reform of the church by the civil power.
761—763	Establishment and rule of the canons by Chrodegaud, bishop of Metz.
767	Council of Gentilly.
769	Charlemagne interdicts the abuse of the right of asylum in the churches.
772	Pope Adrian I. gives a collection of canons to Charlemagne.
774	Charlemagne extends Pepin's donation to the church of Rome.
780	Benedict d'Aniane undertakes the reform of monastic life.
785	Theodulf, bishop of Orleans.
786	Especial bishops established in certain monasteries.
790—794	Condemnation of the worshipping of images by the Gallo-Frankish church—Caroline works composed on this subject by Alcuin, and sent to the pope by the order of Charlemagne.
790—799	Heresy of the adoptians—Opposed by Alcuin, and condemned by the Gallo-Frankish church.
798	Leidrade, archbishop of Lyons.
809	The Gallo-Frankish church adopts the doctrine, that the Holy Ghost proceeds from the Father and the Son.
813	Five councils held the same year labor at the reform of ecclesiastical discipline.
816	Rules of canons and canonesses adopted at the council of Aix-la-Chapelle—Louis le Debonnaire gives the force of law to the treatise of ecclesiastical offices by Amalaire, priest of Metz.
817	Reform of the monasteries ordered by a council of abbots and monks held at Aix-la-Chapelle.
820—877	Progress of the independence and temporal power of the bishops—Decline of royalty.

A.D.
823—824 Proofs of the right of the emperor of the west to interfere in the election of the popes.
826 Harold and his wife, Danish princes, with their suite are baptized in the palace of Louis le Debonnaire.
About 830. Ideas and attempts of Agobard, archbishop of Lyons, after the example of Claude, bishop of Turin, to reform the abuses of the church, particularly the worship of relics and the adoration of images.
831—865 The writings of Paschase-Radbert give rise to a controversy upon transubstantiation and the immaculate conception.
833 Council of Compiegne.
835 Council of Thionville.
836 Council of Aix-la-Chapelle.
840—877 Progress of the papal power at the expense, 1st, of the power of temporal sovereigns; 2d, of the power of the bishops and the national churches—Relations of Nicholas I. with the government of the Gallo-Frankish church.
About 843 Appearance of the False Decretals.
844 Council of Thionville.
845—882 Hincmar, archbishop of Reims.
847—861 Saint Prudentius, archbishop of Reims.
849—869 Controversy upon predestination and grace—Contest between Gottschalk and Hincmar.
852—875 Saint Remy, archbishop of Lyons.
853 Council of Soissons.
853—866 Affair of Wulfad and the other priest ordained by Ebbo, archbishop of Troyes.
856—869 Affair of the divorce of Lothair and Teutberge.
858 Letters of counsel and reproach from the bishop of Gaul to Louis le Germanique.
862—866 Affair of Rhotade, bishop of Soissons.
869—878 Affair of Hincmar, bishop of Laon.
876 Ansegise, archbishop of Sens, is instituted primate of Gaul and Germany by pope John VIII.
— Council of Pontion.
887 Council of Mayence.
909 Council of Trosley.
910 Foundation of the abbey of Cluny by William the Pious, duke of Aquitaine.
912 Rollo and a great number of Normans embrace Christianity.
926—942 Saint Odo, bishop of Cluny, reforms his monastery and several others, which being authorized by the pope, unite in one congregation—First example of common government in a monastic order.
943 Struggle between the Christian Normans and the Normans that remained pagans.
991 Gerbert, archbishop of Reims, pope in 999.
993 Canonization of Ulrich, bishop of Augsburg, by Pope John XV.—First example of papal canonization—The bishops continue to declare saints in their diocese.

A.D.	
Towards the end of the century.	Odillo, abbot of Cluny, institutes the feast of All Souls. Institution of the office of the Virgin. Progress of simony, disorder in the manners of the clergy, and superstitions of all kinds amongst the people—Infinite number of saints and relics—Extension of penances and absolutions. The popes declare themselves more and more the adversaries of the disorder in the church, and attempt to put a stop to it. Private individuals rise against abuses and superstitions, amongst others, Leutard, in the environs of Châlons-sur-Saone. The monasteries labor to escape from the jurisdiction of the bishops.

VI.

Chronological Table of the principal Events of the Literary History of Gaul, from the Fifth to the Tenth Century.

Fifth Century.

Name.	Date.	Condition in Life.	Works.
Rutilius Numatianus, of Toulouse, or Poictiers.	Died after 418.	Civil magistrate	A poem, entitled *Itinerarium*; or, *De Reditu*, from Rome to Gaul.
Sulpicius Severus, of Aquitaine	Died after 420.	Ecclesiastic.	1. The Life of Saint Martin of Tours; 2. A Sacred History, from the Creation to 400; 3. Dialogues on the Monks of the East, and a Life of St. Martin.
Evagrius.	Beginning of the 5th century.	Idem.	1. Controversy between Theophilus, a Christian, and Simon, a Jew; 2. Dialogue between Zacheus, a Christian, and Apollonius, a philosopher.
Saint Paulin, of Bordeaux.	354—431	Bishop of Nola.	1. Letters; 2. Short poems; 3. a sermon upon charity; 4. Several lost works

Name.	Date.	Condition in Life.	Works.
Cassien (John) of Provence.	350—433	Bishop of Nola.	1. A treatise on monastic institutions; 2. Conferences on monastic life; 3. Several works on theology.
Palladius, of Poictiers.	Beginning of the 5th century.	Jurisconsult.	A poem upon agriculture.
Saint Prosper, of Aquitaine.	Died towards 463.	Ecclesiastic.	1. A poem upon the question of predestination and grace, entitled, *Of Ingrates*; 2. A chronicle from the creation of the world until 455; 3. Several theological writings and letters.
Mamertius Claudienus, of Vienne.	Died about 474.	Idem.	1. A treatise upon the nature of the soul; 2. Hymn upon the passion, *pange lingua*; 3. Letters.
Salvienus, of the north of Gaul.	Died about the end of the 5th century.	Ecclesiastic.	1. A treatise upon avarice; 2. A treatise on the government of God, or Providence; 3. Letters; 4. Lost writings.
Sidonius Apollinaris, born at Lyons.	430—488	Bishop of Clermont.	1. Nine books of letters; 2. Poetry; 3. Lost writings.
Faust of Breton origin.	Died towards the end of the 5th century.	Idem	1. A treatise upon grace; 2. Letters, wherein he treats of several philosophical and theological questions; 3. Sermons.
Gennade, of Provence.	Died at the end of the 5th century.	Idem	1. A treatise, or catalogue of illustrious men, or ecclesiastical authors; 2. A treatise on ecclesiastical doctrines.
Pomerius, of	End of the	Idem.	1. A treatise on con-

Name.	Date.	Condition in Life.	Works.
African origin, resided at Arles.	5th century.		templative life; 2. A treatise on the nature of the soul; lost.
Sixth Century.			
Saint Ernodius, of Arles.	473—521.	Bishop of Paris.	1. Panegyric of Theodoric, king of the Ostrogoths; 2. Life of St. Epiphanius, bishop of Paris; 3. Letters; 4. Poems; 5. Theological writings.
Saint Avitus (Alcimus Ecdicius) of Auvergne.	Died in 525.	Bishop of Vienne.	1. Two religious poems; 2. Letters; 3. Lost Sermons; 4. Lost Poems.
St. Cesaire, of Châlons-sur-Saône.	470—542.	Bishop of Arles.	1. Sermons; 2. A treatise upon grace and free will; lost.
Saint Cyprien, of Arles.	Died about 546.	Bishop of Toulon.	Life of St. Cesaire.
Saint Gregory, of Auvergne.	544—595.	Bishop of Tours.	1. An ecclesiastical history of the Franks; 2. On the glory of martyrs; 3. On the glory of confessors; 4. Lives of the fathers; 5. The miracles of Saint Martin; 6. Several theological writings; lost.
Marius, of Autun.	532—596.	Bishop of Avenche.	A chronicle extending from 455 to the year 581.
Joseph of Touraine.	Towards the end of the 5th century.	A Jew.	A history of the Jews, in Hebrew.
Seventh Century.			
Saint Fortunatus, of Ceneda, in Italy.	530, Beginning of the 7th century.	Bishop of Poietiers	1. Sacred and profane poems; 2. Lives of the saints.
St. Colomban, of Irish origin.	Died in 1615.	Abbot of Luxeuil.	1. Poems; 2. Homilies; 3. Letters; 4 Short theological writings.

Name.	Date.	Condition in Life.	Works.
Marculf.	Towards the middle of the 7th century.	A monk.	Collection of formulæ, or models of public and private acts.
Frédégaire, of Burgundy.	Towards the middle of the 7th century.	A monk.	A chronicle from the creation until the year 641.
Jonas, of Italian origin.	Idem.	Abbot of Saint Amand.	The life of St Colomban.
Saint Ouen, of Sanci, near Soissons.	609—683.	Archbishop of Rouen.	The life of Saint Eloy.

Eighth Century.

An anonymous historian.	Beginning of the 8th century.	... ...	Les Gestes des Francs, a chronicle extending to the year 584.
Saint Boniface (Winfried), Anglo-Saxon.	680—755.	Archbishop of Mayence.	1. Letters; 2. Sermons; 3. Theological writings; lost.
Ambroise Autbert, probably of Aquitaine,	Died in 778.	Abbot of Saint Vincent near Benevento.	1. A Commentary upon the Apocalypse; 2. Sermons; 3. A treatise on combating vice.
An anonymous historian.	Towards the end of the 8th century.	... ...	The Life of Dagobert I.
Turpin.	Died in 800.	Archbishop of Reims.	It is to him that has been attributed the fabulous chronicle entitled, Histoire de la Vie de Charlemagne et de Roland.

Ninth Century.

Alcuin in England, Yorkshire.	735—804.	Abbot of Saint Martin of Tours.	1. Commentaries upon the Scriptures; 2. Philosophical and literary writings; 3. Poems; 4. Letters.
Anonymous.	Beginning of 9th century.		Annales de l'Histoire des Francs
Angilbert in Neustria.	Died in 814.	Counsellor of Charlemagne,	1. Poems; 2. A relation of what he

Name.	Date.	Condition in Life.	Works
Leidrade, originally from Norica.	Died towards 816.	abbot of St. Regnier. Archbishop of Lyons.	had done for his monastery. 1. Letters; 2. Theological writings.
Smaragde.	Died about 820.	Abbot of St. Mihiel.	1. Moral treatise; 2. Commentaries on the New Testament; 3. A Grammar.
Saint Benedict, of Aniane, in Septimania.	751—821.	Abbot of Aniane and Inde.	1. The Code of Monastic Rules; 2. The Concordance of the rules; 3. Writings on Theology.
Theodulf, an Italian Goth.	Died in 821.	Bishop of Orleans.	1. Instruction schools; 2. Theological writings; 3. Poems.
Adalhard, born in Austrasia.	753—826.	Counsellor to Charlemagne, abbot of Corbie.	1. Statutes for the abbey of Corbie; 2. Letters; 3. A treatise *De Ordine Palatii*, reproduced by Hincmar.
Dungal, of Irish origin.	Died about 834.	A hermit, near St. Denis.	1. A letter to Charlemagne on the pretended eclipses of the sun in the year 810; 2. A treatise in favor of the worship of images; 3. Poems.
Halitgaire.	Died in 831.	Bishop of Cambray.	1. A penitential; 2 A treatise on the lives and duties of priests.
Ansegise of Burgundy.	Died in 833.	Counsellor to Charlemagne, abbot of Fontenelle.	The first collection of the capitularies of Charlemagne and Louis Le Debonnaire, in four books.
Friedgies, an Anglo-Saxon by birth	Died in 834.	Abbot of Saint Martin of Tours.	1. A philosophical treatise on Chaos and Darkness; 2. Poems.
Ermold le Noir, from Septimania.	Died towards the middle of the 9th century.	Abbot of Aniane	A poem on the life and actions of Louis le Debonnaire.

Name.	Date.	Condition in Life.	Works.
Amalaire, in Austrasia.	Died in 837.	A priest at Metz.	1. The rule of the Canonesses; 2. A treatise on the ecclesiastical offices; 3. Letters.
Eginhard in Austrasia.	Died in 839.	Counsellor to Charlemagne, abbot of Seligenstadt.	1. The life of Charlemagne; 2. Annals; 3. Letters.
Agobard, originally of Spain.	779—840.	Archbishop of Lyons.	1. Theological writings; 2. Letters; 3. Poems.
Hilduin.	Died about 840.	Abbot of Saint Denis.	The Areopagites, destined to prove that Denys the Areopagite is the same as St. Denis, first bishop of Paris.
Dodane.	Died in the middle of the 9th century.	Duchess of Septimania.	A manual containing counsels to her sons.
Jonas in Aquitaine.	Died in 842.	Bishop of Orleans.	1. A treatise on the institution of laymen; 2. On the institution of the king; 3. On Images.
Saint Ardon, Smaragde, in Septimania.	Died in 843.	A monk at Aniane.	The life of St. Benedict d'Aniane.
Benedict in Belgium.	Towards the middle of the 9th century.	Deacon at Mayence.	A collection of the capitularies of the kings of the Francs, in three books, added to the four books collected by Angesise.
Thegan, in Austrasia.	Died in 846.	Chorepiscopus of Trèves.	The life of Louis le Debonnaire.
An anonymous writer called the Astronomer.	In the first half of the 9th century.	.. ..	The life of Louis le Debonnaire.
Walfried Strabo, in Germany.	807—849.	Abbot of Reichenau	1. A commentary on the whole of the Bible; 2. The life of Saint Gall; 3. Theological writings; 4. Poems; amongst others a

Name.	Date.	Condition in Life.	Works.
Frecult.	Died in 850.	Bishop of Lisieux.	descriptive poem, entitled *Hortulus*. An universal history from the creation of the world until the end of the sixth century.
Angelome in Burgundy.	Died about 855.	A monk at Luxeuil.	Commentaries upon several parts of the Bible.
Raban-Maur, in Austrasia.	776—856.	Archbishop of Mayence.	Fifty-one works on theology, philosophy, philology, chronology; Letters, &c.
Nithard in Austrasia.	Died in 859.	Duke of Maritime France, monk at Saint Riquier.	The history of the dissensions of the sons of Louis le Debonnaire.
Florus, in Burgundy.	Died about 860.	A priest at Lyons.	1. Theological writings, amongst others, a refutation of the treatise on predestination, by John Scotus; 2. Poems; amongst others, a complaint on the division of the empire after Louis le Debonnaire.
Saint Prudentius, in Spain.	Died about 861.	Bishop of Troyes.	Theological writings; amongst others, on predestination, and against John Scotus.
Loup (Servat), in Burgundy.	Died about 862.	Abbot of Ferrieres in Gatinais.	1. Theological writings; amongst others, on predestination; 2. Letters; 3. A history of the emperors; lost.
Radbert (Paschase), in the diocese of Soissons	Died in 865.	Abbot of Corbie.	1. Theological writings; amongst others, a treatise on the Eucharist; 2. The life of Wala, abbot of Corbie.
Ratramne.	Died in 868.	Monk at Corbie.	Theological writings; amongst others, on transubstan-

Name.	Date.	Condition in Life.	Works.
Gottschalk, of Saxon origin.	Died in 869.	Monk at Orbais.	tiation and predestination. Writings on predestination.
Otfried.	Died about 870.	Monk at Weissemburg.	A paraphrased translation of the Gospel, in German rhymed verse.
Milon.	Died in 872.	Monk at Saint Amand.	Poems; amongst others, a poem on sobriety, dedicated to Charles le Chauve; and a pastoral entitled, the Combat of Winter and Spring.
Jean, called the Scot, or Erigena, in Ireland.	Died between 872 and 877.	Layman.	Several philosophical works: 1. On divine predestination; 2. On the division of nature; 3. The translation of the pretended writings of Dionysius the Areopagite.
Usuard.	About the middle of the ninth century.	Monk at Saint Germain des Pres.	A great martyrology.
Saint Remy	Died in 875	Archbishop of Lyons.	Theological works; amongst others, on predestination and free will.
Saint Adon, in the diocese of Sens.	800—875.	Archbishop of Vienne.	1. Theological writings; 2. A universal chronicle.
Isaac.	Died in 880	Bishop of Langres.	An extensive collection of canons.
Henric, at Hery, near Auxerre.	834—881.	Monk at St. Germain d'Auxerre.	The life of St. Germain d'Auxerre, in verse, in six books.
Hincmar.	Died in 882	Archbishop of Reims.	1. Theological writings; amongst others, on predestination; 2. Political writings and counsels; 3. Letters.
Anonymous.	.. ..	.. ..	The annals of St. Bertin, by several writers, in part by

CIVILIZATION IN FRANCE.   245

Name.	Date.	Condition in Life.	Works.
A monk of Saint Gaul, Anonymous.	The end of the ninth century.	.. ..	St. Prudence, bishop of Troyes, and perhaps by Hincmar. Des faits et gestes de Charlemagne.

Tenth Century.

Name.	Date.	Condition in Life.	Works.
Remy in Burgundy.	Died about 908.	Monk at St. Germain d'Auxerre.	1. Commentaries on the Bible; 2. Theological works; 3. Commentaries on the ancient grammarians and rhetoricians.
Reginon.	Died in 915.	Abbot of Prüm	1. A chronology from the birth of Jesus Christ until the year 906; 2. A collection of canonical rules.
Ahbon	Died about 924.	Monk at Saint Germain des Pres.	A poem on the siege of Paris by the Normans in 885.
Hucbald, in Flanders.	840—930.	Monk at Saint Amand.	1. Poems; among others, a poem in honor of the Bald, dedicated to Chas. le Chauve, in which all the words begin with c; 2. Lives of the saints.
Saint Odon, in le Maine.	879—942	Abbot of Cluny.	1 Theological writings; 2. The lives of the saints, especially that of Saint Gregory of Tours; 3. Poems.
John, of Italian origin.	About the middle of the 10th century.	Monk.	The life of St. Odon, abbot of Cluny.
Frodoard, at Epernay.	894—966.	Canon at Reims.	1. Poems; 2. The history of the church of Reims; 3. A chronicle from 919 to 966.
Helperic.	About the end of the 10th century.	Schoolmaster of Grand Fel	A treatise on computation or supputation of time as re-

Name.	Date	Condition in Life.	Works.
John.	About the end of the 10th century.	Abbot of Saint Arnould at Metz.	gards the ecclesiastical calendar. Several lives of the saints; amongst others that of John de Verdiere, abbot of Gorze, and the relation of his embassy in Spain to Abderrahman, caliph of Cordova.
Adson, in Transjuran Burgundy.	Died in 992.	Abbot of Montier en Der.	1. A treatise on the Antichrist, celebrated in the middle ages; 2. The lives of the saints.
Arnoult.	End of the 10th century.	Bishop of Orleans.	Letters entitled *de Cartilagine* (on the Cartilage), remarkable as an essay at anatomical studies. They are inedited.
Gerbert, at Aurillac.	Died in 1003.	Pope, under the name of Silvester II.	1. Works on mathematics; 2. On philosophy; 3. On theology; 4. Poems; 5. Letters.

VII.

Chronological Table of the Councils and Canonical Legislation of Gaul, from the Fourth to the Tenth Century.[1]

Date.	Place.	Present.	Object of the Council, Rules, &c.
314	Arles	33 bishops, 14 priests, 25 deacons, 8 clerks.	This council was convoked by Constantine, to pronounce on the subject of the Donatists; and of Cecilian, bishop of Carthage. *Rules.*—That each priest reside in the place in which he was ordained.

It will be at once seen that in this abstract I have only inserted the most important of the canons.

Date.	Place.	Present.	Object of the Council, Rules, &c.
			That the faithful who become governors of provinces receive letters of communion, in order that the bishop of the place they inhabit may be able to watch, and excommunicate them, if they act contrary to the discipline. That the priests and deacons who quit the places assigned to them, shall be deposed. The council orders that Easter should be celebrated everywhere the same day; excommunicates those who carry arms in time of peace, usurious clerks, and calumniators; forbids deacons to celebrate the office; orders that absolution shall be received in the same place where excommunication was pronounced; forbids bishops to encroach reciprocally on their rights, and interdicts to the deacons of towns the power of doing anything without the consent of the priests.
343	Cologne.	14 bishops, 10 envoys from bishops	Euphratus, bishop of Cologne, having denied the divinity of Jesus Christ, the faithful and clergy of Cologne denounce him as a heretic, and he is condemned and deposed.
353	Arles.	. .	This council, at which the emperor Constantius assisted, and the Arians prevailed, deposed Paul, bishop of Trèves, who would not sign the condemnation of Saint Athanasius.
356	Beziers.	.. ..	This council, convoked by Saturnin, bishop of Arles, and which decided nothing, banished Saint Hilary, bishop of Poictiers, to Phrygia.
359	In Gaul.	.. .	This council condemned the Arian formula adopted at Sirmium.
360	Paris.	. ..	This council condemned the

Date.	Place.	Present.	Object of the Council, Rules, &c.
374	Valence	21 bishops.	Arian formula of Rimini; communicated this resolution to the bishops of the east, and excommunicated Saturnin, bishop of Arles. *Rules.*—It is forbidden to confess a crime, whether true or false, in order to escape from holy orders. The council forbids the ordaining those who have been twice married, or who have married a widow. It excommunicates virgins consecrated to God if they marry, and those who, after their baptism, sacrifice to demons, or make use of pagan purifications.
383 Date uncertain.	Nimes.		
385	Bordeaux.	.. ..	This council was held at the request of Ithace against the Priscillianists. Instantius was deprived of his bishopric; Priscillian appealed to the emperor, who put him to death.
386	Trèves.[1]	.. ..	This council declared Ithace absolved from the death of the Priscillianists, Saint Martin there communicated with him, for which he never forgave himself.
395	Turin.	.. ..	This council treated only of affairs of discipline, and the pretensions to primacy of the bishops of Marseilles, as well as the rivality of the bishops of Vienne and Arles. *Rules.*—That no bishop shall receive a clerk of another bishop and ordain him for himself. That no one who has been rejected

---

[1] We have, as usual, preferred the date of Sirmond to that of Labbe, because the events of these two councils clearly prove, that that of Bordeaux must have taken place before that of Trèves. I can only conclude that Sulpicius Severus deceived himself, when he said that after the year 384 St. Martin was present at no council; or, which is very possible, it is an error of the copyist.

Date.	Place.	Present.	Object of the Council, Rules, &c.
			shall be admitted to the communion.
That those who have had children after their ordination, shall be excluded from the major orders.

Fifth Century.

Date.	Place.	Present.	Object of the Council, Rules, &c.
429	In Gaul. Place uncertain.	.. ..	This numerous council assembled in compliance with the wishes of the Bretons, who demanded from the bishops of Gaul succor against the heresy of Pelagius; the council sent them Saint Germain and St. Loup.
439	Riez.	13 bishops, 1 bishop's envoy.	This council was held on the subject of the bishop of Embrun, who had been consecrated by two bishops only. Several canons of discipline were made at it.
Rules.—That if two bishops only shall ordain a bishop, they shall, for the future, be excluded from all ordinations and councils.
That when a bishop dies, the nearest bishop shall take charge of his diocese.
That no person shall interfere with the consecration of a bishop without having been invited to do so by the metropolitan.
That it be permitted to country priests to give the blessing, to consecrate virgins, to confirm neophytes, and that they conduct themselves as superiors to the priests, and inferiors to the bishops.[1]
That a council be held twice a year.
441	Orange	16 bishops, 1 priest for a bishop	This council was engaged only on affairs of discipline.
Rules.—That no one shall re-

[1] This passage proves that chorepiscopi, or rural bishops, are meant; a class superior to priests, but inferior to the bishops.

Date.	Place	Present.	Object of the Council, Rules, &c.
			duce to servitude those who belong to the church. That one council shall not be dissolved without indicating another, the rigor of the weather preventing the holding two councils a year. That the functions of an infirm bishop shall be fulfilled by another bishop, and not by priests. The council forbids repeating confirmation, delivering up those who take refuge in a church; forbids a bishop to communicate with him who has excommunicated another bishop, or to ordain deaconesses; orders that some of the graces of the church be granted to idiots, and that catechumens shall be present at the reading of the Gospel.
442	Vaison.	.. ..	This council was occupied with affairs of discipline. *Rules*—That those who retain the offerings of the dead shall be excommunicated. If a bishop does not acquiesce in his sentence, he can appeal to a synod.[1]
444	Vienne.	.. ..	This council was presided over by Saint Hilary. Chelidonius, bishop of Besançon, was deposed for having married a widow. *Rules*—That the priests shall receive the holy Chrism every year at Easter, from the nearest bishop, and not at their own mere discretion.
About 452	Arles.[2]	44 bishops	This council was held against the Novatians, the Photinians, or Paulinists, the Bonosians, the Arians, the Eutychians. Several canons of discipline were made at

---

[1] The judgments of the metropolitan are doubtless here referred to.
[2] We find among the canons of the council of Arles, twenty which belong, as it would appear, to that of Orange; they are distinguished by the titles C. d'O.

Date.	Place.	Present.	Object of the Council, Rules, &c.
			it. The council also was engaged with the *lapsi*, that is to say, those who had given way during the persecution. *Rules.*—That no one shall be consecrated a bishop without a letter from the metropolitan, or from three provincial bishops. That in a contested election the metropolitan must vote with the majority. The ordination of a clerk out of his diocese, and without the approbation of his bishop, is null. A bishop who does not come to the council, or who quits it before the end, is excommunicated. A bishop is guilty of sacrilege who neglects to extirpate the custom of adoring fountains, trees, and stones. When there are priests present, deacons must not administer the body of Jesus Christ. Actors shall be excommunicated. That penance shall not be given to married people without their mutual consent. *C. d'O.* The causes of clerks must, under pain of excommunication, be brought before the bishop. *C. d'O.* If a bishop builds a church in the diocese of another bishop, which cannot be prevented without a crime, he must not think he has therefore the right of dedicating it; that is reserved for the bishop in whose diocese it stands; but he will have the privilege of placing what clerks he pleases therein. To avoid simony in the election of bishops, the bishops shall name three persons, among whom the clergy and the people shall choose. The council forbids the clerks to practise usury, to charge themselves with the conduct of other

Date.	Place.	Present.	Object of the Council, Rules, &c
			people's affairs, to have in their house, after they have passed the deaconship, other women than their grandmother, their mother, their daughter, their niece, or their wife, converted like themselves. The canons of the council of Orange give to priests the power of confirming a dying heretic, grant penance to the clerks, permit them to absolve dying persons without penance, on condition of their performing penance if they recover. They grant baptism to demoniacs, and those who have suddenly lost the use of speech, and excommunicate any person who, having lost his serfs, owing to their having taken refuge in a church, shall possess himself of the serfs of that church.
About 453	Angers.	8 bishops.	This council was held on the occasion of the consecration of Talasius, bishop of Angers. *Rules.*—That those who renounce the priesthood for the army shall be excommunicated. That monks who wander about without letters of leave shall be excommunicated. That a bishop shall not advance the clerk of another bishop.
455	Arles.	13 bishops.	This council assembled to terminate the quarrel existing between several bishops and Faust, abbot of Lerens.
461	Tours	8 bishops, 1 bishop's envoy.	This council was composed of bishops assembled for the feast of St. Martin. Several canons of discipline were made. *Rule.*—That a clerk shall not travel without letters from his bishop. That a clerk who has permission to marry, shall not marry a widow.

Date.	Place.	Present.	Object of the Council, Rules, &c.
			If a clerk is guilty of drunkenness, he must be punished according to his order.
About 465	Vannes.	6 bishops.	This council was composed of bishops assembled for the purpose of the consecration of the bishop of Vannes. It discussed points of discipline. *Rules.*—That without the permission of his abbot, a monk shall not ask for a private cell. That each abbot shall have but one monastery. That, under pain of excommunication, no clerk shall practise divination by Saints' names,⁴ or the Holy Scriptures. The council forbids clerks to be present at Jewish wedding-feasts or entertainments; orders all who are in town to attend at matins; and prescribes for all the province (Brittany) one order of ceremonies and chant.
475	Arles	30 bishops.	This council was also held against the predestinarians.
About 475	Lyons.	. ..	This council was held against the predestinarians. We are ignorant of what passed.

Sixth Century.

506	Agde.	25 bishops, 8 priests, 2 deacons, representatives of their bishops.	This council was not occupied with dogma. All its canons, of which 24 out of 70 belong to the council of Epaone, are upon discipline. The twenty-four rules of the council of Epaone will be found in their place. Saint Cesaire presided at this council. Gratian adds canons taken from various authors; one against sorcerers, another against usurers; the first of all forbids to bishops and priests the effusion of blood; there is another against quarrelsome persons, scandal-mongers, and calumniators. At the end of

Date.	Place.	Present.	Object of the Council, Rules, &c.
			this council is a letter from Theodoric to the Roman senate, which appears to be the result of it, and in which priests are forbidden to sell the goods of the church. *Rules.*—If a bishop has pronounced an unjust, or too severe excommunication, and warned by the neighboring bishops, he does not withdraw it, they must not refuse the communion to those who have been deprived of it. All that is given to a bishop becomes the property of the church. 　The council prescribes the tonsure of clerks, the fast of Lent, and the communion at the three great feasts. 　Freedmen are protected by the church. 　Every person must be present at mass every Sunday, and not to leave until the conclusion, under the penalty of being publicly reprimanded by the bishop. The bishop can dispose of the minor goods of the church, and of his vagrant serfs. 　The clerk who shall suppress or deliver up the titles of possession belonging to the church, shall be excommunicated, and condemned to pay out of his own property the damage which shall accrue thence to the church. 　Priests, deacons, and sub-deacons, are forbidden to be present at wedding feasts. 　A clerk guilty of drunkenness, shall, according to his order, be deprived of the communion during thirty days, or submitted to a corporal punishment, *corporali supplicio.* 　The council deprives of his priesthood the clerk who robs the church; orders that a young clerk shall not be preferred to an elder one; if, however, the latter cannot fulfil the duties of an archdeaconate, he shall have the title,

Date.	Place.	Present.	Object of the Council, Rules, &c
			and the bishop must choose some one to exercise the functions. This council fixes, at the age of forty years, the time when virgins take the veil, at twenty-five that of the deaconship, at thirty that of priesthood and episcopacy. It forbids conferring the monastic order upon married men without the consent of their wives; it renews a canon of the council of Vaison, upon the care to be taken of exposed children. It forbids the celebration of great feasts out of the parish; to sell or to give the goods of the church; to build new monasteries without the permission of the bishop; to build monasteries for men near those of the women, and to ordain penitents. It commands the church to defend freedmen, and to distribute the salaries of priests according to their merits. It also regulates several rules of worship.
511	Orleans.	32 bishops,	This council was convoked by Clovis, on the advice of Saint Remy, whose signature, however, is not to be found. Many bishops were there from the kingdom of the Visigoths, which had just been conquered by Clovis. *Rules.*—This council made several canons upon the right of asylum, and prescribed that the criminal and serf who had taken refuge in the church, should not be delivered up until they had stipulated for their safety. That no secular person shall be ordained without an order from the king or the judge, and that the children and the grandchildren of clerks shall be under the authority of the bishop, instead of that of their parents. That no one shall be excommunicated for having, without proof, claimed anything belonging to the church; that the ab-

Date.	Place.	Present.	Object of the Council, Rules, &c.
			bots shall be subject to the bishops, and the monks to the abbots. That no person shall celebrate Easter in the country. That the bishop, if not ill, must on Sunday attend the nearest church. That if, through humanity, the bishop has lent land to be cultivated, the length of time must not occasion any prescription. That no monk, instigated by ambition or vanity, shall, without the permission of his abbot, abandon his brethren to build a separate cell; that any professed monk who marries shall be expelled the ecclesiastical order. The council also orders, that if a bishop has ordained a serf without the permission of his master, he must indemnify the latter for his loss, but the clerk will remain ordained; it forbids any one to marry the widow of a priest or deacon; places under the power of the bishops the real property given to the church, and secures to them a third part of the offerings; enjoins them to provide the poor and sick with clothes and nourishment, and regulates several articles of worship.
515	St. Maurice.	4 bishops, 8 counts.	This council was convoked by king Sigismond, converted to the Catholic faith, upon the subject of the foundation or restoration of the monastery of Saint Maurice, and the rules to be established therein.
516	Lyons.	.. ..	It is known by a letter from Avitus, that this council was held, and that he assisted at it. Nothing else has come down to us concerning it.
517	Epaone, in the	25 bishops.	There exist two circular letters by which Avitus and Viventiolus

Date.	Place.	Present.	Object of the Council, Rules, &c.
	Vienese, now Jena, in Savoy.		convoke to this council the bishops of their provinces: Avitus insists upon the importance of making a good choice of priests charged in times of sickness with signing for their bishop. Viventiolus declares that clerks are obliged to come to the council, while it is only permitted to the laity, that the people may know that which is regulated by the bishops. *Rules.*—That priests, bishops, and deacons, shall not possess sporting dogs or falcons. That an abbot shall not, without the authorization of the bishop, sell the goods of the abbey, neither shall he enfranchise its serfs, for it seems unjust that while the monks are obliged to work every day upon the land, their serfs should enjoy repose and liberty. That no bishop shall sell the goods of the church without the approbation of his metropolitan; he may only conclude useful exchanges. If an abbot, convicted of fault, is refractory, and will not receive a successor from his bishop, the affair must be taken before the metropolitan. If any one has killed a serf, without the consent of the judge, he must expiate this effusion of blood by a penance of two years. The council imposes the same penance on those Catholics who have fallen into heresy. That if a serf, guilty of atrocious crimes, seeks refuge in a church, he shall only be exempted from corporal punishment. The council declares null the donations or legacies made by priests and bishops of the goods of the church; it forbids priests to serve a church in another diocese, without the consent of their bishop; to be present at the feasts

Date.	Place.	Present.	Object of the Council, Rules, &c.
			given by heretics; it permits the laity to accuse clerks; it forbids placing the relics of the saints in country oratories, unless there are priests in the neighborhood to serve them; it forbids bishops and clerks to receive women after the vesper hour; orders all the provincial bishops to conform themselves to the order of offices established by the metropolitan. It forbids the young monks and clerks to enter the monasteries for women, unless they go to see a mother or a sister. It orders all the noble citizens to come at Easter and Christmas, to receive the bishop's blessing. We must add to the canons of the council of Epaone, several rules which belong to it, and which have been placed in the council of Agde of 506; these are their principal provisions:
			Bishops are allowed to dispose of their own goods, but not of those of the church; the council condemns to restitution out of their own property, those priests and deacons who have disposed of the property of the church, and declares null the enfranchisements that they have made. It forbids clerks to practise magic; it will not allow the ordination of factious, usurious, and vindictive clerks; it forbids the clerks that are not consecrated to enter the sacristy, and to touch the sacred utensils; and to the deacons to sit down in the presence of the priests.
517	Lyons.	11 bishops.	This council was held on the occasion of a certain Stephen, who had married his sister-in-law. There are no canons that call for remark; they are a repetition of some already cited. Fraternal union among the bishops is recommended.

Date.	Place.	Present.	Object of the Council, Rules, &c.
524	Arles.	14 bishops, 4 priests for their bishops.	This council was held and presided over by Saint Cesarius on the occasion of the dedication of the cathedral of Saint Mary. *Rules.*—Although we ought to observe the ordinances of the ancient fathers as to the longer duration of the conversion of the laity, before their ordination, yet as the number of churches augments, and the want of clerks is greater, it is ordered, without prejudice to the ancient rules, that no metropolitan bishop shall make a bishop from the laity; that the bishops shall not make a laic priest, or deacon, until a year of noviciate. That the bishop who has ordained a penitent or a bigamist, shall remain a year without saying mass.
527	Carpentras	16 bishops.	This council was presided over by St. Cesarius; it has but one article. The fathers arranged to meet at Vaison the next year. *Rules.*—That what belongs to a church, shall be distributed to the clerks who serve it, and employed in reparations. That if a bishop has more expenses than money, and there are in his diocese parishes in the contrary situation, he can apply their surplus to his expenses, leaving them the sum necessary to the wants of their churches and clerks.
529	Orange	14 bishops, 8 *viri illustres*.	This council was assembled for the dedication of the cathedral of Orange, built by the prefect Liber; but the true cause of its convocation by St. Cesarius, was a writing by Faust, bishop of Riez, "De gratiâ Dei quâ salvamur," which was suspected of semi-Pelagianism. The council fixed, in 25 canons, the doctrine of St. Augustin, but did not make it into discipline.

Date.	Place.	Present.	Object of the Council, Rules, &c.
529	Valence.	.. ..	This council was convoked by St. Cesarius (who could not preside) against the semi-Pelagians.
529	Vaison.	12 bishops.	This council was presided over by St. Cesarius. *Rules.*—That, as is the salutary custom in Italy, the priests, when they have no wives, shall receive in their houses young lecturers, whom they shall instruct, and thus prepare for themselves worthy successors; and when these are of age, if by the fragility of the flesh, they wish for a wife, they are not to be prevented from marrying. That, the same as in Italy and the Eastern provinces, the *Kyrie eleison* and the *Sanctus, Sanctus,* shall be said every day at the mass. That the pope's name shall be recited in our churches. As, not only in the apostolic seat, but also in the East, Africa, and Italy, the malice of the heretics causes them to deny that the Son of God has always been equal with the Father, after *Gloria,* &c., *Sicut erat in principio,* has been added; and we order that the same shall be observed in all the churches. The council permits all the priests to preach, not only in the towns, but in all the provinces, and prescribes that when they cannot do it, a deacon shall read the homilies of the holy fathers
533	Orleans.	26 bishops, 8 priests.	*Rules.*—That no bishop having received notice from his metropolitan, fail to come to the council or to the consecration of a co-bishop. That the metropolitans convoke each year the bishops to the provincial councils. That the bishops shall receive nothing for the ordinations.

Date.	Place.	Present.	Object of the Council, Rules, &c.
			That no bishop shall refuse to attend the funeral of another bishop, and that he shall demand nothing for his trouble and expenses. That a bishop attending the funeral of a bishop, shall assemble the priests and entrust the goods of the church to persons worthy of confidence. That no person in a church shall sing, drink, or do anything unbecoming. That no one who is unlettered or ignorant of the form of baptism shall be ordained deacon or priest. On account of their frailty, women are excluded from the deaconship. Catholics who return to the worship of idols and eat flesh offered to idols, or animals killed by the bite of a beast, or suffocated, shall be excommunicated. That no priest shall live with secular persons without the permission of the bishops. The council condemns to degradation the deacon who shall marry in captivity, and the clerks who disdain to acquit themselves of their functions. It excommunicates abbots who resist bishops. It renews the ancient form for the consecration of the metropolitan, and orders that after being chosen by the provincial bishops, the clerks, and the people, he shall be consecrated by the provincial bishops. It forbids marriages between Christians and Jews.
535	Clermont.	Bishops.	The council was held the 11th year of his reign, by Theodebert, king of Austrasia, who was more favorable to the clergy than his father had been. *Rules* —That no bishop shall dare to propose any affair to the council before those which regard the amendment of manners,

Date.	Place.	Present.	Object of the Council, Rules, &c.
			the severity of the rule, and the saving of souls.
That bishoprics shall be given according to merit, and not to those who merely ask for them.
That the clerks shall not rise against the bishops by the help of the power of the laity.
That those who demand from kings the property of the church, and by a horrible cupidity seize the goods of the poor, shall be excluded from the communion, and the donation shall be null.
That Jews shall not be constituted judges over Christian people.
That if a bishop will not by canonical rigor prevent the priests and deacons from having commerce of any kind with women, he shall himself be excommunicated.
The council forbids priests private oratories to celebrate the great feasts away from the cathedral church.
Canons derived from different authors.—That the priests shall inform the people where the inns are situated. The innkeepers must not refuse to lodge any traveller, and must not make him pay for anything more than the market price, or the affair must be taken before the priest, who will oblige them to sell with humanity.
There shall be no action against a bishop who has without interference possessed the diocese of another bishop during thirty years. (Some words are wanting here, but it is evident that the council recommends that in this case the limits of the dioceses shall not be confounded.)
As regards priests who are accused of fornication, or any capital crime, and who have no colleagues to swear with them, as to he

Date.	Place.	Present.	Object of the Council, Rules, &c.
			innocence, they must be judged by the canons. A bishop may, with the concurrence of the clerks, help his family with the church treasures.
538	Orleans.	19 bishops, 7 priests.	*Rules.*—If clerks placed under the patronage of any of the laity, shall make it a pretence to disobey their bishop, and refuse to fulfil their functions, they must be separated from other clerks and shall receive nothing from the church It shall be in the power of the bishop to decide whether or not the clerks attached to a monastery or a church shall or shall not retain what they possessed before their ordination. If any clerks, as by the inspiration of the devil happened lately in several places, rebel against authority, unite in conspiracy, and take mutual oaths, or mutually subscribe an agreement to that purpose, nothing shall excuse such presumption, but the affair shall be taken before the synod. That no serf or laborer shall be admitted to ecclesiastical honors. That no one shall be present at divine service with warlike arms. If a judge, knowing that a heretic has re-baptized a catholic, does not seize the heretic and send the affair before the king, for we have catholic kings, he shall be excommunicated during the space of a year. This council repeats the rules of the preceding, concerning the separation of priests from women; sub-deacons are included. We must repeat, says the council, what we know is not observed. It orders, also, as regards the newly converted Christians, on account of the novelty of their faith and conversion, that the forbidden marriages they have contracted previous shall not be broken.

Date.	Place.	Present.	Object of the Council, Rules, &c.
			It renews, also, the anathemas against those who obtain or alienate the goods of the church, it excommunicates, for six months, the bishops who shall make an ordination contrary to the canons; for one year, him who in such a case has deceived the bishop, clerk or witness. It expels from his order the clerk guilty of any capital crime. It directs them not to restore but to buy at a just price the Christian serfs who have sought in the church an asylum against their Jewish masters, who would impose on them anything contrary to their religion, or shall not have fulfilled the promises made when they were restored upon a former occasion. It refers clerks, who complain of the bishops, to the synodal judgment. It complains, that the people have been told that one may not travel, or cook, or clean houses or one's person on a Sunday; it declares these observances more Jewish than Christian, and holds permitted all that was allowed before; it excludes the cultivation of land, which would prevent the attending church. It forbids people to leave church before the end of mass. It interdicts, also, " for by the grace of God, we have catholic kings," from Holy Saturday until Easter Monday, the Jews from mixing with the Christians in any place or on any occasion.
541	Orleans.	38 bishops, 11 priests, 1 abbot each for 1 bishop.	The council was occupied with discipline. *Rules.*—The council orders the celebration of Easter according to the usage of Rome, and decides that each time there is a doubt upon the epoch of a solemnity, the apostolical usage ought to be observed.

Date.	Place.	Present.	Object of the Council, Rules, &c.
			That the parish priests receive the decrees of the canons, so that they or their people cannot excuse themselves on the plea of ignorance of what is necessary for their salvation. If a bishop, who has left none of his own property, has disposed of that of the church, it must return to the church; but if from the serfs of the church he has made a number of freedmen, they remain free, but they must not fall away from their allegiance to the church. If bishops quarrel among themselves for lands or other possessions, on being warned by the letters of their brothers, they must arrange between themselves or submit to arbitrators. Bishops, priests, and deacons, are exempt from the wardship of the administration, because it is just to retain for Christians what the law of the world did for the pagan priests. That the slaves of the priests and of the church must neither pillage nor make prisoners, for it is iniquitous that ecclesiastical discipline should be stained by the crimes of the servants of those who frequent the sacrament of redemption. Serfs who have fled to the church under pretext of marriage, and believing that thus they can marry, must be returned to their masters or parents; and the clerks must not protect such unions. If parishes are placed in the hands of powerful men, and the clerks, warned by the archdeacon of the city, neglect to acquit themselves of their duty towards the house of the Lord, they must be corrected according to ecclesiastical discipline. If Christians, slaves of the Jews, have fled from their masters

Date.	Place.	Present.	Object of the Council, Rules, &c
			and demand their liberty, we order that, as in the ancient laws, having given a just price they be set at liberty. If any one desires to have a chapel on his own premises, he must assign sufficient land for it and furnish it in with clerks, who will celebrate the offices in a proper manner. The council orders also that the consecration of a bishop shall take place in the town which he is to govern; it forbids proprietors of chapels to receive strange clerks without the consent of the bishop of the place. It forbids heirs to take what has been left to the church; it also forbids any one to marry a girl without the consent of her parents. It excommunicates those proprietors of chapels who would hinder the clerks who serve them from acquitting themselves of what they owe to the divine service. It excludes from ordination those who descend from unemancipated serfs, and assures to the churches the return of all of which the bishops have given out the usufruct.
549	Orleans	50 bishops, 21 priests, archdeacons or abbots, each representing a bishop.	This council condemned the errors of the Eutychians, the Nestorians, and according to Baluze, of the Arians, whose heresy was reaching Orleans. *Rules.*—A serf shall not be ordained, even though he be free, against the will of his master. If it has been done, the serf must be returned to his master; but if he exacts from him services incompatible with the honor of the ecclesiastical order, then the bishop shall give two serfs to the master, and take the one who has been ordained.

Date.	Place.	Present.	Object of the Council, Rules, &c.
549 or 550	Clermont.	10 bishops.	This council assembled a short time after that of Orleans. *Rules.*—As we have discovered that several people reduce again to servitude those, who, according to the custom of the country, have been set at liberty in the churches, we order that every one shall keep possession of the liberty he has received; and if this liberty is attacked, justice must be defended by the church. 　The prisoners must be visited every Sunday by the archdeacon, or some one proposed by the church, that all their wants may be attended to. 　The veil may not be given to virgins when the will of their parents, or their own, leads to the monastery, until three years' trial. 　A bishop knowing that there are leperous persons on his territory, or in the town, must furnish them with all that is necessary. 　A master who has not kept the word he gave to his serf to induce him to leave the church, shall be excommunicated. If the serf refuse to leave the church upon the word of his master, he can employ force, that the church may not suffer from calumny, as if she withheld serfs. 　If a master is a pagan or a heretic, he must present Christians worthy of confidence to swear for him. 　No one may be permitted to obtain a bishopric with the help of presents, but, with the consent of the king, the pontiff elected by the clergy and the people must, as prescribed in the ancient rules, be consecrated by the metropolitan, or some one commissioned in his place, and the provincial bishops. 　No one shall be made bishop over those who refuse to have him, and (it would be a crime)

Date.	Place.	Present.	Object of the Council, Rules, &c.
			the consent of the clergy and citizens must not be constrained by the oppression of persons in power; if it be so, the bishop who has been elected more by violence than by a legitimate election, shall be for ever deprived of the usurped pontifical honor. Excommunication may not be lightly pronounced. Priests may not at an unfitting time see even their near relations Bishops may not ordain in a diocese vacant by the death of its bishop. No bishop must be placed above another, unless the latter has been guilty of some crime.
About 550	Toul.	.. ..	This council was convoked by Theodebald, king of Austrasia. Nicet, bishop of Trèves, had excommunicated several Franks for incestuous marriages. This irritating them, they insulted the bishop. The issue of this council is not known; its epoch is not precise.
550	Metz	.. ..	Saint Gall, bishop of Clermont, being dead, the bishops present at his funeral wished to consecrate as his successor Cato, who was elected by a great part of the people; but the archdeacon Cautin, coming to king Theodebald, acquainted him with the death of the archbishop, but concealed the rest. The king gave him the bishopric; and the bishops, then at Metz, consecrated him, and he was bishop in spite of his flock, by the violence that the king employed towards the deputies of Clermont.
554	Arles.	11 bishops, 8 priests, deacons, and archdeacons.	*Rules.*—No priest shall depose a deacon or subdeacon without the consent of his bishop. The clerk shall not waste the property which has been **given**

Date.	Place.	Present.	Object of the Council, Rules, &c.
			him for his use by the bishop. If a young clerk does so, he must be corrected by the discipline of the church; if he is old, he must be looked upon as an assassin of the poor. The council also made several rules for keeping under the spiritual and temporal power of the bishop, the monasteries of men and women. It forbids abbots to travel without the permission of the bishop.
555	In Armorica, place uncertain.		This council excommunicated Maclou, bishop of Vannes, who, after the death of his brother, Chann, count of Brittany, quitted his bishop for the countship and a wife.
556	Paris	27 bishops.	This council, convoked by Childebert, king of Paris, and presided over by Sapandus, bishop of Arles, deposed and shut up in a monastery Saffaracus, bishop of Paris: Eusebius his successor.
557	Paris	6 bishops.	This council was assembled to prevent by laws the dispersion of the goods of the churches, that the Frank kings gave to the first-comers. *Rules.*—Several laws against the detainers of church property, those who receive it from the kings, those who attack the personal property of the bishops, because the goods of the bishops are the property of the church. It forbids bishops to try to get possession of another's goods, and orders, without prejudice to royal liberality, the restitution thereof to the legitimate proprietor. It forbids any one to carry off or to marry, under favor of the king, a girl or a widow without the consent of her parents. It annuls the ordination of a bishop named by the king against the will of

Date.	Place.	Present.	Object of the Council, Rules, &c.
			the metropolitan and the provincial bishops, and the citizens; and as in several things ancient customs are neglected, the council renews and recommends the observance of the ancient laws. The council also orders the church and the priests to observe the will of the defunct as regards serfs left by will to keep the tombs.
563	Saintes.	.. ..	This council elected Heraclius in the place of Emerius whom Clotaire had made bishop of Saintes, Clotaire being dead in the interval, but Charibert made them receive Emerius, and imposed fines on the bishops, amongst others, on Leontius, the metropolitan of Bordeaux, who had convoked and presided at the council.
567	Lyons	8 bishops, 5 priests, 1 deacon.	This council was convoked by king Gontran, to judge Salone, bishop of Embrun, and Sagittaire, bishop of Gap, who were thorough brigands. They were deposed by the council; but they appealed to Pope John, and were by his order reinstated in their sees. *Rules.*—As to the ruin of their souls many have made captives by violence and treason, if they neglect to restore those they have taken captive, as the king orders, to the place where they have long lived in repose, they must be deprived of communion with the church. The council orders that discussions between bishops must be decided by the metropolitan, and that no bishop shall give communion to him who has excommunicated another bishop. That wills by which clerks, or other persons, have left anything to the church, shall always be valid, whatever fault may be in the form thereof. It forbids bishops to reclaim the liberalities of their predecessors.

Date.	Place.	Present.	Object of the Council, Rules, &c.
567	Tours.	7 bishops.	This council was assembled during the wars of the sons of Clotaire, and when the kings made use of the goods of the church to meet the expenses they incurred. Saint Redegonde wrote to the council to demand the confirmation of her rule. Her demand was granted. *Rules.*--This council, like many others, strongly recommends concord amongst the bishops. It orders that citizens and country priests shall nourish their poor, that they may not be obliged to go to other cities; it reiterates all prohibitions about women, and orders several precautions that suspicion may not fall upon the clerks. It forbids priests and monks to sleep together; it excommunicates the judge who shall refuse to separate a monk from the wife he has taken since his profession; it regulates the monks' fasts; it forbids several pagan superstitions; it renews all the menaces against those who, whilst our lords make war upon each other, invade or reclaim the goods of the church; and declares those judges and lords excommunicated who oppress the poor in spite of being warned by the bishop. The council orders that bishops only shall give letters of recommendation; that before sending away an abbot or an archpriest, they take counsel of all their priests and abbots, under penalty of being themselves excommunicated. It excommunicates priests who do not keep the rules of celibacy; prescribes that they shall help each other when one of them is insulted by indocile clerks. It forbids women to enter monasteries of men.
573	Paris.	21 bishops,	This council was assembled to

Date.	Place.	Present.	Object of the Council, Rules, &c.
575	Lyons.	1 priest	decide the affair of Promotus, who had been consecrated bishop of Chateaudun, against all canonical rule. The council declared him deposed, according to the demand made by Pappolus, bishop of Chartres, administrator of the church of Chateaudun during the vacancy
577	Paris.		This council judged the affair of Pretextat.
578	Auxerre	The bishop of Auxerre, 7 abbots, 34 priests, 3 deacons, all from the diocese of Auxerre.	This synod was held by Annachaire, bishop of Auxerre; nothing was discussed but questions of discipline and ceremonies. *Rules.*—This synod forbids many pagan superstitions; it orders all priests to attend the synod in May, and the abbots to come to the council in November. It forbids repasts in churches, and allowing young girls and secular persons to sing there. No clerk shall summon any one, but he shall authorize his brother, or some other layman, to do it. Every layman, who has despised the warnings of his archpriest, shall be excluded from the church so long as his disobedience shall last, and shall pay besides the fine that our glorious king has imposed. The synod forbids two masses to be said the same day on the same altar; to put a corpse upon a corpse; to receive the offering of those who have committed suicide; it also forbids clerks to hear or celebrate mass unless they be fasting; priests or deacons to assist at executions, or at sentences of death. No clerk shall summon another before the secular judge; priests may not sing or dance at feasts; abbots and monks may not be godfathers. It regulates the penance of an abbot who has not

Date.	Place.	Present.	Object of the Council, Rules, &c.
			enforced the observance of the laws upon celibacy; his penance ought to take place in another monastery than that of which he is the head.
579	Châlons.	.. ..	This council was convoked by Gontran to judge anew Sagittaire and Salone. They were condemned as guilty of high treason and being traitors to their country, the bishops having found that their other crimes could be expiated by canonical penance. The council consecrated a bishop for Maurienne, and subjected it to the bishop of Vienne.
579	Saintes.	.. ..	The council recommended to the mercy of Heraclius the count Nantinius, whom he had excommunicated, and who demanded absolution. The bishop granted it.
580	Braines	.. ..	This council judged the affair of Gregory of Tours, accused by one Leudaste. The cause was gained by Leudaste.
581	Lyon.	.. ..	This council reprimanded several bishops for negligence.
581	Macon.	21 bishops	This council was convoked by Gontran. *Rules.*—No clerk shall wear silk or other secular vestments that do not become his profession. A judge who has without sufficient cause—that is to say, without a charge of manslaughter, theft, or craft, arrested a priest, shall be excommunicated. No Jew shall be made judge over Christians, nor shall they be permitted to receive taxes. The council forbids Christians to serve Jews, and gives to Christians, serfs of Jews, the power of redeeming their liberty. The council made a law upon

Date.	Place.	Present.	Object of the Council, Rules, &c.
			the letters from bishops to other bishops concerning the redemption of captives, recommending that their authenticity be examined. It orders bishops to take care of the lepers found in the territory of their city, that they may not go to other cities
583	Lyon.	8 bishops, 12 bishops' legates.	
584	Valence	17 bishops.	The council confirmed the donations that Gontran, his wife and daughter, had made to churches.
585	Macon	43 bishops, 15 envoys, 16 bishops without sees.	The council convoked by Gontran, was composed of all the bishops under him, amongst whom several had been deprived of their sees by the Goths. He then wrote to all the bishops and judges of his kingdom to make them execute the decrees of the council. It was in this council that took place the celebrated discussion, of which it has so often been said, the question was whether woman had a soul. The fact is, that a bishop insisted that woman ought not to be called *homo;* but he submitted to these two reasons, that the Scripture says that God created man, male and female; and that Jesus Christ, son of a woman, is called the Son of Man. *Rules.*—The council orders that Sunday shall be more exactly observed; that every Christian shall present offerings; that the tithes shall be paid regularly, and that no baptisms shall be celebrated except in the time prescribed, unless it is a matter of necessity. One of the canons commences thus:—It behoves us to bring to their first state all those things of the holy church that we know are degenerated by the lapse of time.

Date.	Place.	Present.	Object of the Council, Rules, &c.
			That no priest being intoxicated, or having broken his fast, dare to celebrate the sacrifice.
The council made a law for protecting freedmen before the church, and charged their bishops to plead their cause. It also regulates, that if any powerful person has a quarrel with a bishop, the affair must be carried before the metropolitan, and no violence employed against the bishop; it orders the same to be observed as to priests and deacons.
It forbids the judges to decide about widows and orphans, without having informed the bishop, their natural protector, or, in his absence, one of his priests, and to decide all in deliberating with them.
It forbids bishops to have their houses protected by dogs, as being contrary to hospitality. It forbids one corpse to be put in the sepulchre of another without the permission of those to whom it belongs. It regulates all the marks of honor that a layman ought to render to a clerk in meeting him, and the manner in which the clerk ought to respond.
The council forbids clerks to assist at the trial of criminals.
It orders that all the demands be judged according to the laws and canons, "for treading under foot the laws and rules, those who are near the king, and are inflated by the power of the world, usurp the goods of others, and without judicial action or proof, not only deprive the poor of their fields, but eject them from their dwellings."
587	Andelot.	. .	This assemblage of bishops and nobles counselled and confirmed the peace between Gontran and Childebert.

Date.	Place.	Present.	Object of the Council, Rules, &c
588	Clermont.	.. ..	This council was held by Sulpice, bishop of Bourges, with his suffragans, about certain parishes, which the bishops of Cahors and Rhodez were disputing; the latter gained the cause.
588	Place uncertain.	.. ..	This council was occupied with several crimes, amongst others, with the murder of Pretextat, archbishop of Rouen.
589	Sourcey	.. ..	This council ordered that the entry of the town be granted to Drontegisile, bishop of Soissons.
589	Poitiers	.. ..	This assembly excommunicated Chrodielde and the nuns of the monastery of St. Radegonde.
589	Châlons.	The bishops who were with Gontran.	This assembly confirmed the excommunication pronounced by the council of Poitiers.
589 590	Norbonne	7 bishops	This council was convoked by Recared, king of the Visigoths. *Rules.*—The council forbids clerks to wear purple vestments; to stop upon public places; to mix in the conversations, which are held there; and to meet in councils or plots, under the patronage of the laity, which had been already forbidden by the council of Nicea (of Chalcedonia, according to Labbe). It orders abbots not to inflict upon the guilty imprisoned in the monasteries any other penance than that imposed by the bishops. The council forbids certain pagan superstitions, and condemns the guilty, if they are freemen, to penance; if they are slaves, to the rod. It orders clerks to be subordinate to their superiors; forbids those who are at the altar to quit it during the celebration of mass; it forbids, under penalty of a fine, the Jews interring their dead with chants.

Date.	Place.	Present.	Object of the Council, Rules, &c.
590	On the confines of Auvergne, of Gerardin and Rouergue.		This council judged the affair of Tetradia, divorced from Didier, and first wife of Euladius, who claimed the property she had taken in flying to rejoin Didier.
590	Poitiers.	6 bishops	This council judged the quarrel between Chrodielde and the abbess of the monastery of Poitiers.
590	Metz.	.. ..	Gilles, bishop of Reims, was deposed in this council for the crime of high treason. Chrodielde and Basine were received into grace.
591	Nanterre.	.. ..	The little king, Clotaire II., was baptized in this assembly.
594	Châlons.	.. ..	This council regulated the manner in which the offices should be said in the monastery of Saint Marcel.

Seventh Century.

	Châlons	.. ..	Queen Brunehault, in this council, deposed Saint Didier, bishop of Vienne.
615	Paris.	.. ..	This council was convoked by Clotaire II. *Rules.*—No bishop shall choose a coadjutor for himself. No judge shall arrest a clerk without the knowledge of a bishop. The council forbids any one to touch the goods of a deceased ecclesiastic until his will is made known. It forbids bishops and all who have power, whether clergy or secular, to seize the goods or rights of a bishop. It forbids bishops and archdeacons to take possession of what has been left by a priest or an abbot, and to despoil the church under pretext of the good of the church.

Date.	Place.	Present.	Object of the Council, Rules, &c.
A little after the preceding.	Place uncertain.		It forbids Jews to demand from princes any authority over Christians, and orders that he who has obtained it shall be baptized with all his family. *Rules*—The council forbids making a layman archpriest, unless it be because the merit of his person has made the bishops judge it necessary for the consolation of the church, and the defence of the parishioners. If freedmen have sold themselves, when they are able to give the sum for which they sold themselves, they ought to receive their liberty; if amongst such persons, the husband has a free wife, or the wife a free husband, their children shall be free. The council forbids celebrating in the monasteries, unless by the permission of the bishops, baptisms and masses for the dead, or interring the laity there. It forbids depriving without reason, archpriests and the archdeacons.
625	Reims.	41 bishops	There are after this council synodal statutes of the church of Reims, but they are thought to be of much later date; they contain nothing of importance. *Rules.*—The council renews the laws against the conspiracy of priests, and the snares they hold out for their bishops. It orders bishops to seek out and convert the heretics that may be found in Gaul. It orders that those whose lives shall be saved by their seeking refuge in the churches shall promise before being set at liberty to accomplish the canonical penance. If a Christian is forced to sell his slaves, he may not sell them to any but Christians, under pain of excommunication. If Jews wish to make their Christian slaves adopt their persuasion, **or**

Date.	Place.	Present.	Object of the Council, Rules, &c.
			make them suffer cruel torments, they shall return into the power of the fisc. The council forbids receiving the accusation of persons who are not free, and reducing freedmen to servitude; it forbids, as did almost all the preceding councils, to regard as a bishop him who is not a native of the place, and who has not been chosen by the will of all the people, with the consent of the provincial bishops; it forbids bishops to break the sacred vases unless it is for the redemption of captives.
627	Mâcon	.. ..	Agrestius, monk of Luxeuil, rigorously attacked the rule of St. Columban; the abbot Eustache defended it; and the council sanctioned it.
628	Clichy.	Bishops and nobles convoked by Clotaire.	The council of Clichy was occupied with public peace and ecclesiastical discipline.
633	Clichy	16 bishops, king Dagobert and some noble laymen.	This council treated of fugitives and the asylum of the church of Saint Denis.
638	Paris.	9 bishops, king Dagobert, 3 noble laymen.	This council confirmed the privileges of the church of Saint Denis.
645	Orleans.	.. ..	This council was assembled by Saint Eloy against a Greek who preached the heresy of the Monothelites. He was opposed by bishop Sauve, and driven from Gaul.
648	Bourges.	Provincial synod.	
650	Châlons	39 bishops, 5 abbots, 1 archdeacon.	The council of Châlons depose Agapius, and Bobon, bishops of Digne. *Rules.*—The council forbids consecrating at the same time two bishops for one town; confiding the property of parishes and the

Date.	Place.	Present.	Object of the Council, Rules, &c
			parishes themselves to laymen; selling slaves beyond the dominion of the king (Clovis II.). It forbids judges to visit parishes and monasteries, which are under the jurisdiction of bishops, and to send before them clerks and abbots, to make them prepare lodgings. It forbids electing two abbots for one monastery, or one abbot to choose his successor, or abbots and monks to seek the protection of the nobles, and to go to the prince without the permission of the bishop; it complains that those nobles who have chapels shake the allegiance of their clerks to the jurisdiction of the ordinary. It forbids carrying arms in church, or attacking any one there to kill or wound him: it also forbids that women should sing indecent songs there
About 658	Nantes.	.. ..	Nivard, bishop of Reims, consented in this assembly to the renovation of the monastery of Hautvilliers, near Marne.
664	Paris.	25 bishops	These bishops confirmed the privileges granted to the church of Saint Denis by Landry, bishop of Paris. Labbe mentions this assembly but does not reckon it.
669	Clichy	Bishops and nobles	King Clovis in this assembly had the privileges of the church of Saint Denis committed to writing.
670	Autur.	.. ..	This council, held by Saint Leger, was only occupied with monastic discipline, and prescribed nothing new on this subject. *Rules.*—Let the priest, or deacon, who does not know perfectly by heart the symbol of Saint Athanasius, be condemned by his bishop. No layman shall be looked upon as catholic who does not go to communicate at Christmas, at Easter, and at Whitsuntide. No woman shall mount to the altar.

Date.	Place.	Present.	Object of the Council, Rules, &c.
About 670	Sens.	34 bishops.	This council confirmed the privileges of the monastery of Saint Pierre-le-Vif.
679	Place uncertain	.. ..	This council condemned the Monothelites, and sent three legates to the pope, two bishops, and one deacon.
683 or 684	In a royal palace.	.. ..	Ebroin deposed in this council. Saint Leger, and Lambert, bishop of Maestricht.
688	Id	.. ..	Saint Leger and Ebroin being dead, three bishops disputed for the body of Saint Leger; the council adjudged it to Ansoald, bishop of Poitiers.
692	Rouen	16 bishops, 4 abbots, 1 legate and many of the clergy.	This council granted several privileges to the monastery of Fontanelles, upon condition that it should not swerve from the rule of Saint Benedict.

Eighth Century.

719	Maestricht.	.. ..	Saint Willibrod and St. Swithbert presided at this synod, which sent Saint Boniface and several other missionaries to preach the gospel to the Germans.
742	Germany	Carloman, 7 bishops named, several others, and their priests, noble laymen.	Carloman convoked this council which was held at Augsburg or at Ratisbon; he had just arrived from Italy, and had received from pope Zachary the order to hold this council. It is Carloman who speaks in these canons. *Rules.*—By the counsel of holy priests and my nobles, we institute bishops for the cities; we place Boniface at their head, and we order that synods shall be held every year. Priests are forbidden to carry arms, except those who are necessary in the armies to say mass, and to hear the confessions of sinners.

Date.	Place.	Present.	Object of the Council, Rules, &c
			Parish priests must submit to their bishops, and render them an account of their conduct every year. One must be cautious with strange and unknown bishops. Unknown priests and bishops may not be admitted to the holy mystery. The bishops, with the aid of the count (Gravio), must watch that the people do not fall into any pagan superstition. (Several dispositions follow regarding the conduct of the priests.)
743	Leptines	.. ..	This council was held by Pepin; it confirmed the decrees of the council of Germany. Pepin placed at the head of the bishops whom he had chosen, Abel, archbishop of Reims, and Adorbert, archbishop of Sens. Saint Boniface presided at this council; the object of it was to reform the clergy; the bishops, priests, and all the clerks promised to change their habits, and to conduct themselves according to the ancient canons; the monks received the rule of Saint Benedict; chastisements were denounced against those, male or female, who should be guilty of adultery. It is Pepin who speaks. At the end of this council are found several pieces which appear to belong to it: the renunciation by the Saxons of the worship of Odin, in the German language; a list of the pagan superstitions of the Germans; an allocution on illicit marriages, one on morals, and one against the Jewish observance of the sabbath; also the canons given by Boniface; they contain nothing new. *Rules.*—We order that he who is in possession of a house, shall give a sol to the church or monastery.

Date.	Place.	Present.	Object of the Council, Rules, &c
			We order, as my father ordered before, that he who has practised any pagan superstition, be condemned to a fine of fifteen sous. Canons and statutes decreed by the synod held by Boniface, according to the order of the Roman pontiff and the prayer of the principal Franks and Gauls. These canons commence and finish by a profession of obedience to the pope, whom they engage to consult and obey in all things; they promise also to ask from him the Pallium. The metropolitan must hold a council every year; every bishop on his return from council must assemble his priests and his abbots and exhort them to observe its decrees; every bishop must visit his diocese every year; every priest must at Lent render a complete account of his conduct to his bishop. The metropolitans must watch the bishops and inquire about their zeal. If a bishop cannot correct his priests, he must carry the affair to the archbishops, as the Roman church has insisted upon my making a vow to indicate to her those priests whom I could never correct.
744	Soissons.	23 bishops, several clerks and laymen.	This council, with the consent of the princes and the people, condemned the heresy of Adalbert; it made several canons of no interest; it is signed by Pepin and Radbod.
745	Germany.	. ..	This council deposed on the demand of Saint Boniface, the bishop of Mayence, who had killed some one in war. Carloman, who had convoked this council by the advice of Boniface, and his brother Pepin, gave to Boniface the bishopric of Mayence, which was made metropolitan of Germany.

Date.	Place.	Present.	Object of the Council, Rules, &c.
748	Duren.	.. ..	This council was convoked by Pepin to occupy itself with the repair of churches and the affairs of the poor, widows and orphans, to whom it was urgent that justice should be rendered.
752	Vermerie.	.. ..	This council was held in the presence of Pepin. *Rules.*—The council forbids giving a woman the veil against her will, and in this case declares her at liberty; the priest who has done it is disgraced. A freeman who has married a wife, believing her to be free, can marry again upon learning that she is not; and so for a woman, unless her husband has sold himself through poverty, and she has consented to it, and the price of the sale has kept her. He who knows that the woman he marries is a serf must keep her. A serf who has a concubine who is a serf, can quit her and receive another from the hands of his master; but he would do better to keep her. If a man is obliged to fly, and his wife refuse to accompany him, he can marry again after he has done penance. If a freed serf has commerce with a woman who is a serf, he must marry her if the master give his consent; if not, so long as she lives he may not have another wife. He who permits his wife to take the veil cannot marry again.
752	Metz.	, ..	This council was held under king Pepin; all its dispositions bear the mark of civil authority. *Rules.*—The count must force the priests to attend the synod. No one shall, under any pretext, stop the pilgrims who are travelling to Rome. A livre may not contain more

Date.	Place.	Present.	Object of the Council, Rules, &c.
			than 22 sous, of which one must be for the coiner. Franchises must be preserved. This council confiscates the goods of those who make forbidden marriages, and condemns to pecuniary and corporal punishment those who aid or tolerate them.
755	Verne.	Nearly all the bishops of Gaul	The council was held by the order and in the presence of king Pepin. *Rules.*—There must be bishops in every town. All must obey the bishops whom we have constituted metropolitans, from this time until we can do it more canonically. There shall be every year two synods, one in the calends of March, in the presence of the king, and in whatsoever place he please; the other in October, and in the place that the bishops shall have chosen in March. All the ecclesiastics that have been so directed by the metropolitan shall come to the second synod. The bishop shall have the power of correcting his clergy and the monks. Those men who say they have been tonsured for the love of God, and who live on their property, and according to their fancy, shall be shut up in a monastery, or shall lead a canonical life under the direction of the bishop. If a monastery has fallen into the hands of laymen, so that the bishop cannot amend it, and the monks wish for the salvation of their souls to leave it, and to enter another, they must be permitted to do so. Bishops who have no diocese must not exercise any function in the diocese of other bishops. As the people have been per-

Date.	Place.	Present.	Object of the Council, Rules, &c
			suaded that they may not on Sunday go on horseback, on oxen, or in carriages, or travel or prepare their nourishment, or cleanse themselves, or their houses (and as this is more Jewish than Christian), we have decided that Sunday may be kept as it has been hitherto. We think that we ought to abstain from cultivating the land, that we may have more facility to come to church; if any one does work that is interdicted, his chastisement does not belong to the laity, but to the priests. All laymen, whether noble or not, must be married publicly. No church may remain more than three months without a bishop. Royal monasteries must render account of their income to the king; those of the episcopacy, to the bishop.
756	Lentines.	.. ..	This council was held by king Pepin, who endeavored to procure the restitution of church property: not being able to succeed, they imposed a rent of twelve deniers on the farms on this property, and they ordered a levy of ninths and tenths with the same view.
757	Compiegne.	20 bishops, 14 ecclesiastics.	This council was held by king Pepin in the general assembly of the people. *Rules.*—All the canons of this council regard marriage; they permit the wife of a leper to marry another man, if she has the consent of her husband; and the man who has married in a fief to which he has followed his lord, after the death of this lord, if he is despoiled of the fief which he received, and has left the wife he received at the same time, and married again in his own country, is permitted to regard this second wife as legitimate.

Date.	Place.	Present.	Object of the Council, Rules, &c.
758	Compiegne	..	This assemb.y, which perhaps ought not to be counted here, was that in which Tassilon, duke of Bavaria, swore fidelity to Pepin.
759	Germany.	. ..	Guarin and Ruithard, employed by the fisc, condemned to prison for disorderly conduct, Othmar, abbot of Saint Gall, whose only crime appears to be that he had complained and still complained of their exactions.
761	Wolwich.	.. ..	Pepin held this assembly in Auvergne; they disputed against heresies on the Trinity Pepin made many donations to the neighboring churches.
763	Nevers.	.. ..	Pepin held this assembly; it has left nothing regarding the churc.
764	Worms.		
765	Attigny.	27 bishops, 17 abbots.	Nothing remains of this assembly except the methods taken by its members to assure themselves a great number of masses and prayers after their death.
766	Orleans.		
767	Gentilly.		In this assembly, held, like the preceding, by Pepin, there was a discussion between the Greeks and the Romans touching the Trinity and the procession of the Holy Ghost and images.
767	Bourges.		
768	Saint Denis.		
770	Worms.		
771	Valenciennes		
772	Worms.		
773	In Bavaria.	5 bishops 13 abbots.	
773	Geneva.		
775	Duren.		
776	Worms.	.. ..	Many Saxons were baptized in this assembly

Date.	Place.	Present.	Object of the Council, Rules, &c.
777	Paderborn.	.. ..	In this one also
779	Duren.	.. ..	These rules bear the title of capitularies, but they are nevertheless canons of the ecclesiastical assemblies held by Charlemagne. *Rules.*—Bishops who are not ordained must be so without delay. Churches cannot give asylum to men condemned to death. There are many other dispositions, but they relate more to public police, than to ecclesiastical discipline.
780	Near Lippe.	.. ..	This council was occupied with the erection of episcopal sees in Saxony, and the construction of several churches.
782	Near Lippe, or at Cologne.		
785	Paderborn.	.. ..	Witikind was baptized.
786	Paderborn	.. ..	They occupied themselves with the affairs of the church of Saxony.
786	Worms.		
787	Worms.		
788	Ingelheim		
798	Narbonne	29 bishops, Didier, the pope's legate; 3 envoys from bishops, and one chancellor.	This council treated of the heresy of Felix, bishop of Urgel, and the limits of the diocese of Narbonne. Under the date of 789, there is a collection of capitularies, given by Charlemagne upon ecclesiastical discipline; the council of Soissons calls them synodals; they are in a great part taken from Eastern canons and the decrees of the popes. Charlemagne held that year an assembly at Aix la Chapelle.
790	Worms.		
792	Ratisbon.	.. ..	This council condemned Felix, bishop of Urgel, who said Jesus Christ was the adopted son of God.

Date.	Place.	Present.	Object of the Council, Rules, &c.
794	Francfort.	The bishops of Gaul, Germany, and Italy, 2 legates from the pope.	This council condemned for the third time, Felix and Elpaud, archbishop of Toledo, who held the same opinion as Felix. The council rejected with anathema the doctrine of the council of Constantinople upon the worship of images, regarding it as idolatrous. *Rules.*—The council ordered a maximum price for the sale of goods, and ordered the new money to be received. It forbids avaricious cellarers to be chosen in monasteries. Abbots may not blind or mutilate their monks; ecclesiastics and monks may not drink in an ale-house; clerks of the king's chapel may not communicate with clerks who are rebellious to their bishop. Bishops may not absent themselves from their diocese more than three weeks. Bishops may not be ignorant of the canons and the rules; they may not invoke new saints; the sacred woods must be destroyed.
797	Aix-la-Chapelle.	.. ..	This council was occupied with the subject of the construction of the monastery of St. Paul at Rome
799	Aix-la-Chapelle	.. ..	This council received the abjuration of Felix.
799	Ratisbon.	.. ..	The date of this council is uncertain, amongst other things it treats of the chor-bishops or country-bishops. Traces of it are only to be found in the capitularies of Charlemagne.
800	Tours. Place uncertain. Worms.	.. ..	Nothing is left of these councils and their date; it is only known that they occupied themselves as to the manner in which the priests could purge themselves from the crimes of which they were accused.

Ninth Century.

Date.	Place.	Present.	Object of the Council, Rules, &c.
802	Aix-la-Chapelle.	.. ..	This council was occupied with the reform of monastic and ecclesiastical discipline. All who were present swore fidelity to the emperor.
809	Aix-la-Chapelle.	.. .	This council treated of the question of the procession of the Holy Ghost which had been raised by John, a Jerusalem monk; he sent a legation to the pope to have his decision. The council was also occupied with discipline, but nothing was decided.
813	Arles.	.. .	These five councils of 813 were held by order of Charlemagne, for the reform of ecclesiastical discipline; much is repetition; the general intention was to oppose the ignorance, grossness, and violence that pervaded the clergy; all recommend to the priests and bishops retirement from the affairs of the world, goodness and study, and interdict them avarice, &c. These dispositions so often repeated in several councils, announce the progress that the secular spirit was making every day in the clergy. There are also several questions upon tithes, the observation of the Sabbath, monastic discipline, and the stability of ecclesiastics. These councils recommended a great preparation for communion, and seem to desire that the laity should not communicate so often. *Rules.*—The council orders that the bishops shall carefully instruct the priests and the people regarding baptism and the mysteries of the faith. They must preach not only in the towns, but also in the parishes. Bishops must protect the poor against oppression, and address

Date.	Place.	Present.	Object of the Council, Rules, &c.
			themselves to the king to procure the cessation of it. It forbids the laity to receive money from the priests to recommend them to benefices.
813	Mayence.	30 bishops, 25 abbots.	*Rules.*—The council orders that powerful persons, counts, bishops, &c., may only buy the goods of the poor in public under pain of nullity. It prescribes rules for the canonical life of the clerks. It forbids holding assemblies for temporal affairs in the church. It recommends the priests teaching the people the Creed and the Lord's Prayer, at least, in the vulgar tongue, if they cannot learn them otherwise, and declares free the clerks and the monks tonsured against their will.
813	Reims	.. ..	*Rules.*—The council forbids a priest to pass from an inferior title to a superior one; monks may not attend secular pleadings; a town or monastery may not have more servants of God in it than it can well contain.
813	Tours	.. ..	*Rules.*—The council recommends bishops to read, and, if possible, to retain by heart the gospel and the epistles of Saint Paul; not to give way to excesses at table; not to amuse themselves with games of actors, and to exhort priests to fly them, and also the chase. It forbids priests to give the communion, indiscriminately, to all those who attend mass. It recommends all the faithful, rich or poor, to submit to the bishops.
813	Châlons.	.. ..	This council was occupied with the administration of penance, and it pronounces anathemas against those penitential works whose errors are certain, and the

Date.	Place.	Present.	Object of the Council, Rules, &c.
			authors uncertain. Their appreciation of sins was very unequal. The council counts eight sins, from which it is difficult to keep; these are the deadly sins; and hatred is comprised therein. It is, without doubt, this which makes the eighth. *Rules.*—The council forbids bishops to require a private oath from the priests they ordain. It forbids separating the serfs united in marriage; it condemns to penitence, but does not separate from their husbands those women who to gain this end have their children confirmed. Some think that we ought to confess our sins to God alone, others that we ought to confess them to the priests; both one and the other are useful in the church of God. The confession which is made to God purges from sin; that made to the priest teaches us how to purge ourselves of them, for God is the author, and the distributor of health and salvation, and he accords much by the invisible effect of his power, and much by the action of the doctors. The council declares that confession ought to be entire.
814	Lyons	.. ..	This council named Agobard archbishop of Lyons, in the place of Leidrade, who had retired in a monastery at Soissons.
814	Noyon	11 bishops, 8 abbots, 4 counts, several of the clergy.	This council, which was held by Wulfaire, archbishop of Reims, and his suffragans, terminated a dispute about boundaries between the bishops of Soissons and Noyon.
	Trèves.	.. ..	The date of this council, held by Hetton, archbishop of Trèves, is uncertain.
816	Aix-la-		*Rules.*—This council, accord-

Date.	Place.	Present.	Object of the Council, Rules, &c.
	Chapelle.		ing to the order of Louis le Debonnaire, made two regulations, one for the canons in 145 articles; the other for the nuns in 28. Louis sent copies of it to each metropolitan, with the order to see them observed in their provinces These two rules are extracted from the fathers and the councils, and contain nothing of any importance except the growing tendency to impose monastic life upon the clergy. This rule of the canons differs very slightly from that of a monastery. *Rules.*—This rule given to the nuns, as well as a multitude of canons at this epoch, shows the difficulty the bishops had to reduce them to the obedience they wished to impose on them: the following dispositions recur continually: Abbesses must submit to the bishops; abbesses may not go out without the permission of the bishop; abbesses may not give the veil, nor take upon themselves any sacerdotal functions. We see, too, that they had a great difficulty in making them keep the cloister; for the councils frequently forbid their receiving men, monks, or priests, at forbidden hours, and without necessity.
817	Aix-la-Chapell.	.. ..	This council was composed of abbots and monks alone; they only treated of monastic discipline.
818	Aix-la-Chapelle	.. ..	This council condemned several bishops who had taken the part of his nephew Bernard against Louis le Debonnaire.
818	Vannes.		
819	Aix-la-Chapelle.		
820	Thionville.	.. ..	This council was held by the archbishops of Mayence, Cologne,

Date.	Place.	Present.	Object of the Council, Rules, &c.
			Trèves, Reims, their suffragans, and the deputies of the other provinces of Gaul, pronounced ecclesiastical punishment and fines against those who should be found guilty towards clerks.
822	Attigny.	.. .	It was in this council that Louis le Debonnaire submitted to do penance.
823	Compiegne.	.. ..	This council was occupied with ecclesiastical goods usurped by the laity. The legates of pope Paschal were there.
824	Paris.	.. ..	This council was occupied about the worship of idols. The authors of the collection regard as forged the acts which bear its name, but have no knowledge of the real acts. The council was held on the occasion of two legates being sent on the same question to the pope by the emperor of the east. The council also sent its acts by two legates to the pope. *Rules.*—The canons of this council are contained in three books. In the first, in thirty-four articles, the council established the distinction of the two powers, and placed that of the priests much above that of the kings. It announces to the clergy the necessity of correcting themselves; it insists upon the right administration of baptism, and the necessity of well explaining the meaning of it to the people; it declares against simony, against the avarice of the bishops, which it endeavors to check, by renewing the ancient dispositions as to the goods of the church; it also makes several rules which apply to manners It demands that two councils be held every year in each province, and that the priests, deacons, and all those who are aggrieved attend them.

Date.	Place.	Present.	Object of the Council, Rules, &c.
			The council assimilate the chor-bishops to the seventy disciples of Jesus Christ, and complain that they wish to assume the functions of a bishop. The council orders bishops to watch the schools with care, and to summon the scholars to the provincial council. It interdicts commerce, and the occupations of a farmer to the priests and monks, and enjoins exact residence to the bishops and priests. It forbids bishops who are not in want to take the fourth part of the offerings; it forbids priests to give the veil, and women to take it themselves; it complains bitterly that women serve at the altar and even give to the people the body and blood of Jesus Christ. It forbids, unless in a case of absolute necessity, to say mass in houses and gardens; it forbids forcing the priests to do so—at any rate, it cannot be done without an altar consecrated by the bishop. It also forbids celebrating mass without having any one to respond. The second book of the council treats of the duties of kings. It is there declared that, " No king ought to think he holds his kingdom from his ancestors, but from God." The rest of the book treats of submission to the king, the duties of Christians, and the respect to be shown in churches, in thirteen articles. The third book is a letter from the bishops to the king, in which they give him an account of all that has passed in the council, and indicate to him the rules they wish particularly to be observed. Besides those we have mentioned, they added others. They demand that schools should be founded in three places in the empire, that the efforts of his father and his own should not

Date.	Place.	Present.	Object of the Council, Rules, &c.
			perish by negligence. They demand that he send from the palace a crowd of priests and monks, who reside there in spite of their bishops. They complain against the custom of celebrating Service on holy days in the chapels of the palace. In short, they give the king several counsels, in which the tone is very different to the habits of respect the bishops had contracted with Charlemagne.
826	Ingelheim.	.. ..	This council was occupied with the affairs of the church. Louis le Debonnaire received there the envoys from the pope, and from the Holy Land.
829	Paris.	.. ..	Louis le Debonnaire convoked these councils of Paris, Mayence, Lyons, and Toulouse, which were held in the same year, 829. He indicated the bishops who should compose it, the questions to be treated, and the capitularies they should adopt. Of these councils we have only that of Paris. It is probable that they much resembled each other.
829 829 829 829	Mayence. Lyon. Toulouse. Worms.	.. ..	This council confirmed the resolutions of the four preceding ones.
830	Lyon.	7 bishops, 2 chor-bishops, 13 abbots, priests, or deacons, 14 proxies.	The synod confirmed the donation that had been made to the monastery of Saint Pierre de Bezon by Alberic, bishop of Langres.
831	Nimeguen.	.. ..	This assembly deposed Jesse, bishop of Amiens, who had taken part against Louis le Debonnaire.
833	Worms.	26 bishops, 5 abbots.	Alderic, archbishop of Sens, permitted in this council, that the

Date.	Place.	Present.	Object of the Council, Rules, &c.
			abbey of Saint Remy should be removed.
833	Compiegne.	.. ..	This assembly deprived Louis le Debonnaire of the crown.
834	Saint Denis.	.. ..	This assembly again admitted Louis to the communion and the empire.
834	Attigny.	.. ..	This assembly was occupied with the bad state of the church. The bishops referred to lay judges the decision of a question of marriage, reserving for themselves the power of applying a penance, if it must take place.
835	Metz.	.. ..	Louis complained in this council of Ebbon, archbishop of Reims, who had excommunicated him. Ebbon chose judges from amongst the bishops according to the African canons.
835	Thionville.	43 bishops.	Louis again received absolution in this council. Ebbon was condemned, and abdicated
836	Aix-la-Chapelle	.. ..	This council was assembled by the order of Louis le Debonnaire, to deliberate upon three objects which form the matter of its three books: 1st, the lives of the bishops, twelve articles; 2d, the doctrine of the bishops, twelve articles, and the doctrine and lives of the inferior orders of the clergy, sixteen articles; lastly, 3d, the person of the king, his children, and his servants, twenty-five articles. The last articles of this book have, however, no direct connection with its title, and are generally dispositions. The council also addressed to Pepin, king of Aquitaine, a treatise, in three books, in which it confirmed, by the authority of the Scriptures, the things it had ordered. The first book has thirty-eight articles;

Date.	Place.	Present.	Object of the Council, Rules, &c.
			the second, thirty-one; the third, twenty-seven. They are all citations, narrations, and reflections, and contain no positive disposition. As to the canons, they are only the repetition of the preceding councils. The third book, that part which relates to the king, and to several other points, is the copy, sometimes abridged, of the third book of the sixth council of Paris. *Rules.*—The council recommends to the priests to watch that the faithful who are confided to them be baptized and confirmed, know the Creed and the Lord's prayer, and how they ought to conduct themselves; and that they be corrected of their faults as they ought, and do not die without confession, sacerdotal prayers, and extreme unction. It recommends that there should not be in the monasteries for women dark places and corners, where they can offend God without being seen. It recommends that, where it is possible, every church have its priest, who will govern it himself, or under the conduct of a priest of superior grade. It forbids fasting, marrying, and pleading on Sunday. It recommends communion every Sunday.
836	Cremieu, in the Lyonnais	. ..	Agobard, archbishop of Lyons, and Bernard, bishop of Vienne, had been deposed by the council of Thionville for having deposed Louis le Debonnaire. This council was assembled to judge them, but nothing could be decided, on account of their absence. They were at last restored to grace.
839	Châlons.	.. ..	This assembly regulated the affairs of the church and the state. In 841, an assembly was held

Date.	Place.	Present.	Object of the Council, Rules, &c.
			at Ingelheim, at which twenty bishops assisted, and several of the clergy; by the order of Lothaire, then emperor, it returned to Ebbon the see of Reims, from which he had been deposed.
841	Auxerre.	20 bishops, 4 abbots.	This assembly ordered a fast of three days on the occasion of the battle which had just taken place at Fontenay.
842	Bourges.	.. ..	This council, held by the partisans of Charles le Chauve, approved the deposition of Ebbon.
843	Toulouse.		Nothing remains of this assembly but the capitularies of Charles le Chauve. We can easily perceive that they were given at the solicitations of simple priests; they are only given while awaiting a general council. *Rules.*—The bishops must not take it ill if the priests lay claims before the king; they must not insist upon a too strong protestation from the priests, they must not demand it when they are not making the visit of their diocese, and they must only demand it once when they visit it twice; they must not divide the parishes to receive double; they must not constrain the priests to attend more than twice a-year at the councils.
843	Coulaine.	.. ..	This assembly was held by Charles le Chauve; the capitularies which remain recommend the observance of the duties towards God and the royal power· they offer nothing curious.
844	Loire, in Anjou.	.. ..	The canons of this council are to the same effect as the preceding; it appears that they relate to the rebellion of Count Lambert.
844	Thionville.	.. .	This assembly was presided

Date.	Place.	Present.	Object of the Council, Rules, &c
814	Vern	.. .	over by Droyon, bishop of Metz; it was held in the place called the Judgment Seat. The three sons of Louis le Debonnaire here made peace, and passed several capitularies, which had for their object to order the affairs of the church. *Rules.*—Bishops must be ordained for the vacant sees, and those who have lost theirs must take them again. The monasteries confided to the laity must be given in charge to religious persons, male or female. Ecclesiastical property must not be invaded. This council had nearly the same aim as the preceding one; it was presided over by Ebroin, bishop of Poitiers. *Rules.*—Send persons to chastise those who contemn the divine and human laws; let religious men visit the monasteries, to inquire into the relaxation of discipline. Clerks and monks who have deserted must be returned to their churches and convents. Ecclesiastical goods must be returned; the churches must be provided with pastors. Those bishops who do not go to war, whether it be on account of the feebleness of their body, or by the indulgence of the king, must confide their men to one of the faithful, that the military service may not suffer by it. Kings and bishops may not reside long with the bishops; and they must not oppose themselves to the holding of the provincial councils. No novelty must be adopted in the explanation of the Scriptures. Bishops must have some one to instruct the country priests. Laymen must not employ the

Date.	Place.	Present.	Object of the Council, Rules, &c
			priests of the church in the care of their farms. The king may not take canons into his service without the consent of the bishops. Do not demand from the priests illicit tributes upon the tithes and the goods of the church.
845	Beauvais.	.. ..	This council was held by Charles le Chauve and his bishops; it is for the same end as the two others.
845	Meaux.	.. ..	This council repeated and confirmed the canons of the preceding councils; it made a great many new ones, of which several repeated ancient dispositions; all are in the same spirit as the three preceding ones: ecclesiastical reform and the restitution of goods and immunities.
846	Vannes.	.. ..	Nomenoe, prince of Brittany, after having expelled several bishops, named others, augmented the number of sees, assembled the bishops on his side, and had himself crowned king.
846 or rather 847	Paris.	20 bishops, 5 abbots.	This council forbade Ebbon the diocese of Reims, until he submitted to his judgment about which the pope was occupied. They terminated what they could not finish at the council of Meaux. *Rules.*—The prince must give to the bishops, powers signed with his seal, that when they need civil authority, they can so accomplish their divine ministry. Royal chapels must not be confided to laymen, but to ecclesiastics.
847	Mayence.	13 bishops, many of the clergy	Raban, archbishop of Mayence, held this council with his suffragans and their clergy; the council was occupied with discipline, and reclaimed the rights and im-

Date.	Place.	Present.	Object of the Council, Rules, &c.
			munities of the church. It condemned a prophetess, named Thiota, who announced the end of the world, and denounced the ecclesiastical orders. *Rules.*—No penance shall be imposed on the dying, but they must be contented with their confession, and the alms and prayers of their friends, and they must give them the viatic, and pray for them; if they get well, they must submit to the penance. The council grants Christian interment and the prayers of the church to criminals executing, after they have confessed.
848	Mayence.	.. ..	This council condemned the monk Gottschalk, who maintained the doctrine of predestination; Raban presided at the council; Gottschalk was sent to Hincmar, archbishop of Reims.
848	Lyon.	.. ..	This council was occupied with the affair of a priest, named Goldegaire; it offers nothing interesting.
848	Limoges.	.. ..	This council grants the demand of the canons of the church of St. Martin, who desired to be made monks. The bishop of Limoges consented with reluctance.
849	Chartres.	.. ..	Charles, brother of Pepin, demanded and received the tonsure in this council.
849	Kiersy.	16 bishops, 3 abbots, several of the clergy.	This council condemned Gottschalk again, had him beaten with rods, and put in prison.
849	Paris, according to some, Tours.	22 bishops.	This council was held at the invitation of Lantraun, archbishop of Tours, on the subject of Nomenoe, and addressed him a letter of reproach, in which it menaced him with excommunication.

Date.	Place.	Present.	Object of the Council, Rules, &c.
850	Moret.		
851	Soissons.	.. ..	Pepin, king of Aquitaine, was in this council deposed and tonsured.
852	Mayence.		
852	Sens, date uncertain.	13 bishops, 2 abbots.	This council confirmed the privileges of the monastery of Saint Remy.
853	Sens.	.. ..	This council refused to consecrate bishop of Chartres, Burchard, recommended by Charles le Chauve, but who was unworthy of it.
853	Soissons	27 bishops, 6 abbots, several of the clergy	This council admitted Burchard to the episcopacy; it was occupied in supplying the wants of several churches; on points of general discipline, and ordinations made by Ebbon, predecessor of Hinemar, at Reims; they were annulled. Charles le Chauve consulted the council upon the instructions that he should give to his envoys; they were approved. *Rules.*—Instructions of Charles le Chauve. Our envoys must take care, how the lords take it ill, when the bishops or their servants strike their serfs with their rods, to correct them; they must know that then they will be submitted to our ban and to a rigorous chastisement. Our faithful must know that we have declared to the synod, that what we should grant of the goods of the church to an unreasonable demand, were it to a bishop or to an abbot, will not avail; they must then take care not to make such demands.
853	Kiersy	.. ..	This council made four canons against Gottschalk, and excommunicated again a nobleman, named Fulere, who had left his wife to espouse another.

Date.	Place	Present.	Object of the Council, Rules, &c.
853	Vermerie.	22 bishops.	This council looked to the affairs of many churches.
855	Valence.	18 bishops, and many of the clergy.	This council made many canons about predestination, and about particular interests and objects of discipline. It was favorable to Gottschalk. *Rules.*—That the bishops take care not to ordain persons unworthy of the ministry. The council blamed the custom of taking the oath, in judicial proceedings, because it necessarily led to perjury. It blamed also the judgment by battle, and refused to those who were slain Christian burial. It recommended the erection of schools of science, divine, humane, and for church singing, seeing that the long interruption of study, ignorance of the faith, and the neglect of all sciences, had invaded many of the churches of God. That there is nothing reprehensible in the priests' service towards the bishops.
857	Kiersy.	.. ..	This council was held for ecclesiastical reform, and convoked by Charles le Chauve.
857	Mayence	.. ..	This council discussed questions concerning ecclesiastical law.
858	Kiersy.	The archbishop of Rouen and his suffragans, the suffragans of Reims.	This council addressed to Louis le Germanique, who was invading the states of Charles le Chauve, a letter of advice and reproach.
858	Soissons.	.. .	This council was held by order of Louis le Germanique, who had entered Gaul, sword in hand.
359	Metz.	6 bishops, 3 archbish-	This council occupied itself with the quarrels of Louis and Charles

Date.	Place.	Present.	Object of the Council, Rules, &c.
859	Langres.	ops. 2 archbishops, many bishops.	*Rules.*—This council made 16 canons, which were confirmed at the council of Toul or Savonieres, and which are only found there. The six first confirmed the canons of the council of Valence in favor of Gottschalk. The twelfth canon recommended that each congregation have a superior of its order.
859	Langres.	8 bishops.	
859	Toul.	The bishops of twelve provinces.	This council occupied itself with the peace between Louis and Charles; with the complaints of Charles against many bishops; with the Breton bishops, and points of discipline.
860	Aix-la-Chapelle.	.. ..	These two councils were held for the divorce of Lothaire and Teutberge, at a month apart; they pronounced the divorce
860	Aix-la-Chapelle.	7 bishops.	
860	Coblentz.	2 abbots, 10 bishops, and many of the laity.	This council occupied itself with the peace between the kings; they here made a treaty.
860	Toul ou Savoniers.	40 bishops, from 14 provinces.	This council made some canons about discipline.
860	Toul ou Tusey.	.. ..	This council occupied itself about the affair of Ingeltrude, wife of count Boson, who had quitted her.
861	Soissons.	.. ..	Hincmar excommunicated in this provincial synod, Rothade, bishop of Soissons.
862	Sens.	.. ..	It is not known precisely where this council was held, which deposed Heriman, bishop of Nevers
862	Aix-la-Chapelle.	5 bishops.	This council permitted Lothaire the Second to espouse another wife than Teutberge
862	Sablonières.	.. ..	This council occupied itself with the accusation brought

Date.	Place.	Present.	Object of the Council, Rules, &c.
			against Lothaire II., protecting Ingeltrude and Judith, the daughter of Charles le Chauve, who, without his consent, had espoused the count Baudouin.
862	Pitres.	37 bishops, 11 abbots, many ecclesiastics.	This council confirmed the privileges of many monasteries, and took many measures to re-establish the order in the state and church.
862	Soissons.	.. ..	This council occupied itself about the affair of Judith.
862	Soissons.	.. ..	This council occupied itself about the affair of Kothade, who, in the council of Pitres, had appealed to the pope; he was deposed.
863	Senlis.	.. ..	According to Pagi, this council is the same as the preceding.
863	Metz.	.. ..	This council, composed of bishops of the kingdom of Lothaire, approved his divorce; the pope annulled the judgment, and excommunicated the bishops.
863	Place uncertain in Aquitaine.	.. ..	This council excommunicated Etienne, count of Auvergne; it was held by order of pope Nicholas, who had some legates here.
863	Vermerie.	.. ..	This council occupied itself about the abbey of Saint Calais, which the bishop of Mans claimed as under his jurisdiction; it pronounced in favor of the abbey.
866	Soissons.	35 bishops.	This council was held by order of Pope Nicholas, who, after having ordained that it should restore to Rothade his bishopric, wished to do the same for Wulfade and the clerks ordained by Ebbon, since his deposition by Hincmar: it did as he desired.
866	Troyes	20 bishops,	Hincmar was attacked in this

Date.	Place.	Present.	Object of the Council, Rules, &c.
		of 6 provinces.	council by some bishops who wished to please the king; however, he finished by prevailing, and made it give an account to the pope of all that had passed, as he had ordered. Pope Adrian wrote to this council that it should consecrate no other bishops than such as should be named by the emperor; the bishops refused.
868	Place uncertain.	Bishops of Gaul and Bourgoyne.	This council was occupied about discipline.
868	Worms.		
869	Vermeriæ.	29 bishops.	Hincmar, bishop of Laon, and nephew of Hincmar, archbishop of Reims, accused before this council, by Charles le Chauve, and by his uncle, of having made some unjust excommunications, failed in his oaths to the king, and unjustly deprived some clerks of their benefices; he appealed to the pope.
869	Metz.	.. ..	This council gave to Charles le Chauve the kingdom of his nephew Lothaire, who had died in Italy.
869	Pitres.	12 bishops.	
870	Attigny.	Bishops of 10 provinces.	Hincmar, bishop of Laon, again accused, again appealed to the pope.
870	Cologne.		This council treated of discipline.
871	Douzy-les-Prés.	22 bishops, 8 envoys of bishops, 8 ecclesiastics.	This council deposed the bishop of Laon.
873	Châlons.	5 bishops, 1 rural bishop, many of the clergy.	This council was occupied with a discussion between two churches of Châlons.
873	Cologne.	11 bishops, 5 priests, 1 deacon.	This council confirmed the privileges accorded to the prebendaries of the cathedral of Cologne.

Date	Place.	Present.	Object of the Council, Rules, &c.
873	Senlis.	Bishops of 2 provinces.	This council, convoked by Charles le Chauve, degraded from the order of deacon, his son, Carloman.
874	Douzy-les-Près.		This council was occupied with forbidden marriages, and the invasion of church property.
875	Châlons.	46 bishops.	This council confirmed the privileges of the monastery of Tournus
876	Pontion.	2 legates, 5 bishops, 3 abbots.	This council was held a little after the coronation of Charles le Chauve, as emperor, it confirmed the acts of the council which he had held at Pavia, just before. *Capitularies of the council of Pontion.*—That the holy Roman church be honored and revered by all, as the mother of all churches, and that no one dare to act unjustly against her right and power, and that she have power and fitting strength to show towards the universal church a pastoral solicitude, and to invoke for all, by her holy prayers, the Author of all things. And that respect be paid by all towards the lord John, our spiritual father, sovereign pontiff, and universal pope ; that all receive, with great veneration, the things that, according to his sacred ministry, he has decided in his apostolic authority, and that we render to him, in all things, the obedience which is his due. That the imperial dignity be respected by all, and that no one disobey with impunity that which the emperor shall ordain, by letters or by messages. *The Capitularies enact:* That the bishops lead, with their clerks, a canonical life ; that they treat the counts and vassals of the king as sons, and that these shall honor them as fathers ; that the

Date.	Place.	Present.	Object of the Council, Rules, &c.
			bishops shall have the authority of the missi dominici; that the bishops and the counts, in their circuits, shall not lodge at the houses of the poor unless invited.
878	In Neustria.	.. ..	This council, presided over by Hincmar, received the complaints of the emperor Louis III. against the devastation that had been committed in his states by Hugues, the son of Lothaire II., and Waldrade; the council menaced Hugues with excommunication.
878	Troyes.	Pope John and 29 bishops.	This council excommunicated, by command of pope John, Lambert, duke of Spoleto, Adalbert, Formoso, bishop of Porto, and their partisans. It heard the complaint of Hincmar, bishop of Laon; confirmed many privileges and made many canons. It excommunicated also those who invaded the property of the churches. The pope here crowned Louis le Begue.
879	Mantaille in the Viennoise.	29 bishops.	This council, composed of bishops and grandees of the kingdom of Arles, gave to Boson the title of king.
881	Fimes	.. ..	This council was held in the church of St. Macre, in a place now named Fimes, and which is between the diocese of Reims and Soissons; the council occupied itself with discipline and ecclesiastical reforms.
883	Toulouse.	The bishops of Septimania and Aquitaine.	The account of this council is found in the life of St. Theodard, archbishop of Narbonne; being curious as a picture of manners, we give an extract, while agreeing with father Labbe, that its authenticity is doubtful: "The Jews of Toulouse complained to king Carloman of the

Date.	Place.	Present.	Object of the Council, Rules, &c.
			injuries that they suffered from the bishop and people of this town, who, three times a year, beat and maltreated one of them; the affair was referred to a council of bishops of Septimania and Aquitaine; the discussion was opened there; the Jews complaining of the injustice of the treatment they suffered, the Christians calling it a just chastisement. "Then Theodard, who was very young, with the permission of the bishop of Toulouse, spoke, and produced two acts, one of Charlemagne, the other of Louis le Debonnaire, which established that the Jews of Toulouse, having called Abderrahman to France, Charles had only allowed them their lives, upon the condition that, on Christmas day, Good Friday, and Ascension-day, one of them should receive before the door of the church a beating from the hand of a notable, and make an offering of three pounds of wax. "The bishops having heard these things, and being consulted by the duke, cried out, 'far be it from us to oppose anything to this just and equitable decision of the king.' "The discussion between Theodard and the Jews continued and warmed. The Jews pronounced against Jesus Christ such blasphemies, that the duke, furious, menaced them with the last extremities; then they threw themselves at the feet of the bishop, entreating him to obtain their pardon from the duke, in such a manner, that, remaining subject to the torture the emperor had decreed for them, they might live in peace and safety. "The duke consented, after some resistance, but adding the following condition, suggested by Theodard; that the Jew who was

Date.	Place.	Present.	Object of the Council, Rules, &c.
	.	.	to be scourged, before being struck, should declare, in a loud voice, before all the assembly; 'It is just that the heads of the Jews should be submitted to the blows of the Christians; because they would not submit to Jesus of Nazareth, Lord of lords, and King of kings.' If the Jew refused this, then he should be struck seven times, that it might be accomplished which was written in their law: *I will punish you sevenfold, lifting up myself against you.* "The bishops approved of this, the duke added it, and the king confirmed it."
896	Châlons.	9 bishops and a chancellor.	This council confirmed the privileges of many churches.
896	Near Port Nimes.	19 bishops.	Theodard, archbishop of Narbonne, held this council against Selva, a Spanish clerk, who had ordained himself archbishop of Tarragona contrary to the canons, and had ordained, in spite of Theodard, Eumiza to be bishop of Gerona; they were both deposed, and their episcopal vestments torn off them; they had the rings taken from their fingers, and their pastoral staffs broken over their heads.
896	Cologne.	5 bishops, 4 abbots, some clerks, and some of the laity.	This council made many canons against those who took possession of church property, those who oppressed the poor, and those who contracted forbidden marriages.
888	St. Maurice.	Bishops and grandees.	This council elected for king of Transjuran Burgundy, and crowned Rodolph, the son of Conrad the Second.
888	Mayence.	The archbishop of Mayence, of Co-	This council was held the first year of the reign of Arnold, with the object of reforming the disci-

Date.	Place.	Present.	Object of the Council, Rules, &c.
		logne, of Trèves, and their suffragans.	pline, and repairing the disorders occasioned by the invasions of the Normans. *Rules.*—The council forbids that for the future the priests should have any women in their house, even their own sister, on account of the disorders resulting there from. It forbids that a clerk of an inferior order should accuse a clerk of an order superior to his own; it regulates how many witnesses should be required for judgment; for a bishop, 72: a priest-cardinal, 40; a deacon-cardinal, of Rome, 26; a sub-deacon, an acolyte, 7. That the witnesses should be men of good repute, having wife and children. This canon is taken from the council of Rome. That the witnesses should be at least fourteen years of age.
888	Metz.	4 bishops of Belgium, 1 abbot, clerks, laity.	This council ordered a fast of three days and solemn prayers, to obtain peace and the retreat of the Normans. *Rules.*—That no lord shall receive anything of the tithes of his church, and that the priest who serves the church shall take them wholly for the divine office. That a priest shall have only one church; unless his own have been joined from all antiquity to a chapel which may not be separated from it.
889	Saint Jangoul.	4 bishops, abbots, 6 counts.	This assembly (*placitum*) was occupied by the order of the queen Ermengarde, widow of Boson, with a complaint of the monks of Guiny against a certain Bernard, who had seized some of their property.
890	Valence.	Bishops and grandees of the kingdom of Arles.	This council made Louis, son of Boson, king.

Date.	Place.	Present.	Object of the Council, Rules, &c.
890	Worms.	The archbishop of Reims, his suffragans, the archbishops of Cologne and Hamburg, many neighboring bishops.	This council occupied itself with the quarrel of the archbishops of Cologne and Hamburg, who were disputing for the church of Bremen. It was held by order of the pope Formosus.
891	Mehun-sur-Loire.	16 bishops.	This council decided that no one should be elected abbot of St. Pierre de Sens but by the brethren.
892	Vienne.	The bishops of the kingdom of Arles, 2 legates.	*Rules.*—Let laymen who have killed, mutilated, maimed, dishonored a priest, do penance, and seek to amend themselves. That no one possess himself fraudulently of the alms of a dying or sick bishop or priest. That laymen neither give nor dispose of churches without the consent of the bishops on which they are dependent, and that they exact no tribute, under form of gift, of priests, at their entry upon churches: that they extort from them nothing by violence.
893	Reims.	.. ..	Foulques, archbishop of Reims, crowned in this council Charles le Simple, competitor of Eudes.
894	Châlons.	4 bishops.	This council admits to the proof of the communion a priest accused of having poisoned the bishop of Autun.
895	Tribur.	22 bishops.	This council, composed almost entirely of German bishops, occupied itself with ecclesiastical reform, by order of king Arnould. *Rules.*—That the Wehrgeld, given for the death of a priest, be divided into three parts—one for the church, the other for his bishop, the third for his parents. It is a sacrilege, calling for pe-

Date.	Place.	Present	Object of the Council, Rules, &c.
			nance, to enter a church with a sword unsheathed. If a bishop in his progress has fixed for the canonical assembly the same day that the count, wittingly, or unwittingly, has fixed upon for holding his court, let all, including the count himself, leave the court to attend the bishop's assembly; but if the bishop in his own town and the count have named the same day for their respective assembly, let him who first named the day have the preference, always saving the dignity and power of the bishop. Any priest who, even under compulsion, has committed homicide, shall be deposed. When necessity requires it, persons may be buried out of the parish appertaining to the cathedral church; in such cases, let the parish be selected in which the person has paid tithe. It is a frightful thing, and hereby interdicted, to claim any money for the ground in which a person is buried. That none of the laity be buried in the churches. That in a quarrel between a layman and a priest, the layman be interrogated by oath, the priest by the communion, because the priest ought not to swear. In memory of the blessed Peter the Apostle, we honor the holy apostolical seat of Rome, in such manner that this church, mother of the sacerdotal dignity, is for us the mistress of ecclesiastical right. If, then, which may God prevent, some priest working against our ministry, being accused to us of having brought a forged letter from the apostolic seat, or anything that could not thence, that it may be in the power of the bishop to keep him in prison until, by letters or message, he has

Date.	Place.	Present.	Object of the Council, Rules, &c.
			called upon his apostolic sublimity to explain, by a worthy legate, the rules of the Roman law, and that which we ought to do to conform to it. If a church is the property of many coheritors, let them agree among themselves, that the service of God shall not suffer; but if, in place of this, they do not agree in the choice of a priest, and that quarrels happen between themselves, or between the priests, let the bishop take the relic from the church, shut and seal the door with his seal, in order that they may not celebrate any office until they shall have provided themselves with a priest worthy to take care of the holy place, and procure the salvation of the people of God. The count is not allowed to force any penitent to plead. That whoever has committed adultery with a woman cannot marry her. If a husband, dishonored by his wife, wishes to kill her, and she flies to the bishop, he should endeavor to dissuade the husband from his project, and if he does not succeed, he ought not to deliver her up to be killed, but to put her carefully in a place chosen by herself, where she can live safely. If persons who live in adultery make to themselves mutual donations, let it serve for their child, but they shall have nothing in common when they separate. The council makes many other canons regarding illegal marriages, and penitential canons.
Uncertain date.	Nantes	.. ..	This council occupied itself with discipline. We are ignorant of its date; its third and tenth canons are transcribed from the seventh book of the capitularies collected by Benedict Diacre Sir-

Date.	Place.	Present.	Object of the Council, Rules, &c.
			mond does not think it impossible that the canons belong to the grand council held at Nantes in 658, which Frodoard mentions. We have left them in the place that Labbe assigned to them. *Rules.*—That the priests before celebrating mass, Sundays and fête days, interrogate the people if there is any one from another parish, in spite of his own priest; send him from the mass, and oblige him to go to his own parish: if he finds persons engaged in rancorous quarrels, let him reconcile them. The council exempts from the obligation of attending mass in their parish those who are travelling or pleading. That the priests be aware that the tithes and offerings are the revenue of the poor and strangers, and that they are not given to them, but only confided to them, and for them to render an account thereof to God. The council orders that before making an ordination, the bishop assemble the priests and prudent men, versed in the law of God, and question them on the life, the birth, the country, the age, and education of those who are to be ordained, the place where they have been instructed, if they are learned, if they know the law of the Lord, above all, if they are of the catholic faith. The council occupies itself afterwards with confraternities, confines them to objects which relate to salvation, to offerings, to keeping in repair the church lights, and the monthly prayers, the alms, the funerals, and other pious objects. It recommends, when meetings are necessary, and that a repast follows, it should be modest and frugal, and that all should be orderly. Priests and the laity met in these confraternities. The

Date.	Place.	Present.	Object of the Council, Rules, &c.
			council complain of women speaking of public affairs, at public assemblies, unless with the permission of their bishop, and for their affairs, or commanded by him. The council recommend to the bishops and priests, to strive to abolish the pagan superstitions.
897	Port, in the Nimois.	4 bishops, 8 ecclesiastics.	This council ordered the bishop of Maguelonne to restore to the church of St. John the Baptist the domains that he had awarded to the church of St. Andrew.

Tenth Century.

900	Reims.	12 bishops.	This council excommunicated the murderers of the archbishop Foulques.
906	Barcelona.	8 bishops.	Although this council took place in Spain, we give it here because it was composed of suffragans from Narbonne; discussed the rights of this metropolis, and that the following one, upon the same affair, was held in France, and that, at this epoch, the count Vico of Barcelona was a fief of France. This council agitated the question whether the church of Osona, at present, belonged to Narbonne.
907	Saint Tiberi, in the diocese of Agde.	10 bishops.	This council freed the church of Osona from all dependence and service towards the church of Narbonne; Aurnste, archbishop of Narbonne, agreed to it.
909	Jonquieres, diocese of Maguelonne.	11 bishops.	This council gave absolution and benediction to count Suniaire and all his family.
909	Troli, in the Soissonnais.	12 bishops.	This council occupied itself with ecclesiastical reform; it cited frequently the capitularies and decrees of the popes; it finished its session by a profession of its faith, upon advices from Rome that the

Date.	Place.	Present.	Object of the Council, Rules, &c.
			Greek heresy, regarding the procession of the Holy Spirit, was still alive in the East. *Rules.*—This council complained of the state of the monastic orders; a great number of monasteries have been destroyed by the pagans; in the monasteries of men or women dwell lay abbots, with their wives, their children, their soldiers, and their dogs; and if one presents the rules to them they reply, as Isaiah, "I know not how to read." The council extends to all products the obligation to pay tithe. Some, perhaps, may say, I am not a laborer, I have neither land nor flocks for which I can give tithe; let every one know, be he a military man, a merchant, or artisan, that the source from whence he draws his living comes from God, and to him he ought to give tithe. The council attributes to the non-payment of tithes, the devastation of pagans and bad seasons. The council prohibits, according to the capitularies, secret marriages, from which result many disorders, which give birth to the blind, the lame, the deformed, &c.; it is necessary that the priest who performs the marriage interrogate the parties, to ascertain if the woman is a relation of her future husband, or spouse of another, or adulteress. The council requires the oath of seven witnesses to convict a priest of having lived with a woman; if these fail, he can justify himself by his sole oath. The council renews a canon of the council of Valencia, in Spain, which forbids the parents of a bishop dying without a will to take possession of his property before the ordination of his successor, or the consent of the me-

Date.	Place.	Present.	Object of the Council, Rules, &c.
			tropolitan, for fear that they possess themselves at the same time of things belonging to the church.
91.	Fontaine Couverte, near Narbonne.	.. ..	This council occupied itself with a quarrel between the bishops of Urgel and of Pallarie, on a question of boundary.
912	Tours.	The archbishop of Tours and his suffragans.	This council decided that the festival of the translation of the remains of St. Martin should be celebrated. One finds at this epoch, the canons of Gautier, archbishop of Sens: Constitutiones ex concilio Galteri, archiepiscopi Senonensi; this appears to indicate that he held a council, but we have no other indications; these canons of discipline are not important.
915	Châlons.	7 bishops.	This council occupied itself with discipline, and received restitution of the goods of the church, which had been usurped by Rodolph, Count of Macon, alarmed with a menace of excommunication.
921	Troli.	.. ..	This council gave absolution to Count Erlebald, who had died excommunicated.
922	Coblentz	8 bishops, many clergy.	This council, at which Charles le Simple and Henry L'Oiseleur were present, made many canons of discipline. *Rules.*—If the laity have chapels, it is against law and reason that they receive tithes and nourish with it their dogs and their mistresses: it is better that the priests should receive it. It is asked, what ought to be done with one who has seduced and sold a Christian; we are of opinion he is guilty of homicide. Let a layman who wishes to give away his property know that he cannot give away the tithes of

Date.	Place.	Present.	Object of the Council, Rules, &c.
			the church where it is situated; if he does so, the act will be null, and he will be himself under the censure of the church.
923	Place not known, in the Remois.	The archbishop of Reims and his suffragans.	This council imposed a penance on those who were at the battle of Soissons, between Charles le Simple and king Robert.
924	.. ..	Bishops; many counts.	Etienne, bishop of Cambray, received at this council satisfaction from Count Isaac; he gave him absolution.
926	Charlieu.	3 bishops.	This synod restored to the monastery of Charlieu, ten churches which had been taken from it.
927	Troli.	6 bishops.	This council, convoked by order of Count Heribert, whose son aged five years had been elected archbishop of Reims, was held in despite of king Raoul, and admitted to penance count Herlnin, who had remarried during the life of his wife.
927	Duisberg.	.. ..	This council excommunicated those who had blinded Bruno, bishop of Metz.
932	Erfurt	13 bishops, many clergy.	This council prohibits calling a Law Court seven days before Christmas, fifteen before Easter, seven before Saint John, in order that all have the facility of going to church to pray. It prohibits imposing extraordinary fasts.
933	Chateau-Thierry.	.. ..	This council consecrated the bishop of Beauvais.
935	Fismes	7 bishops.	This council anathematized those who usurped the goods of the church.
941	Soissons.	The suffragans of the diocese of Reims.	This council decided in favor of Hugues, son of Heribert, against Hartaud, who pretended also to the archbishopric of Reims; the

Date.	Place.	Present.	Object of the Council, Rules, &c.
			bishops went to Reims and consecrated him there.
942 or 943	Bonn.	22 bishops.	We are ignorant of the positive date of this council, or if two were held consecutively; there is nothing remaining of them.
943	Binden in Germany.	.. ..	There is no account of this council.
944	Trenorch, or Tourneux.	7 bishops; many clergy.	Convoked by order of Duke Gilbert; this council decided, that the relics which had been transported from the monastery of Trenorch to that of St. Porcien in Auvergne, should be returned.
947	At Fontaine, diocese of Elne, in Roussillon.	.. ..	This council, deposed, by order of pope Agapetus, and restored immediately the bishops of Gerona and Urgel; it granted to the bishop of Elne the highest rank, after the archbishop of Narbonne. (The see of Elne has since been transferred to Perpignan.)
947	Verdun.	8 bishops; many abbots.	This council adjudged to Artaud the see of Reims.
948	.. ..	Mouson, archbishop of Trèves, and his suffragans; some bishops of the diocese of Reims.	This council adjudged anew the see of Reims to Artaud, and interdicted the communion to Hugues, until the general council convoked for the month of August.
948	Ingelheim.	31 bishops.	This council confirmed that which the preceding had done, and excommunicated the Count Hugues, for having driven from his see the bishop of Laon. It also made many canons of discipline.
948	Laon	.. ..	This council cited, by letters of Marin, the pope's legate, the Count Hugues to repentance.
948	Trèves.	5 bishops,	This council excommunicated

Date.	Place.	Present.	Object of the Council, Rules, &c
		1 legate.	the Count Hugues, and some bishops ordained by bishop Hugues, and many other persons.
952	Augsburg.	25 bishops.	This council, composed of bishops of Germany, Italy, and Eastern Gaul, made canons of discipline, which have nothing new in them.
953	St. Thierry, in the Remois.	3 bishops.	This council was held against the Count Hainold, whose excommunication was deferred at the demand of the king.
955	The place uncertain, upon the confines of Burgundy.	.. ..	This council excommunicated the Count Iodard, who retained the domains of the church of St. Symphorian.
962	Upon the Marne, near Meaux.	13 bishops.	This council was convoked on the occasion of the death of Artaud. Many bishops wished the see of Reims to be given to Hugues; others refused. The council then consulted the pope, and, by his advice, elected and consecrated Odalric.
972	Mount Saint Mary, in the Tardenois.	The archbishop of Reims and his suffragans, ten in all; 5 abbés, 8 archdeacons.	This council confirmed the decree of Adalberon, archbishop of Reims, who put in the hermitage of Mouson monks instead of canons. The pope, being consulted, appointed and confirmed it.
972	Ingelheim.	.. ..	This council refused to Odalric, bishop of Augsburg, permission to quit his bishopric for a monastic life, because of the disorder which would ensue in the election of his successor.
975	Reims.	.. ..	This council, presided over by a legate, excommunicated Thibaud, bishop of Amiens, ordained formerly by Hugues, archbishop of Reims, and already excommunicated for another reason.

Date.	Place.	Present.	Object of the Council, Rules, &c.
980	Sens.	6 bishops, 4 churchmen.	Sevin, archbishop of Sens, restored at this council much property to the monastery of Saint Pierre le Vif.

SECOND COURSE

LECTURE THE FIRST.

Object of the course—Elements of national unity—They exist and begin to be developed in France towards the end of the 10th century—Thence dates French civilization—The feudal period will be the subject of this course—It includes the 11th, 12th, and 13th centuries, from Hugh Capet to Philippe de Valois—Proof that these are the limits of the feudal period—Plan of the course: History; 1st, of society; 2d, of the human mind, during the feudal period—The history of society resolves itself into, 1st, history of civil society; 2d, history of religious society—The history of the human mind resolves itself into, 1st, history of learned literature; 2d, history of national literature in the vulgar tongue—Importance of the middle ages in the history of French civilization—The present state of opinions concerning the middle ages—Is it true that there is danger in historical impartiality and poetical sympathy for this period?—Utility of this study.

In commencing the last course, I was obliged to determine its subject, and to explain the motives of my choice. At present I have not any thing of the kind to do. The subject of our study is known; the route is traced. I endeavored to place you in the presence of the origins of French civilization under the first two races; I propose to follow it through all its vicissitudes, in its long and glorious development up to the eve of our own times. I now, therefore again take up the subject where we left it, that is to say, at the end of the tenth century, at the accession of the Capetians.

As I told you in concluding the past course, it is there that French civilization commences. Hitherto, you will recollect, we have spoken of Gaulish, Roman, Gallo-Roman, Frankish, Gallo-Frankish, civilization; we were obliged to make use of foreign names which did not belong to us, in order to express with any fulness, a society without unity, without fixedness, without entirety. Dating from the end of the tenth century, there is no longer any thing of this kind; it is now with the French, with French civilization, that we have to occupy ourselves.

And yet it was at this very epoch that all national and political unity was disappearing from our land. All books say this, and all facts show it. It was the epoch when the feudal system, that is to say, the dismemberment of the people and of power, entirely prevailed. At the eleventh century, the soil which we call France was covered with petty nations and petty sovereigns, almost strangers one to the other, almost independent of each other. Even the very shadow of a central government, of a general nation, seemed to have disappeared.

How comes it that really French civilization and history commence exactly at the moment when it was almost impossible to discover a France?

It is because, in the life of nations, the external visible unity, the unity of name and government, although important, is not the first, the most real, not that which truly constitutes a nation. There is a more profound, more powerful unity: that which results, not from the identity of government and destiny, but from the similarity of social elements, from the similarity of institutions, manners, ideas, sentiments, languages; the unity which resides in the men themselves whom the society unites together, and not in the forms of their junction; moral unity, in point of fact, far superior to political unity, and which alone can give it a solid foundation.

Well, it is at the end of the tenth century that the cradle of this at once unique and complex being, which has become the French nation, is placed. She required many centuries and long efforts to extricate herself, and to produce herself in her simplicity and grandeur. Still, at this epoch, her elements existed, and we begin to catch glimpses of the work of their development. In the times which we studied in the last course, from the fifth to the tenth century, under Charlemagne, for example, external political unity was often greater and stronger than at the epoch with which we are about to occupy ourselves. But if you go thoroughly into the matter, into the moral state of the men themselves, you find there is an utter absence of unity. The races are profoundly different, and even hostile; the laws, traditions, manners, languages, likewise differ and struggle; situations, social relations have neither generality nor fixedness. At the end of the tenth and at the commencement of the eleventh century, there was no kind of political unity like tha' of Charlemagne, but races began to amalgamate; diversity of laws according to origin is no longer the principle of all legislation. Social situations have acquired some fixedness; institutions not the same, but throughout analogous, the feudal institutions prevailed, or nearly so, over all the land. In place of the radical, imperishable diversity of the Latin language and the Germanic languages, two languages began to be formed, the Roman language of the south, and the Roman language of the north, doubtless different, but still of the same origin, of the same character, and destined one day to become amalgamated. Diversity also began to be effaced from the soul of men, from their moral existence. The German is less addicted to his Germanic traditions and habits; he gradually detaches himself from the past to belong to his present situation. It is the same with the Roman; he thinks less of the ancient empire, of its fall, and of the sentiments which it gave rise to in him. Over conquerors and conquered, the new, actual facts, which are common to them, daily exercise more influence. In a word, political unity is almost null, real diversity still very great, and yet at bottom there is more of true unity than there has been for five centuries. We begin to catch glimpses of the elements of a nation; and the proof is, that from this epoch the tendency of all these social elements to conjoin, to assimilate and form themselves into great masses, that is to say, the tendency towards national unity, and thence towards political unity, becomes the dominant characteristic, the great fact of the history of French civilization, the general and constant fact around which all our study will turn.

The development of this fact, the triumph of this tendency, has made the fortune of France. It is by this especially that she has outstripped the other nations of the continent in the career of civilization. Look at Spain, Italy, even Germany: what is it that they want? They have progressed far more slowly than France towards moral unity, towards the formation into a single people. Even there where moral unity has been formed, or nearly so, as in Italy and Germany, its transformation into political unity, the birth of a general government, has been slackened or almost entirely stopped. France, more happy, arrived more rapidly and more completely at that double unity, not the only principle, but the only pledge of the strength and grandeur nations. It was at the end of the tenth century that it, so to speak, commenced its progress towards this important result. It is, therefore, from this epoch that French civilization really dates; it is there that we may begin to study it under its true name.

The feudal period, that is, the period when the feudal system was the dominant fact of our country, will be the subject of the present course.

It is comprehended between Hugh Capet and Philippe de Valois, that is, it embraces the eleventh, twelfth, and thirteenth centuries.

That these are the true limits, the career of the feudal system, it is easy I think to establish.

The peculiar general character of feudalism, as I have just repeated, and as every one knows, is the dismemberment of the people and of power into a multitude of petty nations and petty sovereigns; the absence of any universal nation, of any central government. Let us see the limits in which this fact is contained. These limits will necessarily be those of the feudal period.

We may, if I do not deceive myself, recognise them especially by three symptoms.

1. To what enemies did feudalism succumb? Who opposed it in France? Two powers; royalty on the one hand, on the other, the commons. By royalty a central government was formed in France; by the commons was formed a universal nation, which grouped itself around the central government.

At the end of the tenth century, royalty and the commons were not visible, or at all events scarcely visible. At the commencement of the fourteenth century, royalty was the head of the state, the commons were the body of the nation. The two forces to which the feudal system was to succumb had then attained, not, indeed, their entire development, but a decided preponderance. By this symptom we may then say that there the feudal period, properly so called, stops, since the absence of any universal nation, and of all central power, is its essential characteristic.

Here is a second symptom which assigns the same limits to the feudal period.

From the tenth to the fourteenth century, wars, which were then the principal event of history, have, at least the greater part of them, the same characteristic. They are internal, civil wars, as it were in the bosom of feudalism itself It is a suzerain who endeavors to acquire the territory of his vassals; vassals who dispute among themselves certain portions of the territory. Such appear to us, with the exception of the crusades, almost all the wars of Louis le Gros of Philip August, Saint Louis, and Philippe le Bel. It is from the very nature of the feudal society that their causes and effects arise.

With the fourteenth century the character of war changed Then began the foreign wars; no longer a vassal against suzerain, or vassal against vassal, but nation against nation, government against government. On the accession of Philippe de Valois, the great wars between the French and the English broke out—the claims of the kings of England, not upon any particular fief, but upon the whole land, and upon the throne of France—and they continued up to Louis XI. They were no longer feudal, bu. national wars; a certain proof that the feudal period stopped at this limit, that another society had already commenced.

Lastly, if we address ourselves to a third kind of indication, if we interrogate the great events which we are accustomed, and with reason, to look upon as the result, as the expression of feudal society, we shall find that they are all included within the epoch of which we speak. The crusades, that great adventure of feudalism, and its popular glory, finished, or nearly finished, with Saint Louis and the thirteenth century; we hear afterwards but a futile echo of them. Chivalry, that poetical daughter, that ideal, so to speak, of the feudal system, is equally enclosed in the same limits. In the fourteenth century it was on the decline, and a knight-errant already appears a ridiculous personage. Romantic and chivalrous literature, the troubadours, the trouveres, in a word, all the institutions, all the facts which may be looked upon as the results, the companions of feudalism, alike belong to the eleventh, twelfth, and thirteenth centuries. That, therefore, is evidently the feudal period; and when I confine it to these limits, I do not adopt an arbitrary, purely conventional classification; it is the fact.

Now, how shall we study this epoch? What method will best make it known to us?

It will, I hope, be borne in mind, that I have regarded civilization as the result of two great facts; the development, on the one hand, of society, on the other, of individual man. I have therefore always been careful to retrace external and internal civilization, the history of society and the history of man, of human relations and of human ideas, political history and intellectual history.

We shall follow the same method here; we shall examine the feudal period from this twofold point of view.

From the political point of view, in confining ourselves to the history of society, we shall find from the tenth to the fourteenth century, as from the fifth to the tenth, two societies closely bordering on each other, dovetailed, as it were, into one another, yet essentially distinct: the civil society and the religious society, the church and the state; we shall study them separately, as we have hitherto done.

Civil society is to be considered, first, in the facts which constitute it, and which show us what it has been; secondly, in the legislative and political movements which emanate from it, and upon which its character is imprinted.

The three great facts of the feudal period, the three facts whose nature and relations comprehend the history of civilization during these three centuries, are—1, the possessors of fiefs, the feudal association itself; 2, above and by the side of the feudal association, in intimate relation with it, and yet reposing upon other principles, and applying itself to create a distinct existence, royalty; 3, below and by the side of the feudal association, also in intimate relation with it, and yet also reposing upon other principles, and laboring to separate itself, the commons. The history of these three facts, and of their reciprocal action is, at this epoch, the history of civil society.

With regard to the written monuments that remain to us, there are four principal ones: two collections of laws which modern learning, wrongly I think, would call codes; and two works of jurisconsults. The legislative monuments are—1. The collection of the ordinances of the kings of France, and especially the *établissements* of Saint Louis. 2. His *assises* of the Frank kingdom of Jerusalem, drawn up by order of Godefry de Bouillon, which reproduce the image of the feudal society more completely and more faithfully than any other document.

The two works of jurisconsults are—1. The *Coutume de Beauvaisis*, by Beaumanoir. 2. The *Traité de l'ancienne Jurisprudence des Français; ou Conseils à un Ami*, by Pierre de Fontaines.

I shall study with you these monuments of the feudal legislation as I have studied the barbarian laws and capitularies, by carefully analyzing them, and attempting to thoroughly comprehend their contents, and to exactly understand their nature.

From civil society we shall pass to religious society; we shall consider it, as we have already done, 1. In itself, in its peculiar and internal organization. 2. In its relations with civil society, with the state. 3. Finally, in its relations with the external government of the universal church—that is, with papacy.

The history of society, if I do not deceive myself, will thus be completed; we shall then enter into the history of the human mind. At this epoch it resides in two great facts, two distinct literatures : 1. A learned literature, written in Latin, addressed solely to the learned classes, lay or ecclesiastical, and which contains the theology and philosophy of the time. 2. A national, popular literature, entirely in the vulgar tongue, addressed to the whole community, particularly to idlers and to the lower classes. Whosoever neglects either of these two facts, whoever does not thoroughly understand these two literatures, who does not see them marching abreast, rarely close to each other, rarely acting upon one another, but both powerful and holding an important place, who does not see all this, will have but an incomplete and false idea of the intellectual history of this epoch, of the state and progress of mind.

Such, in its whole, is the plan of the present course.

Here, most assuredly, is a vast field opened to our study. There is here enough long to excite and nourish learned curiosity. But is so great an epoch of our history—is France in the rudest crisis of her development—in a word, the middle ages, are they with us a mere matter of learning, a mere object of curiosity? Have we not the most universal and pressing interest in thoroughly understanding it? Has the past no other value attached to it than for erudition? has it become totally foreign to the present, to our life?

Two facts, if I mistake not, two contemporary visible facts, prove that such is not the case.

The imagination at the present day is evidently gratified in carrying itself back towards this epoch. Its traditions, its manners, its adventures, its monuments, have an attraction for the public which cannot be mistaken. We may, upon this subject, interrogate letters and the arts; we may open the histories, romance, poems of our time; we may enter the furniture and curiosity shops; everywhere we shall see the middle ages cultivated, reproduced, occupying the thought, amusing the taste of that portion of the public which has time to spare for its intellectual wants and pleasures.

At the same time there is manifested, on the part of some enlightened and honorable men, sincere friends to the learning and progress of humanity, an increasing aversion towards this epoch and all which recalls it. In their eyes, those who there seek inspirations, or merely poetical pleasure, carry literature back towards barbarism; in their eyes, those who, from a political point of view, and amidst an enormous mass of error and of evil, seek to find in it any thing of good, those, whether they wish it or not, favor the system of despotism and privilege. These unrelenting enemies of the middle ages deplore the blindness of the public who can take any pleasure in going back, merely in imagination, amidst those barbarous ages, and seem to predict, if this despotism continues, the return of all the absurdities, of all the evils, which then weighed upon nations.

This clearly proves that the middle ages are quite other than a matter of learning to us; that they correspond to interests more real, more direct than those of historical erudition and criticism, to sentiments more general, more full of life than that of mere curiosity.

How can we be surprised at this? The twofold fact which I spoke of is exactly the result, and as it were a new form of the two essential characteristics of the middle ages, the two facts by which that epoch has held so great a place in the history of our civilization, and influenced posterior ages so powerfully.

On the one hand, it is impossible to overlook the fact that there is the cradle of modern societies and manners. Thence date—1. Modern languages, and especially our own. 2. Modern literatures, precisely in all that there is in them of the national, the original, of the foreign to all mere learning, to all imitation of other times, of other countries. 3. The greater portion of modern monuments, monuments in which, for many centuries, the people have assembled, and still continue to assemble, churches, palaces, town-halls, works of art and public utility of every kind. 4. Almost all historical families, families who have played a part and placed their name in the various phases of our destiny. 5. A large number of national events, important in themselves and for a long time popular, the crusades, chivalry; in a word, almost every thing which for centuries has filled and agitated the imagination of the French people.

This is evidently the heroic age of modern nations, among others, of France. What more natural than its poetical affluence and attraction?

By the side of this fact, however, we encounter another no less incontestable: the social state of the middle ages was constantly insupportable and odious, and especially so in France. Never did the cradle of a nation inspire it with such antipathy; the feudal system, its institutions and principles, never obtained that unhesitating adhesion, the result of habit, which nations have often given to the very worst systems of social organization. France constantly struggled to escape from them, to abolish them. Whosoever dealt them a blow, kings, jurisconsults, the church, was sanctioned and became popular; despotism itself, when it seemed a means of deliverance from them, was accepted as a benefit.

The eighteenth century and the French revolution have been for us the last phase, the definite expression of this fact of our history. When they broke forth, the social state of the middle ages had long been changed, enervated, dissolved. Yet it was against its consequences and recollections that, in the popular mind and intention, this great shock was more especially accomplished. The society which then perished, was the society which the Germanic invasion had created in the west, and of which feudalism was the first and essential form. It was, in truth, no longer in existence: yet it was against it that the revolution was directed.

But precisely because of this fact, precisely because the eighteenth century and the revolution were the definitive explosion of the national antipathy to the social state of the middle ages, two things were inevitably destined to happen, and in fact did happen: 1. In their violent efforts against the memory and remains of this epoch, the eighteenth century and the revolution would necessarily fail in impartiality towards it, and would not recognise the good which might be met with in it; and it would in like manner overlook its poetical character, its merit, and its attractions as the cradle of certain elements of the national life. The epochs in which he critical spirit dominates, that is to say, those which occupy themselves more especially with examining and demolishing, generally understand but little of the poetica times, those times when man complacently gives himself to the impulsion of his manners and the facts which surround him. They understand more especially little of what there is of the true and poetical in the times against which they make war. Open the writings of the eighteenth century, those at least which really have the character of the epoch, and contributed to the great revolution then accomplished; you will see that the human mind there shows itself very little sensible of the poetical merit of any social state much differing from the type which they then conceived and followed, especially of the poetical merit of the rude and unrefined times, and, among those times, of the middle ages. The *Essai sur les mœurs et l'esprit des nations* is in this way the most faithful image of the general disposition of the age: look there for the history of the middle ages: you will see that Voltaire incessantly applied himself to the task of extracting all that is gross, absurd, odious, calamitous, in this epoch. He was right, thoroughly right in the definitive judgment which he gave of it, and in his efforts to abolish its remains. But that is all that he sees of it; he thinks only of judging and abolishing, in his historical writings, that is to say, in his works of polemical criticism; for Voltaire has done other things than criticism. Voltaire was also a poet, and when he gave himself up to his imagination, to his poetical instincts, he found impressions greatly differing from his judgment. He has spoken of the middle ages elsewhere than in the *Essai sur les mœurs et l'esprit des nations*, and how has he spoken of it?

> "Oh! l'heureux temps que celui de ces fables,
> Des bons démons, des esprits familiers,
> Des farfadets, aux mortels secourables!
> On écoutait tous ces faits admirables
> Dans son château, près d'un large foyer.
> Le père et l'oncle, et la mère et la fille,
> Et les voisins, et toute la famille,
> Ouvraient l'oreille à monsieur l'aumônier,
> Qui leur faisait des contes de sorcier.
> On a banni les démons et les fées;
> Sous la raison les grâces étouffées
> Livrent nos cœurs à l'insipidité;
> Le raisonner tristement s'accrédite;
> On court, hélas! après la vérité:
> Ah! croyez-moi, l'erreur a son mérite."

Voltaire is wrong to call the poetical side of these old times *erreur;* Poetry there doubtless associated herself with many errors; but in herself she was true, although of a truth very different from philosophical truth, and she answered to very legitimate wants of human nature. This incidental observation, however, is of but little importance; what is necessary to be remarked, is the singular contrast between Voltaire the poet, and Voltaire the critic. The poet acutely feels for the middle ages impressions to which the critic shows himself an entire stranger; the one deplores the loss of those impressions which the other applies himself to destroy: nothing, surely, better manifests that want of political impartiality and poetical sympathy in the eighteenth century, of which I just now spoke.

We are now in the reaction against the tendency of the age which preceded us. This fact is evidenced in the direction now taken, at least for the most part, by historical studies, by works of general literature following the public taste, and also in the indignation of the exclusive partisans of the eighteenth century. Is this indignation legitimate? Is the danger denounced from this reaction so great? is there any danger at all?

In a literary point of view I shall not absolutely deny it. I would not say that there is not some exaggeration, something of mania in this return of the imagination towards the middle ages, and that good sense and good taste have not a little suffered from it. The reaction, followed with much talent, appears to me, upon the whole, a groping rather than a regeneration. In my opinion, it proceeds from very distinguished men, sometimes sincerely inspired, but who often deviate in seeking a good vein, rather than from people who have found one, and are working it with confidence. But in truth, in the actual state of society and mind, the evil cannot become very grave. Are not publicity and criticism always at hand in the literary world as well as in the political world, and always ready to render everywhere the same services, to warn, restrain, to combat, in fine, to prevent us from falling under the exclusive domination of a coterie or system? They do not spare the new school; and the public, the genuine and general public, while receiving it with gentleness, does not seem disposed to become subjected by it. It judges it, and sometimes even rebukes it rather roughly

Nothing, therefore, seems to me to indicate that barbarism is about to resume sway over the national taste.

Besides, we must take life where life manifests itself; the wind, from whatever quarter it blows; talent, wherever it has pleased Heaven to bestow it. For we need above all things in the literary world talent and life. The worst that can happen to us here is immobility and sterility.

Is danger to political impartiality the character of the reaction which they deplore? This must be absolutely denied. Impartiality will never be a popular tendency, the error of the masses; they are governed by simple, exclusive ideas and passions; there is no fear of their ever judging too favorably of the middle ages and their social state. Present interests, national traditions in this respect preserve, if not all their potency, at least sufficient influence to prevent all excess. The impartiality which is spoken of will scarcely penetrate below the regions of science and of philosophical discussion.

And what is it in these regions themselves, and among the very men who most pique themselves on it? Does it impel them in any way towards the doctrines of the middle ages? to any approbation of their institutions—of their social state? Not in the least degree. The principles upon which modern societies rest, the progress and the requirements of reason and of human liberty, have certainly not firmer, more zealous defenders, than the partisans of historical impartiality; they are first in the breach, and more exposed than any others to the blows of their enemies. They have no esteem for the old forms, the fanatic and tyrannical classification of feudal France, the work of force, which ages and enormous labors have had such difficulty in reforming. What they claim is a full and free judgment of this past of the country. They do not believe that it was absolutely destitute of virtue, liberty, or reason, nor that we are entitled to contemn it for its errors and fallings off in a career in which, even in the present day, after such progress, so many victories, we are ourselves advancing so laboriously.

There is evidently therein no danger either for the liberty of the human mind, or for the good organization of society.

Might there not be, on the other hand, great advantages ir this historical impartiality, this poetical sympathy for ancien France?

And first, is it nothing to have a source of emotions an

pleasures opened to the imagination? All this long epoch, all this old history, in which one hitherto saw nothing but absurdity and barbarism, becomes for us rich in great memories, in noble adventures, in events and sentiments in which we feel a vivid interest. It is a domain restored to that need of emotion, of sympathy, which, thanks to God, nothing can stifle in our nature. The imagination plays an immense part in the life of men and of nations. In order to occupy it, to satisfy it, an actual energetic passion is necessary, like that which animated the eighteenth century and the revolution, a rich and varied spectacle. The present alone, the present without passion, the calm and regular present, does not suffice for the human soul; it feels narrow and poor in it; it desires more extension, more variety. Hence the importance and the charm of the past, of national traditions, of all that portion of the life of nations in which imagination wanders and freely enjoys itself, amidst a space far more vast than actual life. Nations may one moment, under the influence of a violent crisis, deny their past—even curse it; they cannot forget it, nor long or absolutely detach themselves from it. On a certain occasion, in one of the ephemeral parliaments held in England under Cromwell, in that which took the name of one of its members, a ridiculous personage, in the Barebone parliament, a fanatic arose, and demanded that in all the offices, in all public establishments, they should destroy the archives, the records, all the written monuments of old England. This was an excess of that fever which sometimes seizes nations, amidst the most useful, the most glorious regenerations; Cromwell, more sensible, had the proposition rejected. Is it to be supposed that it would long have had the assent of England, that it would truly have attained its end?

In my opinion, the school of the eighteenth century has more than once committed this mistake of not comprehending the whole of the part which imagination plays in the life of man and of society. It has attacked, cried down, on the one hand, every thing ancient, on the other, all which assumed to be eternal, history and religion: that is, it has seemed to dispute, to wish to take from men the past and the future, in order to concentrate them in the present. The mistake explains itself, even excuses itself by the ardor of he struggle then on foot, and by the empire of the passion of the moment, which satisfied those requirements of emotion and of imagination, imperishable in human nature. But it is no less serious, and of serious consequence. It were easy to show the proof and effects of this in a thousand details of our contemporaneous history.

It has, moreover, been made matter of complaint, and with reason, that our history was not national, that we were in want of associations, of popular traditions. To this fact some of the faults of our literature, and even of our character, have been imputed. Should it then be extended beyond these natural limits? Is it to be regretted that the past should again become something for us, that we should again take some interest in it?

In a political point of view, and in an entirely positive aim, this were a valuable advantage. The power of associations in fixing and fertilizing institutions, is very great. Our institutions are beneficial and powerful; they rest upon truly national interests, upon ideas which have penetrated deeply into minds. Still they are young; they do not claim the authority of a long experience, at all events not of a long national experience. It was in the name of reason, of philosophy, that they first appeared: they took birth in doctrines: a noble origin, but for some time subject to the uncertainties, the vicissitudes of the human mind. What more useful than to make them thus strike root in the past; to unite the principles and guarantees of our social order to principles half seen, to guarantees sought in the same path through ages? Facts are at present popular; facts have favor and credit. Well, let the institutions, the ideas which are dear to us, be strongly established in the bosom of facts, of the facts of all time; let the trace of them be everywhere found; let them everywhere reappear in our history. They will thence derive force, and we ourselves dignity; for a nation has higher esteem for itself, and has greater pride in itself, when it can thus, in a long series of ages, prolong its destiny and its sentiments.

Lastly, another advantage, an advantage of an entirely different nature, but no less considerable, must result to us from impartiality towards the middle ages, and from an attentive and familiar contemplation of that epoch.

That the social reform which is brought about in our times under our eyes, is immense, no man of sense can deny. Never were human relations regulated with more justice; never has the result been a more general well-being.

Not only is social reform great, but I am convinced that a correspondent moral reform has also been accomplished; that, perhaps, at no epoch has there been, upon the whole, so much propriety in human life, so many men living regularly, that never has less public force been necessary to repress individual wills. Practical morality, I am convinced, has made almost as much progress as the well-being and the prosperity of the country.

But under another point of view we have, I think, much to gain, and we are justly reproachable. We have lived for fifty years under the influence of general ideas, more and more accredited and powerful, under the weight of formidable, almost indescribable events. Thence has resulted a certain weakness, a certain effeminacy in minds and in characters. Individual wills and convictions want energy and confidence in themselves. They think with a common opinion, they obey a general impulse, they give way to an external necessity. Whether to resist or to act, each has but little idea of his own strength, little confidence in his own thoughts. The individuality, in a word, the inward and personal energy of man, is weak and timid. Amidst the progress of general liberty, men seem to have lost the proud sentiment of their own liberty.

Such were not the middle ages; the social condition of those ages was deplorable; human morality very inferior, according to what is told us, to that of our times. But in men, individuality was strong—will, energetic.

There were then few general ideas which governed all minds, few events which, in all parts of the territory, in all situations, weighed upon characters. The individual displayed himself upon his own account, according to his own inclination, irregularly, and with confidence; the moral nature of man appeared here and there with all its ambition, all its energy. A spectacle not only dramatic and attractive, but instructive and useful; which offers us nothing to regret, nothing to imitate, but much to learn from, were it only by constantly recalling our attention to that wherein we are deficient, by showing us what a man may do when he knows how to believe and to will.

Such merits certainly will justify the care which we shall take in our study; and it will, I hope, be seen, that in being just, fully just towards this great epoch, there is for us no danger and some benefit.

SECOND LECTURE.

Necessity for studying the progressive formation of the feudal system—It is often forgotten that social facts form themselves but slowly, and in forming themselves, undergo many vicissitudes—Analysis of the feudal system in its essential elements. They are three in number: 1. The nature of territorial property; 2. Amalgamation of sovereignty and property; 3. Hierarchical organization of the feudal association—State of territorial property from the 5th to the 10th century—Origin and meaning of the word *feodum*—It is synonymous with *beneficium*—History of benefices, from the 8th to the 10th century—Examination of the system of Montesquieu concerning the legal gradation of the duration of benefices—Causes of the increase of the number of benefices—Almost all landed property became feudal.

It has been shown that the feudal period embraces the eleventh, twelfth, and thirteenth centuries. Before entering upon it, before studying it in itself and according to the plan which I have drawn out, it is necessary that we should have some distinct idea of the origins of feudalism; it is necessary to follow it, and to present it to our minds in all the various phases of its progressive formation, from the fifth to the tenth century.

I intentionally say, its progressive formation. No great fact, no social state, makes its appearance complete and at once; it is formed slowly, successively; it is the result of a multitude of different facts, of different dates and origins, which modify and combine themselves in a thousand ways before constituting a whole, presenting itself in a clear and systematic form, receiving a special name and standing through a long life.

This is so simple, so evident a truth, that, at first sight, it seems useless to call it to mind; it is, however, necessary to do so, for it has been and is constantly forgotten. An historical epoch is generally studied when it has ceased, a social condition when it has disappeared. It is, then, in their entirety, under their complete and definitive form that that epoch and that condition are presented to the mind of the observer or the historian. He is easily led to suppose that it has always been thus; he easily forgets that those facts, which he contemplates in all their development, commenced, increased, and while increasing underwent numerous metamorphoses; and he proposes to see, and everywhere seeks them, such as he knew and conceived them at the time of their full maturity.

Numerous and various errors arise from this inclination, in the history even of beings whose unity and whose permanence is the greatest and most visible in the history of men. Why are there so many contradictions and uncertainties concerning the character and moral destinies of Mahomet, of Cromwell, or of Napoleon? Why those problems concerning their sincerity or hypocrisy, their egoism or patriotism? Because people want to see them, as it were, simultaneously, and as having co-existent in them dispositions and ideas which were successively developed; because they forget that, without losing their essential identity, they greatly and constantly changed; that the vicissitudes of their external destiny corresponded to internal revolutions, often unseen by their contemporaries, but real and powerful. If they followed them step by step, from their first appearance in the world until their death, if they were present at that secret work of their moral nature amidst the mobility and activity of their life, they would perceive many of those incoherences, those absurdities which surprise them, disappear, or at least become attenuated; and then only would they truly know and understand them.

If it be thus in the history of individual beings, the most simple of all, and whose duration is so short, with how much more reason is it in the history of societies, of those general facts, so vast, so complex, and which extend through so many centuries! It is here especially that there is danger of overlooking the variety of origins, the complication and slowness of formation. We have a striking example of this in the matter which occupies us. Few historical problems have been more differently and eagerly debated than that as to when and how the feudal system commenced. To speak only of French scholars and publicists, Chantereau-Lefevre, Salvaing, Brussel, de Boulainvilliers, Dubos, Mably, Montesquieu, and many others: each forms a different idea of it. Whence arises this diversity? It is that they have almost all proposed to find the feudal system entire even in its very cradle, to find it such as they see it is at the epoch of its full development. Feudalism has, as it were, entered at once into their mind; and it is in this condition, at this stage of its history, that they have everywhere sought it. And as, notwithstanding, each of them has applied himself more particularly to such and such a characteristic of the feudal system, and has made it to consist in one particular element rather than another, they have been led into immensely different ideas of the epoch and mode of its formation; ideas which may be easily rectified and reconciled as soon as people will consent not to forget that feudalism took five centuries in forming, and that its numerous elements, during this long epoch, belong to very different elements and origins.

It is according to this idea, and never losing sight of it, that I shall endeavor to trace the history of its progressive formation, rapidly and as a preparation to the study of feudalism itself.

To succeed in this, it is necessary—first, to determine the principal facts, the essential elements of this social condition; I mean the facts which properly constitute it, and distinguish it from all others. Secondly, to follow these facts through their successive transformations, each isolately and in itself, and in the junctions and combinations which at the end of five centuries resulted in feudalism.

The essential facts, the constituent elements of the feudal system may, I think, be reduced to three.

1. The particular nature of territorial property, real, full, hereditary, and yet derived from a superior, imposing certain personal obligations on its possessor, under pain of forfeiture, in a word, wanting in that complete independence which is now its characteristic.

2. The amalgamation of sovereignty with property, I mean the attribution to the proprietor of the soil over all the inhabitants of that soil, of the whole or nearly the whole of those rights which constitute what we now call sovereignty, and which are now possessed only by the government, the public power.

3. The hierarchical system of legislative, judicial, military institutions, which united the possessors of fiefs among themselves, and formed them into a general society.

These, if I am not mistaken, are the truly essential and constitutive facts of feudalism. It would be easy to resolve it into a larger number of elements, to assign to it a greater number of characteristics; but these, I think, are the principal, and contain all the others. I shall therefore confine myself to them, and sum them up by saying, that properly to comprehend the progressive development of feudalism, we have to study: first, the history of territorial property, that is, the state of lands; secondly, the history of sovereignty and of the social state, that is, the state of persons; thirdly, the history of the political system, that is, the state of institutions.

I enter at once into the matter; the history of territorial property will now occupy us.

At the end of the tenth century, when feudalism was definitively constituted, its territorial element, as you know, bore the name of *fief*, (*feodum, feudum*.) A writer replete with sense and learning, Brussel, in his *Examen de l'usage général des Fiefs aux* 11, 12, 13, *et* 14 *siècles*, says, that the word *fief* (*feodum*) did not originally mean the land itself, the body of the domain, but only what in feudal language is called the *tenure* of the land, that is, its relation of dependence towards such or such a suzerain:

"Thus," says he, "when king Louis le Jeune notifies by a charter of the year 1167, that count Henry of Champagne has granted the *fief* of Savegny to Bartholomew, bishop of Beauvais, it is only to be understood from this, that count Henry had granted the dependence of Savegny to the bishop of Beauvais; so that this land which had hitherto been held immediately from the count of Champagne was thenceforward only to hold of him as a sub-fief."

I think that Brussel is mistaken. It is very improbable that the name of feudal property meant at first only the quality, the attribute of that property, and not the thing itself. When the first lands which became fiefs were given, it was not suzerainty alone which was conferred; the donors evidently gave the land itself. At a later period, when the feudal system and its ideas had gained some firmness and development, then they might have distinguished the *tenure* of the domain, have given one apart from the other, and designated it by a particular word. It may be that at this epoch the word *fief* was often used for the *tenure*, independently of the body of the land. But such could not have been the primitive meaning of *feodum*; the domain and the tenure were surely originally confounded in language as in fact.

However this may be, the word is only found at a late period in the documents of our history. It appears for the first time in a charter of Charles le Gros, in 884. It is there repeated three times, and almost at the same epoch it is also met with elsewhere. Its etymology is uncertain; many have been assigned to it. I shall point out but two of them, as those alone which I consider probable. According to some, (and this is the opinion of most of the French jurisconsults, of Cujas among others,) the word *feodum* is of Latin origin; it comes from the word *fides*, and means the land in consideration of which people were bound to fidelity towards a suzerain. According to others, and especially according to German writers, *feodum* is of German origin, and comes from two ancient words, of which one has disappeared from the German languages, while the other still exists in many, particularly in the English, from the word *fe, fee*, reward, recompense, and from the radical *od*, property, goods, possession; so that *feodum* means a property given in recompense, by way of pay or reward.

The Germanic origin seems to me far more probable than the Latin origin: first, because of the very construction of the word, and next, because that, at the time when it was introduced into our territory, it was from Germany that it came; lastly, because, in our ancient Latin documents, this kind of property bears a different name—that of *beneficium*. The word *beneficium* very frequently occurs in our historical documents from the fifth to the tenth century, and these evidently indicate the same condition of territorial property which, at the end of the eleventh century, took the name of *feodum*. For a long time after this epoch, the two words are synonymous; so that in the very charter referred to, of Charles le Gros, down to a charter of the emperor Frederic I., of 1162, *feodum* and *beneficium* are used indifferently.

In order, therefore, to the study of the history of the *feoda* from the fifth to the tenth century, it is necessary to look at that of the *beneficia*. What we say of benefices will apply to fiefs, because the two words, at different dates, are the expression of the same fact.

From the earliest times of our history, immediately after the invasion and establishment of the Germans upon Gallic soil, we find benefices appear. This kind of territorial property is contradistinguished from another, which bears the name of *alodium*. The word *alod, alodium*, means an estate which the possessor holds of no one, which imposed no obligation upon him towards any one.

There is reason to suppose that the first freeholds were lands which, under various forms, and without general or systematic division, were appropriated among themselves by the conquering Germans, Franks, Burgundians, or Visigoths, at the time of their establishment. These were entirely independent; they were gained by conquest, by lot, not from a superior. They were called *alod,* that is to say, according to some, *lot, chance;* according to others, full, independent property, (Al-od.)

The word *beneficium,* on the contrary, meant from its origin (it is on the very face of it) an estate received from a superior by way of recompense, of favor, and which required certain duties and services towards him. You know that the German chiefs, to attract or attach their companions to them, made them presents of arms, of horses, supported them and maintained them in their train. The gifts of estates, the benefices, succeeded, or at least were added to presents of moveables. But thence there was to result, and in fact soon did result, a considerable change in the relations between the chief and his companions. The presents of arms, horses, banquets, retained the companions around the chief, and made them lead a life in common. The gifts of estates, on the contrary, were an infallible cause of separation. Among the men to whom their chiefs gave benefices, many soon wished to establish themselves upon those benefices, to live also upon their own estates, there to become in their turn the centre of a small society. Thus, by their very nature, the new gifts of the chief to his companions dispersed the band, and changed the principles as well as the forms of the society.

There was a second difference, fertile in results: the quantity of arms, horses, in a word, of personal presents, which a chief might make to his men was unlimited. It was a matter of pillage; a new expedition always procured the means of giving. It could not be so with presents of estates. There was doubtless much to share in the Roman empire, but still the mine was not inexhaustible; and when a chief had given away the lands of a country where he was fixed, he had nothing more to give, in order to gain other companions, unless by constantly recommencing the wandering life, by constantly changing residence and country, a habit which gradually disappeared. Thence a twofold fact is everywhere visible, from the fifth to the ninth century. On the one hand, the constant efforts of the givers of benefices to resume them when it suited them, and to make them a means of acquiring other companions; on the other, the equally constant effort of the beneficiaries to ensure themselves the full and unalterable possession of the estates, and to free themselves from their obligations towards the chief from whom they held them, but with whom they no longer lived, and whose whole fate they no longer shared.

From this twofold effort there resulted a continual instability in properties of this kind. Some resumed them, others retained them by force, and all accused each other of usurpation.

This was the fact; but what was the right? what was the legal condition of benefices, and of the tie formed between the givers and the receivers? Let us see the system of most political historians, especially of Montesquieu, Robertson, and Mably.

They think the benefices were: 1, entirely revocable; the giver could take them back when he pleased; 2, temporary, conceded for a fixed time, a year, five years, ten years; 3, for life, granted during the life of the beneficiary; 4, lastly, hereditary. Arbitrary revocability, temporary concession, life possession, and hereditary property, such, in their opinions, are the four conditions through which beneficiary property passed from the fifth to the tenth century; such was the progression of facts from the conquest to the complete establishment of feudalism.

I think this system is alike controverted by historical testimonies and by moral probabilities. And first, how can we conceive to ourselves the absolute, arbitrary revocability of benefices? In the expression alone, there is something repugnant to the very nature of human relations. Unless those relations be the work of force, as is the case between master and slave, the prisoner of war and the conqueror, it is not probable, it is not possible, that all the advantage, all the right should belong to only one of the interested parties. How could a free man, a warrior, who voluntarily united himself to a chief, have subjected himself to this condition, that the chief might do as he pleased with regard to him, and, for example, take from him to-morrow, without motive, of his mere whim, the domain which he has given him to-day? In the voluntary relations of free creatures, whatever the inequality may be, there is always a certain reciprocity, certain mutual conditions ; *à priori*, entire and arbitrary revocability, cannot have been, at any epoch, the legal and recognised state of benefices.

Historical testimonies agree with moral probabilities. Let us see in what terms Montesquieu describes the system, and upon what text he founds it:

" It cannot be doubted but that at first fiefs were revocable. We see in Gregory of Tours that there was taken from Sunegisile and Galloman, all which they held from the fisc, and that they had only left to them what they held in property.[1] Gontran, raising his nephew Childebert to the throne, had a secret conference with him, and pointed out to him those to whom he should give fiefs and those from whom he should take them away.[2] In a formula of Marculf, the king gives in exchange, not only benefices which his son held, but also those which another had held.[3] The law of the Lombards contradistinguishes benefices from property.[4] Historians, formulæ, the codes of different barbarous nations, all the monuments which remain to us, are unanimous. Lastly, those who wrote the Book of Fiefs,[5] inform us that at first the lords could withdraw them at will, then they were assured for a year, and afterwards they were given for life."[6]

With the exception of the last authority, that of the Book of Fiefs, of which I shall immediately speak, it is evident that all these texts prove a fact, and not a law ; the actual, not the legal condition of benefices. Doubtless the king, or any giver of benefices who found himself more powerful than the receiver, took back his gifts when he felt the desire or need.

The instability, the violent struggle was incessant ; but that it was the legal state of this kind of property, that the possessors of fiefs acknowledged the right of the givers to take them back when they pleased, there is no evidence to show. On the contrary, we find the beneficiaries everywhere exclaiming against the iniquity of such spoliation, and maintaining that the benefices should only be taken from them when they, on their side, were wanting in the promised

---

[1] L. ix., c. 38. [2] L. vii., c. 33. [3] L. i., f. 30.
[4] L. iii., tit. 8, 33. [5] L. i., tit. 1.
[6] *Esprit des Lois*, l. xxx., c. 16.

faith—when they had been unfaithful towards the patron of whom they held them. On condition of the fidelity of the beneficiary, the possession of the benefice should be stable and peaceable : that is the law, the moral rule established in minds. I will select a few texts out of a hundred :

" Let all which has been given to a church, to the priests, or to any other person, by the munificence of the said princes of glorious memory, rest fixedly with them."[1]

" If any land be taken from any one, *without fault on his part*, let it be returned to him."[2]

" Charles the Great suffered no lord, from any impulse of anger, to withdraw his benefices from his vassal without reason."[3]

" We will that our faithful hold as settled that no person henceforward, of whatever rank or condition he be, shall be robbed or despoiled of his benefices by our arbitrary will, or by the artifice or unjust avidity of any other person without a just judgment dictated by equity and reason."[4]

With regard to the Book of Fiefs, drawn up at a far posterior epoch, from the twelfth to the thirteenth century, and by the jurisconsults of the time, it most probably committed the same error as Montesquieu : it converted the fact into a law.

The very first step, then, of that systematic progression which it is said the beneficiary property observed in its development, bears no inquiry. I pass to the second. Did it for some time assume the legal form of a concession with a fixed term, a kind of bailment or farming?

Unless I am mistaken, there is something in the very nature of such a concession which is repugnant to a social state so irregular and violent as that of the times of which we speak. Contracts for a fixed term, for precise conditions and of short duration, are delicate combinations, difficult to get observed, which can only be put in practice in advanced and well-regulated societies, and where there exists a power capable of enforcing their execution. If we look closely into the civil life of barbaric nations, or nations bordering upon barbarism, if we run our eye over the Formulæ of Mar-

---

[1] Baluze, *Recueil des Capitulaires*, vol. i., col. 8. Ordonnance of Clotaire, 1st or 2d.
[2] Bal., vol. i., col. 14 ; Treaty of Andelot, in 587.
[3] *Vie de Charlemagne*, by Eginhard.
[4] *Capit. de Charles le Chauve*, in 844 ; Bal., vol. ii., col. 5.

cult, almost all the agreements which we find there are either of a prompt, immediate execution, or concluded for perpetuity, or at least for life. We find very few agreements for a limited time: such agreements are more complicated, and they would be deficient in guarantees. Guarantees also would have been wanting to temporary benefices; and, the term of concession arrived, the giver would have had great difficulty in regaining possession of his domain.

We however find, from the sixth to the ninth century, benefices which appear temporary. Their origin, I think, was this:

In the Roman legislation, the gratuitous concession of the usufruct of a property for a limited, and generally a short time, was called *precarium*. After the fall of the empire, the churches often leased out their properties for a fixed rent, by a contract also called *precarium*, the term of which was commonly one year. In some instances, doubtless to ensure the protection or divert the hostility of a neighboring power, a church gratuitously conceded to him this temporary enjoyment of some domain. In some instances, also, the concessionary, availing himself of his power, did not pay the agreed rent, and yet retained the concession. Undoubtedly the use or abuse of these *precaria*, or temporary benefices of church property, were frequent enough; for, in the course of the seventh century, we find the kings and mayors of the palace employing their credit, or rather their authority, with the churches, to obtain usufructs of this kind for their clients: " At the recommendation of the illustrious Ebroin, mayor of the palace, the said John obtained from the monastery of St. Denis the domain called *Taberniacum*, by precarious tenure."[1] When Charles Martel seized a portion of the domains of the church to distribute them among his warriors, the church exclaimed against the sacrilege, the spoliation; and she had good right so to do. Pepin, become chief of the Franks, needed to reconcile himself with the church; she demanded her domains. But how to return them to her? It would be necessary to dispossess men of whom Pepin had even more need than he had of the church, and who would more efficaciously defend themselves. To extricate himself from this embarrassment, Pepin and his brother Carloman decreed the following capitulary:

Recueil des Historiens de France, vol. v., p. 701.

"With the consent of the servants of God and of the Christian people, and because of the wars which threaten us, and the attacks of nations which surround us, we have decided that, for the maintenance of our warriors, and with the help of the indulgence of God, we shall retain for some time, as *precaria*, and subject to the payment of a rent, a portion of the properties of the churches; on this condition, that each year there shall be paid to the proprietary church or monastery one *solidus*, that is to say, twelve deniers for each farm; and that if he who enjoys the said property die, the church shall re-enter into possession. If we are constrained to it by necessity and so order it, the *precarium* shall be renewed, and a second shall be drawn up. But let them heed that the churches or monasteries whose properties shall be thus lent *in precario* do not suffer want: if that happens, let the church and the house of God be again put in full possession of their property."[1]

Here you perceive between the church and the new possessors of her domains there is a kind of transference placed under the guarantee of the king. Pepin indeed, and his first successors, took much trouble to make it observed; their capitularies incessantly order men to pay the rent due to the churches, or to give up the domains, or to renew the *precaria*. Most of these domains, as you may suppose, were never given up, and the rent was very irregularly paid. Thence, however, arose temporary benefices, lands held for a fixed time, generally for five years. But this fact cannot be considered as a legal state of beneficiary property in general, as one of the degrees through which it passed. It is rather an accident, a special form of certain benefices; and a very unimportant form, for the conditions which it imposed were scarcely ever respected.

From being temporary, it is said, benefices became of life duration: this is their third degree. It is far more than a degree in their history—it is their veritable, primitive, habitual state, the common character of this kind of concession It was thus willed by the very nature of the relations which benefices were destined to perpetuate. Before the invasion, when the Germans wandered upon the Roman frontiers, the relation between the chief and the companions was purely personal. The companion assuredly engaged neither his

---

[1] *Capit. du Roi Carloman*, in 743; Bal., vol. i., col. 149.

family nor his race; he engaged only himself. After the establishment, and when the Germans had passed from the wandering life to the state of proprietors, it still continued the same; the tie between the giver and the beneficiary was still considered personal and for life; the benefice must have been so too. Most of the documents of the epoch, in fact, expressly say as much, or take it for granted. I shall cite but a few texts of various dates, from the sixth to the ninth century; they will place the matter beyond doubt.

In 585, "Wandelin, who had brought up the young king, Childebert, died; all the property which he had received from the fisc returned to the fisc."[1]

In 660, under Theodoric, king of Austrasia, "after the death of Warratum, who had enjoyed it, the domain called *Latiniacum* returns to our fisc."[2]

In 694, under Childebert II., "the domain called *Napsiniacum*, which had been ceded to the illustrious Pannichius, returned to our fisc after his death."[3]

"Let those who hold a benefice from us be careful to improve it."[4]

"Whoever holds a benefice from us must take care, *as much as may be done with the aid of God*, that none of the slaves which form part of it die from hunger, and must not sell the products of the soil on his own account, until he has provided for their subsistence."[5]

"In 889, king Eudes conferred a domain upon Ricabod, his vassal, in benefice and usufruct, with this clause, that if Ricabod had a son, the benefice should pass to that son, but only for his life."[6]

Neither, then, is this a crisis of the development of beneficiary property, a degree through which it passed; it was its general and primitive condition.

At all epochs, however, amidst life benefices we find hereditary benefices. There is no reason to be surprised at this; and the so prompt tendency to hereditary possession which manifests itself in the history of benefices is not to be solely attributed to the avidity of the possessors: it arose from the very nature of territorial possession. Succession

---

[1] *Grégoire de Tours*, l. viii., c. 22.
[2] Mabillon, *de Re Diplomatica*, l. vi., p. 471.   [3] Mabillon, p. 476.
[4] *Capit. de Charlemagne*, in 813; Bal., t. i., col. 507.
[5] Ibid., a. 794; Bal., t. i., col. 264.   [6] Mabillon, *ut sup.*, p. 556

was its normal, almost necessary state, the end towards which it tended, even from its birth. Out of many reasons, I shall mention but two. From the time that a man possesses and improves an estate, whatever the manner of his possession or of his improvement, he employs upon it means which he does not draw from the soil, but from himself; by the labors which he spends upon it, by the buildings with which he covers it, he adds a certain value to the estate, and, to speak in the present language of political economy, he invests therein a certain capital, which, if he at any time leaves, he cannot entirely nor conveniently carry away—a capital which becomes more or less incorporated with the soil, and which cannot be entirely separated from it. Thence arises, and by the instincts of reason and justice, a certain natural tendency of all territorial property to become hereditary; a tendency especially powerful when society, still rude, knows not how to estimate the value which the possessor who is leaving it has added to the soil, and to indemnify him by other means.

Another cause concurred to the same effect. Except in extraordinary states of society, man cannot be constantly moving about and leading a wandering life in the country which he calls his native land; it is a need, a moral inclination with him to fix himself somewhere, to plant himself in a certain place: in the bosom of the political country a domestic country is necessary to him, to which he may attach himself, where he may establish his family. It is therefore the constant effort of the cultivator, of the possessor, to become perpetual proprietor.

Accordingly, by its very nature, and independently of all external circumstance, beneficiary property tended to become hereditary. This tendency, in fact, manifests itself even at the very origin of benefices, and at all epochs, it sometimes attained its end. The treaty of Andelot, concluded in 587, between Gontran and Childebert II., in speaking of the beneficiaries of queen Clotilde, sets forth:

"Let the lands which it pleases the queen to confer upon any one belong to him in perpetuity, and at no time be taken from him."[1]

The Formulæ of Marculf contain the following, which

---

[1] Bal., vol. i., col. 13.

proves that hereditary concession, as early as the end of the seventh century, was a common practice.

"We have conceded to the illustrious —— the domain called ——. We order, by the present decree, which is always to endure, that he shall keep the said domain in perpetuity, shall possess it as proprietor, and shall leave possession of it to his descendants, or to whom he will."[1]

Dating from Louis le Débonnaire, concessions of this kind became frequent; examples abound in the diplomas of this prince and of Charles le Chauve. At length the latter, in 877, formally recognises the hereditability of benefices, and, at the end of the ninth century, this was their common and prevalent condition; as in the sixth and seventh centuries the occupation for life had been the general fact.

Still, even at the ninth century, and although hereditary right prevailed, it was not yet an evident law, nor was it regarded as indubitable. The following is a fact which will clearly show what the state of mind was in this respect:

In 795, Charlemagne had given to a man named John, who had conquered the Saracens in the country of Barcelona, a domain called Fontes, situated near Narbonne, "in order that the said John and his descendants may enjoy it without trouble or rent, as long as they remain faithful to us and to our sons." In 814, Charlemagne died; in 815, the same John presented himself to Louis le Débonnaire with the hereditary donation which he held from Charlemagne, and solicited its confirmation. Louis confirmed it, and added other land, "to the end that the said John, his sons, and their posterity, may enjoy it in virtue of our gift." In 844, the emperor Louis and the beneficiary John, are dead; Teutfried, son of John, presents himself to Charles le Chauve with the two anterior gifts, asks him to confirm them anew and Charles does so, "to the end that thou and thy posterity possess their property without any rent."

Thus, despite the hereditary right of the title, whenever the beneficiary or the giver died, the possessor of the benefice thought it necessary that he should be confirmed in his possession; so strongly was the primitive idea of the personality of this relation and the right which resulted from it, engraved upon minds.[2]

---

[1] L. i., b. 14.   [2] *Essai sur l'Histoire de France*, p. 145.

At the end of the tenth century, when we enter truly into the feudal period, we no longer find any thing of the kind ; the right of fiefs, inheritance, is no longer cal'ed into doubt by any one, it has no longer any need of confirmation.

As I said, historical testimonies agree with moral probabilities. Beneficiary property, from the fifth to the tenth century, did not pass through four successive and regular states—arbitrary revocability, temporary concession, lifelong, and hereditary concession. These four states are met with at all epochs. The primitive predominance of life concession, and the constant tendency to inheritance, which in the end triumphed, these only are the general conclusions which may be deduced from monuments, the true characters of the transition from benefices to fiefs.

At the same time that this transition was brought about, and beneficiary property became hereditary and stable, it also became general—that is, territorial property almost everywhere took this form. At first, you will recollect, there was a large number of freeholds, that is to say, properties entirely independent, which were not held from any one, and which owed nothing to any one. From the fifth to the tenth century, freehold property, without entirely disappearing, became gradually less extensive, and the beneficiary condition became the common condition of territorial property. The following are the principal causes of this :—

It must not be supposed that when the barbarians seized upon the Roman world, they divided the territory into lots more or less considerable, and that each, taking one for himself, established himself upon it. Nothing of the kind happened. The chiefs, the men of importance, appropriated a large extent of land to themselves, and most of their companions, their men, continued to live with them in their houses, always attached to their person. Freemen, Franks, Burgundians, &c., living upon the estates of others, is a fact which is met with at every step in the monuments of the sixth, seventh, and eighth centuries.

But the inclination and desire for territorial property were not long in spreading. In proportion as the habits of the wandering life left them, a greater number of men wished to become proprietors. Besides, money was rare ; land, so to speak, was the most common, the most disposable coin ; it was employed to repay all sorts of services. The possessors of large domains distributed them among their companions by

way of payment. We read in the capitularies of Charlemagne,

"Let any steward (*villicus*) of one of our domains, who
possesses a benefice, send a substitute into our domain to
overlook in his stead the works and all the care of our
land."[1]

"Let those of the keepers of our horses (*poledrarii*) who
are free men, and possess benefices in the locality of their
employment, live upon the product of their benefices."[2]

And every great proprietor, ecclesiastic or layman, Eginhard or Charlemagne, paid in this way most of the free men
whom he employed. Thence arose the rapid division of
landed property, and the multitude of petty benefices.

A second cause, usurpation, also greatly increased their
number. Powerful chiefs, who had taken possession of a
vast territory, had little means of actually occupying and preserving it from invasion. It was easy for neighbors, for the
first comer, to establish himself upon it, and to appropriate
to himself such and such part of it. It so happened in many
places. In the anonymous life of Louis le Débonnaire, we
read :

" In 715, Charlemagne, sending back his son Louis into
Aquitaine, asked him how it happened that, being a king, he
was so parsimonious as to offer nothing to any one, not even
his blessing, unless it was asked of him. Louis informed
his father that the great men of the kingdom occupying
themselves only with their own interests, and neglecting the
public interests, the royal domains were everywhere converted into private properties; hence it happened that he
himself was king only in name, and in want almost of everything. Charlemagne wishing to remedy this evil, but fear-
ing that his son would lose somewhat of the affection of the
great men, if he were to take again through wisdom what he
had allowed them to usurp through improvidence, sent his
own messengers into Aquitaine, Willbert, afterwards archbishop of Rouen, and count Richard, inspectors of the royal
domains, and ordered them to procure the restoration to the
king of the domains which had formerly belonged to him,
which was done."[3]

And when, in 846, the bishops gave advice to Charles le

---

[1] *Capit. of Charlemagne, de Villis;* Bal., vol. i. col. 333.
[2] Ibid., c. 338. [3] *Historiens de France,* t. iv., p. 90.

Chauve, as to the best means of elevating his dignity and power:

"Many public domains," say they to him, "have been taken from you, some by force, and some by fraud; and because men have made false reports, and unjust demands of you, they have retained them by way either of benefices, or freeholds. It appears to us useful and necessary that you should send into the countries of your kingdom, firm and faithful messengers, taken from each order; they shall carefully draw up a list of the estates which, in the time of your father and grandfather, belonged to the royal domain, and of those which formed the benefices of vassals; they shall examine what each now withholds of them, and shall render a true account thereof to you. When you find that there is reason, utility, justice, or sincerity, whether in the donation or in the taking possession, things shall remain in their present state. But when you see that there is unreasonableness, or rather fraud, then, with the counsel of your faithful, reform this evil in such a manner that reason, prudence, or justice be not overlooked, and that at the same time your dignity be not debased, nor reduced by necessity to that which is unbecoming it. Your house cannot be filled with servants to do their duties, if you have not the means of recompensing their merits, or of alleviating their poverty."[1]

The greater part of the lands thus usurped certainly did not re-enter into the domain of the first possessor, king or subject. It was too difficult to dispossess the usurpers; but they undertook to hold them as benefices, and to observe the obligations attending them. A new, and I think very influential cause, of the extension of beneficiary property.

There were also many deserted, uncultivated lands; men driven from their dwellings, or still leading a wandering life, or monks, established themselves upon them and cultivated them. When they had become valuable, some powerful neighbor often demanded them, in order afterwards to concede them, by way of benefices, to those who occupied them.

Lastly, a fourth cause powerfully contributed to make the beneficiary condition the common condition of territorial property; by a practice known under the name of *recommendation*, numerous freeholds were converted into benefices. The proprietor of a freehold presented himself before some

---

[1] Bal., vol. ii., col. 31.

neighbor, some powerful man, whom he wished to select as a patron, and holding in his hand either a clod of turf, or a branch of a tree, he ceded to him his freehold, which he immediately resumed by way of benefice, to enjoy according to the rules and duties, but also with the privileges of this new condition.

This practice was allied with the ancient German manners, with the primitive relation of chief and companions. Then also free men recommended themselves to another man, that is, they selected a chief for themselves. But this was an entirely personal and perfectly free relation. When it pleased him, the companion quitted his chief and took another; the engagement entered into between them was purely moral, and rested on their will alone. Immediately after the territorial establishment, the same liberty continued to exist; they could recommend themselves, that is to say, they could select for a patron whom they wished, and might change him at their will. Still, in proportion as society became a little strengthened, attempts were made to introduce some regularity into these proceedings and relations. The law of the Visigoths declares:

"If any one has given arms, or aught else, to a man whom he receives into his patronage, let those gifts remain to him who received them. If the latter choose another patron, let him be free to recommend himself to whom he wills; this cannot be interdicted to a free man, for he belongs to himself; but let him return to the patron from whom he separates all which he has received from him."[1]

And we read in a capitulary of Pepin, son of Charlemagne, and king of Italy:

"If any one, occupying the portion of land which has fallen to him, choose another lord, whether the count or any other man, let him have full liberty to leave him; but let him not retain or carry away any of the things which he possesses, and let all revert to the domain of his first lord."[2]

Matters soon proceeded still farther. Men were in the transition from the wandering life to the sedentary life. It was above all things necessary to put an end to the fluctuation, the disorder of situations; in this direction tended the effort of superior men who aimed at the progression of so-

---

[1] *Laws of the Visigoths*, l. v., tit. 3, c. 1.
[2] *Capit. de Charlemagne*, in 813; Bal., vol. i., col. 510

ciety. Charlemagne undertook to determine, on the one hand, under what circumstance the client might quit his patron; and on the other, to impose upon all free men the necessity of recommending themselves to a patron, that is to say, of placing themselves under the authority and responsibility of a superior. We read in his capitularies:

"Let no man who has received the value of a solidus from his lord quit him, unless his lord has sought to kill him, or to strike him with a stick, or to dishonor his wife or daughter, or to despoil him of his heritage."[1]

"If any free man quit his lord against the will of the latter, and go into the kingdom of another, let not the king receive him into his patronage, and not allow his men to receive him."[2]

"Let no one buy a horse, a beast of burden, an ox, or any thing else, without knowing him who sells it, or of what country he is, where he lives, and who is his lord."[3]

In 858, the bishops wrote to Louis le Germanique: "We bishops, sacred to the Lord, we are not, like the laity, obliged to recommend ourselves to any patron."[4]

Charlemagne did not obtain all he wished; for a long time still an extreme fluctuation pervaded this class of relations. Yet his genius was not mistaken as to the true need of the time, his labors had ever in view the natural course of things. The necessity and fixedness of the recommendation of persons and lands prevailed more and more. Many freehold proprietors were weak, not in a state to defend themselves; they had need of a protector; others became weary of their isolation: free and masters, it is true, in their domain, they had no tie, no influence beyond it; they held no place in that hierarchy of beneficiaries which was become the general society. They wished to enter into it, and to participate in the movement of the period. Thus was brought about the metamorphosis of the greater part of the freeholds into benefices; a metamorphosis less complete in the South of France, where the feudal system did not pervade all things, and where many freeholds continued to exist, but which was not the less general, and which made the

---

[1] *Capit. de Pepin,* king of Italy, in 795; Bal., vol. i., col. 597.
[2] *Capit. de Charlemagne,* in 806; Bal., t. i., col. 443.
[3] *Capit.* of the year 806, vol. i., col. 450.
[4] Ibid., vol. i., col. 118.

beneficiary condition the common condition of territoria property.

Such was the state in which it found itself at the close of the tenth century, after going through the vicissitudes which I have attempted to trace; and not only did most lands become fiefs at this epoch, but the feudal character gradually penetrated into all kinds of properties. At that time almost every thing was given in fief: the *gruerie* or forest jurisdiction; the right of hunting therein; a share in the *péage* (toll-money) or in the *rouage* (wine-toll) of a place; the convoy or escort of merchants going to fairs; the office of judge in the palace of the prince or high lord; the mint-offices in those of his towns where money was coined; the letting of the places in which fairs were held; the houses where the public stoves were; the *common ovens* of towns; lastly, down to the *swarms of bees* which might be found in forests.[1] The whole civil order, in a word, became feudal We shall see the same revolution in the political order.

---

[1] *Usage Général des Fiefs*, by Brussel, t. i., p. 42.

THIRD LECTURE.

Of the amalgamation of sovereignty and property, the second characteristic of the feudal system—True meaning of this fact—Its origin—It comes neither from the Roman society nor from the German band—Is it the result of conquest only?—Of the system of feudal publicists on this subject—Two forms of society in Germany, the tribe and the band—Social organization of the tribe—Domestic sovereignty is there distinct from political sovereignty—Twofold origin of domestic sovereignty among the ancient Germans—It arose from family and from conquest—What became of the organization of the German tribe, and especially of domestic sovereignty after the establishment of the Germans in Gaul—What it retained of the family spirit gradually diminished; what it retained of conquest became dominant—Recapitulation and true character of feudal sovereignty.

We have studied the first of the great facts which constitute and characterize the feudal system; I mean the special nature of landed property, in its progressive development from the fifth to the tenth century. I now approach the second of these facts, the amalgamation of sovereignty and property.

It is first of all necessary to come to an understanding as to the meaning of these words, and as to the limits of the fact itself. Our business here is solely with the sovereignty of the possessor of the fief in his domains, and over their inhabitants. Beyond the fief, and in his relations with other possessors of fiefs, superior or inferior, and whatever the inequality between them, the lord was not a sovereign. No one in this association possessed the sovereignty. There other principles and other forms prevailed, which we shall study in treating of the third characteristic of the feudal system, that is to say, the hierarchical organization of the general society which the possessors of fiefs formed among themselves.

When I speak of the amalgamation of sovereignty and of property, I repeat that I speak solely of the sovereignty of the possessor of the fief within his own domains, and over their inhabitants not themselves possessors of fiefs.

The fact thus limited, its certainty is incontestable. At the eleventh century, feudalism once well established, the possessor of the fief, great or small, possessed all the rights of sovereignty in his domains. No external or distant power gave laws there, established taxes, or administered justice; the proprietor alone possessed all this power.

Such, at least in principle and in the common thought, was feudal right. This right was often overlooked, then disputed, and lastly usurped by the superior and powerful lords, among others by the kings. It did not the less exist, nor was it the less claimed as primitive and fundamental. When the publicist friends of feudalism complain that the sovereignty of the simple lords was usurped by great barons, and that of the great barons by kings, they are quite accurate; such was the case. Originally, in the right, in the spirit of the system, each lord exercised the legislative, judicial, and military powers in his domains; he made war, coined money, &c.; in a word, he was a sovereign.

Nothing of the kind existed before the full development of the feudal system immediately after the invasion, in the sixth and seventh centuries. We then see the germ, the first rudiments of feudal sovereignty; but by its side, and even above it, there still exist imperial royalty, military royalty, the Roman administration, the assemblies and jurisdiction of free men. Various powers and systems coexisted and struggled with each other. The sovereignty was not concentred within each fief, and in the hands of its possessor.

How was the fact brought about from the fifth to the tenth century? How were all other sovereignties abolished, or at least effaced, in order to leave only that of the lord within his domain and over its inhabitants?

Assuredly it was not from Roman society that this fact could have taken its origin, for that contained nothing resembling it. So far from sovereignty there being inherent in property, and disseminated, as here, over the face of the country, it was not even politically divided; it resided wholly and completely in the centre of the empire, and in the hands of the emperor. The emperor alone made laws, imposed taxes, possessed the jurisdiction, regulated war and peace, in fact governed, either of himself or by his delegates. The remains of the municipal system still visible in cities, consisted of some administrative privileges, and in a certain degree of independence, which did not extend to the limits of sovereignty. A master, agents, and subjects—such was the entire social organization of the Roman empire, always excepting slaves, who remained under the domestic jurisdiction.

It is evidently not from the bosom of Roman society that feudal sovereignty could have taken birth.

Nor could it have arisen from the German bands which invaded the Roman empire. There nothing resembling the amalgamation of sovereignty and power can be met with; for property (I mean landed property) is incompatible with the wandering life, and with regard to persons, the chief of such a band possessed no sovereignty over his companions; he had no right to give them laws, to tax them, or of himself to administer justice to them. There reigned common deliberation, personal independence, and a great equality of rights, although the principle of an aristocratical society germinated there, and at a later period was to develop itself.

Did the amalgamation of sovereignty and property take rise from conquest alone? and did the conquerors divide the territory and its inhabitants between them, to reign as sovereign each in his portion, in the sole right of the strongest?

This is what many publicists have believed and maintained. Correctly speaking, in truth, this is the idea which constitutes the basis of the system of all the defenders of the feudal régime, of M. de Boulainvilliers, for example. They do not formally express it; they do not say openly that force alone founded the sovereignty of the possessors of fiefs; but this is their principle, the only possible principle of their theory. The soil had been conquered, and with the soil, the inhabitants; thence the amalgamation of sovereignty and property. Both of them passed, and legitimately passed, to the bravest. Unless M. de Boulainvilliers takes this fact for granted, the whole of his system falls to the ground.

In fact as in right, M. de Boulainvilliers and the publicists of this school are mistaken. The amalgamation of sovereignty and property, that great characteristic of the feudal system, was not so simple, so purely material, so brutal, thus to speak, a fact so foreign both to the organization of the two societies which the invasion brought into contact, the Roman society and the German society, or to the general principles of social organization.

Let us seek its true origin; you will see, I think, that it is more complex, more remote, than the simple right of conquest.

When I spoke in the last course, of ancient Germany, I

distinguished the two societies, or rather the two modes of social organization, differing in their principles and their results, which were visible there; on the one hand, the tribe or horde, and on the other, the band.

The tribe was a sedentary society, formed of neighboring proprietors, living on the produce of their lands and their herds.

The band was a wandering society, composed of warriors united around a chief, either for some special expedition, or to seek fortune at a distance, and living by pillage.

That these two societies coexisted among the Germans and were essentially distinct, Cæsar, Tacitus, Ammianus Marcellinus, all the monuments, all the traditions of ancient Germany prove to us. Most of the nations mentioned by Tacitus, whose names fill his treatise *Upon the Manners of the Germans*, are tribes or confederations of tribes. The greater part of the invasions which ended in the destruction of the Roman empire, especially the first, were effected by wandering bands, who had quitted the German tribes to seek booty and adventures.

The ascendency of the chief over his companions formed the band, and pressed it around him. This was its origin. It was governed by common deliberation; personal independence and warlike equality played a great part in it.

The organization of the tribe was less irregular and less simple.

Its primitive element, its political unity, to speak in the language of publicists, was not the individual, the warrior, but the family, the chief of the family. The tribe, or the portion of the tribe which inhabited the same territory, was composed of families, of the proprietary heads of families established near each other. The proprietary heads of families were its true citizens, the *cives optimo jure* of the Romans.

The dwellings of the families of the German tribe were not contiguous, and at a distance from the lands to be cultivated, as they are in our towns and villages; each chief of a family was established amidst his own lands; his family, and all who cultivated them with him, whether free or not, relations, laborers, or slaves, were established on them like himself, dispersed here and there, like their dwellings, over the face of the domains. The domains of the different chiefs of the family were adjacent, but not their dwellings.

It is in this way that the villages of the Indian tribes are still constructed in North America; in Europe, most of the villages of Corsica, and still nearer to us, at our very door, a large number of the villages of Normandy. There also the dwellings are not contiguous; each farmer, each small proprietor, lives in the midst of his fields, in an enclosure, called *masure, mansura,* dwelling, the *mansus* of our ancient documents.

I dwell upon these circumstances, because they arise from the social organization of the tribe, and assist its proper comprehension. The general assembly of the tribe was formed of all the proprietary heads of families. They met, under the direction of the most aged, (*grau, grav,* the count, become at a later period, the lord,) to discuss together of common affairs, to administer justice upon important occasions, to occupy themselves with religious ceremonies in which the whole tribe was interested, &c. The political sovereignty belonged to this assembly.

By political sovereignty, I mean the government of the general affairs of the tribe. To that, in fact, the jurisdiction of the assembly was confined; it did not penetrate into the domains of the chief of the family; with him no authority had a right to interfere. By title of proprietor and chief of the family, he alone was sovereign there.

In the domains of the proprietary head of a family, and under his authority, lived: 1, his family, properly so called, his children and their families, grouped around him; 2, the laborers who cultivated his lands, some free, others enjoying only a half-freedom. These *Coloni* held certain portions of his domains from the chief of the family, and cultivated them on their own account, subject to a certain ground-rent. They did not by this acquire any right of property over these lands; yet they and their children established themselves there; they possessed and cultivated them hereditarily. Between them and the proprietary head of the family there were formed those ties which rest upon no title, confer no legal right, and nevertheless are true ties, a moral element of society; 3, after the bond-laborers came the slaves, properly so called, employed either in the house or to cultivate, for the chiefs of the family, those lands which he had not ceded to any one, and which generally lay immediately around his habitation.

Such was the extent of the family, and, so to speak, **the** contents of the domain. All this internal population, of very different conditions, was placed under the jurisdiction of the proprietary head of the family; no public power interfered; *every man was master in his own house;* such was already the maxim of the ancient German society. Proprietor and magistrate, the chief of the family was even priest, it appears, for that portion of domestic worship which could subsist at that epoch.

What was the origin of this organization of the tribes in Germany? Should we see in it a first step, and, in some measure, an anticipated repetition of what happened at the sixth century, after the establishment of the Germans upon the Roman territory—that is to say, the result of a conquest? These proprietary chiefs of families, are they conquerors come from afar, and who have seized the soil and its inhabitants? Those laborers who cultivate the soil on payment of a rent, and under the authority of the proprietor, are they the conquered, dispossessed entirely or in part, and reduced to an inferior condition?

Or is this an example of the social organization which has been called the patriarchal system, which arose among pastoral and agricultural nations, from the progressive extension of the natural family and from the agricultural life, of which the annals of the East, especially those of the Arabs and the Hebrews, offer the model: which at every step remind us of the narratives of the Bible, and which also appeared, at least under its most essential features, in the bosom of the Roman republic, in the situation of the *pater familias*, at once proprietor, magistrate, and priest, in the midst of his domain, of his children, and of his slaves?

This last explanation is that which most of the German writers have adopted and maintain. Passionate admirers of the ancient institutions, of the ancient manners of their country, they find in this organization of the tribes, not a complete and regular model, but all the good principles of the social system. In the family, the domestic magistracy; beyond the family, political liberty; the chiefs of the family governing the inferior classes by the ascendency of property and position, and then regulating in common the affairs of the tribe; is not this, say they, the best union of power and liberty? What system better respects the natural elements, the necessary conditions of the social order? Can we see there the work of conquest and of force? Must we not, on the contrary, there recognise the simple and spontaneous development of human relations ?

I, for many reasons, cannot entirely adopt this system.

And, first, the Germans appear to me to carry into their researches and ideas upon this subject a disposition of mind which I must characterize with some precision, for, unless I am mistaken, it exercises a great influence over them.

When, under some broad point of view, or under some essential relation, a social state appears to them good and beautiful, they conceive for it an exclusive admiration and sympathy. They are generally inclined to admire, and to be overcome with passion; the imperfections, the interruptions, the bad side of things, strike them but little. Singular contrast! In the purely intellectual sphere, in the research for and combination of ideas, no nation has more extension of mind, more philosophical impartiality. When the question is of facts which address themselves to the imagination, which arouse moral emotions, they easily fall into prejudices and narrow views; their imagination then wants fidelity, truth; they are without poetical impartiality—in fact, they do not see things from all points of view, and such as they really are.

This disposition has often governed them in the study of ancient Germany, of its origins, its national manners. What they found there great, moral, truly liberal, has struck them, has filled them with enthusiasm; and here their inquiry has stopped; to this has their imagination been limited. It is with these elements only that they have reconstructed their primitive society.

There is a second cause of error. Most of the national documents which the Germans make use of in order to study the ancient Germanic institutions, are of an epoch far posterior to that which occupies them, far posterior to the second, third, fourth, and fifth centuries. Before the conversion of Germany to Christianity—that is to say, before the eighth century—there existed no really national monuments, for then the German languages were not written. Of these times there only remain vague, incomplete traditions, preserved by writers of a period far less remote. Till then, we know the Germans only through Latin writers, or through the western chroniclers; there are consequently many anachronisms in the picture which the Germans trace of the ancient social state of their country. They refer to the third and fourth centuries facts derived from monuments of the ninth, tenth, and eleventh centuries. I do not say that there is not in these monuments some revelation, some echo of the ancient Germanic society; but these inferences from premises antecedent to them three, four, five, and six centuries, are extremely delicate and difficult. We run great risk of deceiving ourselves in such inductions, and when we undertake this work with an exclusive and passionate turn of imagination, the chance of error becomes infinitely greater.

Lastly, numerous positive texts, Cæsar, Tacitus, Ammianus Marcellinus, attest that before the great invasion, between the Rhine, the Elbe, and the Danube, nations of the *same race* and of *different race* often expelled, enslaved, exterminated one another, and that the organization of the ancient German tribe, especially the situation of the agricultural laborers, was more than once the result of conquest. I have already had occasion, in our last course, to point out some of these texts;[1] I shall here repeat the most explicit of them:

"'The slaves in general," says Tacitus, " are not arranged in their several employments in household affairs, as is the practice at Rome; each has his separate habitation or home The master considers him as an agrarian dependent, who is obliged to furnish, by way of rent, a certain quantity of grain, of cattle, or of wearing apparel. The slave does this, and there his servitude ends. All domestic matters are managed by the master's own wife and children. To punish a slave with stripes, to load him with chains, or condemn him to hard labor, is unusual; they kill their slaves sometimes, not out of ordinary severity or discipline, but from violence or sudden impulse, as they would kill an enemy."

" In the neighborhood of the Teucteres were formerly the Bructeres; it is said, however, that now the Chamaves and the Angrivarians possess the district, having, in concert with the adjoining tribes, expelled and entirely extirpated the ancient inhabitants."

"'The Marcomanians are the most eminent for their strength and military glory; the very territory they occupy is the reward of their valor, they having dispossessed its former owners, the Boians."[2]

Go through the treatise *On the Manners of the Germans*—at every step you will find phrases and words which indicate the same fact.

---

[1] Lecture VII. vol. ii. [2] *De Morib. Germ.*, c. 25, 33, 42.

In the social state of ancient Germany, and especially in that of the sedentary and agricultural tribe, I therefore believe the share of conquest, of force, much greater than the German historians generally suppose it to be. I believe the domestic sovereignty of the chief of the proprietary family was much more tyrannical, the conditions of the laborers much worse than they imagine. This, in my opinion, is indicated not only by moral probabilities, not only by the Latin writers whom I have just spoken of, but down to the national documents which the Germans call to the support of their ideas; among others, by all the wrecks of the ancient Germanic poetry. I regret that I have not time to dwell upon this. It would, I think, be easy to prove how far their pictures of their ancient condition is from the truth.

Still, having brought all these restrictions to bear upon the favorite system of the Germans in this matter, I think with them, that the organization of the German tribe, and the relations of the various classes of the inhabitants, is not wholly attributable to conquest, to force. The sovereignty of the proprietary chief of the family, in his domains, was not exclusively that of the conqueror over the conquered, of the master over the slaves or demi-slaves; there was, in fact, something of the patriarchal system; the family, its relations, its habits, its sentiments, were, in part at least, the source of this state of society.

And first, the mere fact that this is a general opinion in Germany, a public belief, prevalent in all classes, is at once a strong presumption that it was so. A nation does not deceive itself to such a degree as to its origins, and the feeling with which they inspire it. That antipathy which we elsewhere encounter towards the ancient social state of the country, does not exist in Germany. The first relations between the superior and inferior classes, between proprietors and cultivators, have not left those mournful traditions, those unhappy recollections, with which our history is filled. The German population has not constantly struggled to escape from its origins, to abolish its old institutions. There is, then, evidently something besides conquest and tyranny.

The common opinion is right, it is conformable with facts. The general invasion of the country by foreigners, the struggle of races, the struggle of languages, the profound hostility of social situations, nothing, or scarcely any thing of all this was found in Germany, at least in a great part of Germany

The feudal system was established there played an important part there, and still weighs heavily upon the people, although less so than elsewhere. There were at all times many free and proprietary peasants, many independent properties, not in the least fettered with the bonds of feudalism.

We therefore cannot refuse to recognise in the organization of the ancient German tribe, and chiefly in the domestic sovereignty of the proprietary chief of the family, another origin than conquest, another character, a character more moral, more free than that of force. This origin is the patriarchal system, of a system analogous to it; this character is that of the life of the family. Very probably, the German tribe was originally the development, the extension of one and the same family; very probably a large portion of the inhabitants of the domain, many of these hereditary laborers, subject to a rent, were relations of the proprietary chief of the family. There was herein, very probably, somewhat of that social organization which has long subsisted in the *clans* of the Scotch Highlands, and the *septs* of Ireland; a: organization which the novels of Sir Walter Scott have rendered familiar to all minds; which, at the first glance, and judging from external appearances, resembles the feudal system, but is still radically different, for it evidently arose from the family; it perpetuates its ties through centuries, and maintains affectionate sentiments in spite of the profound inequality of social conditions; it has rights recognised and respected, where political guarantees are entirely wanting; in fine, morality and liberty in a system where, without this origin and its influence, there would have been only oppression and degradation.

Such, also, was doubtless the influence which, in the Germanic tribe, had introduced something of the relations and manners of the clan.

From these details there result, if I mistake not, two great facts:

1. In the German tribe, the sovereignty, as to all the general affairs of the tribe, belonged to the assembly of the proprietary chiefs of the families; as to all which passed in the interior of such domain, to the chief of the family himself; that is to say, that there was a political, collective sovereignty, and a sovereignty domestic, individual, and inherent to property.

2. The domestic sovereignty of proprietors had a twofold origin, a twofold character. On the one hand the ties and habits of the family; the proprietary chief was a chief of the clan, surrounded by his relations, whatever might be the distance of relationship and the diversity of condition; on the other hand, conquest and force: there also had been portions of territory occupied at the sword's point, conquered, dispossessed, and reduced to servitude or nearly so.

Thus in this organization of the ancient Germanic tribe, there are seen the three great social systems, the three great origins of sovereignty: first, the association among equal and free men, where political sovereignty is developed; secondly, the primitive natural association, that of the family, where the sole and patriarchal sovereignty prevails; thirdly, the compulsory association, the result of conquest, and subject to despotic sovereignty.

Upon the narrow and obscure theatre of the tribe of the Cherusci or of the Hermundures, or other such, there existed then, as early as the third century, all the essential principles, all the great forms of human society.

Let us now transport ourselves to the sixth century, after the invasion, between the Rhine, the ocean, the Pyrenees, and the Alps, and let us see what necessarily happened then.

And first, it was not the German tribes, but the band which went into the Gallo-Roman territory, seized upon it, and established itself there. Of the two original societies of Germany, that which was not resident, but wandering, whose basis was the individual, not the family, and which was devoted, not to an agricultural life, but to warfare; this became one of the primitive elements of our civilization.

In Germany, it was the agricultural tribe, among us it was the warlike band, which is seen at the cradle of society.

Once established, it is true, once impelled to quit the wandering for the sedentary life, and pillage for property, the Germanic band must have wished to reproduce the institutions, the habits of its native country; the organization of the tribe must have been the source, the model of the system which it attempted to adopt.

This, in fact, was what happened. We see the German band, in proportion as it fixes itself upon our territory, attempting to transplant thither the social condition which I have just described, more especially that twofold sovereignty: political, in general affairs, belonging to the assembly of the chiefs of the family; domestic, in the interior of the domains of each proprietary chief of a family, and exercised by him alone.

But what changes must the change of situation and of external circumstances have introduced into the new society!

Let us first see what political sovereignty became.

In Germany, the tribe was generally established upon a contracted territory. The tribes reciprocally confined and narrowed themselves, surrounding themselves, as Cæsar says, with vast deserts, for better security. The chiefs of families lived near to one another, and could easily meet to treat of their common affairs. The sovereignty of the general assembly was natural and possible.

After the invasion into the empire an immense territory was thrown open to the expeditions and eager avidity of the conquerors. They dispersed themselves throughout it in every direction. The chief of them occupied vast domains. They were too far from each other to meet often, and deliberate in common. The political sovereignty of the general assembly became impracticable, was doomed to perish, and, in fact, did perish, giving place to another system, to that hierarchical organization of proprietors, of which I shall speak, in discussing the feudal association and its institutions.

The domestic sovereignty, that of the proprietary chief of the family over the inhabitants of his domains, had equal alterations to undergo.

It was not with his relations, with his clan alone, that the German chief had effected his conquests, and found himself established in his new domains. The band which had followed him was composed of warriors of various families of the tribe, often men of different tribes. Tacitus expressly says as much: "If the tribe in which they were born becomes torpid in the laziness of a long peace, the principal among the young men go to seek nations who are engaged in war; for repose is unknown to this people; the warriors acquire celebrity only in the midst of danger, and it is only by war, by enterprises, that they can preserve a sufficient troop of companions."[1]

The ties between the chief and his companions were thus often the ties of war, not of family. Hence arose a great change in the character of their relations in the new estab-

---

[1] *De Mor. Germ.*, c. 14.

lishment. There was no longer that community of habits traditions, sentiments, which might exist in Germany among the proprietary chiefs and the laborers of their domains; in its place was the comradeship of warriors, a principle of association which was far less strong, far less powerful, far less moral.

The proprietary chief, moreover, found himself, in Gaul, surrounded by a foreign, hostile population, of different race, language, manners, and from whom he had incessantly to guard himself. The Roman Gauls were still the inhabitants, the cultivators of his domains; while in Germany the greater part were Germans like himself. A new and powerful cause of weakness in that patriarchal character, which domestic sovereignty had in Germany.

In his new settlement he was not long surrounded even by those of his countrymen who had formed part, if not of his family, at least of his band. Yet, as I have already had occasion to say several times, this band broke not up immediately into individuals, eager to separate, and to go and inhabit each his own domain. The principal chiefs occupied vast territories, and many of their companions continued to live with them in their homes. Accordingly we find in the documents of the sixth, seventh, and eighth centuries, and even later, a great number of free men, of German origin, and designated under the names of *arimanni, erimanni, herimanni, hermanni,* among the Lombards,[1] and of *rachimburgi, rathimburgi, regimburgi,*[2] among the Franks. Many German

---

[1] The *arimanni* incessantly recur in the Lombard laws, and in the Italian monuments, from the 7th to the 12th century. Their name is written *crimanni, eremanni, harimanni, haremanni, herimanni, hermanni,* variations more especially arising from the difficulty of writing the Teutonic sounds; and all leads us to suppose that the *Germani,* named in many acts, of which many refer to the 9th century, are no others than the *arimanni* or *hermanni;* so that the national name of the Germans would have no other origin than that of *herimanni,* free men. People differ as to the etymology of this latter word: according to some, it comes from *heer,* (army, war,) and the *heermanni* are warriors.; according to others, it comes from *ehre,* (honor,) and means free men *par excellence,* citizens invested with all the rights of political liberty, the *cires optimo jure* of the Roman law. This latter explanation is adopted by Mier (*Osnabrückische Geschichte,* in the preface *et passim*) and by M. de Savigny.—*History of the Roman Law,* &c., vol. i. p. 160, 175.

[2] The *rachimburgi,* often mentioned in the Salic law, are so also in many formulæ of the time, and even in acts of the 10th century: the variations of orthography are still more numerous than for the *arimanni ,*

writers, M. de Savigny among others, have thought to recognise, under these names, a condition, a particular class, the ancient free men and independent proprietors, the true citizens of the German tribe before the invasion; and they have thence inferred the prolonged continuation of the ancient social organization of the Germans in their new country. I think they are mistaken. I have carefully examined this question in my *Essais sur l'Histoire de France*. I shall here quote my words; I have no reason to change them:

" 'The names of *arimanni* and of *rachimburgi* are evidently applied to free men; they mean even (as every thing leads us to suppose) the free men in general, the acting citizens. The Lombard *arimanni* sit in courts or public assemblies in quality of judges, march to war under the orders of the count, appear as witnesses in civil actions; the Frank *rachimburgi* exercise the same right.

" It is equally certain that these words do not mean magistrates, men invested with special functions, judicial or otherwise, and distinct, by this title, from the rest of the citizens. In numerous documents, the *arimanni* are mentioned as witnesses, or simple warriors; the same name is given to the free citizens of town. The Frank *rachimburgi* also appear when there is no public function to fill; the word *rachimburgi* is often translated by that of *boni homines*. Every thing shows that these names are applied to free men, to citizens in general, and not to any special magistrate, to any public power.

" But these free men, these ahrimans, these rachimburgs, were they distinct from the leuds or beneficiaries, as from slaves? Did they form a class of independent citizens, united only among themselves and to the state,—whose social condition, in a word, was other than that of the men who, under the name of *recommended, leudes, faithful, antrustians*, or *vassals*, had entered into a particular association, and

---

we find *rachimburgi, rathimburgi, racimburgi, racineburgi, recyneburgi, racimburdi, regimburgi, raimburgi*. Most of the learned derive this word from *racha*, (cause, process,) or from *recht*, (right, justice,) which would exclusively represent the *rachimburgi* under the character of judges. M. de Savigny thinks, with the celebrated historian *Muller*, that it comes from the ancient Teutonic word *rek*, (great powerful,) which forms the termination of so many German proper names, and occurs again in *reich*, (rich;) so that the *rachimburgi*, called also *boni homines*, would be merely powerful, notable men, the *ricos hombres* of the Spaniards.—*History of the Roman Law*, &c., vol. i. p. 184.

lived in the dependence and under the protection of a superior?

"The monuments and facts alleged even by the defenders of this opinion, prove that it is ill founded, and that the leudes, the vassals of a lord, were called ahrimans or rachimburgs, as much as if veritable citizens alone were spoken of, men who were strangers to all individual independence.

"A man comes to place himself under the faith of the king, declares himself his faithful, his vassal; he comes, says the formula, *cum arimannia sua*—that is to say, followed by his warriors. Here, then, are ahrimans who are already leudes, the vassals of a man, and about to become the arriere-vassals of the king. They do not the less remain ahrimans—that is to say, free men, for that is all that this word means; it indicates liberty in general, and not a social condition distinct from that of the leudes, of the vassals.

"In a diploma of the tenth century, the emperor, Otho I., gives a fortress to a convent, 'with all the freemen, commonly called ahrimans.' In the eleventh century, the emperor Henry IV. made a similar donation to a monastery, and the ahrimans who inhabit the domain are here also included. Concessions of this kind were long common; many documents prove it, and a council of the tenth century forbade counts 'to give the ahrimans of their counties in benefice to their men.' In fact, the counts, originally at least, had no right by that title only to dispose of the lands of their county, nor of the free men who inhabited it. It was for the latter themselves to choose the superior to whom they wished to be attached.

"The quality of ahriman, therefore did not exclude that of leude, of vassal: ahrimans were the leudes of the man upon whose lands they lived, and when these lands were given in benefice they became the leudes of the new beneficiary.

"I do not find any texts with regard to the rachimburgs, where it is evident that this denomination was applied to leudes as well as to men absolutely free. Often employed in the Salic law, it is more rare than that of ahriman in the monuments of posterior ages; but all things authorize us to form the same judgment as to the meaning of this term that we see formed upon analogous terms. Both the one and the other mean men free and in possession of the rights attendant upon liberty, but not a particular class of citizens placed in a condition distinct on the one hand from that of slaves, and on the other from that of the leudes, or vassals."[1]

Not only did the ahrimans, the rachimburgs, not form a class distinct on the one hand from that of the bond-laborers, or slaves, on the other from that of the leudes, or vassals, but they could not fail soon to range themselves under one or other of these two conditions. How, in the house with, and by the side of, a chief who had become a great proprietor, and who was in possession of a thousand means of influence, and whose superiority increased daily, how, I say, could they long preserve that equality, that independence, which the companions of the same band formerly enjoyed? It is evident that it could not be. Those freemen who after the invasion still lived for some time with their chief, before long were divided into two classes; some received benefices, and, become proprietors in their turn, entered into the feudal association, with which we shall occupy ourselves at a later stage of our progress; the others, always fixed within the interior of the domains of their ancient chief, fell either into an entirely servile condition, or else into that of laborers cultivating a part of the land, liable to certain payments or rents.

You see what must result from this sovereignty of the ancient Germanic tribe which I have just described. In the new territorial establishment, it experienced a profound alteration; it lost its character of the family; it could not continue to attach itself to the common sentiments, to those traditions, those ties of parentage which in ancient Germany, united the proprietary head of the family with most of the inhabitants of his domains. This element of the organization of the Germanic tribe disappeared, or nearly so, when it was transplanted into Gaul. The element which became dominant was that of conquest, of force; and its predominance was the necessary result of the situation in which the proprietary heads of families found themselves in Gaul, a situation radically different from that in which they were placed in Germany.

Thus, this fusion of sovereignty and power, which we have remarked as one of the great characteristics of the feudal system, was not, properly speaking, new: it was not the result of conquest only; an analogous fact existed in Germany, in the heart of the German tribe: there also the pro-

---

[1] *Essais sur l'Histoire de France*, pp. 237–241.

rietary head of the family was sovereign within his domains; there also took place the fusion of sovereignty and property. But in Germany this fusion was accomplished under the influence of two principles; on the one hand, under the influence of the spirit of family, of the organization of clan; on the other, under the influence of conquest, of force. These two principles had, in the domestic sovereignty of the proprietary chief of the family in Germany, parts altogether unequal, and which it would be difficult to estimate. In Gaul, the share of the patriarchal system, of the organization of the clan, became greatly impaired; that of conquest, of force, on the contrary, took a great development, and became, if not the only, at least the dominant principle of that fusion of sovereignty and property which is, I repeat, one of the great characteristics of the feudal system.

There is therefore nothing, or at least nothing important to conclude from this fact in Germany, with regard to this fact in our country. I do not say that there is nothing remaining among us of the ancient German habits; I do not say that the spirit of the family, the idea that all the inhabitants of one domain, of one territory, are connected in some moral relations, and in a kind of parentage, had no influence in the French feudal system. I only say that this influence was very confined, very inferior to that of conquest.

Such, if I mistake not, was the transformation of this fact from the fourth to the tenth century. Thus, on its removal from Germany did it become wholly different in our country. In our next lecture we shall occupy ourselves with the third characteristic of the feudal system, that is to say, the relations of the possessors of fiefs among themselves, and the hierarchical organization of their society in itself.

FOURTH LECTURE.

General association of the possessors of fiefs among themselves; third characteristic of the feudal system—From the very nature of its elements this association must have been weak and irregular—It, in fact, always was so—Fallacy of the view which the apologists of this system trace of the feudal hierarchy—Its incoherency and weakness were especially great at the close of the 10th century—The formation of this hierarchy from the 5th to the 10th century—Three systems of institution are seen together after the German invasion: free institutions, monarchical institutions, aristocratical institutions—Comparative history of these three systems—Decline of the two first—Triumph of the third, which yet remains incomplete and disordered.

The two first characteristics of the feudal system, the special nature of landed property, and the fusion of sovereignty and property in each fief, we are well acquainted with. We know how they were formed; we have seen them take birth and grow, from the fifth to the tenth century. Let us now leave the interior of the fief, let us examine the relations of the possessors of fiefs among themselves, the progressive development of the organization which united them, or rather which was reputed to unite them in one and the same society. This, as you know, is the third of the great facts which constitute the feudal system.

I said the organization which was reputed to unite them: the union, in fact, of the possessors of fiefs among themselves, their organization into a general society, was far more a principle than a fact, far more nominal than real. The very nature of the elements of such an association lead us to presume this. What is the tie, the cement of a great society? It is the need which one of the partial, local associations which compose it has of the others; the necessity in which they are placed of having recourse to one another, in order to exercise their rights, for the accomplishment of the various public functions, for legislation, for the administration of justice, of finances, of war, &c. If each family, each town, each territorial circumscription finds within itself, in its own bosom, every thing of which it has any need in a political point of view; if it forms a complete petty state, which has nothing to receive from elsewhere, nothing to give elsewhere it will not adhere to other families, to other towns, to other local circumscriptions; there would be no society between them. The dispersion of sovereignty and government into the various parts, among the different members of the state, that it is which constitutes a state; that is, the external tie of general society, which brings and retains together its elements.

Now, the fusion of sovereignty and property, and its concentration within the domain, in the hands of its possessor, had exactly the effect of isolating the proprietor of the fief from other similar proprietors; each fief formed, as it were, a small, complete state, whose inhabitants had nothing, or almost nothing, to seek beyond it, which sufficed to itself, in matters of legislation, administration, of justice, taxes, war, &c. In a society formed of such elements, it was an inevitable consequence that the general tie should be weak, rarely felt, easily broken. The possessors of fiefs had, it is true, common affairs, reciprocal rights and duties. There was, moreover, the inclination natural to man, of continually extending his relations, of aggrandizing, of animating his social existence more and more, of constantly seeking, as it were, new citizens, and new ties with them. In fine, at the epoch with which we occupy ourselves, the Christian church, a society always one, and strongly constituted, incessantly labored to introduce something of its unity, its entirety, into the civil society; and this work was not fruitless. But it is not the less evident that, from the nature of its elements, and especially from the fusion of sovereignty and property, from the almost entire *localization* of power, if such a term be allowed, the general association of the possessors of fiefs must have had very little compactness, very little activity; that but very little entirety or unity could have prevailed in it.

And such, in fact, was the case; history fully confirms the inductions drawn from the very nature of this social state. Its apologists have applied themselves to the bringing prominently forward the reciprocal rights and duties of the possessors of fiefs; they have vaunted the skilful gradation of the ties which united them among themselves, from the weakest to the most powerful, in such a way that none were isolated, and yet that each remained free and master of himself. According to them, the independence of individuals was never more happily reconciled with the harmony of the whole. A chimerical idea, a purely logical hypothesis. Doubtless, in principle, the possessors of fiefs were united to each other, and their hierarchical association appears skilfully organized. But in fact, this organization was never real and efficacious; feudalism could never draw from its bosom a principle of order and unity sufficient to form a general, and, however little, regulated society. Its elements, that is to say, the possessors of fiefs, were always in a state of disunion and war among themselves, continually obliged to have recourse to force, because no supreme, truly public, power was present to maintain between them justice and peace, that is, society; and to create such a power, to fuse all its scattered and even hostile elements into a single and true society, it was necessary to have recourse to other principles, to other institutions, to institutions and principles foreign and even hostile to the feudal system. As you already know, it was by royalty on the one hand, and on the other by the idea of the nation in general, and of its rights, that political unity has prevailed among us, that the *State* has been constituted; and it was always at the expense of the possessors of fiefs by the weakening and progressive abolition of the feudal system, that we have approached this end.

It, therefore, must not be expected that we shall find that systematical and general organization of the possessors of fiefs among themselves, which I have pointed out as the third great characteristic of the feudal system, clearly and entirely realized in facts. The character belongs to it, and distinguishes it from every other social state; but it has never had its full development, its efficacious and regular application; the feudal hierarchy has never been really constituted, has not lived according to the rules and forms which the publicists assign to it. The special nature of landed property, the fusion of sovereignty and property, are simple, evident facts, which are shown in history, just as they are conceived in theory. But the feudal society in its entirety is an imaginary edifice, constructed after the event in the minds of learned men, and the materials only of which have existed in our territory, always unconnected and imperfect.

If such was its state during the course of the feudal period, how much more must it have been so at the commencement of this period, towards the end of the tenth century. Feudalism had then scarcely arisen out of the chaos of barbarism; it was arising from it as a kind of *pis-aller*, as the system nearest allied to that which was coming to a close, as the sole form which the growing society could take. The incoherence, the want of entirety, would necessarily be much greater than at a later period. The feudal association would be still farther removed from that state of unity, of regularity, which it never attained. The close of the tenth and the commencement of the eleventh century, are, in fact, in the feudal epoch, the period when feudalism appeared most disordered, the most destitute of general organization. We there see the possessors of fiefs forming themselves into an infinity of small groups, of which some count, duke, or mere seigneur, became the chief, according to the chances of place or events, remaining almost strangers to each other. Sometimes these local associations seemed to preserve relations among themselves, to adhere to a common centre; but we soon find that this appearance is fallacious. We see, for example, the name of the king of France still inscribed by such or such a lord of Aquitaine at the head of his acts, but it is the name of a king already dead; they render homage to royalty, but are ignorant as to who is its actual depositary. At no epoch was the parcelling out of territory among the possessors of fiefs so great, and their independence so complete; at no epoch had the hierarchical tie which should have united them so little reality.

In studying, therefore, from the fifth to the tenth century, the progressive formation of this third characteristic of the feudal system, we shall not arrive at results so prompt, so positive, as in the study of the two first. We shall not see the feudal organization appear, and clearly develop itself before our eyes, as was the case with regard to the special nature of landed property, and the amalgamation of sovereignty and property; we shall see but the germs, we shall witness only the first efforts at formation of that system which was never thoroughly perfected; we shall encounter here and there upon our own soil, the materials of that edifice which was never regularly constructed, or, more correctly speaking, we shall see every other social edifice fall, every other system vanish. From the fifth to the tenth century, no principle of social and political unity was able to preserve or acquire the empire; all those which formerly prevailed were conquered, abolished; and it was above their ruins that the rude and incomplete attempts at feudal organization appeared. It is, therefore, less the progressive formation of the general association, of the possessors of fiefs, than the progressive destruction of every other great social system, which I shall endeavor to retrace.

Immediately after the invasion and establishment of the Germans in Gaul, three principles of social organization, three systems of institutions co-exist and are present together: 1, the system of free institutions; 2, the system of aristocratical institutions; 3, the system of monarchical institutions.

The system of free institutions has its origin: 1st, in Germany, in the general assembly of the proprietary chiefs of family of the tribe, and in the common deliberation and personal independence of the warriors who formed the band: 2d, in Gaul, in the remains of the municipal system, in the heart of cities.

The system of aristocratical institutions has its origin: 1st, in Germany, in the domestic sovereignty of the proprietary chiefs of family, and in the patronage of the chief of the band over his companions: 2d, in Gaul, in the very unequal subdivision of landed property, concentrated in the hands of a small number of great proprietors, and in their domination of the mass of the population, laborers or slaves, who cultivate their domains, or serve them in their houses.

The system of monarchical institutions has its origin: 1st, in Germany, in military royalty, that is to say, the command of the chief of the band, and in the religious character inherent to certain families: 2d, in Gaul, in the traditions of the Roman empire, and in the doctrines of the Christian church.

These are the three great systems of institutions, the three principles essentially different, which the fall of the empire and the German invasion brought into the presence of each other, and which were to concur in the formation of the new society.

What were, from the fifth to the tenth century, the destinies of these three systems each in itself, and in their amalgamation?

Let us first speak of the system of free institutions.

It perpetuates and manifests itself from the fifth to the

tenth century: 1st, in the local assemblies, where the conquerors established in various parts of the territory assembled, and together discussed their affairs; 2d, in the general assemblies of the nation; 3d, in the remains of the municipal system, in the heart of cities:

That the local assemblies of the ancient Germans called *mâls*[1] in their language, and *placita* in Latin, continued after the invasion, cannot be doubted; the text of their laws gives evidence of it at every step. The following are some instances:

"If any one convened to the *mâl* does not repair thither, let him be condemned to pay fifteen *solidi*, unless he has been kept back by some lawful impediment."[2]

"If any one has need of witnesses in order that they may give testimony at the *mâl*, he who has need of them must convene them."[3]

"Let the assembly (*conventus*) be according to ancient custom in each hundred, before the count or his envoy, and before the hundred-man."[4]

"Let the court (*placitum*) take place every Saturday, or such day as shall please the count, or the hundred-man, in every week, when there is but little tranquillity in the province: when there is greater tranquillity, let the assembly take place every fortnight in each hundred, as it is ordered here above."[5]

"Let the court be held every calend, or every fortnight if necessary, to inquire into causes, in order that peace may reign in the provinces."[6]

These assemblies were composed of all the free men settled in the territorial circumscription; all had not only the right, but were obliged to repair thither.

"If any free man neglect to come to the court, and do not present himself to the count, or to his delegate, or to the hundred-man, let him be condemned to pay fifteen *solidi*. Let no person, whether vassal of the duke or of the count, or otherwise, neglect to come to the court, to the end that

---

[1] From the ancient German word, *mahl*, which signifies *meeting*, *assembly*, and is still found in many words, as *mahlzet*, repast, time of meeting; *mahlstatt*, place where the tribunal meets, &c.
[2] Salic Law, t. 1, c. 1, b. 16.
[3] Law of the Rip., t. 1, c. 1, t. lxvi., c i., &c.
[4] Law of the Allem., t. xxxvi., c. 1.   [5] *Ibidem*, c. 2.
[6] Law of the Boiares, t. xv., c. 1.

the poor may not be prevented from prosecuting their causes."¹

"Let all free men meet on the days fixed, where the judge shall direct, and let no person dare omit coming to the court. Let all who live in the county, whether vassal of the king or duke, or any other, come to the court, and let him who shall neglect to come be condemned to pay fifteen *solidi*."²

It is not easy to enumerate the attributes, the occupations of these assemblies, for they discussed every thing in them, all the common interests of the men who were assembled at them; but their principal business was to administer justice: all causes, all disputes were carried thither, to be submitted to the decision of free and notable men, of the *rachimburgs*, whose duty it was to declare, to show what was the law.

"If any rachimburgs sitting in any *mâl* have not declared the law, when a cause shall have been debated between two persons, he who prosecutes the cause must say to them three times, 'Tell us the Salic law;' if they will not say it, he who prosecutes the cause must say to them again, 'I require you to declare the law between my adversary and me.' The day being named for this purpose, seven of these rachimburgs shall each pay nine sols. If they do not then choose to declare the law . . . . nor give assurance of payment, then let a second day be appointed them, and then let each of them be condemned to pay fifteen sols."³

"If any one is prosecuting his cause, and the rachimburgs have not chosen to declare the Ripuarian law between the parties, then let him against whom they have pronounced an adverse sentence, say, 'I summon you to tell me the law.' Let those who have not chosen to declare it, and have afterwards been convicted of it, each of them pay fifteen sols fine."⁴

"If any one gain his cause in the mäl and by law . . . the rachimburgs must explain to him the law by which the cause has been decided. The plaintiff must act according to law, invite the officer to go to the house of the other, in order to take of his goods what he legally owes in respect of the cause."⁵

---

[1] Law of the Allem., t. xxxvi., c. 4.
[2] Law of the Boiares, t. xv., c. 1.
[3] Salic Law, t. lx.
[4] Law of the Rip., t. lv.
[5] Salic Law, tit. lix.

Not only did they administer justice in the *mâls*, not only did they deliberate there upon common affairs, but most civil affairs, most contracts were there completed, and thence only acquired the publicity, the authenticity which it is the duty of the notaries and public officers to give them in the present day:

"If any one sell any thing to another, and if the buyer wish to have an act of sale, he must demand it in full *mâl*, immediately put down the price, receiving the articles, and then let the act be written. If the article be of little value, let the act be attested by seven witnesses; if of much value, by twelve."[1]

Such was the state of local assemblies in the first ages following the invasion; they were not long so real and genuine as the texts seem to indicate. You may observe that, according to these very texts, it was more especially among the Germans still established upon the frontiers, or even in the interior of Germany, that the national *mâls* appear active and frequent. The laws of the Germans, of the Boiares, of the Ripuarian Franks, speak of them more frequently and in a more authoritative tone than those of the Salian Franks, further advanced into the interior of Gaul, and amidst the Roman population. There, indeed, the local *mâls* soon fell into disuse, into such disuse, that at the end of the Carlovingian race, the local chiefs, counts, viscounts, or others, convoked them in order to have the right of fining the free men who did not attend them. A capitulary of Louis le Débonnaire is entitled:

"Of vicars and hundred-men who, more out of cupidity than to administer justice, frequently hold courts and thus trouble the people too much."[2]

And Charlemagne, in order to remedy this abuse, had already reduced to three a year, the number of those local courts which the first barbarous laws convoked every month every fortnight, or even every week.

"With regard to the local courts which free men are to attend, the decrees of our father must be observed; namely that only three general courts are to be held in the year, and that no person shall be forced to attend them, except the accused or the accuser, or him who is called to give evidence. With regard to other courts held by hundred-men,

---

[1] Law of the Rip., t. lix., c. 1.   [2] Bal., i., coll. 617.

let none be convoked to them, except him who pleads, him who judges, and him who gives evidence."[1]

Who were these judges who were bound to attend local assemblies, when most free men were exempt from them? The *scabini*, or sheriffs, the real magistrates, charged by the prince with administering justice, instead of the citizens, who refused the burden. That is the true meaning of the word *scabini*, (in German *schöffen*, judges,) which many writers have confounded with the *rachimburgi* of the Salic law; and this innovation of Charlemagne suffices to prove into what decay the ancient local *mâls*, that is to say, the system of free institutions applied to civil life, had fallen at this period:

"Let no person be convoked to the court, but the plaintiff and the defendant in each cause, except seven *scabini*, who must be present at all hearings."[2]

With much stronger reason, the same decay would strike this system in the political sphere, in the general assemblies of the nation. Among men living at a distance from one another, and who had no longer the same interests, and the same destiny, these great meetings became difficult and artificial. Accordingly, the *Champs-de-Mars*, the *placita generalia*, became more and more rare and futile under the Merovingians. In the earliest ages we still frequently meet with them, because the warriors often made new expeditions in common; the band still met to attempt new adventures. Gradually, as the sedentary life prevailed, the general assemblies disappeared, and those which bear the name are of an entirely different nature; they have no longer either one or the other of these two characteristics. Sometimes they are solemn meetings, where people came, in virtue of an ancient custom, to bring to the chief or king presents which form a part of his wealth; sometimes the kings, after having struggled against their leudes, their beneficiaries, the one to resume, the other to retain their fees, entered into a negotiation with them, which led to meetings of which the name calls to mind the ancient national assemblies, but which, in fact, are only conferences, congresses, where great proprietors, petty sovereigns, discuss their interests and arrange their disputes. Such were, in 587, the assembly which concluded the treaty of Andelot; in 615, under Clotaire II. that of Paris, whence

---

[1] *Capit. of Louis le Débon.*, in 819; Bal., t. i., col. 616.
[2] *Capit. of Charlemagne*, in 803; Bal., t. i., col. 394–465.

issued the ordinance which bears its name, and many other
meetings in no way national, in no way resembling the assembly of the tribe, or the German band, but which were yet
called *placita generalia.*

With the first Carlovingians, the general assemblies renewed their primitive character, the military character. The
establishment of the second race was, as you know, up to a
certain point, a second invasion of Western Gaul by the German bands. We accordingly see these bands meet periodically to prosecute their expeditions further, and to secure
their conquests by new ones. This was the predominant
feature of the *Champs-de-Mars,* become the *Champs-de-Mai* of
Pepin le Bref. We meet under his reign with more than
ten great meetings of this kind. Under Charlemagne they
are still more frequent, and their character assumes higher
dignity. They are no longer mere military meetings, great
national reviews. Charlemagne made them a means of
government. Most of you, I think, remember what I said in
the last course upon this subject, and the fragments which I
quoted from the small treatise of Hincmar, *De Ordine Palatii,*
where he gives a detailed account of these assemblies, of
their composition, and of their labors. Charlemagne convoked almost all his agents, and, to speak the language of
our times, the functionaries of his empire, dukes, counts,
viscounts, vicars, hundred-men, scabini, &c. His object
was to learn through them what was passing around, to communicate his wishes to them, to discipline them to his will,
and thus to introduce some entirety, some order, into that
immense and incessantly agitated body, of which he claimed
to be the soul. These, assuredly, are not the ancient
assemblies of the German warriors, those assemblies where
personal independence prevailed, and where Clovis was constrained to allow each to take his share of the booty.

Under Louis le Débonnaire, the *placita generalia* are still
frequent, but disorder and war penetrate them, and make instruments of them. Under Charles le Chauve, they resume
the characteristic of which I have just spoken; they are no
longer any thing but conferences, congresses, where the king
struggles with greater or less success against vassals who
isolate themselves more and more, and whom he can neither
retain nor repress. After Charles le Chauve, and towards
the close of the Carlovingian race, even these congresses
ceased Sovereignty decidedly became local; royalty had

no longer even the simple claim to figure as the centre of the state. To the ancient national assemblies the feudal courts were about to succeed, the assembly of the vassals around the sovereign.

With regard to the wrecks of the Roman municipal system, the third element of the free institutions of this epoch, I shall not repeat what I have already said in our last course; nor shall I anticipate what I shall have to say when we are occupied with the regeneration of the commons. I confine myself to calling to mind, that the *curia*, its rights and institutions, have never disappeared from our territory, especially in the south of Gaul, and that we may equally attest their decay and their perpetuity from the fifth to the tenth century.

Such was the fate of the system of free institutions in this long interval. You see that all its principles grew more and more enervated, that all its means of action were broken. Had the monarchical institutions any better fortune?

I have said that among the Germans royalty had a twofold origin; that it was military and religious.

As being military, royalty was elective; a famous chief proclaimed an expedition to draw around him companions; he had no right, no coercive means; whoever chose came; warriors rallied around a chief of their choice; he was their king while it pleased them to follow him: this was election, if not according to political forms, at least in its principle and its liberty.

Inasmuch as it was religious, royalty was hereditary; for the religious character was the property, so to speak, of certain families descended from heroes, from national demi-gods, from Odin, Tuisco, &c.; and this character could be neither lost nor transferred. There is scarcely any Germanic nation in which we do not meet with these royal families; the Gothic and Anglo-Saxon princes descend from Odin; among the Franks, the Merovingians, in virtue of an analogous origin, alone wear long hair.

In passing over the Roman soil, Germanic royalty there found other principles, other elements which were profoundly to modify its character; there imperial royalty dominated, an institution specially symbolical, and a symbol purely political. The emperor had succeeded to the Roman people; as the representative of the Roman people, he appropriated its rights, its majesty; by this title he called himself sovereign. Imperial royalty was the personification of the republic; and as Louis XIV. said, *L'Etat c'est moi,* the successor of Augustus might say, *The Roman people, it is I.*

Beside imperial royalty arose Christian royalty, also a symbolical institution, but a symbol of a different nature, a symbol purely religious. The king, according to Christian ideas, was the delegate and representative of the Divinity. I just now spoke of the religious origin of barbarous royalty: it had, however, nothing symbolical about it; the families which passed for the descendants of the national demi-gods were thus invested with a positive and personal character. In Christian royalty, on the contrary, there is nothing personal or positive; it is a type, an image of the invisible and only sovereign Being.

Thus, under a twofold point of view, Roman royalty essentially differed from barbarous royalty; political or religious, this was a personal prerogative; political or religious, that was a pure symbol, a social fiction.

Such, so to speak, are the four origins of modern royalty, the four principles which, after the invasion, sought to combine in its production. We see then labor commence under the Merovingians. The Frank kings are, and wish to remain, chiefs of warriors—at the same time they take advantage of their barbaric religious descent; they adopt the Roman maxims, and endeavor to stand forth as the representatives of the state; in fine, they call themselves, and make the clergy call them, the images and representatives of God upon earth.

For minds so rude and simple as those of the barbarians of the sixth century, these notions and combinations were too complicated. They were, accordingly, not successful; and Merovingian royalty—precisely, if I mistake not, by reason of the uncertainty of its character and of its basis—soon fell into complete decay. When it began to reappear with vigor in the person of the Carlovingians, it had undergone a great metamorphosis. The first Carlovingians were pure military chiefs. In the eyes of their German countrymen, they had none of that religious character with which the family of the long-haired kings was invested. Neither Pepin de Herstall nor Charles Martel in any way gave themselves out as the descendants of Odin, or other Germanic demi-gods;

they were simply great proprietors and chiefs of warriors. Germanic royalty, then, reappeared at this time with the military character only. Every one knows how eagerly Pepin sought to add to it the Christian religious character. A stranger to all the traditions, to all the religious creeds of ancient Germany, he desired to support himself by new religious creeds, already far more powerful. Charlemagne went still further; he undertook again to give the character of imperial royalty to Frankish royalty, to again make it a political symbol, himself to resume the rank of representative of the state which the Roman emperors occupied. And he labored at this by the most efficacious means; not by the sole pomp of ceremonies and language, but by really resuscitating the imperial power, the Roman administration, and that *omnipresence*, as it were, of royalty, at all parts of the earth, which, amidst the universal decline, had constituted the whole strength of that great despotism.

This is the true characteristic of the government of Charlemagne. I shall not repeat here what I said concerning it in the last course; but some extracts from his capitularies will show how carefully he was occupied with all things, desired to know every thing, to be everywhere, either in person or by his delegates—in fine, to present himself to the minds of the people as the universal mover and source of the entire government.

"Let the counts and their vicars be well acquainted with the law, to the end that no judge may decide unjustly in their presence, nor unduly alter the law."[1]

"We will and order that our counts do not remit the sitting of their courts, nor abridge them unduly, in order to give themselves to the chase or to other pleasures."[2]

"Let no count hold his courts unless he be fasting, and of composed mind."[3]

"Let each bishop, each abbot, each count, have a good registrar, and let not the scribes write in an illegible manner."[4]

"We will, that with regard to the jurisdiction and affairs which have hitherto belonged to the counts, our envoys shall acquit themselves of their mission four times in the year: in

---

[1] *Capit. of Charlemagne*, in 803; Bal., tom. 1, col. 396.
[2] Year 807; Bal., tom. i., col. 459.   [3] Year 803; ibid., col. 393.
[4] Year 805; ibid., col. 421.

winter, in the month of January; in spring, in the month of April; in summer, in the month of July; and in autumn, in the month of October. Each time, they shall hold courts where the counts of the neighboring counties shall meet."[1]

"Each time that one of our envoys shall observe in his legation that any thing happens otherwise than as we have ordered it, not only shall he take care to reform it, but he shall give us a detailed account of the abuses which he may discover."[2]

"Let our envoys select, in each place, *scabini*, advocates and notaries, and on their return let them bring us their names in writing."[3]

"Whenever they find bad vicars, advocates, or hundred-men, let them be removed, and others selected who know how and are willing to judge affairs according to equity. If they find a corrupt count, let them inform us of the same."[4]

"We will that each of our envoys carefully watch that each of the men whom we have charged with the government of our people, acquit himself justly of his office, in a manner agreeable to God, honorable to us, and useful to our subjects. Let the said envoys, therefore, make a point of knowing if the orders contained in the capitularies which we transmitted to them last year, are executed according to the will of God and our own. We will that in the middle of the month of May, our envoys, each in his legation, convoke in one place all the bishops, abbots, our vassals, our advocates, vicars, abbesses, as well as the representatives of all the lords whom any imperious necessity prevents repairing thither themselves; and if it be more convenient, especially with a view to the poor people, that this meeting be held in two or three different places instead of one, let it be so. Let each count bring thither his vicars, his hundred-men, and also three or four of his most notable sheriffs. In this assembly, let them first occupy themselves with the state of the Christian religion, and the condition of the ecclesiastical order. Then let our envoys inform themselves, from all present, of the manner in which each acquits himself of the employment which we have confided to him; let them learn if concord reigns among our officers, and whether they mutually give each other help in their functions. Let them

---

[1] Year 812; Bal., col. 493. [2] Ibid. [3] Year 803; ibid., col. 393.
[4] Bal., t. i., c. 396, year 805; ibid., c. 426.

make this inquiry with the most careful diligence, and in such a way that we may from them know the truth of all things; and if they learn that in any place there is an affair, the decision of which requires their presence, let them repair thither, and regulate it in virtue of our authority."[1]

Surely, nothing less resembles barbaric royalty than such a mode of government; nothing more forcibly calls to mind the spirit and administration of the empire; of that power which represented the state, and acted almost alone in the state. That is the system which, without being thoroughly aware of it, without having reconstructed its theory, Charlemagne labored to restore; and he knew very well what was the principal obstacle to this enterprise; he knew very well that the rising feudal system, the independence and the rights of proprietary beneficiaries in their domains, the fusion of sovereignty and property, were the most dangerous enemies of that sovereignty and administrative royalty to which he aspired. Accordingly, he struggled incessantly against these enemies, and endeavored to restrain and to divide the power of the proprietors as much as in him lay.

"He never," says the monk of Saint Gall, "confided the administration of more than one county to his counts, except it were those which were situated on the frontiers, or in the neighborhood of barbarians. He never, unless impelled by really powerful motives, conceded to a bishop, in benefice, an abbey or church of the royal domain; and when his counsellors or favorites asked him why he acted thus, he answered them: 'With this property or that farm, with this little abbey or that church, I acquire the faith of a vassal as good, even better than this bishop or that count.'"[2]

He did more; he attempted to pierce through, if I may so express myself, all private properties, in order to enter into direct relations with all the inhabitants of his empire. I will explain myself. He only communicated with the mass of the population through the intermediation of the possessors of freeholds or fees, each sovereign in his domains, and chief of the free men, or *coloni*, or serfs who inhabited them. Charlemagne desired that an oath of fidelity, directed and personal, should be given him by all freemen, as to the real

---

[1] *Capit. of Louis le Débon.*, in 823. He but repeats what Charlemagne prescribed. Bal., t. 1, col. 649.
[2] *Recueil des Historiens de France*, t. v., p. 3.

and true sovereign of the state. We find in the formulæ of Marculf, the following letter from him:

"To the count ———. With the consent of the high men of our realm, we have ordered that our glorious son ——— shall reign in the kingdom of ———. Consequently, we order that in all cities, villages, and castles, you convoke and cause to meet in convenient places all your inhabitants, whether Franks, Romans, or any other nation; to the end, that in the presence of the illustrious ———, our envoy, whom we send to you for this purpose, they all swear fidelity and loyal attachment to our son and to us, whether by the holy places, or by such other holy pledge as we transmit to you for that purpose."[1]

When he had been crowned emperor,

"He ordered that every man in his kingdom, layman or ecclesiastic, who had already sworn fidelity to him under the name of king, should renew the same promise to him as Cæsar; and that all those who had not yet taken the said oath should take it, down to the age of twelve."[2]

Lastly, we read in a capitulary of the year 805:

"Let none swear fidelity to any other than to us and to his lord for our utility and that of his lord."[3]

"Such a system evidently tended to free royalty from all feudal relations, to found its empire beyond the hierarchy of persons and lands; in fine, to render it everywhere present, everywhere powerful, in virtue of the public power and by its own right. The attempt succeeded while Charlemagne presided over it. His successors undertook to continue it, that is to say, they ordered what he had done. The demand of the universal oath reappeared in their acts, and even survived their impotence; but it was no longer any more than a futile form. The relations between free men and the king, and his personal power over them, became daily weakened. The obligation of fidelity was no longer real, except between the vassal and his lord. It was to the lords that Charles le Chauve addressed himself, in order to repress the disorders committed on their lands; it was through their authority that he brought his own to bear. He had no direct influence; and although he menaced the lords with making them responsible for the crimes of their men, if they did not prevent or punish them, it is clear that the feudal hierarchy had re-

---

[1] *Marculf,* l. i., f 40   [2] Bal., t. 1, col. 363.   [3] Ibid., col. 425.

gained independence with the empire, and that the attempt of Charlemagne to free royalty from it had failed by the effect of the general course of things and the incapacity of his successors."[1]

At the close of the tenth century, then, the system of monarchical institutions had succeeded no better than the system of free institutions in taking possession of society, and introducing unity and rule into it. All its laws were shaken, all its means of action enervated or inapplicable. The religious character of ancient German royalty had disappeared; the heroic origin of such or such a family was forgotten, as well as many of the traditions of the barbaric life. It had equally lost its primitive military character; the band no longer existed; the wandering and common life had ceased; most of the warriors were established in their own domains. The political character of imperial royalty was incompatible with the new society; there was no longer sovereignty, no longer national majesty, no longer any state in general; how could there be a symbol, a representative of that which no longer existed? The religious Christian character of royalty alone preserved any reality, any influence, and that was but weak and rare; lay proprietors scarcely heeded it; the tumult of their life and the needs of personal independence alone occupied their minds; the bishops and great abbots themselves cared but little about it; they also had become proprietors of fiefs, had assumed the interests and habits of such, and had but little affection towards ideas which in no way accorded with their temporal position. All the bases, I repeat, of the system of monarchical institutions, as well as of the system of free institutions, were shaken, all its vital principles had lost their energy.

It was entirely different with the system of aristocratical institutions. Instead of declining, they were progressing. To be convinced of this, it is only necessary to observe what the elements, whether German or Roman, which constituted it had become. They were all strengthened and developed.

And first, as you have already seen, the domestic sovereignty of the German proprietary chief of the family was transplanted into Gaul; it even became there more complete and more absolute, because the spirit of family which had formerly been associated with it there had disappeared, and

---

[1] *Essais sur l'Histoire de France*, p. 155-160.

the fact of conquest, of force, had become almost its only base. Accordingly, this first aristocratical element of ancient German society became strengthened instead of weakened, in the new social state.

The second, that is to say, the patronage of the chief of the band over his companions, had experienced the same fate; it had changed its form; to the ascendency of the warrior had succeeded the rights of the suzerain over his vassals. But this metamorphosis of relations had given far more energy and solidity to the aristocratical principle that it previously contained. On the one hand, inequality was developed; the possessors of fiefs were far more unequal among themselves than the warriors; on the other, in the ancient band, the companions living together, supported one another, and in common controlled the power of the chief. When they had entered into the condition of proprietors, each found himself isolated, and the superior, the suzerain, had far greater facilities for subduing them. A new progress of the aristocratical system.

With regard to the subdivision of landed property, I think it underwent considerable and rather aristocratical change; it divided itself. Without doubt, the feudal system had this effect at first. At the close of the tenth century, at the commencement of the feudal period, there were many more landed proprietors in Gaul than at the fall of the empire. The territory was divided into smaller lots, more especially into more varied lots; the fiefs were much more different, more unequal, than the domains of the great Gallo-Roman proprietors had been; in this respect, therefore, the aristocratical principle was a little weakened; but assuredly the distribution of landed property was still sufficiently unequal, the land concentrated into a sufficiently limited number of hands, to found a very aristocratic system.

You see, therefore, that while the system of free institutions and that of monarchical institutions were declining, the system of aristocratical institutions, on the contrary, saw its bases strengthen, its principles gain vigor. It had not acquired, it had not given to society in general, a regular form. unity, or entirety; it never will attain that. But, it evidently prevailed; it alone was likely to live, if I may use the expression, alone capable of subduing men, and of giving to other social principles time to regain breath, to reappear one day with better success.

Thus was feudal society prepared, thus was it progressively formed, from the fifth to the tenth century. We have attempted to discover its origins, to follow it in its earliest developments. It now subsists, it covers our land. We shall henceforward study it in itself, and in its maturity.

FIFTH LECTURE.

Method to be followed in the study of the feudal period—The simple fief is the fundamental element, the integrant molecule of feudalism—The simple fief contains: 1, the castle and its proprietors; 2, the village and its inhabitants—Origin of feudal castles—Their multiplication in the 9th and 10th centuries—Causes of this—Efforts of the kings and powerful suzerains to oppose it—Futility of these efforts—Character of the castles of the 11th century—Interior life of the proprietors of fiefs—Their isolation—Their idleness—Their incessant wars, expeditions, and adventures—Influence of the material circumstances of feudal habitations upon the course of civilization—Development of domestic life, condition of women, and of the spirit of family in the interior of castles.

We now approach the special object of this course. We are about to study feudal society in itself, during the period which especially belongs to it, from the time when it may be regarded as truly formed, down to the time when France escaped from it, and passed under the empire of other principles, of other institutions; that is, during the eleventh, twelfth, and thirteenth centuries.

I desire to follow in their entirety the destinies of feudalism during these three centuries. I would wish not to parcel it out, but to keep it constantly entire under your eyes, and make you thus see its successive transformations at a single glance. This would be its true history, the only faithful image of the reality. Unfortunately, this cannot be. In order to study, the human mind is forced to divide, to analyze; it learns nothing unless it be successively and in parts. It is then the work of the imagination and of the reason to reconstruct the demolished edifice, to resuscitate the being destroyed by the scientific scalpel. But it is absolutely necessary to pass through this dissection and its progress; the weakness of the human mind so orders it.

I have already pointed out the classification of our researches upon feudal society. I have said that on the one hand we shall study the social state, and on the other, the intellectual state: in the social state, the civil and the religious society; in the intellectual state, the learned literature, and the popular literature. It is, therefore, with the history of civil society in the feudal period, that we must commence.

Here also we have need to divide, to classify, to study separately; the matter is too vast and too complicated, to allow of it being comprehended all complete and at a single grasp.

Let us at least endeavor to discover and to follow out the least artificial method, that which will the least mutilate facts, which will best respect their integrity and concatenation; the most living method, as it were, the one most neighboring on reality.

If I mistake not, it is the following:

At the end of the tenth century, feudal society was definitively formed; it had attained the plenitude of its existence; it covered and possessed our territory. What was its fundamental element, its political unity? What, so to speak, (I have already made use of this expression,) what was the primitive feudal molecule, that which could not be broken without the feudal character being abolished?

It is evidently the simple fief, the domain possessed by way of fief, by a lord who exercises over the inhabitants that sovereignty inherent, as you know, to property.

It is therefore with the simple fief, considered in itself, that we shall commence our study. We shall first apply ourselves to the proper understanding of this fundamental element of feudalism.

What does the mere, simple fief contain, reduced to its last expression? What is there to study in its enclosure?

First, the possessor himself of the fief, his situation and his life, that is to say, the castle; then the inhabitant of the fief, not possessors, mere cultivators of the domain, and subject to the proprietor that is to say, the village.

These are evidently the two objects to which our attention is called in the study of the simple fief. It is necessary that we should thoroughly know what was the condition and destiny, from the eleventh to the fourteenth century—1, of the feudal castle and its proprietors; 2, of the feudal village and its inhabitants. When we shall have actually lived in the interior of the fief, when we shall really have been present at what passed there, at the revolutions which were accomplished in it, we shall leave it in order to seek the ties which united together the fiefs disseminated throughout the territory; to be present at the relations, whether between suzerains and vassals, or between vassals among themselves.

We shall then study the general association of the possessors of fiefs under the various relations which constitute the political order, that is, in its legislative, military, judicial, and other institutions. We shall endeavor thoroughly to discern: 1, what principles, what ideas presided at these institutions, what were the rational foundations, the political doctrines of feudalism; 2, what the feudal institutions really were, no longer in principle, and conceived systematically, but actually and in application; 3, finally, what results must have been produced, and in fact were produced, whether by the political doctrines, or by the practical institutions of feudalism, for the development of civilization in general.

There feudal society seems to stop. Do we not now know all its elements? is not all its organization unveiled to us? It essentially consists in the hierarchical association of the possessors of fiefs, and in their sovereignty over the inhabitants of their domains. This known, is not all known? have we not arrived at the term of the career which we had to go over?

Certainly not: feudal society, properly so called, even in its triumph, was not, at this epoch, the entire civil society. As I have already had occasion to observe, other elements are there encountered, of another origin and of another character; elements which took place in feudalism, but which were never completely incorporated with it, which have always secretly combated it, and ended by triumphing over it: these are, royalty and the towns. Royalty was both within and without feudalism: feudal in certain points of its situation, in some of its rights, it borrowed from others, other principles, other social facts, not only foreign but hostile to feudalism. It was so also with towns; they reconstituted themselves within the bosom of feudal society, to a certain degree assimilating themselves to it; but they were also attached to other principles, to other facts; and, upon the whole, the difference was greater than the assimilation, as the event has proved.

When, then, we shall have studied feudalism in itself, it will still remain for us to study two other elements of civil society at the same epoch, royalty and the towns. We shall study, on the one hand, what, in their feudal character, they had in common with feudalism; on the other, how they were separated from it, in their peculiar and distinct character.

All these elements of civil society thus properly known,

we shall endeavor to bring them face to face, to unravel the play of their relations ; to fix the true physiognomy, and the principal revolutions of the whole which they formed.

Such will be our progress in the study of civil society in France, during the feudal period. Let us immediately approach it, let us enter, and confine ourselves to the simple fief.

Let us first occupy ourselves with its possessor ; let us study the situation and the life of the sovereign of this little state, the interior of the castle which contained him, and his people.

The single word *castle* awakes the idea of feudal society ; it seems to rise up before us. Nothing can be more natural. These castles which covered our soil, and the ruins of which are still scattered about, it is feudalism which constructed them; their elevation was, so to speak, the declaration of its triumph. Nothing of the kind existed on the Gallo-Roman soil. Before the German invasion, the great proprietors lived either in cities, or in beautiful houses, agreeably situated near cities, or in rich plains upon the banks of rivers. In the country districts, properly so called, were dispersed the *villæ*, a species of farms, great buildings serving for the improvement of estates, and for the dwelling of the laborers or serfs who cultivated them.

Such was the distribution and habitation of the various classes, which the Germanic nations found in Gaul at the time of the invasion.

It must not be supposed that they disliked and were eager to change it ; that they immediately sought the mountains, steep and savage places, in order to construct new and entirely different dwellings. They first established themselves in the habitations of the Gallo-Romans, whether in the cities, or in the *villæ*, amidst the country districts and the agricultural population, and rather in the latter dwellings, whose situation was more conformable to their national habits. Accordingly the *villæ*, of which constant mention is made under the first race, were the same, or almost the same, as they had been before the invasion ; that is to say, they were the centre of improvement and habitation of great domains, buildings scattered throughout the country districts, where barbarians and Romans, conquerors and conquered, masters, free men, laborers, slaves, lived together.

Still a change soon became visible. The invasion continued; disorder and pillage were incessantly renewed; the inhabitants of the country districts, of ancient or new origin, had need to guard themselves, and incessantly keep on the defensive. We find the *villæ* gradually becoming surrounded by moats, ramparts of earth, with some appearances of fortifications. Hence arises a pretended etymology of the word *villa*, which we read in the *Glossary* of Du Cange, thus:

Villa dicitur à vallis, quasi vallata, eo quod vallata sit solum vallatione vallorum, et non munitione murorum. Indè villanus.

The etymology is incorrect; the word *villa* is far anterior to the epoch when the inhabitants of this kind of dwellings had need to surround them with moats or ramparts; the word is commonly derived from *vehilla*, *vehere*, which probably means the place where the agricultural carts were made. But whatever may be its merit, the mere etymology of the word is not the less a remarkable fact; it proves that the *villæ* were not long before they were in a measure fortified.

There is another circumstance which prevents all doubt of this: in certain parts of France, in Normandy, Picardy, &c., the names of many castles terminate with *ville*, Frondeville, Aboville, Méréville, &c.; and many of these castles are not situated, as most feudal castles properly so called were, in steep, isolated places, but amidst rich plains, in valleys upon the site which the *villæ* doubtless formerly occupied: a sure sign that more than one Anglo-Roman *villa* in fortifying itself, and after many vicissitudes, ended by being metamorphosed into a castle.

As for the rest, even before the invasion was consummated, and in order to resist its disorders, to escape its dangers, the population of the country districts had begun, in many places, to seek refuge in the heights, in places difficult of access, and to surround them with fortifications. We read in the life of St. Nicet, bishop of Trèves, written by Fortunat, bishop of Poictiers:

"In going through these districts, Nicet, that apostolic man, that good pastor, constructed there for his flock a protecting fold: he surrounded the hill with thirty towers, which enclosed it on all sides, and thus raised an edifice where formerly was a forest."[1]

I might quote many analogous examples. Is not this evidently a first attempt of that choice of places, and of that

---

[1] *Fortun. Carm.* l. iii., c. 12.

kind of constructions, which were adopted at a later period for feudal castles?

In the dreadful anarchy of the following centuries, the causes which had impelled the population to seek such places of refuge, and to surround them with fortifications, became more and more pressing; it was necessary for it to fly from places easy of access; to fortify its dwelling. And not only did men thus seek security, they also found in it a means of abandoning themselves without fear to depredation, and to secure to themselves its fruits. Among the conquerors, many still led a life of hunting and pillage; they were forced to have a receptacle where they might shut themselves up after an expedition, repel the vengeance of their adversaries, resist the magistrates who attempted to maintain any order in the country. Such was the aim which originally caused the construction of many of the feudal castles. It was more especially after the death of Charlemagne, under the reigns of Louis le Débonnaire and Charles le Chauve, that we find the country covered with these haunts; they even became so numerous and so formidable, that Charles le Chauve, despite his weakness, and for the sake of the public order, as well as of his own authority, thought it his duty to attempt to destroy them. We read in the capitularies drawn up at Pistes in 864:

"We will and expressly order that, whosoever in these times shall, without our consent, have constructed castles, fortifications, and embankments, (*haias*,) shall entirely destroy them between this and the latter end of August, seeing that the neighbors and inhabitants have suffered much uneasiness and many depredations from them; and if any one refuse to demolish these works, let the counts, in whose counties they have been constructed, themselves cause them to be demolished; and if any one resist them, let them immediately inform us. And if the counts neglect to obey us in this, let them know that, according to what is written in these capitularies, and in those of our predecessors, we shall order them to our presence, and we shall ourselves establish in their counties men who can and will cause our orders to be executed."[1]

The tone and precision of the injunctions addressed to all the royal officers, prove the importance which was attached

---

[1] *Cap. of Charles le Chauve*, at Pistes, in 864; Bal., vol. ii., col. 195.

to the matter; but Charles le Chauve was evidently not in a condition to accomplish such a work. We do not find that this capitulary had any effect, and his successors do not even claim its execution. Accordingly, the number of castles went on increasing under the last Carlovingians with extraordinary rapidity. Still the struggle did not cease between those whose interest it was to prevent, and those who felt the need of raising buildings of this kind: we find it protracted to the eleventh, twelfth, and thirteenth centuries And it was not merely between the king and the possessors of fiefs that it subsisted, it also broke out among the possessors of fiefs themselves. It was not a mere question, in fact, of the maintenance of public order in the whole territory, nor of a duty or interest of royalty. Every suzerain saw with displeasure his vassal constructing a castle on his fief, for the vassal thus ensured himself a powerful means of independence and resistance. Local wars then became longer and more fierce, the castle served for aggression as well as for defence, and the powerful, who desired alone to have them, like the weak who had none at all, greatly feared to see them constructed around them. There was here, accordingly, a subject for continual complaints and protest. About the year 1020, and on a similar occasion, Fulbert, bishop of Chartres, wrote to king Robert a letter which I shall quote entire, because it gives a clear and lively idea of the importance which such a dispute must have had:

> 'To his lord Robert, his most gracious king, whom Fulbert, humble bishop of Chartres, prays may remain in the grace of the King of kings.

"We return thanks to your goodness for that you have lately sent us a messenger charged with rejoicing us by bringing news of your good health, and to instruct your majesty of the condition of our affairs, after having demanded from us an account thereof. We then wrote to you concerning the evils done to our church by viscount Geoffrey, of Chateaudun, who shows sufficiently, and even more than enough, that he has no respect for God or your excellency, for he rebuilt the castle of Galardon, formerly destroyed by you; and upon this occasion we may say, *See! the evil comes from the east* upon our church: and lo! again he dares to undertake the building of another castle at Illiers, in the midst of the domains of Saint Mary, concerning which we may well say, and also in good truth, *See! the evil comes from the west.* Now, therefore, forced to write to you by reason of these evils, we bring complaint to your mercy, and ask help and counsel of it; for in this calamity we have received neither aid nor consolation from your son Hugh. Accordingly, penetrated to the depths of our heart with a lively grief, we have already manifested it to such a degree, that, according to our order, our bells, accustomed to announce our joy and gladness, have ceased to sound, as the more to show our sadness; and divine service, which, up to the present time, and by the grace of God, we have been accustomed to celebrate with great rejoicing of heart and mouth, is no longer celebrated, except in a lamentable manner, with a low voice, and almost in silence.

"Thus, therefore, on our knees we implore your pity, with tears of heart and mind, save the holy church of the Mother of God, of which you have willed that we your faithful should be the chief, however unworthy we be thereof, succor those who from you alone, after God, expect their consolation and comfort in the evils with which they are so heavily laden. Consider of the means of delivering us from these sufferings, and of converting our sadness into joy; summon the count Eudes,[1] and enjoin him sharply, in the name of your royal authority, that he should, in all sincerity, give the necessary orders to have destroyed, or that he himself destroy these constructions of diabolical inspiration, for the love of God, and by fidelity towards you, in honor of the holy Mary, and by affection for us, who are always her faithful. If neither you nor he put an end to this evil, which keeps every thing in our country in confusion, what will remain for us to do, but to formally interdict the celebration of all divine service throughout our bishopric? and for ourselves, alas! although greatly against our will, and constrained only by the severest necessity, to exile ourselves to some place, being unable any longer to see with our eyes, or to suffer the oppression of the holy church of God. To the end that we may not be forced to come to this extremity, we again implore your pity with lamentable voice; for God keep us from seeing ourselves constrained to banish ourselves far from you, to have to confess to a foreign king or emperor that you

---

[1] Geoffrey was vassal of Eudes II., count of Chartres, and the latter was the vassal of the king.

would not or could not defend the bride of Christ, the holy church confided to our care!"

Assuredly, the construction of the castles of Galardon and Illiers must have appeared a grave fact, for it to cause a bishop, in the mere hope of making its gravity felt, to silence the bells of his church, and have divine service almost suspended. The successors of Fulbert, in the bishopric of Chartres, took a different course; they fortified the episcopal house, and were in their turn obliged to demolish their fortifications. We read, in a charter granted to Yves, bishop of Chartres, by Stephen, count of Chartres and of Blois, who died in 1101, the following clause:

"If any future bishop cause to be constructed, in the said episcopal house, a tower or ramparts, let that tower and those ramparts alone be demolished, and let the house itself remain standing, with its dependencies."[1]

Doubtless, between Fulbert and Yves, some bishop of Chartres had added such works to his house, and count Stephen wished to prevent their being renewed.

The lords who each held fiefs, often had quarrels among them, arising from the construction of castles, whether within the fief, or on the frontiers of neighboring fiefs.

"In 1228, Guy, count of Forest and Nevers, and Thibaut, count of Champagne, were at war with one another, because of fortresses which they had respectively caused to be constructed upon the borders of their counties of Champagne and Nevers. This war having lasted for a long period, the two counts put it to the arbitration of the cardinal legate, who then gave his judgment as umpire, by which it was said that so long as Guy, count of Forest, should hold the county of Nevers, the fortresses which were on the confines of the county of Champagne, and on those of the county of Nevers, should subsist, and that they might even be fenced around with new works, provided, however, that it was only to the distance of the shot of a cross-bow; but that the counts could not make new fortresses on the same borders, nor suffer others to make them."[2]

And in 1160, under the reign of Louis le Jeune, a charter of his brother Robert, count of Dreux, is expressed in the following terms:

---

[1] Martenne, *Amplis. Collect.*, t. i., p. 621.
[2] Brussel, *Usage des Fiefs*, t. i., p. 383.

"I, Robert count, brother of the king of France, make known to all present and to come, that there was a certain contest between Henry, count of Champagne and Brie, and myself, concerning a certain house which is called Savegny, and a part of which I fortified by a moat of two outlets. The affair has been arranged as follows, namely: that what is already fortified by a moat of two outlets, shall so remain, but that the remainder shall be fortified with a moat of one outlet only, and a fence without battlements.

" If I make war against the said count, or against any other, I shall immediately give him up the said house. I have guarantied it to him on my faith and by hostages, and he has promised me that he will keep the said house, with the ponds and mills, in good faith and without ill design; and that he will immediately return it to me, the war being finished."[1]

It would be easy to multiply this example of the resistance or, more correctly speaking, various resistances, which, down to the middle of the thirteenth century, the construction of castles had to surmount.

It did surmount them, as it happens with every thing which is the work of necessity. At this epoch, there was war everywhere; everywhere would necessarily be also the monuments of war, the means of making it and repelling it. Not only were strong castles constructed, but all things were made into fortifications, haunts, or defensive habitations. Towards the end of the eleventh century, we find, at Nimes. an association called *Les Chevaliers des Arènes.* When the meaning of this is sought, we find that they were knights who had taken up their abode in the Roman amphitheatre, the Arenes still remaining in the present day. It was easy to fortify them: they were strong in themselves. These knights established themselves in them, and intrenched themselves therein when necessary, and this is not an isolated fact; most of the ancient circuses, the arena of Arles, as well as that of Nimes, have been put to the same use, and occupied for some time as a castle. It was not necessary to be a knight, or even a layman, in order to act thus, and to live amidst fortifications. Monasteries, churches, also fortified themselves; they were surrounded by towers, ramparts, and moats; they were assiduously guarded, and long sieges

---

[1] Brussel, *Usage des Fiefs,* t. i., p. 382, note *b.*

were sustained by them. The burghers did like the nobles: towns were fortified. War so constantly menaced them, that, in many of them, a child was kept, at a fixed post and by way of sentinel, in the bell tower of the church, to observe what passed at a distance, and to announce the approach of an enemy. Moreover, the enemy was within the walls, in the neighboring street, in the intermediate house; war might break out, in fact did break out, between one quarter and another, from door to door, and fortifications, like war, penetrated everywhere. Each street had its barriers, each house its tower, its loop-hole, its platform, in the fourteenth century.

"Rhodez was divided into two parts, surrounded with ramparts and towers. One was called the city, the other the borough; the inhabitants of the city and those of the borough made war with each other from time to time; and even when they were at peace, they shut the gates of their enclosure every night, and were more particular in setting the watch upon the walls which separated them, than upon those which protected the town on the side towards the country."[1]

And many other towns, among others Limoges, Auch, Perigueux, Angoulême, Meaux, were the same, or almost the same, as Rhodez.

Would you have a somewhat exact idea of what a castle was, not exactly at the epoch which occupies us, but at a rather posterior epoch? I shall borrow its description from a very recent work, and which as yet is not even finished; a work which, in my opinion, is often deficient in a due sentiment of the ancient times, and in moral truth, but which, concerning the actual state of society in the fourteenth and fifteenth centuries, concerning the employment of time, manners, and domestic, industrial, agricultural life, &c., contains very complete information, collected with a great deal of learning, and well arranged. I speak of the *Histoire des Français des divers Etats, pendant les cinq derniers Siècles,* by M. A. Monteil, the first four volumes of which are published. The author describes, in the following terms, the castle of Montbazon, near Tours, in the fourteenth century.

"First, imagine to yourself a superb position, a steep mountain, bristling with rocks, furrowed with ravines and precipices; upon the declivity is the castle. The small

---

[1] *Histoire des Français de divers états,* by M. A. Monteil, v. ii., p. 196.

houses which surround it set off its grandeur; the Indre seems to turn aside with respect; it forms a large semicircle at its feet.

"This castle must be seen when, at sunrise, the outward galleries glimmer with the armor of the sentinels, and the towers are shown all brilliant with their large, new gratings. Those high buildings must be seen, which fill those who defend them with courage, and with fear those who should be tempted to attack them.

"The door presents itself all covered with heads of boars or wolves, flanked with turrets, and crowned with a high guard-house. Enter, there are three enclosures, three moats, three drawbridges to pass. You find yourself in a large, square court, where are cisterns, and on the right and left the stables, hen-houses, pigeon-houses, coach-houses; the cellars, vaults, and prisons are below; above are the dwelling apartments; above these are the magazine, larders, or salting-rooms and arsenals. All the roofs are bordered with machicolations, parapets, guard-walks, and sentry-boxes. In the middle of the court is the donjon, which contains the archives and the treasure. It is deeply moated all round, and can only be entered by a bridge, almost always raised. Although the walls, like those of the castle, are six feet thick, it is surrounded up to half its height with a chemise, or second wall, of large cut stones.

"This castle has just been rebuilt. There is something light, fresh, laughing, about it, not possessed by the heavy, massive castles of the last century."[1]

This last phrase will cause some astonishment; one would scarcely expect to hear such a castle qualified with the names of *light, fresh, laughing;* and yet the author is right; and, compared with those of the eleventh and twelfth centuries, the castle of Montbazon really merited these titles. The former were entirely the reverse—heavy, massive, and gloomy; there were not so many courts in them, not so much interior space, nor so judicious a distribution of it. All idea of art or convenience was foreign to their construction; they had no monumental character, no idea of the agreeable; defence, safety, was the only thought manifested in them. Men selected the steepest and most savage places; and there, according to the accidents of the ground, the edifice was raised,

---

[1] *Histoire des Français des divers états,* by M. A. Monteil, t. i., p. 101.

destined solely to repel attacks effectually, and to shut up the inhabitants. But buildings thus conceived every one raised, burghers as well as lords, ecclesiastics as well as laymen; the territory was covered with them, and they all had the same character, that of haunts, or asylums.

Now that we know what was the actual state of feudal habitations at their origin, what passed within? What life was led there by the possessor? What influence must have been exercised over him and his people by such a dwelling, and the material circumstances which arose from it? How and in what direction developed itself the petty society contained by the castle, and what was the constitutive element of feudal society?

The first feature of its situation was isolation. At no epoch, perhaps, in the history of any society, do we meet with isolation so complete. Take the patriarchal system, the nations which were formed in the plains of western Asia; take the nomadic nations, the tribes of shepherds; take those German tribes I described in one of the last lectures; be present at the birth of the Greek or Roman society; transport yourself to the midst of those villages which afterwards became Athens; to the seven hills whose population formed Rome: everywhere you will find men in infinitely closer connection, far more disposed to act upon one another, that is to say, to become civilized, for civilization is the result of the reciprocal and continual action of individuals. The primitive social molecule was never elsewhere so isolated, so separated from other like molecules; the distance was never so great between the essential and simple elements of society.

With this first feature, with the isolation of the castle and its inhabitants, was combined a singular indolence. The possessor of the castle had nothing to do; no duties, no regular occupation. Among other nations, at their origin, even in the superior classes, men were occupied, sometimes with public affairs, sometimes with frequent and various kinds of relations with neighboring families. We never find them at a loss how to fill up their time, to satisfy their activity: here they cultivated and improved large estates; there they managed great flocks; elsewhere they hunted for a livelihood; in a word, they had a compulsory activity. Within the castle, the proprietor had nothing to do; it was not he who improved his fields; he did not hunt for his support; he had no political activity, no industrial activity of any kind; never has there been seen such leisure in such isolation.

Men cannot remain in a situation of this kind; they would die of impatience and ennui. The proprietor of the castle thought only of getting out of it. Shut up there when it was absolutely necessary to his safety and independence, he left it as often as he was able, to seek abroad what he was in want of, society, activity. The life of the possessors of fiefs was passed upon the high roads, in adventures. That long series of incursions, pillages, wars, which characterizes the middle ages, was, in a great measure, the effect of the nature of the feudal habitation, and of the material situation amidst which its masters were placed. They everywhere sought the social movement which they could not find within their own castles.

Horrible pictures of the life which the possessors of fiefs led at this epoch, have been seen in many works. These pictures have often been traced with a hostile hand, in a partial design. Upon the whole, however, I do not think them exaggerated. Historical events on the one hand, and contemporaneous monuments on the other, prove that such was in fact, for a very long period, the feudal life, the life of the seigneurs.

Among the contemporaneous monuments, I shall refer you to three only, in my opinion the most striking, and which give the most exact idea of the state of society at this epoch: first, the *Histoire de Louis le Gros,* by Suger; secondly, the *Vie de Guibert de Nogent,* by himself, a book less known, but curious, and to which I shall immediately return; thirdly, *l'Histoire Ecclésiastique et civile de Normandie,* by Orderic Vital. You will there see to what an extent the life of possessors of fiefs was passed away from home, entirely employed in depredations, incursions, disorders of every description.

Consult events instead of monuments. That which has astonished all historians, the crusades, first presents itself to the mind. Can it be supposed that the crusades would be possible among a people who had not been accustomed, brought up from childhood to this wandering, adventurous life? In the twelfth century, the crusades were not nearly so singular as they appear to be to us. The life of the possessors of fiefs, with the exception of the pious motive, was an incursion, a continual crusade in their own country: they here went farther, and from other causes; that is the great difference. For the rest, they did not leave their habits—they did not essentially change their mode of life. Could one conceive in the present day a nation of proprietors, who should suddenly displace itself, abandon their estates or their families, to go, without any absolute necessity, and seek elsewhere such adventures? Nothing of the kind would have been possible, if the daily life of the possessors of fiefs had not been, so to speak, a foretaste of the crusades,—if they had not found themselves all prepared for such expeditions.

Thus, whether you consult monuments or events, it will be seen that the need to seek activity and amusement abroad prevailed in the feudal society at this epoch, and that it had a large share, among other causes, in the material circumstances amidst which the possessors of fiefs lived.

Two characteristic traits manifest themselves in feudalism. The one is the savage and fantastical energy of the development of individual characters: not only are they brutal, ferocious, cruel, but they are so in a singular, strange fashion, such as we might look for in an individual who lives alone, abandoned to himself, to the originality of his nature, and to the caprices of his imagination. The second trait, equally striking, in feudal society, is the stubbornness of manners,—their long opposition to change, to progress. Into no other society have new ideas, or manners, had so much trouble to penetrate. Civilization was more slow and difficult in modern Europe than anywhere else; it was not till after the tenth century that it actually conquered and settled in the territory. Nowhere was, during so long a period, so little progress with so much movement.

How can we but recognise, in these two facts, the influence of the material circumstances under the empire of which the constitutive element of feudal society lived and was developed? Who does not see therein the effect of the situation of the possessor of the fief, isolated within his castle, surrounded by an inferior and a despised population, obliged to seek afar off, and by violent means, the society and activity which he had not about him? The ramparts and moats of the castles formed obstacles to ideas as to enemies, and civilization had as much trouble as war to penetrate and invade them.

But at the same time that the castles opposed so strong a

barrier to civilization, at the same time that it had such difficulty in penetrating therein, they were in some respects a principle of civilization; they protected the development of sentiments and manners which have played a powerful and beneficial part in modern society. There is no one but knows that the domestic life, the spirit of family, and particularly the condition of women, were developed in modern Europe much more completely, more happily, than elsewhere. Among the causes which contributed to this development, must be reckoned as one of the principal, the life of the castle, the situation of the possessor of the fief in his domains. Never, in any other form of society, has the family reduced to its most simple expression,—the husband, the wife, and the children,—been found so bound, so pressed together, separated from all other powerful and rival relation. In the various states of society which I have just enumerated, the chief of the family, without quitting home, had numerous occupations, diversions, which drew him from the interior of his dwelling, which at least prevented that from being the centre of his life. The contrary was the case in feudal society. So long as he remained in his castle, the possessor of the fief lived there with his wife and children, almost his only equals, his only intimate and permanent company. Doubtless, he often left it, and abroad led the brutal and adventurous life which I have just described; but he was obliged to return to it. It was there that he shut himself up in times of danger. Now whenever a man is placed in any particular position, the part of his moral nature which corresponds to that position is forcibly developed in him. If he be obliged to live habitually in the bosom of his family, with his wife and children, the ideas, the sentiments in harmony with this fact cannot fail to have great influence. Thus it happened in feudalism.

Moreover, when the possessor of the fief left his castle to seek war and adventures, his wife remained in it, and in a situation wholly different from that in which women had hitherto almost always been placed. She remained mistress, chatelaine, representing her husband, charged in his absence with the defence and honor of the fief. This elevated and almost sovereign position, in the very bosom of domestic life, often gave to the women of the feudal period a dignity, a courage, virtues, a distinction, which they have displayed nowhere else, and it has doubtless powerfully contributed to their moral development and to the general improvement of their condition.

This is not all. The importance of children, of the eldest son more especially, was much greater in the feudal mansion than anywhere else. There broke forth not only natural affection, and the desire to transmit his property to his children, but also the desire to transmit to them that power, that superior position, that sovereignty, inherent in the domain. The eldest son of the lord was, in the eyes of his father and all his people, a prince, an heir presumptive, the depositary of the glory of a dynasty. So that the weaknesses as well as the good feelings of human nature, domestic pride as well as affection, combined to give the spirit of family more energy and power.

Add to this the influence of Christian ideas, which I here merely point out in passing, and you will comprehend how this life of the castle,—this solitary, gloomy, hard situation, was favorable to the development of domestic life, and to that elevation of the condition of women which holds so great a place in the history of our civilization.

This great and beneficial revolution was accomplished between the ninth and twelfth centuries. We cannot follow the trace of it step by step; we can but very imperfectly mark the particular facts which have served it as steps; for we are deficient in documents. But that at the eleventh century it was almost consummated,—that the position of women was changed,—that the spirit of family, the domestic life, the ideas and sentiments connected with it, acquired a development, an empire, till then unknown, is a general fact which it is impossible to overlook. Many of you will still have before you the spirit of the monuments of the eleventh century, which I placed before you in the last course; compare them with the three pages I shall here quote from the *Vie de Guibert de Nogent*, of which I just now spoke. They have no historical importance, and no other merit than that of showing to what dignity, to what refined and delicate sentiments, women and domestic manners were elevated from the ninth to the eleventh century; but, under this point of view, they appear to me conclusive, and of a genuine interest.

Guibert de Nogent gives an account in this work, both of the public events at which he was present, and of the personal events which passed within his own family. He was born in 1053, in a castle of Beauvaisis. Let us see how he speaks of his mother, and of his relations with her. Call to mind the narrative, or rather the language, (for narrative is entirely wanting,) of writers contemporaneous with Charlemagne, Louis le Débonnaire, and Charles le Chauve, on a similar matter, and say if this is the same condition of relations and of souls.

"I have said, God of mercy and holiness, that I would return thanks to thee for thy goodness. First, I especially return thanks to thee for having given me a chaste and modest mother, and one filled with fear of thee. With regard to her beauty, I should praise it in a worldly and extravagant manner, did I place it anywhere but in a face armed with a severe chastity.... The virtuous expression of my mother, her rare speech, her always tranquil countenance, were not made to encourage the levity of those who beheld her.... and what is very rarely, or scarcely ever seen in women of a high rank, she was as jealous of preserving pure the gifts of God, as she was reserved in blaming women who abused them; and when it happened that a woman, whether within or without her house, became the object of a censure of this kind, she abstained from taking part in it; she was afflicted at hearing it, just as if the censure had fallen on herself.[1].... It was far less from experience than from a kind of awe with which she was inspired from above, that she was accustomed to detest sin; and, as she often said to me, she had so penetrated her soul with the fear of sudden death, that, arrived at a more advanced age, she bitterly regretted no longer experiencing in her aged heart those same stings of pious terror which she had felt in her age of simplicity and ignorance.[2]

"The eighth month of my birth had scarcely elapsed, when my father in the flesh died; .... although my mother was still fair and of fresh age, she resolved to remain a widow, and how great was the firmness which she used to accomplish this vow! How great were the examples of modesty which she gave!... Living in great fear of the Lord, and with an equal love for her neighbors, especially those who were poor, she managed us prudently, us and our pro-

---

[1] *Vie de Guibert de Nogent*, l. i., c. 2, in my *Collection des Mémoires relatifs à l'Histoire de France*, t. ix., p. 346–349.
[2] Ibid., c. 12, p. 385.

perty. . . . Her mouth was so accustomed to continually repeat the name of her dead husband, that it seemed as if her soul had never any other thought; for, whether in praying or distributing alms, even in the most ordinary acts of life, she continually pronounced the name of that man, which showed that her mind was always preoccupied with him. In fact, when the heart is absorbed in a feeling of love, the tongue forms itself in a manner to speak, as it were unconsciously, of him who is its object.[1]

" My mother brought me up with the most tender care. . . Scarcely had I learned the first elements of letters, when, eager to have me instructed, she confided me to a master of grammar. . . . There was shortly before this epoch, and even at this time, so great a scarcity of masters of grammar, that so to speak, scarce one was to be seen in the country, and hardly could they be found in the great towns. . . . He to whom my mother resolved to confide me had learned grammar in a rather advanced age, and was so much the less familiar with this science, as he had devoted himself to it at a later period; but what he wanted in knowledge, he made up for in virtue. . . . From the time that I was placed under his care, he formed in me such a purity, he so thoroughly eradicated from me all the vices which generally accompany youth, that he preserved me from the most frequent dangers. He allowed me to go nowhere except in his company, to sleep nowhere but in my mother's house, to receive a present from no one without her permission. He required me to do every thing with moderation, precision, attention, and exertion. . . . While most children of my age ran here and there, according to their pleasure, and were allowed from time to time the enjoyment of the liberty which belongs to them, I, held in continual restraint, muffled up like a clerk, looked upon the bands of players as if I had been a being above them.

" Every one, seeing how my master excited me to work, hoped at first that such great application would sharpen my wits; but this hope soon diminished, for my master, altogether unskilful at reciting verses, or composing them according to rule, almost every day loaded me with a shower of cuffs and blows, to force me to know what he himself was unable to teach me. . . . Still he showed me so much friend-

---

[1] *Vie de Guibert de Nogent*, c. 4, 12, 13, p. 355, 385, 396, 397.

ship; he occupied himself concerning me with so much solicitude, he watched so assiduously over my safety, that, far from experiencing the fear generally felt at that age, I forgot all his severity, and obeyed with an inexpressible feeling of love.... One day, when I had been struck, having neglected my work for some hours in the evening, I went and sat myself at my mother's knee, severely bruised, and certainly more so than I had deserved. My mother having, according to her custom, asked if I had been beaten that day, I, in order to avoid accusing my master, assured her that I had not. But she pulling aside, whether I would or no, the garment they call a shirt, saw my little arms all black, and the skin of my shoulders all raised up and swollen by the blow of the rod which I had received. At this sight, complaining that they treated me with too much cruelty at so tender an age, all troubled and beside herself, her eyes full of tears, she cried: 'I will no longer have thee become a priest, nor in order to learn letters, that thou thus endure such treatment.' But I, at these words, regarding her with all the rage of which I was capable, said to her: 'I would rather die than cease learning letters, and wishing to be a priest.'"[1]

Who can read this account without being struck with the prodigious development which, in two centuries, has been taken by the domestic sentiments, the importance attached to children, to their education, to all the ties of family? You might search through all the writers of the preceding centuries, and never find any thing resembling it. We cannot, I repeat, give an exact account of the manner in which this revolution was accomplished; we do not follow it in its degrees, but it is incontestable.

I must close this lecture. I have given you a glimpse of the influence which the internal life of the feudal castles exercised over the domestic manners, and to the advantage of the sentiments which arose from it. You will immediately see this life take a great extension; new elements will become joined to it, and will contribute to the progress of civilization. It was in the castles that chivalry took birth and grew. We shall occupy ourselves with it in our next lecture.

---

[1] *Vie de Guibert de Nogent*, l. i., c. 2, in my *Collection des Mémoires relatifs à l'Histoire de France*, c. 4, 5, 6, p. 356, 358, 363, 364.

THE
NEW AMERICAN CYCLOPÆDIA.

EDITED BY
GEORGE RIPLEY AND CHARLES A. DANA.

PUBLISHED BY
D. APPLETON & COMPANY, New York

In 16 Vols. 8vo, Double Columns, 750 Pages each.

Price, Cloth, $5.00; *Sheep,* $6.00; *Half Mor.,* $6.50; *Half Russ.,* $7.50 *per Volume.*

———◦———

EVERY one that reads, every one that mingles in society, is constantly meeting with allusions to subjects on which he needs and desires further information. In conversation, in trade, in professional life, on the farm, in the family, practical questions are continually arising, which no man, well read or not, can always satisfactorily answer. If facilities for reference are at hand, they are consulted, and not only is the curiosity gratified, and the stock of knowledge increased, but perhaps information is gained and ideas are suggested that will directly contribute to the business success of the party concerned.

With a Cyclopædia, embracing every conceivable subject, and having its topics alphabetically arranged, not a moment is lost. The matter in question is found at once, digested, condensed, stripped of all that is irrelevant and unnecessary, and verified by a comparison of the best authorities. Moreover, while only men of fortune can collect a library complete in all the departments of knowledge, a Cyclopædia, worth in itself, for purposes of reference, at least a thousand volumes, is within the reach of all—the clerk, the merchant, the professional man, the farmer, the mechanic. In a country like ours, where the humblest may be called to responsible positions requiring intelligence and general information, the value of such a work can not be over-estimated.

PLAN OF THE CYCLOPÆDIA.

The New American Cyclopædia presents a panoramic view of all human knowledge, as it exists at the present moment. It embraces and popularizes every subject that can be thought of. In its successive volumes is contained an inexhaustible fund of accurate and practical information on Art and Science in all their branches, including Mechanics, Mathematics, Astronomy, Philosophy, Chemistry, and Physiology; on Agriculture, Commerce, and Manufactures; on Law, Medicine, and Theology; on Biography and History, Geography and Ethnology; on Political Economy, the Trades, Inventions, Politics, the Things of Common Life, and General Literature.

The Industrial Arts and those branches of Practical Science which have a direct bearing on our every-day life, such as Domestic Economy, Ventilation, the Heating of Houses, Diet, &c., are treated with the thoroughness which their great importance demands.

The department of Biography is full and complete, embracing the lives of all eminent persons, ancient and modern. In American biography, particularly, great pains have been taken to present the most comprehensive and accurate record that has yet been attempted.

In History, the New American Cyclopædia gives no mere catalogue of barren dates, but a copious and spirited narrative, under their appropriate heads, of the principal events in the annals of the world. So in Geography, it not only serves as a general Gazetteer, but it gives interesting descriptions of the principal localities mentioned, derived from books of travel and other fresh and authentic sources.

As far as is consistent with thoroughness of research and exactness of statement, the popular method has been pursued. The wants of the people in a work of this kind have been carefully kept in view throughout.

It is hardly necessary to add that, throughout the whole, perfect fairness to all sections of country, local institutions, public men, political creeds, and religious denominations, has been a sacred principle and leading aim. Nothing that can be construed into an invidious or offensive allusion has been admitted.

DISTINGUISHING EXCELLENCES.

While we prefer that the work should speak for itself, and that others should herald its excellences, we cannot refrain from calling attention to the following points, in which we take an honest pride in believing that the New American Cyclopædia surpasses all others:—

I. IN ACCURACY AND FRESHNESS OF INFORMATION.—The value of a work of this kind is exactly proportioned to its correctness. It must preclude the necessity of having other books. Its decision must be final. It must be an ultimatum of reference, or it is good for nothing.

II. IN IMPARTIALITY.—Our work has undergone the examination of Argus eyes. It has stood the ordeal. It is pronounced by distinguished men and leading reviews in all parts of the Union, strictly fair and national. Eschewing all expressions of opinion on controverted points of science, philosophy, religion, and politics, it aims at an accurate representation of facts and institutions, of the results of physical research, of the prominent events in the history of the world, of the most significant productions of literature and art, and of the celebrated individuals whose names have become associated with the conspicuous phenomena of their age—doing justice to all men, all creeds, all sections.

III. IN COMPLETENESS.—It treats of every subject, in a terse and condensed style, but fully and exhaustively. It is believed that but few omissions will be found; but whatever topics may, through any oversight, be wanting, are supplied in an Appendix.

IV. IN AMERICAN CHARACTER.—The New Cyclopædia is intended to meet the intellectual wants of the American people. It is not, therefore, modelled after European works of a similar design; but, while it embraces all their excellences, has added to them a peculiar and unmistakable American character. It is the production mainly of American mind.

V. IN PRACTICAL BEARING.—The day of philosophical abstraction and speculation has passed away. This is an age of action. *Cui bono* is the universal touchstone. Feeling this, we have made our Cyclopædia thoroughly practical. No man of action, be his sphere humble or exalted, can afford to do without it.

VI. IN INTEREST OF STYLE.—The cold, formal, and repulsive style usual in works of this kind, has been replaced with a style sparkling and emphatically readable. It has been the aim to interest and please, as well as instruct. Many of our writers are men who hold the foremost rank in general literature, and their articles have been characterized by our best critics as models of elegance, force, and beauty.

VII. IN CONVENIENCE OF FORM.—No ponderous quartos, crowded with fine type that strains the eyes and wearies the brain, are here presented. The volumes are just the right size to handle conveniently; the paper is thick and white, the type large, the binding elegant and durable.

VIII. IN CHEAPNESS.—Our Cyclopædia has been universally pronounced a miracle of cheapness. We determined, at the outset, to enlarge its sphere of usefulness, and make it emphatically a book for the people, by putting it at the lowest possible price.

Such being the character of the New American Cyclopædia, an accurate, fresh, impartial, complete, practical, interesting, convenient, cheap Dictionary of General Knowledge, we ask, who can afford to do without it? Can the merchant, the statesman, the lawyer, the physician, the clergyman, to whom it gives thorough and complete information on every point connected with their several callings? Can the teacher, who is enabled, by the outside information it affords, to make his instructions doubly interesting and profitable? Can the farmer, to whom it offers the latest results of agricultural research and experiment? Can the young man, to whom it affords the means of storing his mind with useful knowledge bearing no any vocation he may have selected? Can the intelligent mechanic, who wishes to understand what he reads in his daily paper? Can the mother of a family, whom it initiates into the mysteries of domestic economy, and teaches a thousand things which more than saves its cost in a single year? In a word, can any intelligent American, who desires to understand the institutions of his country, its past history and present condition, and his own duties as a citizen, deny himself this great American digest of all human knowledge, universally pronounced the best Cyclopædia and the most valuable work ever published?

CONTRIBUTORS TO THE CYCLOPÆDIA.

The best talent in all parts of the country, and many distinguished foreign writers, have been engaged in the New American Cyclopædia. We give below the names of several of the most prominent contributors, from which the public may form some idea of the character of the work.

Hon. GEORGE BANCROFT, LL.D., New York.
Hon. J. R. BARTLETT, late U. S. and Mexican Boundary Commissioner, Providence, R. I.
Rev. HENRY W. BELLOWS, D.D., New York.
Hon. JEREMIAH S. BLACK, U. S. Attorney General, Washington, D. C.
Capt. GEORGE S. BLAKE, U. S. Naval Academy, Annapolis, Md.
Hon. ERASTUS BROOKS, New York.
EDWARD BROWN-SÉQUARD, M.D., London.
JOHN ESTEN COOKE, Esq., Richmond, Va.
Rev. J. W. CUMMINGS, D.D., Pastor of St. Stephen's Church, New York.
Prof. JAMES D. DANA, LL.D., Yale College, New Haven, Conn.
Hon. CHARLES P. DALY, Judge of the Court of Common Pleas, New York.
Hon. CHARLES S. DAVIES, LL.D., Portland, Me.
RALPH WALDO EMERSON, Concord, Mass.
Hon. EDWARD EVERETT, Boston, Mass.
Pres. C. C. FELTON, LL.D., Harvard University, Cambridge, Mass.
D. W. FISKE, Esq., Secretary of the Geographical and Statistical Society, New York.
CHARLES L. FLINT, Esq., Secretary of the Massachusetts Board of Agriculture, Boston, Mass.
JOHN W. FRANCIS, M.D., LL.D.
Prof. CHANDLER R. GILMAN, M.D., College of Physicians and Surgeons, New York.
Prof. HENRY GOADBY, M.D., State Agricultural College of Michigan, Ann Arbor, Mich.
HORACE GREELEY, Esq., New York.
GEORGE W. GREENE, Esq., New York.
R. A. GUILD, Esq., Librarian of Brown University, Providence, R. I.
Prof. CHARLES W. HACKLEY, D.D., Columbia College, New York.
Hon. JAMES HALL, Cincinnati, Ohio.
GERARD HALLOCK, Esq., editor of the "Journal of Commerce," New York.
Prof. A. W. HARKNESS, Brown University, Providence, R. I.
JOHN R. G. HASSARD, Esq., New York.
CHARLES C. HAZEWELL, Esq., Boston, Mass.
M. HEILPRIN, Esq., New York.
RICHARD HILDRETH, Esq., author of "History of the United States," &c., New York.
Rev. THOMAS HILL, President of Antioch College, Ohio.
Hon. GEORGE S. HILLARD, Boston, Mass.

CONTRIBUTORS TO THE CYCLOPÆDIA.

J. S. HITTELL, Esq., San Francisco, Cal.
JAMES T. HODGE, Esq., Cooper Institute, New York.
Prof. L. M. HUBBARD, D.D., University of N. C., Chapel Hill, N. C.
Rev. HENRY N. HUDSON, author of "Lectures on Shakespeare," &c., Litchfield, Conn.
Prof. S. W. JOHNSON, Yale College, New Haven, Conn.
J. C. G. KENNEDY, Esq., Washington, D. C.
Hon. JOHN B. KERR, late U. S. Minister to Central America, Baltimore, Md.
Rev. T. STARR KING, San Francisco, Cal.
CHARLES LANMAN, Esq., Washington, D. C.
CHARLES G. LELAND, Esq., Philadelphia, Pa.
Prof. JAMES R. LOWELL, Harvard University, Cambridge, Mass.
R. SHELTON MACKENZIE, D.C.L., Philadelphia, Pa.
Rev. H. N. MCTYEIRE, D.D., editor "Christian Advocate," Nashville, Tenn.
CHARLES NORDHOFF, Esq., author of "Stories of the Island World," &c., New York.
Rev. SAMUEL OSGOOD, D.D., New York.
Prof. THEOPHILUS PARSONS, LL.D., Harvard University, Cambridge, Mass.
Prof. F. R. PEASLEE, M.D., New York Medical College, New York.
JOHN L. PEYTON, Esq., Staunton, Va.
WILLIAM C. PRIME, author of "Boat Life and Tent Life," &c., New York.
J. H. RAYMOND, LL.D., Principal of the Polytechnic Institute, Brooklyn, New York.
GEORGE SCHEDEL, Esq., late British Consular Agent for Costa Rica, Staten Island, N. Y.
Prof. ALEXANDER G. SCHEM, Dickinson College, Carlisle, Penn.
Hon. FRANCIS SCHROEDER, Jr., late U. S. Minister to Sweden, Paris.
Hon. WILLIAM H. SEWARD, U. S. Senator from New York, Auburn, N. Y.
WILLIAM GILMORE SIMMS, LL.D., Charleston, S. C.
Prof. HENRY B. SMITH, D.D., Union Theological Seminary, New York.
Rev. J. A. SPENCER, D.D., author of "The History of the United States," &c., New York.
Rev. WILLIAM B. SPRAGUE, D.D., Albany, N. Y.
Hon. E. G. SQUIER, author of "The States of Central America," "Nicaragua," &c.
ALEX. W. THAYER, Esq., Berlin, Prussia.
JOHN R. THOMPSON, Esq., editor "Southern Literary Messenger," Richmond, Va.
GEORGE TICKNOR, LL.D., Boston, Mass.
OSMOND TIFFANY, Esq., Springfield, Mass.
R. T. TRALL, M.D., author of "Hydropathic Encyclopædia," New York.
Baron DE TROBRIAND, New York.
W. P. TROWBRIDGE, Esq., U. S. Coast Survey, Washington, D. C.
HENRY T. TUCKERMAN, Esq., New York.
ALEXANDER WALKER, Esq., editor of the "Delta," New Orleans.
CHARLES S. WEYMAN, Esq., New York.
Rev. W. D. WILSON, D.D., Hobart Free College, Geneva, N. Y.
E. L. YOUMANS, Esq., author of "The Hand-Book of Household Science," New York.

OPINIONS OF THE PRESS AND DISTINGUISHED MEN.

In setting forth what the Press think of the New American Cyclopædia, we hardly know where to begin, so numerous and flattering are the notices it has received. We can only give here and there a brief extract from the leading Reviews and Journals, and letters from distinguished men, bearing for the most part on special features of the work.

- The work itself no longer needs commendation at our hands, or at any hands. It has long since established its worth; and, if there be in it any considerable defect, much search will be required to find it.—*North American, Philadelphia, Pa.*
- The great arts of condensation, of clear perception, and striking exposition of the essential parts of their subject have been fully attained; and will give the reader a library of universal knowledge in a convenient compass, arranged for ready use, and attractively presented in the concise and perspicuous style appropriate to such a work.—*Letter from the late Hon.* Thos. H. Benton.
- This work, instead of being a mere dictionary—a stupid epitome of dry facts and dates—is made up of attractive and readable matter; scholarly and sparkling essays; fresh biographies of living and dead celebrities; records of important discoveries and inventions; and information on every subject that has attracted the attention of man up to the present period.—*Examiner, Poughkeepsie, N. Y.*
- I feel quite sure that it will be marked by distinguished ability, and that, when concluded, it will be a vast storehouse of late and very important information—such a work as almost every intelligent person will be glad to have always near him for reference. I can only express the hope that so large an undertaking may be duly sustained, and crowned with ultimate success.—*Letter from the Rt. Rev.* Horatio Potter, (*Prot. Epis.*) *Bishop of N. Y.*
- The editors have done their duty with justice, fairness, and liberality. We see no instance of partisanship or partiality, and, as yet, no proofs of that hostile sectionality of which we have hitherto had reason, in all such publications, to complain.—*Mercury, Charleston, S. C.*
- We esteem it the best and most comprehensive Cyclopædia that has yet been issued from the press of this or any other country.—*News, Savannah, Ga.*
- When completed, this Cyclopædia will be the most complete library of knowledge which has ever been given to the world in the same space since the art of printing was discovered.—*Union, Rochester, N. Y.*
- Its freshness and general thoroughness give it a decided advantage over any other Cyclopædia of its class hitherto issued on either side of the Atlantic.—*Daily Times, N. Y.*
- It is a perfect treasury of knowledge. In all branches of the arts and sciences, in literature, history, biography, and geography.—*Pilot, Boston, Mass.*

OPINIONS OF THE PRESS.

The scientific articles are evidently the productions of learned and accomplished men. Many of the papers deserve especial commendation, as presenting the latest developments in their various departments of research.—*National Intelligencer, Washington, D. C.*

Our own country has never before been so fairly or fully represented in any Cyclopædia. America, her resources, her literature, her politics, and her representative men receive in this work, at least, their full share of attention.—*Post, Boston, Mass.*

To enumerate one half of its excellences would require far more space than newspaper columns afford. To the professional man and the laborer, the citizen and the farmer, it is invaluable as an epitome of all useful knowledge.—*Leader, Cleveland, O.*

There is no conceivable topic which is not here discussed as fully as most persons would care to find it.—*American Agriculturist.*

It should be in every family, for in no other shape can so much useful information be obtained as cheaply. As a book of reference, it is invaluable.—*Indiana Sentinel.*

It is, without doubt, the most complete work of the kind ever published. To prepare it, the publishers have called into requisition the talent of some of the best men our country affords.—*Pennsylvanian, Philadelphia, Pa.*

There can be no doubt that, at least for the use of American readers, and in some respects wherever the English language is spoken, the Cyclopædia will GREATLY SURPASS, in its value as a reference book, any similar compilation that has yet been issued on either side of the Atlantic.—*North American Review.*

Take it all in all—for the strict purposes of an Encyclopædia; for a clear survey of all the departments of human knowledge; for embracing every important topic in this vast range; for lucid and orderly treatment; for statements condensed yet clear; for its portable size—not being too large or too small; for convenience of reference, and for practical utility, especially to American readers; *it is incomparably the best work in the English language.*—*N. Y. Evangelist.*

It is a most extraordinary effort of genial scholarship and of *multum in parvo* erudition. We commend it as a book which the world has long wanted, and which will exert an incalculable influence in Europe as regards creating respect for solid American learning.—*Telegraph, Harrisburgh, Pa.*

It has been truly said that almost every man of note who ever lived and died, of whom there is record, has in it a place; every country, province, race, and tribe; every sea, river, lake and island; every science, religion, and, in short, almost every noun in the language, is descriptively illustrated in the most complete shape in which the information could be condensed.—*Blade, Toledo, O.*

The various subjects are not treated according to the mere routine of technical details, or in the settled formularies of professional science, but, while the information is full, thorough, and accurate, it is given in a genial and attractive style.—*Tribune, Mobile, Ala.*

THE CORRELATION AND CONSERVATION

OF

FORCES.

A SERIES OF EXPOSITIONS BY GROVE, MAYER, HELMHOLTZ, FARADAY, LIEBIG, AND CARPENTER.

WITH

AN INTRODUCTION.

BY E. L. YOUMANS.

The work embraces:

I.—THE CORRELATION OF PHYSICAL FORCES. By W. R. GROVE. (The complete work.)

II.—CELESTIAL DYNAMICS. By DR. J. R. MAYER.

III.—THE INTERACTION OF FORCES. By PROF. HELMHOLTZ.

IV.—THE CONNECTION AND EQUIVALENCE OF FORCES. By PROF. LIEBIG.

V.—ON THE CONSERVATION OF FORCE. By DR. FARADAY.

VI.—ON THE CORRELATION OF PHYSICAL AND VITAL FORCES. By DR. CARPENTER.

Works of Herbert Spencer published by D. Appleton & Co.

The Philosophy of Herbert Spencer.

FIRST PRINCIPLES;

IN TWO PARTS:

I. THE UNKNOWABLE. II. LAWS OF THE KNOWABLE.

In one Volume. 518 pages.

"Mr. Spencer has earned an eminent and commanding position as a metaphysician, and his ability, earnestness, and profundity, are in none of his former volumes so conspicuous as in this. There is not a crude thought, a flippant fling, or an irreverent insinuation in this book, notwithstanding that it has something of the character of a daring and determined raid upon the old philosophies."—*Chicago Journal.*

"This volume, treating of First Principles, like all Mr. Spencer's writings that have fallen under our observation, is distinguished for clearness, earnestness, candor, and that originality and fearlessness which ever mark the true philosophical spirit. His treatment of theological opinions is reverent and respectful, and his suggestions and arguments are such as to deserve, as they will compel, the earnest attention of all thoughtful students of first truths. Agreeing with Hamilton and Mansel in the general, on the unknowableness of the unconditioned, he nevertheless holds that their being is in a form asserted by consciousness."—*Christian Advocate.*

"The literary world has seen but few such authors as Herbert Spencer. There have been metaphysical writers in the same exalted sphere who before him have attempted to reduce the laws of nature to a rational system. But in the highest realm of philosophical investigation he stands head and shoulders above his predecessors; not perhaps purely by force of superior intellect, but partly owing to the greater aid which the light of modern science has afforded him in the prosecution of his difficult task."—*Boston Bulletin.*

"Mr. Spencer is achieving an enviable distinction by his contributions to the country's literature; his system of philosophy is destined to become a work of no small renown. Its appearance at this time is an evidence that our people are not *all* absorbed in war and its tragic events."—*Ohio State Journal.*

"Mr. Spencer's works will undoubtedly receive in this country the attention they merit. There is a broad liberality of tone throughout which will recommend them to thinking, inquiring Americans. Whether, as is asserted, he has established a new system of philosophy, and if so, whether that system is better than all other systems, is yet to be decided; but that his bold and vigorous thought will add something valuable and permanent to human knowledge is undeniable."—*Utica Herald.*

"Herbert Spencer is the foremost among living thinkers. If less erudite than Hamilton, he is quite as original, and is more comprehensive and catholic than Mansel."—*Universalist.*

www.ingramcontent.com/pod-product-compliance
Lightning Source LLC
Chambersburg PA
CBHW030552300426
44111CB00009B/957